Ireland's Golf Courses:
The Complete Guide

Ireland

IRELAND'S
GOLF COURSES
The Complete Guide

VIC ROBBIE
Foreword by PADRAIG HARRINGTON

MAINSTREAM
PUBLISHING

EDINBURGH AND LONDON

First published in Great Britain in 2006 by
MAINSTREAM PUBLISHING COMPANY
(EDINBURGH) LTD
7 Albany Street
Edinburgh EH1 3UG

ISBN 1 84596 073 4

A catalogue record for this book is available
from the British Library

Typeset in Baskerville and Gill Sans

Printed in Germany by
Appl Druck, Wemding

Acknowledgements

The compilation of *Ireland's Golf Courses: The Complete Guide* has taken many willing hands without whose assistance it would not have been possible, and I owe them my sincere thanks. To the club managers, directors of golf, secretaries, captains, professionals and members who have provided the information about their beloved courses; and to those who have allowed me to hack around them in my research. To the Golfing Union of Ireland, the Irish Tourist Boards and the clubs for permission to use the magnificent photographs which capture perfectly the beauty of our Irish courses. To Mainstream Publishing editor Paul Murphy for his patience and attention to detail. To Christine, Gabrielle and Kirstie for all their hard work, good-humoured support and encouragement. To Maia and Jed for their inspiration, and my regular playing partner Nick, who has shown me how great courses should be played.

Vic Robbie

Contents

Foreword

I **GENUINELY BELIEVE THERE IS SOMETHING ABOUT IRISH GOLF COURSES THAT** sets them apart from the rest, and with The K Club near Dublin hosting the Ryder Cup in September 2006, it gives Ireland the opportunity to impress the world. But then, I have to admit, I'm totally biased on the subject.

Having grown up learning to play the game on golf courses in Ireland and then been privileged enough to test myself against many of the best of them as a professional, I can testify to the outstanding quality and sheer variety of our proud golfing heritage. Over the years I have been fortunate enough to hold course records at a number of outstanding Irish courses, perhaps the most satisfying being the 65 recorded at one of my favourite courses, Royal Portrush, when playing as an amateur in the North of Ireland Championship in 1993.

I have played in three Ryder Cups and all the majors, but the more I travel the world to play golf on courses young and old, the more I relish the chance to return home to play on courses that most golfers elsewhere can only dream about. Whether they're parkland or links, Irish courses invariably offer the most wonderful challenges in the most breathtaking settings.

Some of the most accomplished course designers have also played a major part in shaping world-famous courses, such as Royal County Down ('Old' Tom Morris); Ballybunion (Simpson McKenna and Robert Trent Jones, sen.); Portmarnock (W.G. Pickeman and George Ross); Waterville (J.A. Mulcahy); Royal Portrush and Royal Dublin (Harry Colt); Tralee and The K Club (Arnold Palmer); and Mount Juliet (Jack Nicklaus).

By bringing all of the great Irish golf courses together, this book illustrates the range of challenges open to golfers who visit Ireland today. There are the great, world-renowned courses, but there are also many 'hidden gems' waiting to be discovered. The choice seems almost endless. I am sure that the experience, both on and off the course, will live long in the memory regardless of the final scorecard.

I hope you find this book as fascinating as I did and that you enjoy your game on any one of these special Irish golf courses.

Padraig Harrington

Introduction

FEW WOULD DISAGREE WITH IRELAND'S CLAIM TO BE THE MOST POPULAR golfing destination in Europe. With more than 450 courses from the most humble that delight the weekend golfer to the most intimidating that demand the highest skills, Ireland has them all. Now The K Club's hosting of the 36th Ryder Cup has endorsed the country's position in the pantheon of the game.

There cannot be a more dramatic setting for golf, whether it be the Atlantic-lashed links of the West, the outstanding traditional links of the North and East, or the new generation of stunning championship parkland courses, such as The K Club, on the banks of the Liffey 18 miles west of Dublin. All the ingredients are here – beautiful undulating countryside, brooding mountain peaks, cascading rivers, deep lakes and romantic castles. The Emerald Isle already hosts European Tour events and has staged the Walker Cup in the amateur game. Now arguably the world's greatest golf event takes Ireland to a new level.

The Ryder Cup will be worth hundreds of millions of euros in revenue to the community, and Bertie Ahern, Ireland's Taoiseach, has no doubt about its ongoing value to his country, saying, 'It is the launch pad for continued, sustained success with many more of the world's 56 million golfers wanting to come to Ireland.'

Ireland's rise to golfing prominence has been dramatic. When Portmarnock hosted the Canada Cup in 1960, there were only 200 clubs, most of them with nine-hole courses. Since then golf in Ireland has mushroomed into a massive tourist industry, and in 2004, Ireland was voted The International Golf Destination of the Year. In the last 20 years, the number of golf clubs affiliated to the Golfing Union of Ireland has almost doubled to 408. Now the island of Ireland has more courses than any other country of comparable size, and when you consider that only 10 per cent of the population of five million actually play the game, there are plenty of tee times for visitors, who seldom leave disappointed. Ireland welcomes almost half a million golfers each year, generating many hundreds of millions in revenue. For example, Killarney's three courses attract in excess of 40,000 visitors a year to an area which José Maria Olazábal described as 'one of the most beautiful places I have ever seen'.

Nowadays, the great and the good of golf all make regular pilgrimages to play in Ireland. Tom Watson is probably Ireland's greatest ambassador. Some years ago he fell in love with the wild links of Ballybunion, looking for a place to hone his skills in preparation for his assault on the British Open. It worked for him. He won the Old Claret Jug five times. During his visits, he forged such a strong bond with the club, whose links runs hard along the Atlantic coast of Kerry, that he became the club captain for their millennium year. He says with a certain amount of pride, 'It's the best course in the world.'

In recent years, American presidents and top professionals have visited to pit their skills against the best Ireland can offer, the most recent being Bill Clinton, Tiger Woods, Mark O'Meara, David Duval and the late Payne Stewart, who struck up such an affinity with Waterville that the club dedicated a statue to his memory.

Ireland boasts more than a third of the world's links courses. For years its reputation was built on great links – courses like Northern Ireland's magnificent Royal Portrush, the only course outside Scotland and England to host the British Open; the awesome Royal County Down, where the Mountains of Mourne really do sweep down to the sea; Dublin's imposing Portmarnock; the west coast's Ballybunion; and the ruggedly beautiful Waterville. All of these courses are regularly included in the world's top 20.

In the last 15 years, there has been an unprecedented development of outstanding parkland venues such as The K Club, Druids Glen, Mount Juliet, Fota Island and Adare Manor. More recently, PGA National Ireland at Palmerstown House, Carton House and The Heritage have been added to the list of internationally acclaimed courses. Each is a masterpiece, sculpted into beautiful sylvan settings and making full use of the natural contours of the land and abundant water hazards. The great Bobby Jones said that a good course should 'offer problems a man may attempt according to his ability . . . never hopeless for the lesser player nor failing to concern and interest the expert'. He must have had Ireland in mind. It's these new parkland courses that have been attracting the major events. Killarney, Mount Juliet and Druids Glen have all staged the Irish Open, while The K Club has hosted the European Open and Killarney the Curtis Cup.

Many of the great names of the sport have been involved in some way in laying the foundations of Irish golf by employing their skills and knowledge to create some of the finest courses the world has seen. Old Tom Morris was paid four guineas to construct Royal County Down in 1889, while the prolific James Braid, Willie Park, Harry Colt, Harry Vardon and Dr Alister Mackenzie, who conspired with Bobby Jones to build Augusta, have all left their individual stamp on the Emerald Isle. Now the greats of the modern era have got involved as Ireland enters the new millennium as a major force in world golf.

It was in Ireland in the 1980s that Arnold Palmer designed his first course in Europe, the rugged links at Tralee, in an area that provided the setting for the filming of *Ryan's Daughter*. Bounded by water on three sides, there is a clear view of the Atlantic Ocean from every hole and Palmer said at the time, 'I am happy we have one of the world's great links here.' Almost a decade later, he returned to create The K Club, with the promise that it would be 'a blend of pleasure, skill and challenge', and fashioned the perfect arena for the Ryder Cup, with the River Liffey and lakes coming into play in what is a challenge of technique and nerve.

Palmer's great rival Jack Nicklaus, arguably the greatest player the game has known, achieved as good a result at Mount Juliet, having said, 'Building a golf course is my total expression. My golf game can only go on so long. But what I have learned can be put into a piece of ground to last beyond me.'

Robert Trent Jones, who has more of his courses in the top 100 than any other architect, moved heaven, earth and water to create an outstanding parkland set-up complete with huge lakes in the grounds of Adare Manor. Ireland's own Pat Ruddy built the impressive Druids Glen and compatriots Des Smyth, Philip Walton, Christy O'Connor Jr., David Jones and former Walker Cup player Peter McEvoy have all been involved in carrying on the good work of Ireland's most prolific designer, Eddie Hackett.

But it would be wrong to believe that Ireland is split between the old traditional links and the new parklands. Some new and challenging links courses to rival the old were laid down in the 1990s. Pat Ruddy designed the unique 20-hole European links in County Wicklow, which he owns and runs, and the Glashedy Links at Ballyliffin, the most northerly course in Ireland. Robert Trent Jones created the dramatic Cashen Course at Ballybunion. He says, 'It's the finest piece of links land I have ever seen,' and there are many who believe it to be a bigger test than its sister. Bernhard Langer put his stamp on the new Portmarnock Links. But perhaps the most dramatic of all is the Old Head of Kinsale, built on top of 200-foot-high cliffs on a promontory jutting out into the Atlantic.

Then, in 2002, Greg Norman created a masterpiece, Doonbeg, in County Clare. 'Blessed with one of the best pieces of property for a golf course that I have ever seen,' says Norman, 'my name will be indelibly linked with the golfing lore of this great land. For that, I am honoured and humbled. It was from my visits during the construction of Doonbeg that my love of this land and its golf courses swelled. Natural elements shape the land and are central to how the game is experienced in Ireland. That's what makes this place, and its courses, so special.'

It is difficult to pinpoint where golf was first played in Ireland, but one thing we know is that the game was brought to the island by Scots, many of whom were in the army and stationed around the country. There is evidence that golf was played in County Wicklow as far back as 1762, but the Scottish influence appears to have been everywhere.

Ireland's Golf Courses

Royal Belfast is Ireland's oldest club, having been founded in November 1881 by Thomas Sinclair, whose interest in the game was sparked by a visit to Scotland, and a Scottish teacher, George Baillie, who was living in Belfast. Ireland's second oldest, and the Republic's oldest, is the Curragh in County Kildare, which was founded two years later. Golf had first been played here as early as 1857 by Scotsman David Ritchie, who eventually designed the heathland course opposite the Curragh Racecourse, and three years later, the game was first played in County Offaly. Down in the south-west tip of Ireland, golf was first introduced with the arrival of the trans-Atlantic telegraph cable and Waterville was formed in 1885. Further north, Lahinch in County Clare, which is often referred to as the St Andrews of Ireland, was originally laid down by officers of a Scottish regiment, although Tom Morris improved on it in 1892.

Golf has been played at Kerry's Dooks since 1889, when the game was introduced to the local aristocracy by officers from the Royal Horse Artillery attending compulsory training at the nearby Glenbeigh artillery range. Then, in 1891, the Golfing Union of Ireland was formed.

Although its courses speak volumes for Ireland, it has also produced many fine golfers who have been outstanding ambassadors for their country – the great amateur Joe Carr, Fred Daly, the only Irishman to win the British Open, Harry Bradshaw, Christy O'Connor, sen., and his nephew Christy O'Connor Jr., and today's Ryder Cup stars, Darren Clarke, Padraig Harrington and Paul McGinley.

To choose a favourite from Ireland's great array of courses would be like professing a preference for one of your own offspring, but one thing you can be assured of when golfing in the Emerald Isle is the warmth of the *fáilte* and the *craic* at the 19th hole.

The K Club's Key Ryder Cup Holes

SWASHBUCKLING AND CAVALIER WERE JUST SOME OF THE EPITHETS USED TO describe the legendary Arnold Palmer's style of golfing genius. It is why he became arguably the most popular golfer ever and played a significant role in boosting the game's fortunes.

He took that attitude into golf-course design, aiming to make a course a 'blend of pleasure, skill and challenge' and fashioning holes that rewarded the player who would 'go for broke'.

Such was the case with his design of The K Club's Palmer Course, making it the ideal choice to host the 2006 Ryder Cup. The K Club's premier course embodies all those principles, and at 7,337 yards (standard scratch 76), it is a supreme test for the world's best golfers with its reliance on an abundance of water as its first defence. The appeal of water as a hazard is its finality. There is often no way back.

The Ryder Cup is regarded by many as the world's greatest golf event with the golfers of Europe and the USA putting it all on the line for their team, honour and national pride rather than prize money. There can be no more exciting format than matchplay with the players competing against each other and the course in front of a 40,000 crowd and a television audience of millions. One error, one injudicious shot and the Ryder Cup could switch hands, and in recent years, the event has served up many dramatic and tense climaxes.

And there can be no more testing a finishing stretch than on the Palmer Course, specially reconfigured to ensure an exciting 5–4–5 finale for the Ryder Cup spectators.

The customary first eight holes become ten to seventeen for the Ryder Cup, ensuring a grandstand finish with the final three holes favouring the bold, the brave

The 18th hole at The K Club

and the accurate. As The K Club's Director of Golf, John McHenry, says, 'The last three holes are as good a test as anywhere.'

The sixteenth (the members' seventh) could prove to be the most crucial hole over the three days of the event. From the back tees, this mighty double-dogleg, right then left, which is often rated as Ireland's best par 5, measures a hefty 606 yards. However, for the Ryder Cup it will play shorter, ensuring that the player has the choice of risking going for the narrow roller-coaster of a green in two. A good drive gives them the chance to do just that and cut the corner across the flowing waters of the River Liffey if they dare. A lay-up can be just as hazardous, because the green, on an island between two arms of the Liffey, is also protected by bunkers and mature trees.

From the 16th green to the 17th tee is a short walk across a white wrought-iron bridge, built by Courtney &

The Ryder Cup

Stephens of Dublin in 1849, around the back of Straffan House, the luxurious base for the two teams. The walk provides the ideal chance to recover one's senses if the 16th has been an unfortunate experience or to prepare for the next, a devil of a hole. Certainly, Denmark's Thomas Björn might agree, following his experience in the Smurfit European Open in 2005. He started the final round with a four-shot lead but ended up with a share of thirty-third place having found the water on the sixteenth for a bogey, three times hit his drive into the river on the next for a septuple bogey eleven and bogeyed the last. And Ian Woosnam, Europe's captain in 2006, also had something of an altercation here, resulting in his driver being despatched into the Liffey.

The 17th is called 'Half Moon' because it curves left along the banks of the Liffey offering a narrow driving target. McHenry offers his advice: 'Most players hit it right to left, and there's a bale-out area on the right, but it's easy to blow your drive into the trees. You've got to hit it up the right half of the fairway and hope it doesn't draw too much and end up in the river.'

The 18th is quite simply a classic Ryder Cup finishing hole, aptly named the 'Hooker's Graveyard'. At 537 yards, it's a big dogleg right with eight bunkers on a mound obscuring the view of the landing area. Imagine preparing for the second shot, attempting to go for the green with the lake creeping in from the left and a cluster of bunkers awaiting the shot that seeks the safety of the right, and knowing that the outcome of the Ryder Cup depends on it.

Serious preparations were under way years before the event with dress rehearsals in the September of 2004 and 2005 to ensure they got it just right. As McHenry said, 'This is the biggest thing ever to happen to Ireland in sporting terms.'

As is the home captain's prerogative, Woosnam tweaked the course here and there to combat the big-hitting Americans, asking for some new bunkers to be put in, for the inclusion of a tall tree on the corners of doglegs at around 280 yards with a small bushy tree behind to catch the falling ball, and for the collars around the greens to be shaved.

While the course is perfection, the infrastructure is also ideal for an event of this magnitude, and Tom Lehman, the American captain, agrees, claiming that it is the best golf property he has ever visited.

The K Club will play host to 40,000 spectators, 1,100 journalists and 3,000 workers, but it was built for this – the owner, Dr Michael Smurfit, even made a bid to stage the Ryder Cup before the Palmer Course was laid down in 1991.

Whatever the result, the whole of Ireland knows that the successful staging of a Ryder Cup will provide a legacy that lasts many lifetimes.

(More K Club details – page 65.)

Irish Eyes Are Smiling

IT HAS TAKEN TIME FOR THE EMERALD ISLE TO BE AWARDED THE RYDER CUP – an accolade that few would begrudge. Yet although the action has taken place on foreign fields, the Irish have had a major influence on the biennial meeting between the best golfers of Europe and the United States over the years. On more than one occasion, it's been an Irishman whose stroke of genius has had more than Irish eyes smiling.

No one could have envisaged the eventual impact the Ryder Cup would have on golf when Samuel Ryder, who made his fortune from selling penny seed packets, launched the first match between Britain and the USA in 1927.

In 1979, after years of American domination, the Great Britain and Ireland team was expanded to include fellow Europeans, and the resulting events became more competitive, so much so that in the last ten years the Americans have won only once. In recent times, there has been a strong Irish backbone to the team with Darren Clarke, Padraig Harrington and Paul McGinley all playing key roles in Europe's success, especially in the record victory at Oakland Hills in 2004.

Irish pedigree runs through the history of the event. Fred Daly was the first Irishman to play in the event in 1947. Then there was the great Christy O'Connor, known to golf fans in Ireland as 'Himself'. He was a veteran of ten Ryder Cups – only Nick Faldo has played in more matches.

But it is wonderful moments of magic by Irish golfers that are the enduring memories. None more so than Christy O'Connor Jr.'s amazing shot to the last hole at The Belfry in 1989 that virtually ensured Europe's third successive victory. Christy had made the European team as a captain's pick, but he outshone his more illustrious teammates Faldo, Ballesteros and Olazábal on that occasion with a shot that is remembered in detail by all who saw it.

Playing Fred Couples in the final-day singles, the pair had been neck and neck, hole

**Darren Clarke, Paul McGinley and Padraig Harrington, the Irish
members of the winning 2004 European Ryder Cup team**

by hole, and were level coming to the last. As expected, Couples outdrove the Irishman, who was left facing an approach to the green of 221 yards and a 190-yard carry over water. With the words of his captain, Tony Jacklin, ringing in his ears – 'Give it one last swing for Ireland' – O'Connor pulled out his two-iron and hit the ball to four feet from the pin. 'I made a perfect execution,' he recalls. 'It came off 110 per cent.' That unsettled Couples, who missed the green on the right then failed with his putt for par.

O'Connor's Ping two-iron raised £50,000 at a charity auction, and it was later returned to him before being stolen from his car. Although he never recovered the club, that Ryder Cup memory has stayed with him and thousands of golf fans.

It was another Irishman, Eamonn Darcy, who played a key role two years before when he holed the winning putt against Ben Crenshaw at Muirfield Village to ensure Europe would not lose the trophy.

A decade later in 1995, at Oak Hill in New York State, Philip Walton clinched victory for Europe. Afterwards, the team flew home on Concorde and en route to London stopped off in Dublin, where Walton and his teammates received a hero's welcome.

Perhaps the most demonstrative example of Irish success in the Ryder Cup came from Paul McGinley, who sank a winning 10-foot putt on the 18th at The Belfry in 2002. 'It just had to be an Irishman to sink the winning putt,' he says. 'I don't think I'll ever tire of being asked about that putt – I have no problem talking about it all day long.' The celebrations involved McGinley ending up in the lake on the 18th and then being wrapped in the Irish tricolour by his compatriots, Darren Clarke and Padraig Harrington.

As McGinley has said, 'There is something about the Ryder Cup and the Irish.'

Ireland. Home of the green stuff. (And the black stuff.)

You could be forgiven for thinking that Ireland was designed for golf. That'd explain why such a small country has some of the most challenging and enjoyable courses in Europe. And why we're hosting the Ryder Cup 2006. The other great thing about Ireland is win, lose or draw, there's always a great celebration at the 19th. *Come on. Let's play.*

Ireland 2006 *Let's play.*
Discover more at **www.ireland.ie**

Irish Open Championship

YEAR	WINNER	VENUE
1927	G. Duncan	Portmarnock
1928	E.R. Whitcombe	Newcastle
1929	A. Mitchell	Portmarnock
1930	C. Whitcombe	Portrush
1931	E. Kenyon	Royal Dublin
1932	A. Padgham	Cork
1933	E.W. Kenyon	Malone
1934	S. Easterbrook	Portmarnock
1935	E. Whitcombe	Newcastle
1936	R. Whitcombe	Royal Dublin
1937	B. Gadd	Portrush
1938	A. Locke	Portmarnock
1939	A. Lees	Newcastle
1940–45	No championship	
1946	F. Daly	Portmarnock
1947	H. Bradshaw	Portrush
1948	D. Rees	Portmarnock
1949	H. Bradshaw	Belvoir Park
1950	H.O. Pickworth	Royal Dublin
1951–52	No championship	
1953	E.C. Brown	Belvoir Park
1954–74	No championship	

CARROLLS INTERNATIONAL 1963–1974:

1963	B.J. Hunt	Woodbrook
1964	C. O'Connor	Woodbrook
1965	N.C. Coles	Cork
1966	C. O'Connor	Royal Dublin
1967	C. O'Connor	Woodbrook

23

1968	J. Martin	Woodbrook
1969	R.D. Shade	Woodbrook
1970	B. Huggett	Woodbrook
1971	N.C. Coles	Woodbrook
1972	C. O'Connor	Woodbrook
1973	P. McGuirk	Woodbrook
1974	B. Gallacher	Woodbrook

IRISH OPEN CHAMPIONSHIP REVIVED

1975	C. O'Connor Jr.	Woodbrook
1976	B. Crenshaw	Portmarnock
1977	H. Green	Portmarnock
1978	K. Brown	Portmarnock
1979	M. James	Portmarnock
1980	M. James	Portmarnock
1981	S. Torrance	Portmarnock
1982	J. O'Leary	Portmarnock
1983	S. Ballesteros	Royal Dublin
1984	B. Langer	Royal Dublin
1985	S. Ballesteros	Royal Dublin
1986	S. Ballesteros	Portmarnock
1987	B. Langer	Portmarnock
1988	I. Woosnam	Portmarnock
1989	I. Woosnam	Portmarnock
1990	J.M. Olazábal	Portmarnock
1991	N. Faldo	Killarney
1992	N. Faldo	Killarney
1993	N. Faldo	Mount Juliet
1994	B. Langer	Mount Juliet
1995	S. Torrance	Mount Juliet
1996	C. Montgomerie	Druids Glen
1997	C. Montgomerie	Druids Glen
1998	D. Carter	Druids Glen
1999	S. García	Druids Glen
2000	P. Sjoland	Ballybunion
2001	C. Montgomerie	Fota Island
2002	S. Hansen	Fota Island

(after play-off with D. Fichardt, R. Bland, and N. Fasth)

2003	M. Campbell	Portmarnock
2004	Brett Rumford	Baltray
2005	Stephen Dodd	Carton House

How to Use this Guide

THIS BOOK AIMS TO GIVE THE VISITOR TO IRELAND, AND ALSO THE IRISH GOLFER, a comprehensive guide to a great range of courses, which are listed by county in geographical areas and alphabetically by club in the index. Where possible, all the contact information you need is listed – addresses, telephone numbers, fax numbers, email addresses and websites, along with the names of the secretary and professional. There are also directions and suggestions for accommodation where applicable.

To give you an idea of what to expect from the course, we detail the number of holes, yardages – in most cases from the championship or medal tees – par and standard scratch score (SSS). Many clubs in the Republic of Ireland measure their courses in metres rather than yards. When converting, add 10 per cent to the metres to get the yardage. For example, a hole of 500 metres will be approximately 550 yards. In some cases, there is also a description of the club's signature hole.

Clubs operate different restrictions, and wherever possible, these are detailed along with green fees. Please note that green fees are liable to change without notice and that the fees published should be regarded as a guide only. All prices quoted are in the local currency. Prices in Northern Ireland are in pounds sterling, while the Republic, in common with most of Europe, changed their currency to euros in 2002. At the time of going to press, £1 sterling = 1.45 euros. We also state whether clubs have a bar and catering services and list the facilities they provide, such as the hire of buggies and trolleys, clubs and caddies, changing-rooms, putting green, pro-shop, practice ground, driving range and tuition.

While every effort has been made to compile an accurate and complete guide to Ireland's golf courses, the publisher and author cannot be held responsible for any errors, omissions or changes to details.

If you are planning to visit an Irish golf course, you should telephone the club in advance to determine playing times, availability and green fees.

Dublin
and the East

Ireland's Golf Courses

County Cavan

BELTURBET GOLF CLUB

A very tricky, hilly parkland course in excellent order with small elevated greens and few bunkers but many trees. Has been described as one of the best nine-hole courses in Ireland. Founded in 1948.

9 holes parkland, 5,850 metres (6,435 yards) for 18 holes, par 68 (SSS 65).

ADDRESS: Erne Hill, Belturbet, Co. Cavan.
TELEPHONE: +353 (0)49 952 2287.
VISITORS: Welcome.
GREEN FEES: €15 per round weekdays and weekends.
CATERING: Full facilities and bar.
FACILITIES: Locker rooms, putting green, pro-shop, trolleys, club hire.
LOCATION: Half a mile from Belturbet on the Cavan Road.

BLACKLION GOLF CLUB

A scenic and testing parkland course, founded in 1962 and designed by Eddie Hackett, on the shores of Lough McNean.

9 holes parkland, 5,840 metres (6,424 yards) for 18 holes, par 72 (SSS 69). Ladies 4,971 metres (5,468) yards, par 72.

ADDRESS: Toam, Blacklion, Co. Cavan.
TELEPHONE: +353 (0)71 985 3024.
EMAIL: blackliongolfclub@yahoo.ie
WEBSITE: www.blackliongolf.netfirms.com
VISITORS: Mondays, Tuesdays, Wednesdays and Fridays.
GREEN FEES: €15 per round weekdays, €20 weekends and public holidays.

CATERING: Restaurant and bar.
FACILITIES: Locker rooms, chipping/putting practice area, trolleys.
LOCATION: 30 miles north-east of Sligo, 14 miles west of Enniskillen.

CABRA CASTLE GOLF CLUB

Very scenic woodland course with mature trees set in 100 acres. Not difficult but a pleasant experience. Founded in 1979.

9 holes parkland, 5,261 metres (5,787 yards) for 18 holes, par 70 (SSS 68). Ladies 4,853 metres (5,338 yards), par 70 (SSS 72).

SIGNATURE HOLE:
FOURTH (125 yards, par 3) – a profusion of rhododendron bushes on the tee.

ADDRESS: Kingscourt, Co. Cavan.
TELEPHONE: +353 (0)42 966 7030.
FAX: +353 (0)42 966 7039.
EMAIL: sales@cabracastle.com
WEBSITE: www.cabracastle.com
VISITORS: Yes.
GREEN FEES: €15 per round weekdays and weekends.
CATERING: Full facilities in Cabra Castle Hotel.
FACILITIES: Locker rooms, putting green, practice facilities, trolleys, club hire, caddies.
LOCATION: 6 miles south of Carrickmacross, 1 hour from Dublin.
LOCAL HOTELS: Cabra Castle (on the course).

COUNTY CAVAN GOLF CLUB

Attractive and challenging parkland course founded in 1894, with many centuries-old trees and rhododendron bushes adding to the beauty and the degree of difficulty.

18 holes parkland, 5,634 metres (6,197

yards), par 70 (SSS 69). Ladies 4,815 metres (5,296 yards), par 72 (SSS 70).

SIGNATURE HOLE:
TENTH (189 metres [208 yards], par 3) – challenging tee shot from in front of the clubhouse to an undulating green in the shade of an old chestnut tree.

ADDRESS: Arnmore House, Drumelis, Co. Cavan.
TELEPHONE & FAX: +353 (0)49 433 1541.
EMAIL: info@cavangolf.ie
WEBSITE: www.cavangolf.ie
HONORARY SECRETARY: Jim McCorry.
PROFESSIONAL: William Noble +353 (0)49 433 1388.
VISITORS: Welcome.
GREEN FEES: €25 per round weekdays, €30 per round at weekends.
CREDIT CARDS ACCEPTED: All major cards.
CATERING: Restaurant and bar.
FACILITIES: Locker rooms, putting green, practice ground, driving range, pro-shop, buggies, trolleys, club hire.
LOCATION: Off the R198 Killeshandra Road, 1 mile north-west of Cavan.

CROVER HOUSE HOTEL GOLF CLUB

This parkland course slopes down from the hotel towards Lough Sheelin. Ideal for the beginner or the more experienced golfer.
  9 holes parkland, 3,902 metres (4,292 yards) for 18 holes, par 64 (SSS 62). Ladies 3,306 metres (3,636 yards) par 64 (SSS 69).

SIGNATURE HOLE:
NINTH (546 metres, par 5) – good driving hole with difficult approach shot to the green.

ADDRESS: Mountnugent, Co. Cavan.
TELEPHONE: +353 (0)49 854 0832.

FAX: +353 (0)49 854 0356.
EMAIL: crovergolf@eircom.net
WEBSITE: www.croverhousehotel.ie
SECRETARY/MANAGER: Patrick O'Reilly.
VISITORS: Yes.
GREEN FEES: €15.
CREDIT CARDS ACCEPTED: Yes.
CATERING: Yes.
FACILITIES: Locker rooms, putting green, pro-shop, trolleys, club hire.
LOCATION: 4 miles from Ballyjamesduff on shores of Lough Sheelin. 1½ hours from Dublin and 2 hours from Belfast.
LOCAL HOTELS: Crover House Hotel +353 (0)49 854 0206.

SLIEVE RUSSELL HOTEL GOLF AND COUNTRY CLUB

This Paddy Merrigan-designed championship parkland course has established a fine reputation since it opened in 1992. Undulating, sand-based greens and rolling fairways on a 300-acre estate, including 50 acres of lakes, have attracted the 1996 Smurfit Irish PGA Championship and the European Tour's North-west of Ireland Open in 2000 and 2001. It is a challenge from the championship tees, but there are multiple tee positions to suit all standards of golfer.
  18 holes parkland, 7,053 yards, par 72 (SSS 74). Ladies 5,568 yards, par 72 (SSS 72).
  9 holes, par 27.

SIGNATURE HOLE:
THIRTEENTH (529 yards, par 5) – dogleg left around Lough Rud which teases the golfer into risking a lengthy carry over the water to reach the green in two.

ADDRESS: Ballyconnell, Co. Cavan.
TELEPHONE: +353 (0)49 952 5090.
FAX: +353 (0)49 952 6640.

Slieve Russell Hotel Golf and Country Club

EMAIL: Slieve-russell@quinn-hotels.com
WEBSITE: www.quinn-hotels.com
PROFESSIONAL: Liam McCool.
VISITORS: Always welcome – pre-booking advisable. Soft spikes.
GREEN FEES: €72 per round Sundays to Fridays (hotel residents €45), €90 Saturdays (hotel residents €55).
CREDIT CARDS ACCEPTED: All major cards.
CATERING: Restaurant and bar.
FACILITIES: Locker rooms, putting green, practice area, 5-bay floodlit driving range, pro-shop, buggies (€32), trolleys (€3), club hire (€20), bag carriers, tuition.
LOCATION: 18 miles north of Cavan town.
LOCAL HOTELS: Slieve Russell Hotel (on the course).

VIRGINIA GOLF CLUB

Parkland course with narrow, tree-lined fairways overlooking Lough Ramor. Established in 1945.

9 holes parkland, 4,582 yards for 18 holes, par 64 (SSS 62).

ADDRESS: Virginia, Co. Cavan.
TELEPHONE: +353 (0)49 854 8066.
SECRETARY/MANAGER: Pat Murphy.
VISITORS: Welcome. Soft spikes.
GREEN FEES: €15 per round weekdays and weekends.
CATERING: Park Hotel.
FACILITIES: Locker rooms with showers.
LOCATION: 50 miles north of Dublin on the main Dublin–Cavan road.
LOCAL HOTELS: Park Hotel.

County Dublin

BALBRIGGAN GOLF CLUB

Established in 1945, this challenging parkland course about 20 minutes from Dublin Airport has stunning views of the Mountains of Mourne.

18 holes parkland, 5,922 metres (6,514 yards), par 71 (SSS 72). Ladies 5,172 metres (5,689 yards), par 74 (SSS 73).

SIGNATURE HOLE:
FIFTEENTH (392 metres [431 yards], par 4) – sloping gently downhill right to left, the drive is framed by trees right and bunkers left. The further right you go to avoid the bunkers, the longer the second shot becomes. The approach to a generous green has to carry a deeply banked stream that cuts across the front.

ADDRESS: Blackhall, Balbriggan, Co. Dublin.
TELEPHONE: +353 (0)1 841 2229.
FAX: +353 (0)1 841 3927.
EMAIL: balbriggangolfclub@eircom.net
WEBSITE: www.balbriggangolfclub.com
ADMINISTRATION MANAGER: Seamus Rooney.
PROFESSIONAL: Nigel Howley.
VISITORS: Welcome.
GREEN FEES: €35 per round weekdays, €45 at weekends.
CREDIT CARDS ACCEPTED: Yes.
CATERING: Restaurant and bar.
FACILITIES: Locker rooms, practice ground, putting green, tuition, pro-shop, buggies (€25), trolleys (€3).
LOCATION: From Dublin on the main Dublin–Belfast road, take the Balbriggan exit (R132). Just beyond Balrothery, the entrance to the club is on your right. From the north, take the Balbriggan exit (R132) at the start of the Balbriggan bypass, travel through the town and the club is on the left.
LOCAL HOTELS: Bracken Court +353 (0)1 841 3333.

BALCARRICK GOLF CLUB

Founded in 1972. This is a parkland course with water coming into play on ten holes. The feature holes include the eighth, twelfth, fourteenth and seventeenth.

18 holes parkland, 6,191 metres (6,810 yards), par 72 (SSS 73). Ladies 5,093 metres (5,602 yards), par 72 (SSS 71).

ADDRESS: Corballis, Donabate, Co. Dublin.
TELEPHONE: +353 (0)1 843 6957.
FAX: +353 (0)1 843 6228.
EMAIL: balcarr@iol.ie
WEBSITE: www.balcarrickgolfclub.com
PROFESSIONAL: Stephen Rayfus +353 (0)1 843 4034.
VISITORS: Mondays to Fridays are best.
GREEN FEES: €32 per round weekdays, €40 at weekends.
CATERING: Restaurant and bar.
FACILITIES: Locker rooms, practice ground, pro-shop, buggies, trolleys, club hire, tuition.
LOCATION: Off the R126 at Donabate.

BALLINASCORNEY GOLF CLUB

Founded in 1971 in Bohernabreena in County Dublin, the club moved to the current course in 2001. The famed Wicklow Way passes the course, which is overlooked by the Kilmashogue Wood (a local beauty spot) and dominated by the backdrop of the Three Rock Mountain.

9 holes parkland, 4,958 yards for 18 holes, par 66 (SSS 64). Ladies 4,456 yards, par 68 (SSS 65).

ADDRESS: Oldfield Golf Course, Kilmashogue Lane, Rathfarnham, Dublin 16.
TELEPHONE: +353 (0)1 493 7475.
FAX: +353 (0)1 406 9813.
EMAIL: info@ballinascorneygc.com
WEBSITE: www.ballinascorneygc.com
HONORARY SECRETARY: Mark Quinlan.
VISITORS: Yes, weekdays. Telephone for weekend availability.
GREEN FEES: €25 per round.
CREDIT CARDS ACCEPTED: No.
CATERING: Bar food in clubhouse.
FACILITIES: Locker rooms, practice net, putting green, trolleys.
LOCATION: Within easy reach of the M50 motorway and minutes from Rathfarnham village.
LOCAL HOTELS: Taylor's Three Rock, Bewleys.

BEAVERSTOWN GOLF CLUB

Founded in 1985 and designed by Eddie Hackett, this parkland course, which was originally a fruit farm, is a profusion of colour in the spring when the apple trees blossom.

18 holes parkland, 5,972 metres (6,569 yards), par 72. Ladies 5,095 metres (5,604 yards), par 72.

ADDRESS: Donabate, Co. Dublin.
TELEPHONE: +353 (0)1 843 6439.
FAX: +353 (0)1 843 5059.
EMAIL: manager@beaverstown.com
WEBSITE: www.beaverstown.com
PROFESSIONAL: Marcus Casey +353 (0)1 843 4655.
VISITORS: Weekdays, weekends by arrangement. Soft spikes.

GREEN FEES: €48 per round weekdays, €58 at weekends.
CATERING: Restaurant and bar.
FACILITIES: Locker rooms, putting green, practice ground, pro-shop, buggies, trolleys (€2), club hire.
LOCATION: 15 miles north of Dublin, 3 miles from Dublin Airport.

BEECH PARK GOLF CLUB

Undulating but without any heavy climbs, this tree-lined parkland course was established in 1983 and designed by Eddie Hackett. It has its own 'Amen Corner' from the ninth to the thirteenth.

18 holes parkland, 5,762 metres (6,338 yards), par 72 (SSS 70). Ladies 4,878 metres (5,365 yards), par 72 (SSS 71).

SIGNATURE HOLE:
THIRTEENTH (469 metres [516 yards], par 5) – sweeps to the right with water all along the right up to the green.

ADDRESS: Johnstown, Rathcoole, Co. Dublin.
TELEPHONE: +353 (0)1 458 0522/0100.
FAX: +353 (0)1 458 8365.
EMAIL: info@beechpark.ie
WEBSITE: www.beechpark.ie
SECRETARY: Paul Muldowney.
PROFESSIONAL: Zak Rouiller.
VISITORS: Yes.
GREEN FEES: €40.
CREDIT CARDS ACCEPTED: Yes.
CATERING: Restaurant and bar.
FACILITIES: Locker rooms, practice ground, putting green, pro-shop, buggies (€20), trolleys (€3).
LOCATION: South on N7. Turn into Rathcoole village, 2 miles from the village.
LOCAL HOTELS: Ambassador Hotel.

CARRICKMINES GOLF CLUB

Mixture of heathland and parkland, founded in 1900.

9 holes heathland/parkland, 6,063 yards, par 71 (SSS 69). Ladies 5,470 yards, par 72 (SSS 71).

ADDRESS: Golf Lane, Carrickmines, Dublin 18.
TELEPHONE: +353 (0)1 295 5972.
EMAIL: carrickminesgolf@eircom.net
VISITORS: Any day, except for Wednesdays and Saturdays.
GREEN FEES: €33 per round weekdays, €38 at weekends.
CATERING: Bar.
FACILITIES: Locker rooms, putting green, practice ground, trolleys.
LOCATION: 8 miles south of Dublin.

CASTLE GOLF CLUB

This parkland course designed by Harry Colt with five par 3s and three not too demanding par 5s was upgraded in 1999 with reconstruction of all 18 greens to USGA sand-based standard. Founded in 1913, it has wonderful views of the Dublin Mountains.

18 holes parkland, 6,290 yards, par 70.

ADDRESS: Woodside Drive, Rathfarnham, Dublin 14.
TELEPHONE & FAX: +353 (0)1 490 4207.
EMAIL: info@castlegc.ie
WEBSITE: www.castlegc.ie
SECRETARY/MANAGER: John McCormack.
PROFESSIONAL: David Kinsella +353 (0)1 492 0272.
VISITORS: Welcome.
GREEN FEES: €80 per round weekdays, €90 weekends and public holidays.
CATERING: Restaurant and bar.

FACILITIES: Locker rooms, putting green, practice facilities, coaching, pro-shop, trolleys (€3), club hire (€15), caddies on request, tuition.
LOCATION: 5 miles south of Dublin.

CASTLEKNOCK GOLF AND COUNTRY CLUB

Recently opened parkland course, designed by Jonathan Gaunt, with large undulating greens and no sharp inclines. The renowned Irish professional David Jones claims the par 3s, all guarded by lakes, are amongst the best he has seen. More than 10 acres of lakes have been created and water comes into play on seven holes, with marshes on some.

18 holes parkland, 6,700 yards, par 72.

SIGNATURE HOLE:
ELEVENTH (par 3) – set out on a lake of three acres, the green is framed by a sloping Donegal rock wall.

ADDRESS: Porterstown Road, Castleknock, Dublin 15.
TELEPHONE: +353 (0)1 820 5600.
FAX: +353 (0)1 820 5653.
EMAIL: info@castleknockgolfclub.ie
WEBSITE: www.castleknockgolfclub.ie
MANAGER: Paddy Maguire.
VISITORS: Every day. Soft spikes.
GREEN FEES: €90 per round.
CATERING: Restaurant and bar.
FACILITIES: Locker rooms, putting green, practice facilities, club shop, buggies(€35), trolleys (€4), club hire (€25).
LOCATION: 3 miles from Dublin centre alongside Farmleigh House on the outskirts of Castleknock village.
LOCAL HOTELS: Castleknock Hotel (on the course).

CHRISTY O'CONNOR GOLF CLUB

Founded in 1996, this is a challenging parkland course with two very long par 5s and six par 4s over 400 yards.

18 holes parkland, 5,924 metres (6,516 yards), par 70 (SSS 70). Ladies 4,899 metres (5,388 yards), par 70 (SSS 70).

ADDRESS: Silloge Park Golf Course, Ballymum Road, Swords, Co. Dublin.
TELEPHONE: +353 (0)1 862 0464.
FAX: +353 (0)1 844 1250.
VISITORS: Yes.
GREEN FEES: €18 per round weekdays, €25 at weekends.
CATERING: Coffee shop.
FACILITIES: Locker rooms.
LOCATION: Next to Dublin Airport.

CITYWEST HOTEL AND GOLF CLUB

Two parkland courses on 300 acres in the foothills of the Dublin Mountains – the Championship Course, established in 1994, which has hosted several major championships, and the Lakes Course, which opened in 2000. Designer Christy O'Connor Jr. reckons that the last three holes of the Championship Course is one of the best finishing stretches to be found in Ireland. The Lakes Course has eight par 3s and, as you would expect, water comes into play on thirteen of the holes.

CHAMPIONSHIP COURSE: 18 holes parkland, 6,266 yards, par 69 (SSS 71). Ladies 5,451 yards, par 70.

LAKES COURSE: 18 holes parkland, 5,154 yards, par 65 (SSS 65). Ladies 4,112 yards, par 65.

CHAMPIONSHIP COURSE SIGNATURE HOLE: EIGHTEENTH (437 yards, par 4) – tough finishing hole. The drive has a water hazard running the length of the hole on the left side. The approach to the green is over a lake to a well-guarded green that slopes from back to front. Finishing with a par is a real treat.

LAKES COURSE SIGNATURE HOLE: EIGHTEENTH (195 yards, par 3) – lovely finishing hole that is partly surrounded by water. One of many challenging and beautiful short holes on the course. Miss left and there are many bunkers to catch your shot while the water awaits on the right and long. Pin position adds to the challenge of the hole.

ADDRESS: 16 Jigginstown Park, Saggart, Co. Dublin.
TELEPHONE: +353 (0)1 401 0878/0501.
FAX: +353 (0)1 401 0945.
EMAIL: golf@citywesthotel.com
WEBSITE: www.citywesthotel.com
VISITORS: Yes. Soft spikes.
GREEN FEES: Championship course – €45 per round Mondays and Tuesdays (residents €40), €55 Wednesdays and Thursdays (€45), €65 Fridays to Sundays, (€50). Lakes Course – €30 per round Mondays and Tuesdays (€25 residents), €40 Wednesdays and Thursdays (€30), €45 Fridays to Sundays (€40).
FACILITIES: Locker rooms, putting green, practice area, golf academy with 20-bay driving range, buggies (€40), trolleys (€3), caddies on request, club hire (€25).
CATERING: Restaurant and bar.
LOCATION: From Dublin take N7, then turn left on N82.
LOCAL HOTELS: Citywest Hotel (on the course).

CLONTARF GOLF CLUB

This pleasant parkland course has rolling fairways and mature trees. It is relatively short, but its narrow fairways call for accuracy off the tee, and its greens can be fast. Founded in 1912.

18 holes parkland, 5,317 metres (5,848 yards), par 69 (SSS 68). Ladies 4,949 metres (5,443 yards), par 71 (SSS 71).

SIGNATURE HOLE:
TWELFTH (334 metres [367 yards], par 4) – known locally as 'the quarry hole', you drive to a plateau with out of bounds on the right. Approach is to the green in a valley, with two ponds and two greenside bunkers. A large bunker to the rear of the green traps an over-hit shot.

ADDRESS: Donnycarney House, Malahide Road, Dublin 3.
TELEPHONE: +353 (0)1 833 1892.
FAX: +353 (0)1 833 1933.
EMAIL: info.cgc@indigo.ie
WEBSITE: www.clontarfgolfclub.ie
SECRETARY: Arthur Cahill.
PROFESSIONAL: Mark Callan.
VISITORS: Yes.
GREEN FEES: €50 weekdays, €60 at weekends.
CREDIT CARDS ACCEPTED: Yes.
CATERING: Restaurant and bar.
FACILITIES: Locker rooms, practice ground, putting green, pro-shop, buggies limited (€25), trolleys (€3), club hire (€20).
LOCATION: Off the Malahide Road less than 3 miles from the centre of Dublin city and close to Dublin Airport.
LOCAL HOTELS: The Grand Hotel, Malahide +353 (0)1 845 0000; Clontarf Castle Hotel +353 (0)1 833 2321.

CORBALLIS LINKS

Set on the same stretch of links land that hosts The Island Golf Club, this public course offers an unusual mix of par 3s, 4s and 5s coupled with fantastic greens, which former Irish Ryder Cup hero Philip Walton has claimed are some of the best and most consistent in the country. Ruggedly beautiful, it is playable all year round. Established in 2003.

18 holes links, 4,971 metres (5,468 yards), par 65 (SSS 64). Ladies 4,600 metres (5,060 yards), par 64.

ADDRESS: Corballis, Donabate, Co. Dublin.
TELEPHONE: +353 (0)1 843 6583.
FAX: +353 (0)1 822 6668.
EMAIL: corballislinks@golfdublin.com
WEBSITE: www.golfdublin.com
SECRETARY/MANAGER: Austin Levins.
VISITORS: Every day.
GREEN FEES: €20 per round weekdays, €25 at weekends.
CATERING: Bar, snacks, lunch.
FACILITIES: Buggies, trolleys (€2), club hire (€6).
LOCATION: Situated in Donabate on the coast, 25 miles north of Dublin city off the Dublin–Belfast road (N1).
LOCAL HOTELS: The Dunes Hotel.

CORRSTOWN GOLF CLUB

The River Course is parkland with fairway mounds, burns, lakes and a small river meandering through and coming into play on several holes, culminating in a challenging island-green finish. The Orchard Course has mature trees and rolling pastureland, offering a relaxing and enjoyable game. Founded in 1993.

RIVER COURSE – 18 holes parkland, 6,298 metres (6,927 yards), par 72 (SSS 72).

Ladies 5,232 metres (5,755 yards), par 72 (SSS 72).

ORCHARD COURSE – 9 holes parkland, 5,584 metres (6,142 yards) for 18 holes, par 70 (SSS 68). Ladies 5,064 metres (5,570 yards), par 72 (SSS 71).

RIVER COURSE SIGNATURE HOLE: EIGHTEENTH (382 metres [420 yards], par 4) – with an island green, the decision on your approach shot is whether to go for the hole or lay up.

ADDRESS: Corrstown, Kilsallaghan, Co. Dublin.
TELEPHONE: +353 (0)1 864 0533/4.
FAX: +353 (0)1 864 0537.
EMAIL: info@corrstowngolfclub.com
WEBSITE: www.corrstowngolfclub.com
SECRETARY: Michele Jeanes.
PROFESSIONAL: Pat Gittens.
VISITORS: Yes.
GREEN FEES: €50 weekdays, €60 at weekends.
CREDIT CARDS ACCEPTED: Yes.
CATERING: Restaurant and bar.
FACILITIES: Locker rooms, practice ground, putting green, pro-shop, buggies, trolleys.
LOCATION: 6 miles north of Dublin Airport.
LOCAL HOTELS: Great Southern Hotel, Dublin Airport +353 (0)1 844 6000.

DEER PARK HOTEL AND GOLF COURSES

Established in 1974, Deer Park offers four parkland courses in 450 acres of parkland to suit all standards of golfer. There's the eighteen-hole Deer Park course and two nine-hole courses, the Grace O'Malley and St Fintan's, which combine to make the Old Course, plus a 12-hole short course. The Deer Park gets off to a challenging start with the 414-yard first downhill and the green

not visible from the tee. The second is a tricky 225-yard par 3 with mature woodland lining either side of the fairway. In spring, the profusion of cherry blossom trees make it a particularly attractive hole. Set in the grounds of Howth Castle with spectacular views of Dublin Bay and the coastline, H.G. Wells reputedly described this ever-changing panorama as the finest sight west of Naples.

DEER PARK – 18 holes parkland, 6,293 metres (6,922 yards), par 72 (SSS 71). Ladies 4,678 metres (5,145 yards), par 72 (SSS 72).

GRACE O'MALLEY 9 holes parkland and ST FINTAN'S 9 holes parkland as an 18-hole course, 5,927 metres (6,519 yards), par 72 (SSS 72). Ladies 4,983 metres (5,481 yards), par 72, (SSS 72).

SHORT COURSE – 12 holes parkland, 1,598 metres (1,757 yards), par 36.

ADDRESS: Howth, Co. Dublin.
TELEPHONE: +353 (0)1 832 2624.
FAX: +353 (0)1 839 2405.
EMAIL: sales@deerpark.iol.ie
WEBSITE: www.deerpark-hotel.ie
SECRETARY/MANAGER: David Tighe.
VISITORS: Welcome. Restrictions Sunday mornings. Hotel residents on golf-inclusive packages may enjoy unlimited use of the courses for the duration of their stay.
GREEN FEES: €18 per round weekdays, €26 at weekends.
CREDIT CARDS ACCEPTED: Yes.
CATERING: Restaurant and bar.
FACILITIES: Locker rooms, putting green, practice facilities, 18-hole pitch and putt course, buggies (€25), trolleys (€2), club hire (€16), tuition.
LOCATION: 9 miles east of Dublin city centre.
LOCAL HOTELS: Deer Park Hotel on site.

DONABATE GOLF CLUB

This fairly flat parkland course amongst lakes and trees, with water coming into play on nine holes, has sand-based greens and was recently extended to 27 holes. The main course is the red and blue nines and is tight and tree lined. The new clubhouse was built in 2003. Founded in 1925.

27 holes parkland, Red/Blue 5,958 metres (6,553 yards), par 72 (SSS 72); Yellow 2,918 metres (3,209 yards), par 36. Ladies Red/Blue 5,411 metres (5,952 yards), par 73 (SSS 72). Yellow 2,538 metres (2,791 yards), par 36.

BLUE COURSE SIGNATURE HOLE
NINTH (480 yards, par 5).

ADDRESS: Balcarrick, Donabate, Co. Dublin.
TELEPHONE: +353 (0)1 843 6346.
FAX: +353 (0)1 843 4488.
EMAIL: info@donabategolfclub.com
WEBSITE: www.donabategolfclub.com
GOLF ADMINISTRATOR: Brian May.
PROFESSIONAL: Hugh Jackson.
VISITORS: Yes.
GREEN FEES: €50 per round weekdays, €65 weekends and public holidays. Early bird €30 weekdays, €40 weekends and public holidays.
CREDIT CARDS ACCEPTED: MasterCard/Visa.
CATERING: Restaurant and bar.
FACILITIES: Locker rooms, putting green, pro-shop, buggies (€25), trolleys (€3), club hire (€20), tuition.
LOCATION: 10 minutes north of Dublin Airport off M1.
LOCAL HOTELS: Waterside Hotel; White Sands Hotel, Portmarnock +353 (0)1 846 0003; Carnegie Court Hotel.

DUBLIN CITY GOLF CLUB

This is a very tight parkland course founded in 1971 and originally designed by Eddie Hackett with redesign by Frank Clarke. Every hole is different and has a character of its own.

18 holes parkland, 5,568 metres (6,124 yards), par 69 (SSS 67). Ladies 4,838 metres (5,321 yards), par 70 (SSS 69).

ADDRESS: Ballinascorney, Tallaght, Co. Dublin.
TELEPHONE: +353 (0)1 451 2082.
FAX: +353 (0)1 459 8445.
EMAIL: info@dublincitygolf.com
WEBSITE: www.dublincitygolf.com
VISITORS: Yes, weekdays.
GREEN FEES: €25 per round weekdays, €38 at weekends.
CATERING: Bar.
FACILITIES: Locker rooms, putting green, buggies, club hire.
LOCATION: 8 miles south-west of Dublin.

DUBLIN MOUNTAIN GOLF CLUB

Undulating parkland course, founded in 1993.

18 holes parkland, 5,635 metres (6,198 yards), par 71 (SSS 69). Ladies 5,232 metres (5,755 yards), par 73 (SSS 71).

ADDRESS: Gortlum, Brittas, Co. Dublin.
TELEPHONE: +353 (0)1 458 2570.
FAX: +353 (0)1 458 2048.
EMAIL: dmgc@eircom.net
VISITORS: Yes.
GREEN FEES: €18 per round weekdays, €20 at weekends.
CATERING: Snacks.
FACILITIES: Locker rooms, putting green, practice ground, trolleys.
LOCATION: 1 mile east of Brittas, off the R114.

Ireland's Golf Courses

DUN LAOGHAIRE GOLF CLUB

This well-wooded parkland course, designed by Harry Colt in 1918, demands accuracy. The 465-metre (512-yard) par-5 18th has featured in the *Guinness Book of Records* as the venue for the longest recorded drive by an amateur, Tommy Campbell.

18 holes parkland, 5,313 metres (5,844 yards), par 71 (SSS 68).

ADDRESS: Eglinton Park, Tivoli Road, Dun Laoghaire, Co. Dublin.
TELEPHONE: +353 (0)1 280 3916.
FAX: +353 (0)1 280 4868.
EMAIL: dlgc@iol.ie
WEBSITE: www.dunlaoghairegolfclub.ie
PROFESSIONAL: Vincent Carey.
VISITORS: Fridays and Sundays are best.
GREEN FEES: €55 per round.
CREDIT CARDS ACCEPTED: All major cards.
CATERING: Restaurant and bar.
FACILITIES: Locker rooms, putting green, practice ground, pro-shop, trolleys (€3), club hire (€20), tuition.
LOCATION: 7 miles south of Dublin. Dun Laoghaire ferry port, 1 mile.

EDMONDSTOWN GOLF CLUB

Established in 1944, this is a testing parkland course in the foothills of the Dublin Mountains with scenic views. Well maintained.

18 holes parkland, 6,011 metres (6,612 yards), par 71 (SSS 73). Ladies 4,875 metres (5,362 yards), par 72 (SSS 70).

SIGNATURE HOLE:
SIXTH (382 metres [420 yards], par 4) – claimed to be one of the best inland par 4s in Ireland.

ADDRESS: Edmondstown Road, Rathfarnham, Dublin 16, Co. Dublin.
TELEPHONE: +353 (0)1 493 1082.
FAX: +353 (0)1 493 3152.
EMAIL: info@edmondstowngolfclub.ie
WEBSITE: www.edmondstowngolfclub.ie
SECRETARY/MANAGER: Selwyn Davies.
PROFESSIONAL: Gareth McShea +353 (0)1 494 1049.
VISITORS: Welcome.
GREEN FEES: €55 weekdays, €65 at weekends.
CREDIT CARDS ACCEPTED: Yes.
CATERING: Restaurant and bar.
FACILITIES: Locker rooms, practice ground, putting green, pro-shop, buggies (€35), trolleys (€3), club hire (€25 including trolley).
LOCATION: 8 miles south-west of Dublin city centre. Take junction 11 off the M50.
LOCAL HOTELS: Bewley's +353 (0)1 293 5000, Camden Court +353 (0)1 475 9666, Plaza +353 (0)1 462 4200.

ELMGREEN GOLF CENTRE

A public parkland course designed by Eddie Hackett, Elmgreen has a challenging layout with undulating greens and year round playability. The centre also has splendid practice facilities, including an 18-hole pitch-and-putt course and a 24-bay floodlit driving range. Founded in 1996.

18 holes parkland, 5,796 yards, par 71 (SSS 68). Ladies 4,948 yards, par 72 (SSS 69).

ADDRESS: Castleknock, Dublin 15.
TELEPHONE: +353 (0)1 820 0797.
FAX: +353 (0)1 822 6668.
EMAIL: elmgreen@golfdublin.com
WEBSITE: www.golfdublin.com
HEAD PROFESSIONAL: Arnold O'Connor.
VISITORS: Every day. Soft spikes.

GREEN FEES: €25 per round weekdays, €32 at weekends.
CATERING: Restaurant and bar.
FACILITIES: Locker rooms, putting green, floodlit 24-bay driving range, pro-shop, 18-hole pitch-and-putt course, buggies (€32), trolleys (€2), club hire (€20), golf academy, tuition.
LOCATION: 15 minutes north of Dublin city centre at the junction of the M50 and the Navan Road, and 5 minutes' drive from the Castleknock exit from Phoenix Park.
LOCAL HOTELS: Travelodge Dublin, Castleknock.

ELM PARK GOLF AND SPORTS CLUB

Established in 1924, this is an interesting parkland course with a stream coming into play on half of the holes. Paddy Merrigan redesigned all the greens in 2002.

18 holes parkland, 5,380 metres (5,918 yards), par 69 (SSS 69). Ladies 4,974 metres (5,471 yards), par 72.

ADDRESS: Nutley House, Nutley Lane, Donnybrook, Dublin 4.
TELEPHONE: +353 (0)1 269 3438.
FAX: +353 (0)1 269 4505.
EMAIL: office@elmparkgolfclub.ie
WEBSITE: www.elmparkgolfclub.ie
PROFESSIONAL: Seamus Green +353 (0)1 269 2650.
VISITORS: Yes, but you should contact the club in advance. Soft spikes.
GREEN FEES: €70 per round weekdays, €90 at weekends.
CATERING: Restaurant and bar.
FACILITIES: Locker rooms, putting green, practice ground, driving range, buggies, trolleys, club hire, caddies on request.
LOCATION: 2 miles from city centre.
LOCAL HOTELS: Bewley's +353 (0)1 293 5000.

FORREST LITTLE GOLF CLUB

Testing, mature parkland course, with many featured water hazards. Established in 1940, it has been used as a pre-qualifying course for the Irish Open. With large sand-based greens and undulating fairways, it is playable all year round.

18 holes parkland, 5,900 metres (6,490 yards), par 71 (SSS 72). Ladies 5,145 metres (5,659 yards), par 73 (SSS 72).

SIGNATURE HOLE:
TWELFTH (315 metres [346 yards], par 4) – dogleg requiring accuracy from tee and for the second shot as the green is surrounded by a water hazard.

ADDRESS: Cloghran, Co. Dublin.
TELEPHONE: +353 (0)1 840 1763.
FAX: +353 (0)1 890 8499.
EMAIL: margaret@forrestlittle.ie
WEBSITE: www.forrestlittle.ie
SECRETARY/MANAGER: Shirley Sleator.
PROFESSIONAL: Tony Judd.
VISITORS: Yes.
GREEN FEES: €50, weekdays only.
CREDIT CARDS ACCEPTED: Yes.
CATERING: Restaurant and bar.
FACILITIES: Locker rooms, practice ground, putting green, pro-shop, buggies (€25), trolleys (€3).
LOCATION: The course runs parallel to Dublin Airport and is 6 miles north of Dublin on the N1.

FOXROCK GOLF CLUB

Tree-lined parkland course. Founded in 1893.

9 holes parkland, 5,667 metres (6,233 yards), par 70 (SSS 65). Ladies 5,179 metres (5,696 yards), par 72 (SSS 72).

ADDRESS: Torquay Road, Foxrock, Dublin 18, Co. Dublin.
TELEPHONE: +353 (0)1 289 3992.
FAX: +353 (0)1 289 4943.
EMAIL: fgc@foxrockgolfclub.com
WEBSITE: www.foxrockgolfclub.com
PROFESSIONAL: David Walker +353 (0)1 289 3414.
VISITORS: Yes, Monday to Wednesday mornings and Thursdays, Fridays and Sundays with a member. Societies Mondays and Thursdays.
GREEN FEES: €50 per round weekdays and weekends.
CATERING: Restaurant and bar.
FACILITIES: Buggies.
LOCATION: 6 miles from Dublin, off the T7.

GLENCULLEN GOLF CLUB

Parkland course with breathtaking views. Founded in 1998.

9 holes parkland, 4,925 metres (5,417 yards) for 18 holes, par 69 (SSS 65). Ladies 4,580 metres (5,038 yards), par 69.

ADDRESS: Glencullen, Co. Dublin.
TELEPHONE: +353 (0)1 294 0898.
EMAIL: info@glencullengolfclub.ie
WEBSITE: www.glencullengolfclub.ie
PROFESSIONAL: Ray Lucy.
VISITORS: Weekday and weekend afternoons.
GREEN FEES: €17 per round weekdays, €22 at weekends.
CATERING: Snacks.
FACILITIES: Locker rooms, practice ground, trolleys, tuition.
LOCATION: Dublin to Stepaside to Kilternan then 4 miles to Glencullen.
LOCAL HOTELS: Foxes, Lambdoyles, Silver Tassie, Killiney Castle Hotel, Stillorgan Park Hotel, Powerscourt Arms Hotel.

GRANGE GOLF CLUB

Tree-lined parkland course founded in 1910 and designed by James Braid.

18 holes parkland, 5,396 metres (5,935 yards), par 68 (SSS 69). Ladies 4,980 metres (5,478 yards), par 71.

ADDRESS: Whitechurch Road, Rathfarnham, Dublin 16.
TELEPHONE: +353 (0)1 493 2889.
FAX: +353 (0)1 493 9490.
EMAIL: administration@grangegolfclub.ie
WEBSITE: www.grangegc.com
PROFESSIONAL: Declan Leigh.
VISITORS: Mondays, Thursdays and Fridays. Soft spikes.
GREEN FEES: €80 per round.
CREDIT CARDS ACCEPTED: All major cards.
CATERING: Restaurant and bar.
FACILITIES: Locker rooms, putting green, practice ground, club shop, buggies (€30), trolleys, caddies on request, tuition.
LOCATION: 7 miles south of Dublin.

GRANGE CASTLE GOLF CLUB

The latest addition to Dublin's municipal pay-and-play courses, established in 1998, is a parkland course designed by Paddy Merrigan, who also designed The Old Head of Kinsale, Slieve Russell and Faithlegg. Four lakes and fifty strategically positioned bunkers add to the degree of difficulty. Good greens.

18 holes parkland, 5,893 metres (6,482 yards), par 71. Ladies 4,986 metres (5,484 yards), par 73.

SIGNATURE HOLE:
FOURTH (386 metres [425 yards], par 4) – a dogleg which involves a tee shot over water, with a further lake to be negotiated in front of the green.

ADDRESS: Nangor Road, Clondalkin, Dublin 22.
TELEPHONE: +353 (0)1 464 1043.
FAX: +353 (0)1 464 1039.
EMAIL: info@grange-castle.com
WEBSITE: www.grange-castle.com
MANAGER: PGA Sports Management.
VISITORS: Every day. Soft spikes.
GREEN FEES: €21 per round weekdays, €30 at weekends.
CREDIT CARDS ACCEPTED: All major cards.
CATERING: Coffee shop, snacks.
FACILITIES: Locker rooms, putting green, practice facilities, club shop, buggies (€30), trolleys (€3), club hire (€15).
LOCATION: Just off the Naas road, 5 minutes from Newlands Cross in Clondalkin and M50.

HAZEL GROVE GOLF CLUB

Very hilly parkland 18-hole course based on an 11-hole layout. Founded in 1988 and designed by Eddie Hackett.

11 holes parkland, 5,500 yards for 18 holes, par 69 (SSS 66). Ladies 5,076 yards, par 70 (SSS 68).

ADDRESS: Mount Seskin Road, Jobstown, Tallaght, Dublin 24.
TELEPHONE & FAX: +353 (0)1 452 0911.
EMAIL: info@hazelgrove.ie
WEBSITE: www.hazelgrove.ie
SECRETARY/MANAGER: Vincent Dempsey.
VISITORS: Mondays, Wednesdays and Fridays. Phone for availability.
GREEN FEES: €20 per round weekdays, €22 at weekends.
CATERING: Bar and function room.
FACILITIES: Locker rooms, putting green, practice ground, trolleys.
LOCATION: Out of Tallaght on Blessington Road, take second turn left after the Jobstown Inn.

LOCAL HOTELS: Plaza Hotel, Tallaght +353 (0)1 462 4200, Abberley Court Hotel, Tallaght +353 (0)1 459 6000.

HERMITAGE GOLF CLUB

This parkland course was founded in 1905 as nine holes and upgraded by Eddie Hackett. The River Liffey comes into play on a number of holes, namely the tenth and eleventh.

18 holes parkland, 6,064 metres (6,670 yards), par 71 (SSS 71). Ladies 5,318 metres (5,849 yards), par 73 (SSS 73).

ADDRESS: Ballydowd, Lucan, Co. Dublin.
TELEPHONE: +353 (0)1 626 8491.
FAX: +353 (0)1 623 8881.
EMAIL: hermitagegolf@eircom.net
WEBSITE: www.hermitagegolf.ie
PROFESSIONAL: Simon Byrne +355 (0)1 626 8072.
VISITORS: Mondays, Thursdays and Fridays.
GREEN FEES: €80 per round weekdays, €85 at weekends.
CREDIT CARDS ACCEPTED: MasterCard/Visa.
CATERING: Restaurant and bar.
FACILITIES: Locker rooms, putting green, practice ground, driving range, pro-shop, buggies (€35), trolleys (€4), club hire (€20), caddies, tuition.
LOCATION: 6 miles from Dublin on the north-east of Lucan.
LOCAL HOTELS: Bewleys Hotel, Finnstown Hotel, Green Isle Hotel, Moran's Red Cow Hotel, Spa Hotel.

HOLLYSTOWN GOLF CLUB

Mature parkland pay-and-play courses designed by Eddie Hackett, featuring trees, lakes and streams. Founded in 1992 and extended to 27 holes in 1999. The three nine-hole courses, now known as yellow, blue and red, allow for some interesting combinations.

YELLOW – 9 holes parkland, 3,072 yards, par 35. Ladies 2,493 yards, par 35.

BLUE – 9 holes parkland, 3,444 yards, par 36. Ladies 2,648 yards, par 35.

RED – 9 holes parkland, 3,057 yards, par 35. Ladies 2,488 yards, par 36.

ADDRESS: Hollystown, Dublin 15.
TELEPHONE: +353 (0)1 820 7444.
FAX: +353 (0)1 820 7447.
EMAIL: info@hollystown.com
WEBSITE: www.hollystown.com
VISITORS: Every day.
GREEN FEES: €28 per round weekdays, €38 weekends and public holidays.
CREDIT CARDS ACCEPTED: MasterCard/Visa.
CATERING: Restaurant and bar.
FACILITIES: Locker rooms, putting green, practice ground, driving range, club shop, buggies (€25), trolleys (€4), club hire (€20), tuition.
LOCATION: 8 miles off the N3 (Dublin–Cavan road) at Mulhuddart or off the N2 (Dublin–Ashbourne road).
LOCAL HOTELS: Burlington Hotel, Jurys Hotel, Berkeley Court, Mount Herbert, Central Hotel, Stakis Hotel, Moran's Red Cow Hotel, Mont Clare Hotel, Conrad Hotel.

HOLLYWOOD LAKES GOLF CLUB

Testing parkland course with narrow undulating fairways and water hazards on nine holes. Founded in 1991.

18 holes parkland, 6,088 metres (6,696 yards), par 72 (SSS 72). Ladies 5,136 metres (5,649 yards), par 72.

ADDRESS: Hollywood, Ballyboughal, Co. Dublin.
TELEPHONE: +353 (0)1 843 3407.
FAX: +353 (0)1 843 3002.

EMAIL: info@hollywoodlakesgolfclub.com
WEBSITE: www.hollywoodlakesgolfclub.com
MANAGER AND PROFESSIONAL: Sid Baldwin.
VISITORS: Mondays, Tuesdays and Thursdays are best.
GREEN FEES: €35 per round weekdays, €40 Fridays, and €45 weekends and public holidays.
CATERING: Restaurant and bar.
FACILITIES: Locker rooms, putting green, golf shop, driving range, pro-shop, buggies (€30), trolleys (€3), club hire, tuition.
LOCATION: 15 minutes north of Dublin airport via the N1 and the R129 to Ballyboughal.
LOCAL HOTELS: Grand Hotel, Grove Hotel.

HOWTH GOLF CLUB

This challenging heathland course, designed by James Braid in 1916, is situated on the legendary Hill of Howth about 10 miles from Dublin city centre. It commands unrivalled views south over Dublin Bay and the Wicklow Mountains and north to the Mountains of Mourne. Gorse and heather bloom in season and add to the charm of the course.

18 holes heathland, 5,634 metres (6,197 yards), par 71 (SSS 69). Ladies 4,941 metres (5,435 yards), par 72 (SSS 72).

SIGNATURE HOLE:
FIFTEENTH (137 metres [151 yards], par 3) – may demand anything from a three-wood to a pitching wedge depending on the wind direction. Dublin Bay looms in the middle distance, backed by the Wicklow Mountains. The hole is protected by out of bounds at the rear and a stream on the left. Those looking for the member's bounce favour hitting it down the right.

ADDRESS: Carrickbrack Road, Sutton, Dublin 13.

TELEPHONE: +353 (0)1 832 3055.
FAX: +353 (0)1 832 1793.
EMAIL: secretary@howthgolfclub.ie
WEBSITE: www.howthgolfclub.ie
MANAGER: Paul Kennedy.
PROFESSIONAL: John McGuirk.
VISITORS: Yes.
GREEN FEES: €50.
CREDIT CARDS ACCEPTED: Yes.
CATERING: Restaurant and bar.
FACILITIES: Locker rooms, practice ground, putting green, pro-shop, buggies (€25), trolleys (€2), club hire (€25).
LOCATION: 10 miles north-east of Dublin city centre, 2 miles from Sutton Cross on the Sutton side of Hill of Howth.
LOCAL HOTELS: Marine Hotel, Sutton +353 (0)1 839 0000, Deer Park Hotel +353 (0)1 832 2624.

THE ISLAND GOLF CLUB

A classic links course, established in 1890, The Island presents a formidable challenge to test the capabilities of all golfers. Undulating fairways roll through majestic 25-foot high sand dunes. Situated on Corballis Peninsula, the course is just 5 miles north of Dublin Airport and offers magnificent splendour and solitude. It is an Open Championship qualifying course from 2005 to 2010.

18 holes links, 6,203 metres (6,823 yards), par 71 (SSS 73). Ladies 5,403 metres (5,943 yards), par 75.

SIGNATURE HOLE:
THIRTEENTH ('Broadmeadow', 192 metres [211 yards], par 3) – Christy O'Connor, sen., put this hole in the top three of par 3s in Ireland. With a length of 211 yards from the back tee across a valley and the seashore, which is out of bounds, on your right, a par here is always acceptable.

ADDRESS: Corballis, Donabate, Co. Dublin.
TELEPHONE: +353 (0)1 843 6205.
FAX: +353 (0)1 843 6860.
EMAIL: info@theislandgolfclub.com
WEBSITE: www.theislandgolfclub.com
SECRETARY/MANAGER: Peter McDunphy.
PROFESSIONAL: Kevin Kelliher.
VISITORS: Welcome.
GREEN FEES: €125 all week (time restrictions at weekends), €85 early bird.
CREDIT CARDS ACCEPTED: Amex/ MasterCard/Visa.
CATERING: Restaurant and bar.
FACILITIES: Locker rooms, practice ground, putting green, club shop, buggies, trolleys, club hire.
LOCATION: Follow signs for Belfast and the M1 from Dublin. Join the M1 and take the second exit for Donabate. At the roundabout take the third exit, and at the next roundabout, take the second exit (R126). Pass Newbridge House and take the second right (signposted to The Island Golf Club).
LOCAL HOTELS: Waterside Hotel, Donabate +353 (0)1 843 6153, The Grand, Malahide +353 (0)1 845 0000, Carnegie Court, Swords +353 (0)1 840 4384.

KILLINEY GOLF CLUB

Parkland course, established in 1903, on the side of Killiney Hill.

9 holes parkland, 6,431 yards for 18 holes, par 70 (SSS 70). Ladies 5,683 yards, par 72, (SSS 72).

SIGNATURE HOLE:
FIFTH (174 yards, par 3) – the highest point of the course. Original hole restored during centenary year in 2003. Usually into the prevailing east wind to a two-tiered green.

The fifth green at Killiney Golf Club

ADDRESS: Ballinclea Road, Killiney, Co. Dublin.
TELEPHONE: +353 (0)1 285 2823.
FAX: +353 (0)1 285 2861.
EMAIL: killineygolfclub@eircom.net
SECRETARY/MANAGER: Michael F. Walsh.
PROFESSIONAL: Paddy O'Boyle +353 (0)1 285 6294.
VISITORS: Welcome Mondays, Wednesdays, Fridays and Sundays (afternoons). Essential to check with pro-shop in advance. Soft spikes.
GREEN FEES: €55 per round.
CREDIT CARDS ACCEPTED: Yes.

CATERING: Bar and light snacks available daily. Dinner every Tuesday, lunch on Sundays.
CATERING: Bar in new clubhouse.
FACILITIES: Locker rooms, putting green, practice ground, pro-shop, buggies (€25), trolleys (€3), club hire (€35), tuition.
LOCATION: Off the roundabout at Killiney Shopping Centre, Rochestown Avenue, Dun Laoghaire.
LOCAL HOTELS: Fitzpatrick Castle Hotel +353 (0)1 230 5400, Rochestown Lodge +353 (0)1 285 3555.

KILMASHOGUE GOLF CLUB

Parkland course situated at the base of the Three Rock Mountains with a mixture of mature trees, rivers, a lake and finely manicured greens. Established in 1995.

9 holes parkland, 5,320 metres (5,850 yards), par 70 (SSS 70). Ladies 5,185 metres (5,703 yards), par 72 (SSS 71).

SIGNATURE HOLE:
FIFTH (108 yards, par 3).

ADDRESS: St Columba's College, College Road, Whitechurch, Dublin 16.
TELEPHONE: +353 (0)1 493 0729.
EMAIL: kilmashoguegc@eircom.net
WEBSITE: www.kilmashoguegc.ie
SECRETARY: Derek P. Whelan.
VISITORS: With member.
GREEN FEES: With member on request.
CREDIT CARDS ACCEPTED: No.
FACILITIES: Locker rooms, practice net, putting green.
CATERING: No.
LOCATION: From Dublin take the N11 southbound following the signs for Wexford then the R113 (Leopardstown Road). Head for Sandyford and Marlay Park. Pass under the M50 flyover and left again at the roundabout onto Kilmashogue Lane. The entrance to the college is on the left.

KILTERNAN GOLF AND COUNTRY CLUB

The new course and hotel are under construction and will reopen in 2007–08.

ADDRESS: Kilternan Hotel, Enniskerry Road, Kilternan, Co. Dublin.

LUCAN GOLF CLUB

Founded in 1897, this is an undulating parkland course, although the back nine, which features water hazards, is flatter.

18 holes parkland, 5,969 metres (6,565 yards), par 71 (SSS 71). Ladies 5,176 metres (5,693 yards), par 73 (SSS 72).

ADDRESS: Celbridge Road, Lucan, Co. Dublin.
TELEPHONE: +353 (0)1 628 2106.
FAX: +353 (0)1 628 2929.
EMAIL: lucangolf@eircom.net
WEBSITE: www.lucangolfclub.ie
SECRETARY/MANAGER: Tom O'Donnell.
VISITORS: Mondays, Wednesdays and Fridays.
GREEN FEES: €45 per round weekdays, €25 with members only at weekends.
CATERING: Restaurant and bar.
FACILITIES: Locker rooms, putting green, practice ground, practice facilities, buggies (€25), trolleys (€3).
LOCATION: Turn off N4 near the Spa Hotel and take the old Celbridge road to the club.
LOCAL HOTELS: Spa Hotel.

LUTTRELLSTOWN CASTLE GOLF CLUB

A championship parkland course set in the 560-acre grounds of the fifteenth-century Luttrellstown Castle in the Liffey Valley, west of Dublin city. It is renowned for exceptionally well-manicured greens and a magnificent woodland setting. Major course reconstruction is due to be completed in September 2006.

18 holes parkland, 7,021 yards, par 72 (SSS 74).

ADDRESS: Castleknock, Dublin 15.
TELEPHONE: +353 (0)1 808 9988.

FAX: +353 (0)1 808 9989.
EMAIL: golf@luttrellstown.ie
WEBSITE: www.luttrellstown.ie/golf.htm
PROFESSIONAL: Edward Doyle +353 (0)1 808 9980.
VISITORS: Every day but only nine holes in play until course reconstruction is completed.
GREEN FEES: €35.
CATERING: Restaurant and bar.
FACILITIES: Locker rooms, putting green, golf shop, driving range, buggies, trolleys, club hire, caddies, tuition.
LOCATION: Take junction six off the M50 and follow signs to Castleknock and Carpenterstown. The course is 1 mile west of Carpenterstown.
LOCAL HOTELS: Hawthorn Hotel, Lucan Spa Hotel, The Manor Inn.

MALAHIDE GOLF CLUB

One of Ireland's oldest golf clubs, Malahide was founded in 1892 by Nathaniel Hone, reputedly the greatest Irish landscape painter of the period. Set on Dublin's golden north coast beside the beautiful seaside resorts of Malahide and Portmarnock, it offers 27 holes of challenging parkland with a variety of interesting holes, featuring doglegs, water hazards and raised greens.

CHAMPIONSHIP COURSE – 18 holes parkland, 6,066 metres (6,672 yards), par 71 (SSS 72). Ladies 5,200 metres (5,720 yards), par 70 (SSS 70).

9-hole course.

ADDRESS: Beechwood, Malahide, Co. Dublin.
TELEPHONE: +353 (0)1 846 1611.
FAX: +353 (0)1 846 1270.
EMAIL: malgc@clubi.ie
WEBSITE: www.malahidegolfclub.ie

SECRETARY: P.J. Smyth.
PROFESSIONAL: John Murray.
VISITORS: Welcome Mondays to Fridays.
GREEN FEES: €55.
CREDIT CARDS ACCEPTED: MasterCard/Visa.
CATERING: Restaurant and bar.
FACILITIES: Locker rooms, practice ground, putting green, pro-shop, buggies (€30), trolleys (€2.50), club hire (€20).
LOCATION: 3 kilometres from Malahide village, 10 kilometres from Dublin Airport.
LOCAL HOTELS: The Grand, Malahide +353 (0)1 845 0000, White Sands Hotel, Portmarnock +353 (0)1 846 0003.

MARLAY PARK GOLF COURSE

This municipal par-3 course situated within the picturesque Marlay Park complex has good greens, an idyllic setting and a variety of holes.

9 holes parkland, par 27.

ADDRESS: Rathfarnham, Dublin 14.
TELEPHONE: +353 (0)1 495 2100.
FAX: +353 (0)1 295 2639.
EMAIL: stepaside@golfdublin.com
WEBSITE: www.golfdublin.com
VISITORS: Yes, every day.
GREEN FEES: €8 per round weekdays and weekends.
CATERING: Coffee shop, snacks.
FACILITIES: Trolleys (€3).
LOCATION: In Rathfarnham village take a right at the Yellow House pub and Marlay Park is signposted.

MILLTOWN GOLF CLUB

Founded in 1907, this parkland course close to the city of Dublin has views of the Dublin Mountains.

18 holes parkland, 5,638 metres (6,201

yards), par 71 (SSS 69). Ladies 5,208 metres (5,728 yards), par 73 (SSS 73).

ADDRESS: Lower Churchtown Road, Milltown, Co. Dublin.
TELEPHONE: +353 (0)1 497 6090.
FAX: +353 (0)1 497 6008.
EMAIL: info@milltowngolfclub.ie
WEBSITE: www.milltowngolfclub.ie
PROFESSIONAL: John Harnett.
VISITORS: Mondays, Thursdays and Fridays are best. Soft spikes.
GREEN FEES: €80 per round weekdays, €25 with a member at weekends.
CATERING: Restaurant and bar.
FACILITIES: Locker rooms, putting green, practice area, club shop, trolleys, club hire.
LOCATION: 3 miles south of Dublin city centre.
LOCAL HOTELS: Berkeley Court Hotel, Herbert Park Hotel, Jurys Hotel, Montrose Hotel.

NEWLANDS GOLF CLUB

Parkland course designed by James Braid and founded in 1926.

18 holes parkland, 5,897 metres (6,486 yards), par 71 (SSS 70). Ladies 5,095 metres (5,604 yards), par 73 (SSS 72).

ADDRESS: Clondalkin, Co. Dublin.
TELEPHONE: +353 (0)1 459 3157.
FAX: +353 (0)1 459 3498.
EMAIL: info@newlandsgolfclub.com
WEBSITE: www.newlandsgolfclub.com
PROFESSIONAL: Karl O'Donnell +353 (0)1 459 3538.
VISITORS: Yes, societies weekdays.
GREEN FEES: €75 per round weekdays and weekends.
CATERING: Restaurant and bar.
FACILITIES: Locker rooms, putting green,

practice facilities, buggies, trolleys, club hire.
LOCATION: 6 miles from Dublin city centre.

PORTMARNOCK GOLF CLUB

One of the world's great links courses, which has hosted many major championships, including the British Amateur Championship, the Walker Cup, the Canada Cup and the Irish Open. Established in 1894 on duneland north of Dublin city, Bernard Darwin wrote, 'I know of no greater finish in the world than that of the last five holes at Portmarnock.' When Tom Watson prepared here in 1981 for his defence of the British Open title, he said, 'There are no tricks or nasty surprises, only an honest, albeit searching, test of shot-making skills.'

Golf was played here as early as 1858 by the Jamesons, a Scottish family who had founded a distillery in Dublin in 1780 and had used the land as their private golf course.

Often rated as Ireland's best course, many holes deserve to be labelled 'classic'. There is the 411-yard 14th, which Henry Cotton believed to be the best hole in golf. A slight dogleg left, it plays towards the sea, and the problems start with the approach shot. Hit it short and you will catch the two bunkers in the upslope; slightly offline or unlucky and the humps and swales will carry it off track. The fifteenth and the 442-yard fifth, which was regarded as the best by the late Harry Bradshaw, who for forty years was Portmarnock's golf professional and runner-up to Bobby Locke in the 1949 British Open, are also great holes. The sixth, at 603 yards, is a bit of a monster, and the wind is often in your face as you make your approach to a green on top of a hill.

Portmarnock Golf Club

Portmarnock's signature is its fast and true greens, many on plateaux. Darwin recounted the tale of a Scottish professional who 'arrived on the first green in two perfect shots and had ultimately to hole a four-yard putt for a seven'. Located on a small peninsula which extends just briefly southward into the Irish Sea, Portmarnock is bounded by water on three sides and is laid out so that you never play more than two holes in the same direction, which demands a continual assessment of the wind.

In its early days, Portmarnock could be reached only by boat or, at low tide, by horse-drawn carriage. The bell which signalled the last boat of the day still hangs at the caddie master's pavilion near the first tee. There are stunning views. To the south rises the Hill of Howth and Dublin Bay, to the east Ireland's Eye and the Lambay Islands, to the west is the sheltered inlet of the sea and to the north the Mountains of Mourne.

On a windy day, Portmarnock can be a terror, demanding of you only your very best. If that is not good enough, take solace from the fact that even the greats of golf have struggled to handle Portmarnock in a gale. When the great Henry Cotton played here in the Irish Professional Championship, he took a total of 167 blows for the last 36 holes – and still finished only one stroke behind the winner.

CHAMPIONSHIP COURSE – 18 holes links, 7,365 yards, par 72 (SSS 74). Ladies 6,684 yards, par 72 (SSS 71).

C COURSE – 9 holes, 3,460 yards, par 37.

SIGNATURE HOLE:
FIFTEENTH (190 yards, par 3) – Arnold Palmer, who in partnership with Sam Snead won the Canada Cup here, reckons this is the best par 3 in the world. Club selection is invariably a problem. With the beach and out of bounds on the right, those who go left must flirt with a pair of bunkers.

ADDRESS: Golf Links Road, Portmarnock, Co. Dublin.
TELEPHONE: +353 (0)1 846 2968.
FAX: +353 (0)1 846 2601.
EMAIL: secretary@portmarnockgolfclub.ie
WEBSITE: www.portmarnockgolfclub.ie
SECRETARY: John Quigley.
PROFESSIONAL: Joey Purcell +353 (0)1 846 2634.
VISITORS: Mondays, Tuesdays, Thursdays and Fridays. Weekends by prior arrangement.
GREEN FEES: €165 per round weekdays, €190 at weekends.
CREDIT CARDS ACCEPTED: All major cards.
CATERING: Restaurant and bar.
FACILITIES: Locker rooms, putting green, practice ground, overseas memberships available, driving range, pro-shop, trolleys, club hire, caddies, tuition.
LOCATION: 8 miles north-east of Dublin city.
LOCAL HOTELS: Portmarnock Hotel.

PORTMARNOCK HOTEL AND GOLF LINKS

This is a challenging tight links over the same kind of terrain as its more famous neighbour. Designed by Bernhard Langer, who clearly has a liking for pot bunkers, it was opened in 1996. The inspirational use of natural dunes and land features, and the creative use of elevated tees and greens, acutely angled doglegs, and 98 strategically placed bunkers test even the most accomplished of players. Langer said, 'There are very few locations in Europe which could have allowed me the opportunity and landscape to design such a classic championship links. I hope all those who play it discover its magic and its challenging beauty.'

18 holes links, 6,255 metres (6,880 yards), par 71 (SSS 73). Ladies 5,051 metres (5,556 yards), par 71.

ADDRESS: Strand Road, Portmarnock, Co. Dublin.
TELEPHONE: +353 (0)1 846 0611.
FAX: +353 (0)1 846 2442.
EMAIL: golfres@portmarnock.com
WEBSITE: www.portmarnock.com
GOLF DIRECTOR: Moira Cassidy.
VISITORS: Every day, but pre-book.
GREEN FEES: €125 per round weekdays and weekends. Hotel guests €85.
CREDIT CARDS ACCEPTED: Amex/ MasterCard/Visa.
CATERING: Restaurant and bar.
FACILITIES: Locker rooms, putting green, practice ground, pro-shop, buggies (€40), trolleys (€4), club hire (€20–60), caddies on request, tuition.
LOCATION: 20 minutes from Dublin city centre.
LOCAL HOTELS: Portmarnock Hotel.

Ireland's Golf Courses

RATHFARNHAM GOLF CLUB

Club founded in 1899. Parkland course since redesigned by John Jacobs in 1962.

9 holes parkland, 5,424 metres (5,966 yards) for 18 holes, par 71 (SSS 70). Ladies 4,959 metres (5,454 yards), par 73 (SSS 71).

ADDRESS: Newtown, Rathfarnham, Dublin 16.
TELEPHONE: +353 (0)1 493 1201.
FAX: +353 (0)1 493 1561.
EMAIL: rgc@oceanfree.net
PROFESSIONAL: Brian O'Hara.
VISITORS: Yes, weekdays, except Tuesdays. Soft spikes.
GREEN FEES: €40 per round weekdays, €50 at weekends.
CATERING: Restaurant and bar.
FACILITIES: Locker rooms, buggies, trolleys, club hire.
LOCATION: 2 miles from Rathfarnham.

ROGANSTOWN GOLF AND COUNTRY CLUB

Established in 2004 and designed by Christy O'Connor Jr., this championship course is set among peaceful lakes, rolling hills and picturesque homes. The Broadmeadow River flows beside the course and water comes into play on all but six holes. Christy, who has designed 24 courses in Ireland, says, 'The site, on gentle rolling terrain with natural running water, has allowed me to be truly creative, and I've exploited water to the full.' It boasts a classic 592-yard par-5 finishing hole, which is the longest on the course. There are bunkers left and right to catch a wayward drive, more bunkers and a lake to contend with for the second shot, and the green is on a plateau.

18 holes parkland, 6,588 yards, par 71.

SIGNATURE HOLE:
SIXTH (196 yards, par 3) – green is protected by a lake on three sides.

ADDRESS: Roganstown, Swords, Co. Dublin.
TELEPHONE: +353 (0)1 843 3118.
FAX: +353 (0)1 843 3303.
EMAIL: golf@roganstown.com
WEBSITE: www.roganstown.com
SECRETARY/MANAGER: Elaine McLoughlin.
VISITORS: Yes.
GREEN FEES: €50 weekdays, €60 at weekends.
CREDIT CARDS ACCEPTED: Yes.
CATERING: Full catering available.
FACILITIES: Locker rooms, short iron practice ground, pitching and putting greens, golf shop, buggies (€35), electric trolleys (€20), pull trolleys (€3), club hire (€20), shoe hire (€15).
LOCATION: 4 miles north of Dublin Airport.
LOCAL HOTELS: 52-bedroom hotel and leisure club on site.

THE ROYAL DUBLIN GOLF CLUB

Though laid out entirely on flat land on Bull Island in Dublin Bay, Royal Dublin, founded in 1885, is as formidable a links as you are likely to encounter. A traditional out and back course, the two nines must nevertheless be handled quite differently, prevailing winds dramatically changing the aspect of each. The north-east-south-west layout means the back nine is possibly tougher. The club hosted the Irish Open from 1983 to 1985 and Seve Ballesteros, on winning his second Irish Open here, said, 'It was a great test and one of my favourite links courses.' In 1998, Ernie Els, having played the course on his way to the British Open, described the greens as 'the best links greens I have played in a long time'.

18 holes links, 6,493 metres (7,142 yards), par 72 (SSS 74).

The sixth at Roganstown Golf and Country Club

SIGNATURE HOLE:
EIGHTEENTH ('Garden', 432 metres [475 yards], par 4) – one of the best finishing holes in Ireland. Severe dogleg right, playing across out of bounds. Christy O'Connor, sen., says, 'It is pressure all the way. The hole can play shorter than it appears, but it will snap at you if you don't respect it.'

ADDRESS: North Bull Island Nature Reserve, Dollymount, Dublin 3.
TELEPHONE: +353 (0) 1 833 6346.
FAX: +353 (0) 1 833 6504.
EMAIL: info@theroyaldublingolfclub.com
WEBSITE: www.theroyaldublingolfclub.com
SECRETARY/MANAGER: John A. Lambe.

PROFESSIONAL: Leonard Owens +353 (0) 1 833 6477.
VISITORS: Yes.
GREEN FEES: €150 per person per round.
CREDIT CARDS ACCEPTED: Amex/Laser/ MasterCard/Visa.
CATERING: Dining room, grill room and bar.
FACILITIES: Locker rooms, driving range (€3 for 30 balls), putting green, buggies (€35), pro-shop, trolleys (€3), club hire (prices vary).
LOCATION: 3 miles north-east of Dublin centre on coast road to Howth.
LOCAL HOTELS: Clontarf Castle Hotel +353 (0) 1 833 2321, White Sands Hotel, Portmarnock +353 (0) 1 846 0003.

Ireland's Golf Courses

RUSH GOLF CLUB

Established in 1943, this is the most northerly links course in County Dublin with undulating fairways and an abundance of bunkers.

9 holes links, 5,603 metres (6,163 yards) for 18 holes, par 70 (SSS 71). Ladies 4,691 metres (5,160 yards), par 70 (SSS 68).

ADDRESS: Sandy Hills, Rush, Co. Dublin.
TELEPHONE & FAX: +353 (0)1 843 7548.
EMAIL: info@rushgolfclub.com
WEBSITE: www.rushgolfclub.com
SECRETARY/MANAGER: Noeline Quirke.
VISITORS: Yes.
GREEN FEES: €32 per round.
CREDIT CARDS ACCEPTED: Yes.
CATERING: Yes.
FACILITIES: Locker rooms, putting green, trolleys (€3.60).
LOCATION: 20 minutes north of Dublin Airport. Take the first exit off the M1 to Belfast and follow signs to Skerries/Rush.
LOCAL HOTELS: Great Southern Hotel, Dublin Airport +353 (0)1 844 6000, Holiday Inn, Dublin Airport +353 (0)1 808 0500, Bracken Court, Balbriggan +353 (0)1 841 3333.

SKERRIES GOLF CLUB

Tree-lined, undulating parkland course founded in 1905.

18 holes parkland, 6,107 metres (6,682 yards), par 73 (SSS 72).

ADDRESS: Hacketstown, Skerries, Co. Dublin.
TELEPHONE: +353 (0)1 849 1567.
FAX: +353 (0)1 849 1591.
EMAIL: skerriesgolfclub@eircom.net
WEBSITE: www.skerriesgolfclub.ie
PROFESSIONAL: Jimmy Kinsella +353 (0)1 849 0925.

VISITORS: Every day.
GREEN FEES: €50 per round weekdays, €60 at weekends.
CATERING: Restaurant and bar.
FACILITIES: Locker rooms, practice ground, buggies, trolleys.
LOCATION: Off the R127, north of Dublin Airport.
LOCAL HOTELS: The Red Bank Guesthouse, Skerries +353 (0)1 849 0439, The Bracken Court Hotel, Balbriggan +353 (0)1 841 3333, The Pier House Hotel, Skerries +353 (0)1 849 1033.

SLADE VALLEY GOLF CLUB

Established in 1970, this is an undulating but not too demanding parkland course.

18 holes parkland, 5,468 metres (6,014 yards), par 69 (SSS 68). Ladies 4,894 metres (5,383 yards), par 72 (SSS 70).

ADDRESS: Lynch Park, Brittas, Co. Dublin.
TELEPHONE: +353 (0)1 458 2183.
FAX: +353 (0)1 458 2784.
EMAIL: sladevalleygc@eircom.net
PROFESSIONAL: John Dignam.
VISITORS: Thursdays and Fridays are best.
GREEN FEES: €30 per round weekdays, €40 weekends and public holidays.
CREDIT CARDS ACCEPTED: All major cards.
CATERING: Restaurant and bar.
FACILITIES: Locker rooms, putting green, pro-shop, practice facilities, buggies, trolleys.
LOCATION: Off the M7, 8 miles west of Dublin.
LOCAL HOTELS: Downshire House Hotel, Green Isle Hotel.

THE SOUTH COUNTY GOLF CLUB

Established in 2002, this is a testing championship course built to USGA specifications with the Dublin Mountains as a backdrop.

18 holes parkland, 7,039 yards, par 72 (SSS 74). Ladies 5,543 yards, par 72 (SSS 72).

ADDRESS: Lisheen Road, Brittas, Co. Dublin.
TELEPHONE: +353 (0)1 458 2965.
FAX: +353 (0)1 458 2842.
EMAIL: info@southcountygolf.ie
WEBSITE: www.southcountygolf.com
SECRETARY/MANAGER: Roger Yates.
VISITORS: Mondays to Fridays.
GREEN FEES: €55 weekdays and weekends.
CREDIT CARDS ACCEPTED: All major cards.
CATERING: Restaurant and bar.
FACILITIES: Locker rooms, club shop, buggies, trolleys, club hire.
LOCATION: 30 minutes from the centre of Dublin.

ST ANNE'S GOLF CLUB

Founded in 1921 and set on North Bull Island in Dublin Bay, a bird sanctuary under the protection of Unesco. The sand and dunes create a natural links terrain; the island's beach is more than 3 miles long. The course underwent major redevelopment in 2003.

18 holes links, 6,626 yards, par 71 (SSS 73). Ladies 5,710 yards, par 72 (SSS 74).

SIGNATURE HOLE:
SEVENTH (472 yards, par 4) – a dogleg left to a well-defended green.

ADDRESS: Bull Island Nature Reserve, Dollymount, Dublin 5.
TELEPHONE: +353 (0)1 833 6471.
FAX: +353 (0)1 833 4618.
EMAIL: info@stanneslinksgolf.com
WEBSITE: www.stanneslinksgolf.com

SECRETARY: Robbie Gaine.
VISITORS: Mondays, Tuesdays, Thursdays, Fridays and 1 hour on Saturday mornings.
GREEN FEES: €70 per round weekdays, €80 at weekends.
CREDIT CARDS ACCEPTED: All major cards.
CATERING: Restaurant and bar.
FACILITIES: Locker rooms, putting green, practice ground, club shop, buggies (€28), trolleys (€3), club hire (€25).
LOCATION: From Dublin city, head north along the coast road keeping Dublin Bay on your right. Drive past the old wooden bridge and take the next right out along the causeway to the Island. The course is about 100 yards before the end of the road.
LOCAL HOTELS: Clontarf Castle Hotel +353 (0)1 833 2321, White Sands Hotel, Portmarnock +353 (0)1 846 0003.

ST MARGARET'S GOLF AND COUNTRY CLUB

St Margaret's has moved small mountains, flooded lakes and carved out running streams to create a parkland golf course. Opened in 1992, it has hosted international tournaments. Five of the par 4s are more than 400 yards long. There are broad forgiving fairways, neat par 3s and greens that play very true. Sam Torrance claimed that the 458-yard par-4 18th was one of the best finishing holes he'd ever seen.

18 holes parkland, 6,917 yards, par 73 (SSS 73). Ladies 5,770 yards, par 75 (SSS 74).

SIGNATURE HOLE:
EIGHTH (525 yards, par 5) – difficult approach over two large lakes.
ADDRESS: St Margaret's, Co. Dublin.
TELEPHONE: +353 (0)1 864 0400.

St Margaret's Golf and Country Club

FAX: +353 (0)1 864 0408.
EMAIL: reservations@stmargaretsgolf.com
WEBSITE: www.stmargaretsgolf.com
PROFESSIONAL: John Kelly.
VISITORS: Yes, seven days a week.
GREEN FEES: €40.
CREDIT CARDS ACCEPTED: Yes.
CATERING: Restaurant and bar.
FACILITIES: Locker rooms, practice ground,
   putting green, pro-shop, buggies (€35),
   trolleys (€4), club hire (€20), John Kelly
   Golf Academy.
LOCATION: Behind Dublin Airport.
LOCAL HOTELS: Great Southern, Crown
   Plaza, Bewleys.

STACKSTOWN GOLF CLUB

Founded in 1975, this is a hilly parkland
course with panoramic views of Dublin and
the bay. Ryder Cup star Padraig Harrington
is a member here.

18 holes parkland, 6,152 yards, par 71
(SSS 70). Ladies 5,088 yards, par 71.

ADDRESS: Kellystown Road, Rathfarnham,
   Dublin 16.
TELEPHONE: +353 (0)1 494 1993.
FAX: +353 (0)1 494 2338.
EMAIL: stackstowngc@eircom.net
WEBSITE: www.stackstowngolfclub.ie
SECRETARY: Larry Clarke.
PROFESSIONAL: Michael Kavanagh.

VISITORS: Mondays, Thursdays, Fridays and Sundays.
GREEN FEES: €35 per round weekdays, €45 at weekends.
CATERING: Restaurant and bar.
FACILITIES: Locker rooms, pro-shop, golf academy, buggies (€25), trolleys (€2.50), club hire (€15), tuition.
LOCATION: A mile and a half from exit 13 on the M50 for Ticknock.

STEPASIDE GOLF COURSE

This public parkland course, established over 20 years ago, has lush greens and is densely populated by a mixture of mature trees.

9 holes parkland, 5,848 metres (6,432 yards) for 18 holes, par 74. Ladies 5,014 metres (5,515 yards), par 76.

ADDRESS: Stepaside, Co. Dublin.
TELEPHONE: +353 (0)1 295 2859.
FAX: +353 (0)1 295 2639.
EMAIL: stepaside@golfdublin.com
WEBSITE: www.golfdublin.com
VISITORS: Every day.
GREEN FEES: €17 per round weekdays; €24 at weekends.
CATERING: Tea, coffee and light snacks.
FACILITIES: Locker rooms, putting green, practice facilities, shop, trolleys, club hire.
LOCATION: Accessible from the Stillorgan dual carriageway, approximately 25 minutes from Dublin's city centre, just outside the village of Stepaside.
LOCAL HOTELS: Step Inn.

SUTTON GOLF CLUB

Very narrow and tricky seaside links course with heavy rough and well-bunkered greens. Founded in 1890.

9 holes links, 6,153 yards for 18 holes, par 70 (SSS 68). Ladies 5,302 yards, par 70 (SSS 70).

ADDRESS: Cush Point, Sutton, Dublin 13.
TELEPHONE: +353 (0)1 832 2965.
FAX: +353 (0)1 832 1603.
EMAIL: info@suttongolfclub.org
WEBSITE: www.suttongolfclub.org
PROFESSIONAL: Nicky Lynch +353 (0)1 832 1703.
VISITORS: Yes, but restrictions on Tuesdays and Saturdays. Soft spikes.
GREEN FEES: €50 per round weekdays and weekends.
CATERING: Restaurant and bar.
FACILITIES: Locker rooms, putting green, trolleys.
LOCATION: 7 miles north-east of Dublin.
LOCAL HOTELS: Bailey Court Hotel, Howth; Portmarnock Hotel; White Sands Hotel, Portmarnock +353 (0)1 846 0003; Clontarf Castle Hotel +353 (0)1 833 2321; The Grand Hotel, Malahide +353 (0)1 845 0000; Marine Hotel, Sutton +353 (0)1 839 0000.

SWORDS OPEN GOLF COURSE

Founded in 1991, this is a flat parkland course with the Broadmeadow River running through the centre.

18 holes parkland, 5,631 metres (6,194 yards), par 71 (SSS 69). Ladies 4,845 metres (5,329 yards), par 71 (SSS 70).

SIGNATURE HOLE:
SIXTEENTH (360 metres [396 yards], par 4) – Roganstown Bridge, with its many arches, provides an impressive backdrop to the green, and the fairway is shaped with natural contours.

ADDRESS: Balheary Avenue, Swords, Co. Dublin.

The 18th at Westmanstown Golf Club

TELEPHONE: +353 (0)1 840 9819/890 1030.
FAX: +353 (0)1 840 9819.
EMAIL: info@swordsopengolfcourse.com
WEBSITE: www.swordsopengolfcourse.com
SECRETARY/MANAGER: Orla McGuinness.
VISITORS: Every day. Soft spikes.
GREEN FEES: €18 per round weekdays, €25
    weekends and public holidays.
CATERING: Coffee shop.
FACILITIES: Locker rooms, putting green,
    trolleys (€2), club hire (half set €5).
LOCATION: 3 miles west of Swords off the
    Naul–Balboughal road.
LOCAL HOTELS: Roganstown Golf and
    Country Club +353 (0)1 843 3118.

TURVEY HOTEL AND GOLF CLUB

This undulating course, lined with oaks
and beeches, is set in 150 acres of beautiful
parkland with a variety of challenging holes.
Founded in 1994.

18 holes parkland, 5,824 metres (6,406
yards), par 71 (SSS 71). Ladies 5,230 metres
(5,753 yards), par 73 (SSS 74).

SIGNATURE HOLE:
SIXTH (281 metres [309 yards], par 4)
– slight dogleg to the right to an elevated
green in the shade of an imperious
oak. The green is guarded by a pair of
bunkers.

ADDRESS: Turvey Avenue, Donabate, Co. Dublin.
TELEPHONE: +353 (0)1 843 5169.
FAX: +353 (0)1 843 5179.
EMAIL: turveygc@eircom.net
WEBSITE: www.turveygolfclub.com
VISITORS: Mondays to Fridays.
SECRETARY/MANAGER: Sean McNelis.
PROFESSIONAL: Dominic McCarthy.
VISITORS: Welcome weekdays and after 1 p.m. at weekends.
GREEN FEES: €35 per round weekdays, €40 at weekends.
CREDIT CARDS ACCEPTED: MasterCard/Visa.
CATERING: Restaurant and bar.
FACILITIES: Locker rooms, practice ground, putting green, golf shop, buggies (€30), trolleys (€3).
LOCATION: 10 minutes north of Dublin Airport off the M1.
LOCAL HOTELS: Turvey Golf Club Hotel (on the course).

WESTMANSTOWN GOLF CLUB

Parkland course founded in 1988 and designed by Eddie Hackett.

18 holes parkland, 5,826 metres (6,408 yards), par 71 (SSS 71). Ladies 4,900 metres (5,390 yards), par 72 (SSS 70).

SIGNATURE HOLE:
EIGHTEENTH (340 metres [374 yards], par 4) – slight dogleg with water feature.

ADDRESS: Clonsilla, Dublin 15.
TELEPHONE: +353 (0)1 820 5817.
FAX: +353 (0)1 820 5858.
EMAIL: info@westmanstowngolfclub.ie
WEBSITE: www.westmanstowngolfclub.ie
SECRETARY/MANAGER: Stephen Crosbie.
VISITORS: Yes.
GREEN FEES: €45 per round weekdays, €50 at weekends.
CREDIT CARDS ACCEPTED: Yes.
CATERING: Restaurant and bar.
FACILITIES: Locker rooms, putting green, practice ground, golf shop, buggies (€30), trolleys (€3).
LOCATION: Off the M50 motorway at Blanchardstown or take the Lucan exit and follow the signs.
LOCAL HOTELS: Castleknock Golf and Country Club, Spa Hotel, Lucan.

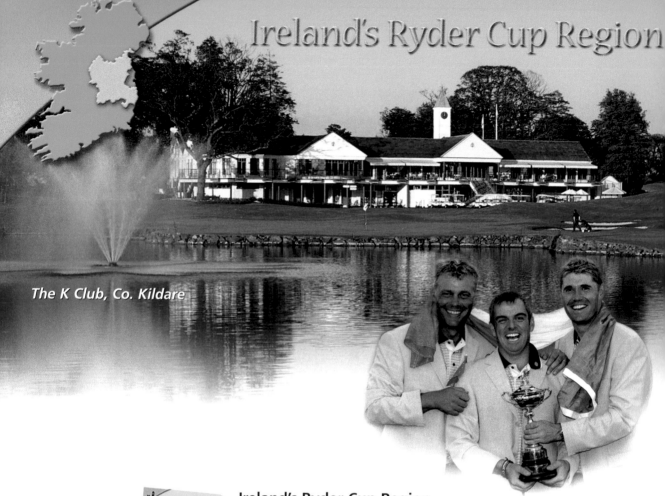

Ireland's Ryder Cup Region

The K Club, Co. Kildare

Ireland's Ryder Cup Region
Simply Number 1 for Quality, Choice and Value.

The K Club, Co. Kildare will soon host one of the world's most prestigious events, *Ryder Cup 2006*.

Almost a quarter of the 400+ golf courses in Ireland can be found in Ireland's East Coast & Midlands, a traditional golfing region quite literally surrounding Dublin. As well as some of Europe's best known courses, you will discover a whole host of lesser known gems which combine to offer a golfing experience that for quality, choice and value is simply unbeatable!

*For your **FREE** Ryder Cup Region Golf Guide and other great golf offers log onto:*

www.rydercupregion.com

East Coast and Midlands Tourism, Dublin Road, Mullingar, Co. Westmeath, Ireland
Tel: +353 (0) 44 48650 Fax: +353 (0) 44 40413
email: info@eastcoastmidlands.ie web: www.eastcoastmidlands.ie

COUNTY KILDARE

ATHY GOLF CLUB

Undulating parkland course formed in 1906 with nine holes and extended to eighteen in 1993. In recent years, there has been major development work, changing the tees on 11 holes, creating a par 5, planting trees and building 33 new bunkers. The 16th and 17th holes are claimed to be among the most difficult consecutive par 4s you will find in Ireland.

18 holes parkland, 6,475 yards, par 72 (SSS 71). Ladies 5,541 yards, par 73 (SSS 73).

SIGNATURE HOLE:
FIFTH (517 yards, par 5) – a tight drive to the top of a hill, then you are faced with either a lay-up or a long second over a river with a lake to the left of the green and two large bunkers to the right.

ADDRESS: Geraldine, Athy, Co. Kildare.
TELEPHONE: +353 (0)59 863 1729.
FAX: +353 (0)59 863 4710.
EMAIL: info@athygolfclub.com
WEBSITE: www.athygolfclub.com
OFFICE MANAGER: Kathleen Gray.
VISITORS: Welcome on all days except Sundays. Phone to check availability.
GREEN FEES: €30 per round Mondays to Fridays, €40 Saturdays and public holidays.
CREDIT CARDS ACCEPTED: MasterCard/Visa.
CATERING: Restaurant and bar. Full catering service available all day, everyday.
FACILITIES: Locker rooms, practice ground, putting green, buggies (€25), trolleys (€3).

LOCATION: 1 ½ miles from the town on the Kildare road, 42 miles from Dublin.
LOCAL HOTELS: Bert House Hotel +353 (0)59 863 2578, Clanard Court Hotel +353 (0)59 864 0666.

Athy Golf Club

BODENSTOWN GOLF CLUB

Two parkland courses with wide fairways and generous greens. Founded in 1973.

BODENSTOWN OLD COURSE – 18 holes parkland, 6,132 metres (6,745 yards), par 72 (SSS 72). Ladies 4,861 metres (5,347 yards), par 72 (SSS 72).

LADYHILL COURSE – 18 holes parkland, 5,618 metres (6,179 yards), par 72.

ADDRESS: Sallins, Co. Kildare.
TELEPHONE: +353 (0)45 897096.
FAX: +353 (0)45 898126.
EMAIL: bodenstown@eircom.net
MANAGER: Rita Mather.
VISITORS: Mondays to Fridays on the Bodenstown Old Course. Every day on the Ladyhill Course.
GREEN FEES: €20 per round weekdays and weekends.
CATERING: Restaurant and bar.
FACILITIES: Locker rooms, putting green, practice ground, driving range, buggies (€30), trolleys (€3), club hire (€13).
LOCATION: Off the R407, 5 miles north of Naas.

CARTON HOUSE

Carton House boasts two outstanding golf courses: the Montgomerie and the O'Meara, named after their famous designers, in the 1,100-acre estate. The Montgomerie is a parkland – almost links in style – creation featuring head-high pot bunkers, contoured trees and tall fescue grasses that separate fast running fairways. It offers a mix of long par 4s and tricky short ones. The course was host to the Irish Open in 2005 and 2006. Although only opened in 2003, Carton has already won prestigious design awards. Colin Montgomerie says,

'You can't call it a links course, but it plays like a links and has all the characteristics of a links. In designing this course, I attempted to go back to a more traditional course.'

The O'Meara makes good use of the estate's historic rolling hills, specimen trees and the River Rye. Feature holes are the fourteenth, fifteenth and sixteenth: two par 3s either side of a par 5 criss-crossing the loops of the river. Carton House is also the home of the Golfing Union of Ireland.

MONTGOMERIE COURSE – 18 holes parkland, 7,301 yards, par 72 (SSS 74). Ladies 5,655 yards, par 72 (SSS 72).

O'MEARA COURSE – 18 holes parkland, 7,006 yards, par 72. Ladies 5,472 yards, par 72.

ADDRESS: Carton House, Maynooth, Co. Kildare.
TELEPHONE: +353 (0)1 505 2000.
FAX: +353 (0)1 628 6555.
EMAIL: reservations@cartonhouse.com
WEBSITE: www.cartonhouse.com
PROFESSIONAL: Francis Howley.
VISITORS: Yes. Soft spikes.
GREEN FEES: €115 per round weekdays, €135 at weekends.
CREDIT CARDS ACCEPTED: Yes.
CATERING: Restaurant and bar.
FACILITIES: Locker rooms, golf academy, practice area, putting greens, club shop, buggies (€40), trolleys (€5), club hire (€40).
LOCATION: 14 miles south-west of Dublin city and 30 minutes from Dublin Airport.
LOCAL HOTELS: Carton House's new hotel with 164 bedrooms and spa is scheduled to open in July 2006.

Above: The Montgomery Course at Carton House

Below: The 15th on the O'Meara Course

CASTLEWARDEN GOLF AND COUNTRY CLUB

This parkland course, founded in 1990 and designed by Tommy Halpin, has elevated tees and water features on four holes.

18 holes parkland, 6,690 yards, par 72 (SSS 71). Ladies 5,865 yards, par 74 (SSS 73).

ADDRESS: Castlewarden, Straffan, Co. Kildare.
TELEPHONE: +353 (0)1 458 9254.
FAX: +353 (0)1 458 8972.
EMAIL: info@castlewardengolfclub.com
WEBSITE: www.castlewardengolfclub.com
VISITORS: Yes, Mondays, Thursdays and Fridays. With a member only at weekends. Soft spikes.
GREEN FEES: €45 per round.
CREDIT CARDS ACCEPTED: MasterCard/Visa.
CATERING: Restaurant and bar.
FACILITIES: Locker rooms, putting green, practice ground, pro-shop, buggies, trolleys, club hire, tuition.
LOCATION: On the Dublin–Kildare road (just off the main Dublin and Cork–Limerick road – N7), 16 miles from the centre of Dublin city.

CELBRIDGE GOLF CLUB

Popular parkland course with good sand-based greens. Founded in 1997.

9 holes parkland, 6,004 yards for 18 holes, par 70 (SSS 70). Ladies 5,302 yards, par 72 (SSS 70).

ADDRESS: Elm Hall, Celbridge, Co. Kildare.
TELEPHONE: +353 (0)1 628 8208.
FAX: +353 (0)1 825 9887.
OWNER: Seamus Lawless.
VISITORS: Yes. Soft spikes.
GREEN FEES: €27 per round weekdays, €30 at weekends.
CATERING: Coffee room.
FACILITIES: Locker rooms, putting green, practice ground, trolleys, club hire.
LOCATION: Main Dublin road from Celbridge. Take the first right opposite Orchard Nurseries.

CILL DARA GOLF CLUB

Moorland course founded in 1920 only a mile from Curragh Racecourse.

9 holes moorland, 5,852 metres (6,402 yards) for 18 holes, par 71 (SSS 70). Ladies 4,962 metres (5,458 yards), par 72 (SSS 70).

SIGNATURE HOLE:
SEVENTH (343 metres [377 yards], par 4) – a difficult dogleg.

ADDRESS: Little Curragh, Kildare, Co. Kildare.
TELEPHONE: +353 (0)45 521295/521433.
FAX: +353 (0)45 531749.
EMAIL: cilldaragc@eircom.net
SECRETARY/MANAGER: Dan Doody.
VISITORS: Yes, but not Wednesdays. Limited Saturday mornings.
GREEN FEES: €20 per round.
CATERING: Bar and meals.
FACILITIES: Locker rooms, putting green, practice ground, pro-shop, buggies (€25), trolleys (€2), tuition.
LOCATION: 2 miles east of Kildare.
LOCAL HOTELS: Stand House +353 (0)45 436180.

CLONGOWES GOLF COURSE

Owned by Clongowes Wood College, this parkland course was designed by Eddie Hackett in 1965. This is a private course with no green fees. Played over by Clane Golf Club (+353 (0)45 868030) and a

Craddockstown Golf Club

separate ladies club.

9 holes parkland, 5,350 yards for 18 holes, par 68 (SSS 64).

ADDRESS: Clane, Co. Kildare.
TELEPHONE: +353 (0)45 868202.
VISITORS: For use of college students and Clane members only.

CRADDOCKSTOWN GOLF CLUB

Easy-walking parkland course on 144 acres. The course was redeveloped in March 2003 by designer Roger Jones and now boasts many water features, fairway mounding, fairway bunkers and greens which are sand based. Craddockstown is 5 miles from the Ryder Cup venue, The K Club.

18 holes parkland, 6,133 metres (6,746 yards), par 72 (SSS 73). Ladies 4,963 metres (5,459 yards), par 73 (SSS 72).

SIGNATURE HOLE:
TENTH (340 metres [374 yards], par 4) – short, but you must be accurate. Lay up with a low iron or fairway wood to avoid the trees on the right and fairway mounding and bunkers. Approach with a mid-iron across a lake to an island green.

ADDRESS: Blessington Road, Naas, Co. Kildare.
TELEPHONE: +353 (0)45 897610.
FAX: +353 (0)45 896968.

EMAIL: gaynolan@craddockstown.com
WEBSITE: www.craddockstown.com
SECRETARY: Gay Nolan.
VISITORS: Welcome.
GREEN FEES: €40 Mondays to Thurdays, €45 Fridays, €50 Saturdays, Sundays and bank holidays.
CREDIT CARDS ACCEPTED: Yes.
CATERING: Restaurant and bar.
FACILITIES: Locker rooms, practice ground, putting green, pro-shop, buggies (€25), trolleys (€3).
LOCATION: A quarter of a mile from Naas town.
LOCAL HOTELS: Killashee House Hotel +353 (0)45 879277, Osprey Hotel +353 (0)45 881111.

THE CURRAGH GOLF CLUB

Founded in 1883, it is the oldest course in the Republic. There is evidence that golf was first played here as early as 1852, having been brought to the area by a Scotsman named David Ritchie, who eventually designed this heathland course opposite the Curragh Racecourse.

18 holes heathland, 6,035 metres (6,638 yards), par 72 (SSS 71). Ladies 4,928 metres (5,420 yards), par 72.

ADDRESS: Curragh Camp, The Curragh, Co. Kildare.
TELEPHONE: +353 (0)45 441714.
FAX: +353 (0)45 442476.
EMAIL: curraghgolf@eircom.net
WEBSITE: www.curraghgolf.com
PROFESSIONAL: Gerry Burke +353 (0)45 441896.
VISITORS: Welcome every day but Tuesday.
GREEN FEES: €32 per round weekdays, €40 at weekends.
CATERING: Restaurant and bar.
FACILITIES: Locker rooms, putting green,

driving range, pro-shop, buggies, trolleys, club hire, tuition.
LOCATION: Off the N7 between Newbridge and Kildare.
LOCAL HOTELS: Keadeen Hotel, Standhouse Hotel.

DUNMURRY SPRINGS GOLF CLUB

Built to USGA specifications, Mel Flanagan has crafted a new parkland course on a 140-acre site. It offers generous fairways, no heavy rough, but undulating greens. It opened in May 2006.

18 holes parkland, 6,757 yards, par 72. Ladies 5,277 yards, par 71.

ADDRESS: Dunmurry Hill, Kildare, Co. Kildare.
TELEPHONE: +353 (0)45 531400.
FAX: +353 (0)45 521595.
EMAIL: info@dunmurrysprings.ie
WEBSITE: www.dunmurrysprings.ie
MANAGER: Simon Holohan.
VISITORS: Yes.
GREEN FEES: €65 Mondays and Tuesdays, €80 Wednesdays to Sundays.
CATERING: Restaurant and bar.
FACILITIES: Locker rooms, putting green, pro-shop, buggies, trolleys, club hire, tuition.
LOCATION: 2 miles north of Kildare town on the R401 between Kildare and Rathangan.

HIGHFIELD GOLF CLUB

Established in 1992, this parkland course, created on farmland, has sensitively integrated the leisure facility with the environment. Unused areas have been left uncultivated and the course contains a network of wildlife corridors incorporating watercourse

Dunmurry Springs Golf Club

banks, hedgerows and mature trees. Several innovative features and water hazards come into play throughout the course, and the clubhouse is a luxurious Canadian cedar-wood log cabin.

18 holes parkland, 6,140 yards, par 70 (SSS 69). Ladies 5,397 yards, par 71.

ADDRESS: Carbury, Co. Kildare.
TELEPHONE & FAX: +353 (0)46 973 1021.
EMAIL: highfieldgolf@eircom.net
WEBSITE: www.highfield-golf.ie
VISITORS: Always welcome, soft spikes.
GREEN FEES: €30 per round weekdays, €40 at weekends.
CATERING: Restaurant and bar.
FACILITIES: Locker rooms, putting green, floodlit driving range, pro-shop, trolleys, club hire, tuition.
LOCATION: Off the R402 to Carbury.
LOCAL HOTELS: Luxury timber lodges (on the course).

THE K CLUB

The Kildare Hotel and Country Club with its two Arnold Palmer-designed championship courses and luxurious five-star hotel is regarded by many as Ireland's premier golfing establishment, and its selection to host the 2006 Ryder Cup only enhanced that reputation.

A magnificently restored Georgian estate, set in 700 acres of rolling woodland

Above: The sixteenth at The K Club, which will be the seventh for the Ryder Cup

Right: The K Club's Smurfit Course

in County Kildare, just 30 minutes from Dublin, Straffan House, whose origins date back to 550 AD, is the centrepiece of the resort. It is sumptuously appointed and ideal as the base for the European and American teams during the event.

The K Club's second equally challenging course is the Smurfit, host to the European Open in 2006, but it is the sweeping Palmer Course that is the jewel in the crown. It opened in 1991, and its blend of challenging parkland and water features immediately marked it out as one of the most important new developments in Europe. There are 14 man-made lakes and the River Liffey to

contend with, and, as you would expect, water comes into play on most holes, depending on your standard of playing skills.

The great Arnold Palmer's cavalier approach to the game endeared him to the fans of the sport, and he incorporates that 'go for broke' attitude in his design of courses. The K Club embodies all his principles, and is as much an enjoyment off the shorter tees as it is a challenge over the 7,212-yard blue tees.

Although Ryder Cup hero Darren Clarke of Northern Ireland holds the course record with an astonishing 60, you underestimate it at your peril for it has more than its fair share of really outstanding holes.

The course is configured differently for the Ryder Cup superstars with holes one to eight becoming ten to seventeen (The K Club's Key Ryder Cup Holes – page 15), but for mere mortals and the members, who prefer it in the original order, the challenges are just as mighty.

There are so many good holes: from beautiful and intriguing short holes to par 4s that demand accurate shot making to spectacular long holes. One of those par 3s is the deceptively pretty 213-yard fifth, which requires a long iron to find the generous green, guarded by water on the right. At the back is a waterfall and all around are impressive houses costing anywhere between £2 to £3 million.

'Arnold's Pick', the double dogleg 13th, is a sweeping downhill 568-yard par 5 with a mound studded with bunkers that the drive has to carry. A large reed-lined pond on the right, a sea of greenside bunkers and overhanging trees also have to be avoided.

'Michael's Favourite' is the 16th, which at 430 yards is the toughest hole on the course; it lies in wait like a highwayman, capable of ambushing an otherwise perfect round. Water seems to be everywhere here with the River Liffey running all the way up the right to an island green.

The 173-yard 17th is another teaser with the Liffey and a tree on the right and bunkers guarding the green on the

front left. It demands an immaculate tee shot. And the 537-yard 18th provides a grandstand finish. Aptly called 'The Hooker's Graveyard', a large lake on the left has to be negotiated.

The stunning Smurfit Course, which opened in 2003, is not just a copy of its more venerable sister. It has a distinct character of its own and is as scenically beautiful as you will get. It could almost be described as an inland links with fescue grasses, deep bunkers and roller-coaster fairways.

The Smurfit has its share of outstanding holes with the pick being the long seventh (*see below*) and a great home hole, a 578-yard par 5 which sweeps right to left around a lake with an island green to finish.

PALMER COURSE – 18 holes parkland, 7,212 yards, par 72 (SSS 76). Ladies 5,459 yards, par 73 (SSS 74).

SMURFIT COURSE – 18 holes parkland, 7,277 yards, par 72 (SSS 75). Ladies 5,443 yards, par 72.

PALMER COURSE SIGNATURE HOLE: SEVENTH (570 yards, par 5) – this mighty double-dogleg, right then left, has been rated as Ireland's best par 5. A good drive gives you the chance to cut the corner across the flowing waters of the River Liffey and make the green in two if you dare. If you lay up, it can be just as hazardous because the green, on an island between two arms of the Liffey, is also protected by bunkers and mature trees.

SMURFIT COURSE SIGNATURE HOLE: SEVENTH ('Quarry', 600 yards, par 5) – named after the Swallow Quarry, a man-made rock face that rises 60 feet out of a lake with a series of waterfalls and cascades. The green is large but perched on an island in the middle of the Liffey.

ADDRESS: Straffan, Co. Kildare.
TELEPHONE: +353 (0)1 601 7300.
FAX: +353 (0)1 601 7399.
EMAIL: golf@kclub.ie
WEBSITE: www.kclub.ie
DIRECTOR OF GOLF: John McHenry.
PROFESSIONAL: Peter O'Hagan.
VISITORS: Yes, but telephone for availability.
GREEN FEES: Palmer Course – €350 per round high season; Smurfit Course – €225 per round.
CREDIT CARDS ACCEPTED: All major cards.
CATERING: Restaurant and bars at both courses.
FACILITIES: Locker rooms, putting green, practice ground, driving range, pro-shops at each course, buggies, trolleys, club hire, caddies, golf academy with John McHenry and Peter O'Hagan.
LOCATION: 23 miles from Dublin Airport, off the M4 junction for Naas. 18 miles from Dublin.
LOCAL HOTELS: The Kildare Hotel and Country Club (on site).

KILKEA CASTLE GOLF CLUB

A championship parkland course, opened in 1996, with two lakes and the River Griese, which comes into play on almost every hole. The par 5 second gives a measure of what is to come, making the golfer combine shot making with good course management. Not until you reach the 17th will you be safe from the river. The 18th has Kilkea Castle, the oldest inhabited castle in Ireland, dating back to 1180, as an imposing backdrop. Mature greens, tees and fairways belie the course's comparative youth. Owner Dave Conway has spent in excess of €8 million on the course and on upgrading the hotel and its facilities.

18 holes parkland, 6,097 metres (6,706 yards, par 72 (SSS 71). Ladies 5,076 metres (5,583 yards), par 72 (SSS 71).

Killeen Golf Club

SIGNATURE HOLE:
SIXTEENTH (177 yards, par 3) – nerve-racking! The river runs diagonally across the front of the green and down the right side. There are trees on the left and a bunker on the right. It is a very difficult green to hold with a ferocious slope towards the front.

ADDRESS: Castledermot, Co. Kildare.
TELEPHONE: +353 (0)503 45555.
FAX: +353 (0)503 45505.
EMAIL: kilkeagolfclub@eircom.net
WEBSITE: www.kilkeacastlehotelgolf.com
SECRETARY/MANAGER: John Kissane.
VISITORS: Every day.
GREEN FEES: €40 per round weekdays, €50 at weekends.

CATERING: Two restaurants and bar.
FACILITIES: Locker rooms, putting green, pro-shop, buggies, trolleys, club hire, caddies on request, tuition.
LOCATION: 40 minutes from Dublin and 15 minutes from Naas. South on the N7, then the M9 and N78 to Athy.
LOCAL HOTELS: Kilkea Castle Hotel.

KILLEEN GOLF CLUB

Parkland course with water hazards on seven holes. Built to USGA specifications with sand-based greens. Founded in 1991.
18 holes parkland, 6,732 yards, par 72 (SSS 72). Ladies 5,374 yards, par 72 (SSS 71).

ADDRESS: Kill, Co. Kildare.
TELEPHONE: +353 (0)45 866003.
FAX: +353 (0)45 875881.
EMAIL: admin@killeengc.ie
WEBSITE: www.killeengolf.com
VISITORS: Mondays, Wednesdays, Thursdays and Fridays are best for visitors. Soft spikes.
GREEN FEES: €35 per round weekdays, €50 at weekends.
CATERING: Restaurant and bar.
FACILITIES: Locker rooms, putting green, club shop, trolleys, club hire.
LOCATION: Off the N7, 2 miles north of Kill. The K Club is 10 minutes away.

KNOCKANALLY GOLF AND COUNTRY CLUB

Championship course standing in 125 acres of parkland with water features on 11 holes. One of the most attractive is the par-3 11th, set amidst overhanging trees and protected front and right by water. The clubhouse is a nineteenth-century Palladian mansion. Established in 1985.

18 holes parkland, 6,424 yards, par 72 (SSS 71). Ladies 5,402 yards, par 73 (SSS 72).

SIGNATURE HOLE:
FIRST (423 yards, par 4) – Christy O'Connor, sen., once described it as the most difficult opening hole in Irish golf. Out of bounds is to the right, and there is a spinney on the left. Requires an accurate approach to a green surrounded by trees, drains and bunkers.

ADDRESS: Donadea, North Kildare, Co. Kildare.
TELEPHONE & FAX: +353 (0)45 869322.
EMAIL: golf@knockanally.com
WEBSITE: www.knockanally.com

MANAGING DIRECTOR: Noel Lyons.
PROFESSIONAL: Martin Darcy.
VISITORS: Yes.
GREEN FEES: €35 weekdays, €50 at weekends.
CREDIT CARDS ACCEPTED: Yes.
CATERING: Restaurant and bar. Functions catered for.
FACILITIES: Locker rooms, practice ground, putting green, pro-shop, buggies, trolleys, club hire.
LOCATION: Off the M4 going west from Dublin, between villages of Kilcock and Enfield. Approximately 25 miles from Dublin city centre.
LOCAL HOTELS: Hamlet Court, Johnstown House Hotel.

MILLICENT GOLF CLUB

Designed by Tommy Halpin in 2001, the course has many daunting hazards, including bunkers, the River Liffey and internal lakes.

18 holes parkland, 7,045 yards, par 73 (SSS 73). Ladies 5,458 yards, par 72 (SSS 72).

SIGNATURE HOLE:
SEVENTEENTH (198 yards, par 3) – carry over water to a small green and large bunkers to the rear.

ADDRESS: Millicent Road, Clane, Co. Kildare.
TELEPHONE: +353 (0)45 893279.
FAX: +353 (0)45 868369.
EMAIL: info@millicentgolfclub.com
WEBSITE: www.millicentgolfclub.com
SECRETARY/MANAGER: Derek Killian.
VISITORS: Yes. Soft spikes mandatory.
GREEN FEES: €32 weekdays, €43 at weekends.
CATERING: Coffee bar.
FACILITIES: Locker rooms, driving range,

putting and chipping green, club shop, buggies (€25), trolleys (€3), club hire (€10), shoe hire.
LOCATION: Take the M50 around Dublin and cross the West Link toll bridge. Take the N4 for Maynooth then head for Straffan and Clane. Take a right 3 miles on at the staggered crossroads heading for Clane.

NAAS GOLF CLUB

Founded in 1896 as a nine-hole course, the club moved to its current location in 1940. A rolling, tree-lined parkland course, the first, eleventh and eighteenth were redesigned by Jeff Howes in 2003. The 11th and 17th have water hazards.

18 holes parkland, 6,173 yards, par 71 (SSS 69). Ladies 5,423 yards, par 72 (SSS 71).

SIGNATURE HOLE:
SEVENTEENTH (178 yards, par 3) – almost surrounded by a lake. Beautiful but daunting!

ADDRESS: Kerdiffstown, Naas, Co. Kildare.
TELEPHONE: +353 (0)45 874644/897509.
FAX: +353 (0)45 896109.
EMAIL: naasgolfclubisdn@eircom.net
WEBSITE: www.naasgolfclub.com
MANAGER: Denis Mahon.
VISITORS: Welcome. Soft spikes.
GREEN FEES: €40 per round weekdays, €45 weekends and public holidays.
CREDIT CARDS ACCEPTED: Yes.
CATERING: Restaurant and bar.
FACILITIES: Locker rooms, putting green, driving range, trolleys (€3).
LOCATION: Off the N7 on the road between Johnstown and Sallins.
LOCAL HOTELS: Osprey Hotel, Naas.

NEWBRIDGE GOLF CLUB

Parkland course opened in 1995 with many water features and USGA sand-based greens. Set in beautiful countryside, more than 40,000 trees have been planted and the course is noted for its wildlife, including herons, moorhens, kingfishers and wild ducks.

18 holes parkland, 6,002 metres (6,602 yards), par 72 (SSS 72). Ladies 4,534 metres (4,987 yards), par 73 (SSS 72).

SIGNATURE HOLE:
EIGHTEENTH (420 metres [463 yards], par 5) – a challenging risk/reward hole that has three different water features.

ADDRESS: Barretstown, Newbridge, Co. Kildare
TELEPHONE: +353 (0)45 486110.
FAX: +353 (0)45 431289.
EMAIL: newbridgegolfclub@eircom.net
WEBSITE: www.newbridgegolfclub.com
MANAGER: Jamie Stafford.
VISITORS: Yes.
GREEN FEES: €22 weekdays, €27 at weekends.
CREDIT CARDS ACCEPTED: No.
CATERING: Restaurant and bar.
FACILITIES: Locker rooms, putting green, pro-shop, buggies (€25), trolleys (€2.50), club hire (€4).
LOCATION: Off the M7, 8 miles south-west of Naas. From the motorway, pass Wyeth and the parish church on the left, turn right at the main bridge to Newbridge College, follow the road right passing Murtagh's shop and Old Connell Weir on the right. Turn left after the sharp bend, head over the bridge and the course is on the left.

Ireland's Golf Courses

PGA NATIONAL IRELAND AT PALMERSTOWN HOUSE

One of the newest courses in Ireland, this 7,419-yard masterpiece from Christy O'Connor Jr. on 320 acres of the sweeping grounds of Palmerstown House is already being tipped by some to become Ireland's number-one rated parkland course.

It's only minutes as the helicopter flies from The K Club, and it's eyeing the crown of its more illustrious and venerable neighbour, the host for the 2006 Ryder Cup. It has already received the ultimate accolade, by being selected to carry the Professional Golfers' Association's branding alongside the PGA National at the Belfry in England and the PGA Centenary at Gleneagles in Scotland.

Sandy Jones, chief executive of the PGA, says, 'It will not be long before it is hosting some of the world's most prestigious golf events. It has been the ambition of the PGA for a number of years to create and develop a spiritual home for the PGA in Ireland. The criteria for choosing a suitable golf venue as our partner was rigorous and that meant only a course deemed by experts to be in the top ten in Ireland could be considered.'

As you travel up the long drive of the 800-acre estate to the luxurious clubhouse, PGA National exudes style. It cost €15 million to build the course and a further €10 million for the clubhouse, which also provides steam rooms and saunas in the opulent locker rooms. Nothing has been left to chance, and the staff pride themselves in attention to detail, even claiming that they maintain their lush fairways like greens.

One thing is certain: no bunker will be left unraked in the pursuit of excellence – there are 300 rakes out there on the course, not to mention 60 electric golf buggies, the most expensive flags, special sprinkler heads and a computer system that shows leader boards and tee times on TV screens.

PGA National is exclusive, but it's not the most expensive course to play in Ireland being fourth behind The K Club, Old Head of Kinsale and Doonbeg in green fees. Whatever the cost, it's an experience not to be missed. Although it was only opened in July 2005, it soon hosted The Irish PGA Championship, won by Padraig Harrington, who said of the new creation, 'It's a really nice course to play. It seems to have got the right balance. It's reasonably tough without going overboard. It's got everything you want in a golf course.'

One visitor said that it was the closest to American conditions outside of the US, and some have compared it to the majestic Loch Lomond course in Scotland, which is praise indeed.

What this course has over some of its older rivals is that it is truly a twenty-first century venue built on an awesome scale. Many of the greens are large – as much as 85 square metres in one case – and flow with devilish undulations.

The land was an old stud farm, and the course, which has three rivers (the Kill, Morrell and Hartwell), was built on marshy land requiring more than 20 miles of drainage; needless to say, water is integral to many of the holes. No more so than on the course's signature hole, the fourth, with its island green.

One of the prettiest par 3s around is the 198-yard third, and it would push the fourth close as the signature hole, but, then again, on PGA National there are any number of well-crafted holes vying for that honour. Facing a long carry with water on the left and in front of the green, the beautiful gardens surrounding the hole and the exotic plants can prove a distraction. The

The eighth green at PGA National Ireland with Palmerstown House in the background

green – three clubs difference from back to front – looks long and narrow, but is larger than it appears. Water behind the green awaits the foolhardy.

Christy has created many a trick for the eyes, which adds to the degree of difficulty, especially on the 565-yard sixth, which is regarded as the hardest hole on the course. Big hitters need to flirt with the trees on the right to have a chance of hitting the green in two. If laying up, the landing area looks small, but this is an optical illusion caused by three large bunkers. Again, from a distance, the green looks small, but it's on three levels.

Christy certainly likes his bunkers, and on the 580-yard ninth, snaking in an S-shape between water and sand, there is a veritable

sea of them on the face of the rise to the green. But once on the green there are great views of the estate and Palmerstown House.

PGA National certainly has its designer's inimitable stamp on it, perhaps more so because he lived on the course for a time. During its building, Christy broke a leg and stayed at Palmerstown House. Owner Jim Mansfield, who also owns the Citywest Hotel and golf courses, had one of the buggies customised so that Christy could put his leg up. Whereas a designer would usually pop in and out and spend a few days on the project, Christy lived on the job.

PGA National is very much a course of two halves: while the front nine has many mature trees and is more parkland, the back is open and not as attractive, but the water is omnipresent. And there are two classic par 5s. Christy's favourite is the 588-yard 14th with two tracts of water to carry as it doglegs left. For the big hitters, it's a 255-yard carry over the water to set up a chance of going for the green in two, but for the average hitter, it's a case of plotting your route between water and large bunkers down the right. Don't be too heavy with the approach because there's a burn at the back of the green.

The 16th is already being hailed as one of the best par 5s in Ireland. It's 560 yards and a classic. The landing area for the drive is between a large bunker on the left and water on the right. The green is almost on an island, and for the big hitters, it looks like a tiny target for the approach shot. There's a bale-out area to the left but that leaves a tricky putt/chip onto a green sloping back down to the water. In the PGA Championship, Padraig Harrington drove 330 yards, hit his six-iron approach downwind across water to three feet, and then, unfortunately, missed the putt.

The home hole, a 448-yard par 4, provides a fitting finish with a green which is almost four-in-one being on four different levels. Again, the drive is over water, but the good selection of tees means you can reduce the amount of water you have to carry.

The Irish PGA set up their headquarters here in 2006, and it is hoped that in time it will host a PGA Academy at which all aspiring Irish professionals will complete their PGA training.

18 holes parkland, 7,419 yards, par 72.

SIGNATURE HOLE:
FOURTH (428 yards, par 4) – played through a funnel of mature trees to an island green. The prevailing easterly wind blows right to left, and if the drive is not perfect, you may consider laying up. Judging distance here can be quite deceptive as the brickwork on the front of the green is the same colour as the roof of the boathouse behind the green, and if your approach is too strong, there's more water at the back.

ADDRESS: PGA National Ireland, Palmerstown House, Johnstown, Co. Kildare.
TELEPHONE: +353 (0)45 906901.
FAX: +353 (0)45 906922.
EMAIL: pganational@palmerstownhouse.com
WEBSITE: www.palmerstownhouse.com
PROFESSIONAL: Edward Pettit, PGA Operations Manager.
VISITORS: Welcome seven days a week.
GREEN FEES: Vary from €130 to €185 depending on the time of year.
CREDIT CARDS ACCEPTED: All major cards.
CATERING: Restaurant and bar. Ability to cater for large groups of up to 220.
FACILITIES: Locker rooms, steam room and sauna, four putting greens, short-game practice area with practice green and bunkers, driving range, golf shop, buggies, trolleys, tuition.
LOCATION: Approximately 30 minutes from Dublin's city centre. Follow the signs for the M50; once on the M50, take the exit for the N7 (the Naas Road). On the N7 after Kill at the traffic lights in Johnstown, go straight on towards the flyover at Naas. At the flyover, follow the signs for Dublin. Once back on the N7, the PGA National Ireland is the second gate on the left-hand side approximately 500 yards after the lights at Johnstown.
LOCAL HOTELS: Thirty four-bedroom golf suites in the clubhouse and a new five-star

The 16th at Woodlands Golf Club

two-hundred-bed hotel overlooking the sixth hole was expected to be completed in time for the Ryder Cup. Also, Citywest Hotel, Saggart.

PINE TREES GOLF COURSE

Short but interesting parkland course with good bunkering and two dykes which intersect the course.

18 holes parkland, 5,080 metres (5,568 yards), par 71 (SSS 69). Ladies 4,246 metres (4,658 yards), par 72 (SSS 72).

ADDRESS: Kilmurray, Clane, Co. Kildare.
TELEPHONE: +353 (0)45 869525.
VISITORS: Every day, including Sunday afternoons.
GREEN FEES: On application.
FACILITIES: Locker rooms, buggies, trolleys.

WOODLANDS GOLF CLUB

This parkland course was recently upgraded to eighteen holes and has a combination of hillocks, slopes and seven lakes. More than 1,500 trees have been planted since 1999. Founded in 1991.

18 holes parkland, 6,020 metres (6,622 yards), par 72 (SSS 71). Ladies 5,079 metres (5,586 yards), par 72 (SSS 72).

ADDRESS: Cooleragh, Coill Dubh, Naas, Co. Kildare.
TELEPHONE: +353 (0)45 860777.
FAX: +353 (0)45 860988.
EMAIL: woodlandsgolf@eircom.net
WEBSITE: www.woodlandsgolf.ie
VISITORS: Weekdays are best. Soft spikes.
GREEN FEES: €30 per round weekdays, €35 at weekends.
CATERING: Restaurant and bar.
FACILITIES: Locker rooms, putting green, club shop.
LOCATION: Off the R403, on the outskirts of Naas.

COUNTY LAOIS

ABBEYLEIX GOLF CLUB

Founded in 1895 and extended to 18 holes in 2000, this parkland course has hills and a lake which comes into play on the fourth and fifth.

18 holes parkland, 6,029 yards, par 72 (SSS 70). Ladies 5,001 yards, par 72 (SSS 70).

ADDRESS: Rathmoyle, Abbeyleix, Co. Laois.
TELEPHONE: +353 (0)502 31450.
FAX: +353 (0)502 30108.
EMAIL: info@abbeyleixgolfclub.ie
WEBSITE: www.abbeyleixgolfclub.ie
PROFESSIONAL: Sean Conlon.
VISITORS: Mondays to Saturdays.
GREEN FEES: €20 per round weekdays, €30 at weekends.
CATERING: Restaurant and bar.
FACILITIES: Locker rooms, putting green, buggies.
LOCATION: Half a mile from the centre of Abbeyleix.
LOCAL HOTELS: Globe House Hotel, Hibernian Hotel, Montague Hotel.

THE HEATH GOLF CLUB

A challenging heathland course on 130 acres which demands accuracy. It has an abundance of gorse, trees and lakes coming into play on the fourth, fifth and eighteenth. Originally the Queen's County Heath Golf Club, it has been in existence since 1891. The nine-hole course was laid out in 1920 and extended to eighteen holes in 1970.

18 holes heathland, 6,120 metres (6,732 yards), par 71 (SSS 71). Ladies 4,986 metres (5,484 yards), par 72 (SSS 70).

ADDRESS: The Heath, Portlaoise, Co. Laois.
TELEPHONE: +353 (0)502 46045.
FAX: +353 (0)502 46866.
EMAIL: info@theheathgc.ie
WEBSITE: www.theheathgc.ie
PROFESSIONAL: Mark O'Boyle +353 (0)502 46622.
VISITORS: Yes.
GREEN FEES: €18 per round weekdays, €34 at weekends.
CATERING: Restaurant and bar.
FACILITIES: Locker rooms, putting green, two practice areas, ten-bay driving range, pro-shop, buggies (€25), trolleys (€2), club hire (€10), caddies, tuition.
LOCATION: South on the N7. Take the first exit on the left at the entrance to the M7, and then the next left, keeping right. The course is 3½ miles north-east of Portlaoise.
LOCAL HOTELS: The Foxrock Inn, Ivyleigh House, Oakville, Ballaghmore House.

THE HERITAGE AT KILLENARD

This new championship course, co-designed by Seve Ballesteros and Jeff Howes, set in beautiful undulating countryside has challenging doglegs and spectacular water features. It hosted the 2005 Irish Seniors Open.

18 holes parkland, 7,319 yards, par 72. Ladies 5,747 yards, par 72.

SIGNATURE HOLE:
FOURTH (214 yards, par 3) – the green is protected on the left by a large bunker complex, with water to the right and back. Prevailing wind pushes shots towards a lake on the right.

The 18th at The Heritage at Killenard

ADDRESS: Killenard, Co. Laois.
TELEPHONE: +353 (0)502 45500.
FAX: +353 (0)502 42392.
EMAIL: info@theheritage.com
WEBSITE: www.theheritage.com
GENERAL MANAGER: Eddie Dunne.
HEAD PROFESSIONAL: Eddie Doyle.
VISITORS: Welcome every day.
GREEN FEES: €115 weekdays, €130 weekends and public holidays.
CREDIT CARDS ACCEPTED: Yes.
CATERING: Full restaurant facilities available.
FACILITIES: Locker rooms, practice ground, putting green, pro-shop, par 3 course, buggies (€50), trolleys, club hire (€50), Seve Ballesteros golf school.
LOCATION: Just off the M7/N7 main Dublin–Cork–Limerick road. 40 miles from Dublin and the airport.
LOCAL HOTELS: Heritage Hotel, Killenard (on the course) +353 (0)502 45500, The Heritage Hotel, Portlaoise +353 (0)502 71900.

MOUNTRATH GOLF CLUB

Picturesque undulating parkland course at the foot of the Slieve Bloom Mountains, founded in 1929. It has lush fairways, well-bunkered greens and the River Nore comes into play on a number of holes.

18 holes parkland, 5,372 metres (6,305 yards), par 71 (SSS 69). Ladies 4,929 metres (5,421 yards).

ADDRESS: Knockanina, Mountrath, Co. Laois.
TELEPHONE: +353 (0)502 32558.
FAX: +353 (0)502 32643.
EMAIL: mountrathgc@eircom.net
WEBSITE: www.mountrathgolfclub.ie
VISITORS: Every day but check availability at weekends. Soft spikes.
GREEN FEES: €20 per round weekdays, €30 at weekends.
CATERING: Bar and snacks.
FACILITIES: Locker rooms, putting green, buggies, trolleys.
LOCATION: 2 miles south of Mountrath, just off the N1.
LOCAL HOTELS: Killeshin Hotel, Montague Hotel, Manor Hotel.

PORTARLINGTON GOLF CLUB

Tough inland course bordered by the River Barrow, which comes into play on the 16th and 17th holes, with tree-lined fairways. A sanctuary for pheasants and mallards lies in the centre of the course. Founded in 1909.

18 holes parkland, 5,906 metres (6,496 yards), par 71 (SSS 71). Ladies 5,152 metres (5,667 yards), par 74 (SSS 74).

SIGNATURE HOLE:
SIXTEENTH (323 metres [355 yards], par 4) – River Barrow on the right, woods on the left and a pond in front of the green.

ADDRESS: Garryhinch, Portarlington, Co. Laois.
TELEPHONE: +353 (0)502 23115.
FAX: +353 (0)502 23044.
EMAIL: portarlingtongc@eircom.net
WEBSITE: www.portarlingtongolf.com
SECRETARY: Frank Higgins.
VISITORS: Welcome.
GREEN FEES: €25 weekdays.
CREDIT CARDS ACCEPTED: Yes.
CATERING: Restaurant and bar. All day catering available.
FACILITIES: Locker rooms, practice ground, putting green, pro-shop, buggies (€20), trolleys (€3).
LOCATION: On the Portarlington–Mountmellick road about 5 kilometres from Portarlington.

LOCAL HOTELS: East End Hotel. All
Portlaoise hotels.

RATHDOWNEY GOLF CLUB

Parkland course with gently sloping hills. A
good test for club golfers with an interesting
mix of holes.

18 holes parkland, 5,864 metres (6,450
yards), par 71 (SSS 70). Ladies 5,057 metres
(5,562 yards), par 73 (SSS 72).

SIGNATURE HOLE:
SIXTH (510 metres [561 yards], par 5)
– challenging long hole which normally
plays into the prevailing wind.

ADDRESS: Coolnaboul West, Rathdowney,
Portlaoise, Co. Laois.
TELEPHONE: +353 (0)505 46170.
FAX: +353 (0)505 46065.
EMAIL: webmaster@rathdowneygolfclub.com
WEBSITE: www.rathdowneygolfclub.com
SECRETARY/MANAGER: Mike Munro.
VISITORS: Weekdays, weekends by
arrangement. Soft spikes.
GREEN FEES: €25 per round weekdays,
weekends and public holidays.
CATERING: Bar and snacks.
FACILITIES: Locker rooms, putting green,
buggies (€25), trolleys (€3).
LOCATION: Signposted from the square in
Rathdowney. Less than a mile from the
square off the Johnstown Road.
LOCAL HOTELS: The Foxrock Inn, Abbeyleix
Manor Hotel, Racket Hall Hotel.

COUNTY LONGFORD

COUNTY LONGFORD GOLF CLUB

This tree-lined parkland course, founded
in 1894, underwent extensive development
during 2003 and 2004. Features a stream
which comes into play from the fourth to
the eighth holes and also on the eighteenth.
18 holes parkland, 6,790 yards, par 72.

ADDRESS: Glack, Dublin Road, Longford,
Co. Longford.
TELEPHONE: +353 (0)43 46310.
FAX: +353 (0)43 47082.
EMAIL: colonggolf@eircom.net
PROFESSIONAL: Cormack Robinson.
VISITORS: Welcome at all times. Soft spikes.
GREEN FEES: €30 per round weekdays, €35
at weekends.
CREDIT CARDS ACCEPTED: All major cards.
CATERING: Restaurant and bar.
FACILITIES: Locker rooms, putting green,
driving range, pro-shop, buggies, trolleys,
club hire, tuition.
LOCATION: South-east of Longford, off the
N4 from Dublin.
LOCAL HOTELS: Longford Arms Hotel.

COUNTY LOUTH

ARDEE GOLF CLUB

This mature parkland course with a stream was founded in 1911 and designed by Eddie Hackett.

18 holes parkland, 6,490 yards, par 71 (SSS 72). Ladies 5,496 yards, par 73 (SSS 72).

ADDRESS: Town Parks, Ardee, Co. Louth.
TELEPHONE: +353 (0)41 685 3227.
FAX: +353 (0)41 685 6137.
EMAIL: ardeegolfclub@eircom.net
WEBSITE: www.ardeegolfclub.com
PROFESSIONAL: Scott Kirkpatrick +353 (0)41 685 7472.
VISITORS: Yes, Mondays, Tuesdays, Thursdays and Fridays. Soft spikes.
GREEN FEES: €35 per day weekdays, €50 at weekends.
CREDIT CARDS ACCEPTED: Diners Club/MasterCard/Visa.
CATERING: Restaurant and bar.
FACILITIES: Locker rooms, putting green, practice ground, driving range, buggies, trolleys, caddies.
LOCATION: Left at the bottom of Main Street, coming from Dublin or Drogheda, then it is 100 yards on your left. Take a right at the flower bed, coming from Dundalk or Carrick Road.
LOCAL HOTELS: Arradale House.

BALLYMASCANLON HOUSE HOTEL GOLF AND LEISURE CLUB

Parkland course designed by the Craddock and Ruddy design team, featuring sand-based greens. Lakes and streams provide natural hazards.

18 holes parkland, 5,763 yards, par 68 (SSS 67). Ladies 4,721 yards, par 71.

ADDRESS: Dundalk, Co. Louth.
TELEPHONE: +353 (0)42 935 8200.
FAX: +353 (0)42 937 1598.
EMAIL: info@ballymascanlon.com
WEBSITE: www.ballymascanlon.com
VISITORS: Yes.
GREEN FEES: €28 per round Mondays to Thursdays, €30 Fridays and €35 at weekends.
CATERING: Restaurant and bar.
FACILITIES: Locker rooms, putting green, club shop, buggies, trolleys, club hire, tuition.
LOCATION: 2 miles north of Dundalk.
LOCAL HOTELS: Ballymascanlon House Hotel (on the course).

CARNBEG GOLF COURSE

Established in 1998, this parkland course, designed by Eddie Hackett and Tom Craddock, is full of undulating dips and mounds and has more than 90 bunkers.

18 holes parkland, 6,321 yards, par 72. Ladies 4,858 yards, par 72.

SIGNATURE HOLE:
ELEVENTH (600 yards, par 5) – a good test of a golfer's abilities and the Cooley peninsula provides a stunning backdrop to this hole.

ADDRESS: Armagh Road, Dundalk, Co. Louth.
TELEPHONE & FAX: +353 (0)42 933 2518.

Ballymascanlon House Hotel Golf and Leisure Club

EMAIL: carnbeggolfcourse@eircom.net
WEBSITE: www.dundalk.parkinn.ie
VISITORS: Always welcome.
GREEN FEES: €20 weekdays, €28 at
   weekends.
CATERING: Restaurant and bar.
FACILITIES: Locker rooms, putting green,
   club shop, buggies, trolleys, club hire,
   tuition.
LOCATION: A few minutes from Dundalk
   town centre. Located on the R177
   (Dundalk–Armagh road), just 1 hour
   from both Dublin and Belfast.
LOCAL HOTELS: Radisson Park Inn Hotel
   (on the course).

COUNTY LOUTH GOLF CLUB

Better known as Baltray, this is a challenging
championship links with great greens. It
hosted the 2004 Nissan Irish Open and
would have hosted more international
events but for its location at the mouth
of the River Boyne. Established in 1892,
the present course was redesigned by
Tom Simpson in 1938. All great courses
have holes on which the good shot is
rewarded and Baltray, hewn out of the Irish
countryside, is no exception. Play your best
game and you will retire to the 19th satisfied
with your labours rather than bemoaning
your bad luck. Its par 3s are excellent,
especially the 173-yard fifth to a green high

County Louth Golf Club

in the dunes. But it is perhaps its par 4s which are its trademark. Not particularly long but, with Simpson's strategic use of bunkers and hazards and with so many of them doglegs of varying degrees, they are an intriguing test of your skills.

The 379-yard fourth is one such example; it is well within range in two shots, but the dunes lining the undulating fairway add to the degree of difficulty. As the course moves towards the sea, the terrain becomes more rugged and the dunes even more imposing with the holes almost built into them. At the par-4 12th, 13th and 14th, driving accuracy is at a premium, but while the play becomes tougher, the views are more scenic.

The view from the 332-yard 14th tee of the River Boyne estuary and the Mountains of Mourne is worth all the challenges. The 15th is a short hole, then there's the last of the splendid par 4s to an amphitheatre green before finishing with another par 3 and the par-5 home hole, which has recently been increased to 559 yards.

18 holes links, 6,936 yards, par 72 (SSS 73). Ladies 5,873 yards, par 75 (SSS 73).

SIGNATURE HOLE:
FOURTEENTH (332 yards, par 4) – shortest par 4 on the course. No bunkers but a tantalising approach and green.

Dundalk Golf Club

ADDRESS: Baltray, Drogheda, Co. Louth.
TELEPHONE: +353 (0)41 988 1530.
FAX: +353 (0)41 988 1531.
EMAIL: reservations@countylouthgolfclub.
    com
WEBSITE: www.countylouthgolfclub.com
SECRETARY/MANAGER: Michael Delany.
PROFESSIONAL: Paddy McGuirk.
VISITORS: Yes.
GREEN FEES: €115 weekdays, €135 at
    weekends.
CREDIT CARDS ACCEPTED: Yes.
CATERING: Restaurant and bar.
FACILITIES: Locker rooms, putting green,
    practice ground, pro-shop, buggies
    (€20), trolleys, club hire, tuition.
LOCATION: 4 miles north-east of Drogheda.
LOCAL HOTELS: Boyne Valley Hotel +353
    (0)41 983 7737, The D Hotel +353 (0)41
    987 7700.

DUNDALK GOLF CLUB

This rolling parkland course surrounded by
mature woodland celebrated its centenary
in 2005. It was upgraded in 1980 by Dave
Thomas and Peter Alliss.

   18 holes parkland, 6,206 metres (6,826
yards), par 72 (SSS 72). Ladies 5,222 metres
(5,744 yards), par 73.

ADDRESS: Blackrock, Dundalk, Co. Louth.
TELEPHONE: +353 (0)42 932 1731.
FAX: +353 (0)42 932 2022.
EMAIL: office@dundalkgolfclub.ie
WEBSITE: www.dundalkgolfclub.ie
PROFESSIONAL: Leslie Walker +353 (0)42
    932 2102.
VISITORS: Best days are Mondays,
    Wednesdays, Thursdays, Fridays and
    Saturdays. Soft spikes.
GREEN FEES: €55 per round.
CREDIT CARDS ACCEPTED: Amex/
    MasterCard/Visa

CATERING: Restaurant and bar.
FACILITIES: Locker rooms, putting green, driving range, pro-shop, buggies (€30), trolleys (€3), club hire (€20), tuition.
LOCATION: Off the R172, 2 miles south of Dundalk.
LOCAL HOTELS: Fairways Hotel.

GREENORE GOLF CLUB

Founded in 1896, the course is a mixture of links and woodland designed by Eddie Hackett. It features rivers, ponds and pine trees and boasts panoramic views of Carlingford.

18 holes links/woodland, 6,647 yards, par 71 (SSS 73). Ladies 5,731 yards, par 74 (SSS 74).

ADDRESS: Greenore, Co. Louth.
TELEPHONE: +353 (0)42 937 3678.
FAX: +353 (0)42 938 3898.
EMAIL: greenoregolfclub@eircom.net
PROFESSIONAL: Robert Giles.
VISITORS: Yes, but prior booking recommended.
GREEN FEES: €35 per round weekdays, €50 at weekends.
CATERING: Restaurant and bar.
FACILITIES: Locker rooms, putting green, practice ground, buggies, trolleys, club hire.
LOCATION: 15 miles north of Dundalk, 12 miles south of Newry.
LOCAL HOTELS: The Heritage Hotel.

KILLIN PARK GOLF CLUB

Opened in 1991, this is an undulating parkland course, designed by Eddie Hackett, with mature woodland and river features. The Castletown River surrounds the fourth and sixth holes. Played over by Killinbeg Golf Club.

18 holes parkland, 5,388 yards, par 69 (SSS 65). Ladies 4,783 yards, par 69 (SSS 68).

ADDRESS: Killin Park, Dundalk, Co. Louth.
TELEPHONE: +353 (0)42 933 9303.
FAX: +353 (0)42 932 0848.
EMAIL: killinbeggolfclub@eircom.net
VISITORS: Yes.
GREEN FEES: €22 weekdays, €27 weekends and public holidays.
CATERING: Bar and meals.
FACILITIES: Locker rooms, buggies, trolleys, club hire, practice net.
LOCATION: 3 miles north-west of Dundalk.

SEAPOINT GOLF CLUB

A championship links course with large manicured greens, designed by Des Smyth on 260 acres and opened in 1993, playable all year. Mature trees border the course on the west and offer a contrast to the links, while water hazards come into play on six of the first nine holes. The closing holes are bordered by the beach and offer magnificent views of the east coast, the Mountains of Mourne and the Irish Sea.

18 holes links, 7,120 yards, par 72 (SSS 75). Ladies 5,630 yards, par 72.

SIGNATURE HOLE:
FOURTEENTH (445 yards, par 4) – a draw is required from the tee otherwise the green will be hidden from view on the approach shot. The second shot requires a fade to a green that is well guarded.

ADDRESS: Seapoint, Termonfeckin, Co. Louth.
TELEPHONE: +353 (0)41 982 2333.
FAX: +353 (0)41 982 2331.
EMAIL: golflinks@seapoint.ie
WEBSITE: www.seapointgolflinks.com
MANAGER: Kevin Carrie.

The 13th at Seapoint Golf Club

PROFESSIONAL: David Carroll.

VISITORS: Welcome Mondays to Fridays with
limited availability on Saturdays.

GREEN FEES: €60 Mondays to Fridays, €75
on Saturdays.

CATERING: Bar. Full catering facilities
provided each day from 9 a.m.

FACILITIES: Locker rooms, driving range,
putting, pitching and chipping areas,
buggies (€25), club hire (€20), trolleys (€3).

LOCATION: On the coast, 30 minutes from
Dublin Airport by the M1.

LOCAL HOTELS: Boyne Valley Hotel +353
(0)41 983 7737, Neptune Beach Hotel
+353 (0)41 982 7107, Glenside Hotel
+353 (0)41 982 9185, Westcourt Hotel
+353 (0)41 983 0965.

TOWNLEY HALL GOLF CLUB

Founded in 1994, this is a relatively flat
parkland course with many sloping greens.
9 holes parkland, 5,865 yards for 18
holes, par 71 (SSS 68). Ladies 5,050 yards,
par 72 (SSS 70).

ADDRESS: Townley Hall, Tullyallen,
Drogheda, Co. Louth.

TELEPHONE & FAX: +353 (0)41 984 2229.

EMAIL: townleyhall@oceanfree.net

PROFESSIONAL: Cathal Barry/Conor
Russell.

VISITORS: Yes. Soft spikes.

GREEN FEES: €15 per round weekdays, €18
at weekends.

CATERING: Snacks.
FACILITIES: Locker rooms, putting green, practice area.
LOCATION: 3 miles from Drogheda on the Drogheda–Cullen road.

COUNTY MEATH

ASHBOURNE GOLF CLUB

Undulating parkland course with fast, true greens. Three man-made lakes and the Broadmeadow River come into play on nine holes. Ashbourne has its own Amen Corner – the four holes from the 11th to the 14th – which separates the men from the boys. Founded in 1994 and designed by Des Smyth.

18 holes parkland, 5,882 metres (6,470 yards), par 71 (SSS 70). Ladies 5,080 metres (5,588 yards), par 72 (SSS 72).

SIGNATURE HOLE:
THIRD (340 metres [374 yards], par 4) – a demanding tee shot followed by a mid-iron approach to a green fronted by the Broadmeadow River.

ADDRESS: Archerstown, Ashbourne, Co. Meath.
TELEPHONE: +353 (0)1 835 2005.
FAX: +353 (0)1 835 9261.
EMAIL: ashgc@iol.ie
WEBSITE: www.ashbournegolfclub.ie
SECRETARY/MANAGER: Jim Clancy.
PROFESSIONAL: John Dwyer +353 (0)1 835 9002.
VISITORS: Mondays to Fridays. Soft spikes.
GREEN FEES: €35 per round weekdays, €45 weekends and public holidays.
CREDIT CARDS ACCEPTED: Yes.

CATERING: Restaurant and bar.
FACILITIES: Locker rooms, putting green, pro-shop, driving range, buggies (€25), trolleys, club hire, caddies on request, tuition.
LOCATION: On the N2, 12 miles from Dublin. Coming from Dublin, take a right in Ashbourne at the Ashbourne House Hotel and continue for half a mile.
LOCAL HOTELS: Ashbourne House Hotel.

BLACK BUSH GOLF CLUB

Generally flat parkland courses opened in 1988. The twenty-seven-hole complex offers the choice of three eighteen-hole courses, each a good test of golf. Lush fairways bordered by maturing trees lead to well protected sand-based greens with strategic bunkering and occasional water hazards.

BLACK BUSH (courses A and B) – 6,849 yards, par 73 (SSS 72).

THOMASTOWN (courses B and C) – 6,343 yards, par 71 (SSS 70).

LAGORE (courses C and A) – 6,599 yards, par 72 (SSS 71).

ADDRESS: Thomastown, Dunshaughlin, Co. Meath
TELEPHONE: +353 (0)1 825 0021.
FAX: +353 (0)1 825 0400.
EMAIL: golf@blackbush.iol.ie
WEBSITE: www.blackbushgolf.ie
ADMINISTRATOR: Kate O'Rourke.
PROFESSIONAL: Shane O'Grady.
VISITORS: Yes.
GREEN FEES: €30 Mondays to Thursdays, €45 Fridays to Sundays.
CREDIT CARDS ACCEPTED: No.
CATERING: Restaurant and bar.
FACILITIES: Locker rooms, practice ground, putting green, pro-shop, buggies (€23), trolleys (€3), club hire (€25).
LOCATION: 1 mile from Dunshaughlin on

the N3 Dublin–Navan road, 20 minutes from Dublin's M50.

LOCAL HOTELS: Ardboyne Hotel, Navan +353 (0)46 902 3119, Ashbourne Court Hotel, Ashbourne +353 (0)1 835 9300.

COUNTY MEATH GOLF CLUB (TRIM)

Parkland course founded in 1898 and redesigned in 1990 by Eddie Hackett. Four very challenging par 5s. The greens are sand-based, some elevated, some two-tiered and all guarded by bunkers.

18 holes parkland, 6,088 metres (6,696 yards), par 73 (SSS 72). Ladies 5,005 metres (5,505 yards), par 73.

ADDRESS: Newtownmoynagh, Trim, Co. Meath.
TELEPHONE: +353 (0)46 943 1463.
FAX: +353 (0)46 943 7554.
EMAIL: sec@trimgolf.net
WEBSITE: www.trimgolf.net
PROFESSIONAL: Robin Machin.
VISITORS: Mondays to Fridays. Soft spikes.
GREEN FEES: €30 per round weekdays, €35 at weekends.
CATERING: Restaurant and bar.
FACILITIES: Locker rooms, putting green, practice ground, pro-shop, buggies, trolleys, tuition.
LOCATION: On the R160, 3 miles south-west of Trim.

GLEBE GOLF COURSE

Natural parkland course with gentle rolling hills.

18 holes parkland, 5,906 metres (6,496 yards), par 73.

ADDRESS: Dunlever, Trim, Co. Meath.
TELEPHONE & FAX: +353 (0)46 943 1926.
EMAIL: glebegc@eircom.net

SECRETARY/MANAGER: Breda Bligh.
VISITORS: Every day.
GREEN FEES: €16 per round weekdays, €19 at weekends.
CATERING: Snacks.
FACILITIES: Locker rooms, putting green, practice area, club shop, trolleys (€2), club hire (€7).
LOCATION: 1 mile from the town centre on Kildalkey Road.

GORMANSTON COLLEGE GOLF COURSE

Parkland course founded in 1961.
9 holes, 2,158 yards, par 32.

ADDRESS: Franciscan College, Gormanston, Co. Meath.
TELEPHONE: +353 (0)1 841 2203.
FAX: +353 (0)1 841 2685.

HEADFORT GOLF CLUB

Established in 1928, this is an attractive 36-hole parkland facility set in the mature woodland of what was formerly the Headfort Estate. The Old Course has hosted PGA Championships and has gentle undulations and mature specimen trees. The recently built New Course was designed by Christy O'Connor Jr., who made maximum use of the two islands on the River Blackwater, and is the tougher of the two courses. Headfort House, built in 1780, and mature trees provide a stunning backdrop to some of the holes.

OLD COURSE – 18 holes parkland, 5,973 metres (6,570 yards), par 72. Ladies 5,148 metres (5,663 yards), par 73.

NEW COURSE – 18 holes parkland, 6,515 metres (7,176 yards), par 72. Ladies 5,010 metres (5,511 yards), par 72.

Headfort Golf Club

OLD COURSE SIGNATURE HOLE:
FIFTEENTH (301 metres [331 yards], par 4) – the tee shot has to be shaped from right to left, and the second shot has to be precise to avoid the out of bounds behind the green and the bunkers all around the target area.

NEW COURSE SIGNATURE HOLE:
TWELFTH (366 metres [402 yards], par 24) – the River Blackwater flows down the right side of the fairway, and the approach shot has to be perfectly struck as the green is almost surrounded by water.

ADDRESS: Navan Road, Kells, Co. Meath.
TELEPHONE: +353 (0)46 924 0146.

TIME SHEETS: +353 (0)46 928 2001.
FAX: +353 (0)46 924 9282.
EMAIL: info@headfortgolfclub.ie
WEBSITE: www.headfortgolfclub.ie
ADMINISTRATION MANAGER: Nora Murphy.
PROFESSIONAL: Brendan McGovern +353 (0)46 924 0639.
VISITORS: Welcome any day. Soft spikes.
GREEN FEES: Old Course – €45 per round Mondays to Thursdays, €50 Fridays to Sundays; New Course – €60 per round Mondays to Thursdays, €65 Fridays to Sundays; Early bird specials (Mon–Thurs 8–11 a.m.) – €35 Old Course, €45 New Course.
CREDIT CARDS ACCEPTED: All major cards accepted.

CATERING: Restaurant and bar.
FACILITIES: Locker rooms, putting green, pro-shop, buggies (€26), trolleys (€3), club hire, tuition.
LOCATION: Take the M50 from Dublin Airport. Then take the N3 Cavan–Navan route, just outside Kells. Approximately 50 minutes from the airport.
LOCAL HOTELS: The Headfort Arms Hotel, Kells (www.headfortarms.ie).

KILCOCK GOLF CLUB

Parkland course with mature trees and water features, established in 1985 and designed by Eddie Hackett. A stream meanders through the course coming into play on eight holes while a new water feature comes into play on a further four holes. Fast, well-manicured and undulating greens.

18 holes parkland, 5,816 metres (6,393 yards), par 72. Ladies 5,147 metres (5,614 yards), par 74.

ADDRESS: Gallow, Kilcock, Co. Meath.
TELEPHONE: +353 (0)1 628 7592/628 4074.
FAX: +353 (0)1 628 7283.
EMAIL: kilcockgolfclub@eircom.net
WEBSITE: www.kilcockgolfclub.com
MANAGER: Seamus Kelly.
VISITORS: Anytime.
GREEN FEES: €25 Mondays to Thursdays, €32 Fridays, €35 weekends and bank holidays.
CREDIT CARDS ACCEPTED: Yes.
CATERING: Restaurant and bar.
FACILITIES: Locker rooms, practice ground, putting green, buggies (€20), trolleys (€3).
LOCATION: 20 miles from Dublin, 5 minutes from the M4/N4.
LOCAL HOTELS: Glenroyal Hotel, Maynooth +353 (0)1 629 0909, Johnstown House Hotel +353 (0)46 954 0000.

LAYTOWN AND BETTYSTOWN GOLF CLUB

Undulating traditional links course, with small, fast greens and strategically placed bunkers, on the Mornington Dunes. Founded in 1909 but recently redesigned by Des Smyth and Declan Branigan.

18 holes links, 5,862 metres (6,448 yards), par 71. Ladies 5,082 metres (5,590 yards), par 73.

ADDRESS: Golf Links Road, Bettystown, Co. Meath.
TELEPHONE: +353 (0)41 982 7170.
FAX: +353 (0)41 982 8506.
EMAIL: links@landb.ie
WEBSITE: www.landb.ie
SECRETARY: Robbie Gaine.
PROFESSIONAL: Bobby Browne +353 (0)41 982 8793.
VISITORS: Mondays to Fridays are best days.
GREEN FEES: €60 per round Mondays to Thursdays, €75 Fridays to Sundays and public holidays.
CATERING: Restaurant and bar.
FACILITIES: Locker rooms, putting green, practice ground, pro-shop, buggies (€25), trolleys (€3), club hire (€15), caddies on request, tuition.
LOCATION: Off the R151, 4 miles east of Drogheda.

MOOR PARK GOLF CLUB

Rolling parkland course founded in 1994 with five man-made lakes.

18 holes parkland, 5,584 metres (6,142 yards), par 71 (SSS 69). Ladies 4,784 metres (5,262 yards), par 72 (SSS 70).

ADDRESS: Mooretown, Navan, Co. Meath.
TELEPHONE & FAX: +353 (0)46 902 7661.
SECRETARY/MANAGER: Martin Fagan.

Ireland's Golf Courses

VISITORS: Any day. Soft spikes.
GREEN FEES: €20 per round weekdays, €25 at weekends.
CATERING: Limited.
FACILITIES: Locker rooms, putting green, buggies (€20), trolleys (€3), club hire (€10).
LOCATION: 3 miles south-east of Navan.

NAVAN GOLF CLUB

Opened in 1998, this parkland course is renowned for its testing, sand-based greens. Designed in two loops with nine holes within Navan racetrack.

18 holes parkland, 6,800 yards, par 72.

SIGNATURE HOLE:
SEVENTH (370 yards, par 4) – a dogleg left that requires an exacting drive and a precise shot to a testing green.

ADDRESS: Proudstown, Navan, Co. Meath.
TELEPHONE: +353 (0)46 907 2888.
FAX: +353 (0)46 907 6722.
EMAIL: jmc@navangolfclub.ie
WEBSITE: www.navangolfclub.ie
SECRETARY/MANAGER: John McCann.
PROFESSIONAL: Emmanuel Riblet.
VISITORS: Yes.
GREEN FEES: €19 per round weekdays, €29 at weekends.
CREDIT CARDS ACCEPTED: Yes.
CATERING: Restaurant and bar. All day catering available.
FACILITIES: Locker rooms, 12-bay driving range, putting green, pro-shop, buggies (€25), trolleys (€3).
LOCATION: 41 kilometres from Dublin, 2 miles outside Navan on the Kingscourt road.
LOCAL HOTELS: Ardboyne Hotel, Navan +353 (0)46 902 3119, Newgrange Hotel +353 (0)46 907 4100.

RATHCORE GOLF AND COUNTRY CLUB

Established in 2004, the course on a 130-acre estate has two ring forts, dating from pre-Christian times, a motte, on which Anglo-Norman knights built a wooden fortress to protect the territory wrested from the hands of the native Irish, and numerous natural springs that come into play on twelve holes.

18 holes parkland, 6,533 yards, par 72 (SSS 74). Ladies 5,332 yards, par 72 (SSS 72).

SIGNATURE HOLE:
FIFTEENTH (406 yards, par 4) – a natural lake borders the fairway on this dogleg. The green is bordered by furze and marsh with two bunkers just short of the hole.

ADDRESS: Rathcore, Enfield, Co. Meath.
TELEPHONE: +353 (0)46 954 1855.
FAX: +353 (0)46 954 2916.
EMAIL: info@rathcoregolfandcountryclub.com
WEBSITE: www.rathcoregolfandcountryclub.com
SECRETARY/MANAGER: Brenda Daly.
VISITORS: Yes.
GREEN FEES: €35 Mondays to Thursdays, €40 Fridays, €45 weekends and bank holidays.
CREDIT CARDS ACCEPTED: Yes.
CATERING: Restaurant and bar.
FACILITIES: Ladies and men's locker rooms, putting green, pro-shop, buggies (€30), trolleys (€10), club hire (€20).
LOCATION: 4 miles from Enfield off the main Dublin–Galway road (M4/N4) and 30 minutes from the M50 (Dublin).
LOCAL HOTELS: Marriott Johnstown House, Enfield +353 (0)46 954 0000, The Hamlet Court Hotel, Enfield +353 (0)46 954 1200.

Rathcore Golf and Country Club

ROYAL TARA GOLF CLUB

Rolling parkland course close to the Hill of Tara, the ancient seat of the kings of Ireland. Founded in 1906, the course was extended from nine to thirteen holes in 1966 and from thirteen to eighteen holes in 1969. In 1995, a new eighteen-hole course was designed by Des Smyth, part of which was on the ground occupied by the old front nine. The main course consists of the Cluide (Blue), named after the Cluide wood through which the course runs, and the Tara (Red) nines. The Bellinter (Yellow) nine is the back nine of the old course.

18 holes parkland, 6,494 yards, par 72 (SSS 71).

9 holes parkland, 3,201 yards, par 35 (SSS 35).

ADDRESS: Bellinter, Navan, Co. Meath.
TELEPHONE: +353 (0)46 902 5508.
FAX: +353 (0)46 902 6684.
EMAIL: info@royaltaragolfclub.com
WEBSITE: www.royaltaragolfclub.com
PROFESSIONAL: Adam Whiston +353 (0)46 902 6009.
VISITORS: All week but pre-book. Soft spikes.
GREEN FEES: €35 per round weekdays, €45 weekends and public holidays.
CATERING: Restaurant and bar.
FACILITIES: Locker rooms, putting green, driving range, pro-shop, buggies, trolleys, club hire, tuition.
LOCATION: 5 miles south of Navan on the N3.
LOCAL HOTELS: Lios na Greine, Bboyne Dale, Athlumney Manor, Pineview House – all Navan.

Ireland's Golf Courses

SOUTH MEATH GOLF CLUB

Parkland course founded in 1997. Currently being extended to 18 holes and expected to be in play in 2007.

9 holes parkland, 5,312 metres (5,843 yards) for 18 holes, par 70 (SSS 67). Ladies 4,058 metres (4,463 yards), par 70 (SSS 69).

ADDRESS: Longwood Road, Trim, Co. Meath.
TELEPHONE: +353 (0)46 943 1471.
EMAIL: smgc@eircom.net
WEBSITE: www.southmeathgolfclub.com
SECRETARY/MANAGER: Joseph Keegan.
VISITORS: Yes.
GREEN FEES: €13 for nine holes and €15 for 18 on weekdays; €15 for nine holes and €17 for 18 at weekends.
FACILITIES: Locker rooms, trolleys, club hire.

SUMMERHILL GOLF CLUB

A mixture of undulating parkland and moorland, this is a tight course with few level stances and can be punishing for big hitters. Recently upgraded to 18 holes, it is open all year with all-weather greens due to the gravel subsoil. Founded in 1993.

18 holes parkland/moorland, 5,827 metres (6,409 yards), par 72 (SSS 71).

ADDRESS: Agher, Rathmolyon, Co. Meath.
TELEPHONE: +353 (0)46 955 7587.
EMAIL: namadrarua@eircom.net
SECRETARY: Mark Nangle.
VISITORS: All times.
GREEN FEES: €15 per round weekdays, €20 at weekends.
CATERING: Meals by arrangement.
FACILITIES: Locker rooms, putting green, practice facilities.
LOCATION: On the M4 from Dublin, take Kilcock exit. It is 6 miles to Summerhill or take the Trim road from Enfield on the M4.
LOCAL HOTELS: Cherryfield B & B, Wells Hotel.

COUNTY MONAGHAN

CASTLEBLAYNEY GOLF CLUB

Hilly parkland course founded in 1984, on the shores of Lough Mucknoo and near Blayney Castle. The club is developing 18 new holes at the Concra Wood Golf and Country Club.

9 holes parkland, 5,382 yards for 18 holes, par 68 (SSS 66). Ladies 4,989 yards, par 72 (SSS 71).

ADDRESS: Onomy, Castleblayney, Co. Monaghan.
TELEPHONE: +353 (0)42 974 9485.
FAX: +353 (0)42 974 0451.
EMAIL: secretary@castleblayneygolfclub.com
WEBSITE: www.castleblayneygolfclub.com
VISITORS: Yes. Soft spikes.
GREEN FEES: €12 per day weekdays, €15 at weekends.
CATERING: Restaurant and bar.
FACILITIES: Locker rooms, putting green, buggies, trolleys, club hire.
LOCATION: On the N2, north of Dublin. The course is near the centre of town.
LOCAL HOTELS: Glencarn Hotel.

CLONES GOLF CLUB

Established in 1913, the club moved to its present location in 1928 as a nine-hole course and was extended to eighteen holes in 2000. The original course was renowned for its dryness and its greens, and the new holes more than match this. Set in Hilton Park with panoramic views of the Drumlins.

18 holes parkland, 5,549 metres (6,103 yards), par 70 (SSS 69). Ladies 4,900 metres (5,390 yards), par 70 (SSS 70).

SIGNATURE HOLE:
FIFTH (410 yards, par 4) – dogleg right. Drive from an elevated tee between two natural lakes. Approach to a two-tiered green protected by three massive bunkers.

ADDRESS: Hilton Park, Clones, Co. Monaghan.
TELEPHONE: +353 (0)47 56017.
FAX: +353 (0)47 56913.
EMAIL: clonesgolfclub@eircom.net
WEBSITE: www.clonesgolf.com
HONORARY SECRETARY: Martin Taylor.
VISITORS: Welcome, but phone in advance at weekends.
GREEN FEES: €30 weekdays and weekends.
CREDIT CARDS ACCEPTED: Yes.
CATERING: Full catering.
FACILITIES: Locker rooms, practice ground, putting green, buggies (€20), trolleys (€2).
LOCATION: 3 miles from Clones on Scotshouse Road.
LOCAL HOTELS: Kilmore Hotel +353 (0)49 433 2288, Creighton Hotel +353 (0)47 51055, Cavan Crystal Hotel +353 (0)49 436 0600, Lennard Arms +353 (0)47 51075, Hillgrove Hotel +353(0)47 81288, Errigal Country House Hotel +353 (0)49 555 6901.

MANNAN CASTLE GOLF CLUB

Parkland course set among the Drumlins of Monaghan. Established in 1993, a second nine was added in 1999, and the final five holes are played along tree-lined fairways through a flat meadowland area. Each hole crosses water at least once with a tempting pond in front of the 18th.

18 holes parkland, 6,082 yards, par 70 (SSS 69). Ladies 5,003 yards, par 70 (SSS 68).

SIGNATURE HOLE:
SECOND (155 yards, par 3) – played from a height down to an island green, walled in at the rear with a pond and a river in the front.

ADDRESS: Carrickmacross, Co. Monaghan.
TELEPHONE & FAX: +353 (0)42 966 3308.
EMAIL: info@mannancastlegolfclub.ie
WEBSITE: www.mannancastlegolfclub.ie
SECRETARY/MANAGER: Rosemary Barry.
PROFESSIONAL: L. Leatham +353 (0)42 933 2295.
VISITORS: Welcome, except before 4 p.m. on Sundays.
GREEN FEES: €25 per day weekdays, €35 at weekends.
CATERING: Restaurant and bar.
FACILITIES: Locker rooms, putting green, practice ground, buggies, trolleys.
LOCATION: 4 miles from Carrickmacross on Crossmaglen Road.
LOCAL HOTELS: Nuremore Hotel, Shirley Arms Hotel.

NUREMORE HOTEL AND COUNTRY CLUB

Championship parkland course, carved out of the Monaghan hillside by designer Eddie Hackett. Each hole has its own distinctive character, and you are never far from a hill

or a lake. Upgraded to 18 holes in 1991, the course was a venue for the 1998 Irish Club Professional Championship.

18 holes parkland, 6,419 yards, par 71 (SSS 69).

SIGNATURE HOLE:
EIGHTEENTH (423 yards, par 4) – out of bounds on the right and four greenside bunkers.
ADDRESS: Carrickmacross, Co. Monaghan.
TELEPHONE: +353 (0)42 966 1438.
FAX: +353 (0)42 966 1853.
EMAIL: nuremore@eire.net.com
WEBSITE: www.nuremore.com
PROFESSIONAL: Maurice Cassidy.

VISITORS: Yes.
GREEN FEES: €35 weekdays, €45 weekends and bank holidays.
CREDIT CARDS ACCEPTED: All major credit cards.
CATERING: Restaurant and bar.
FACILITIES: Locker rooms, putting green, pro-shop, buggies (€35), club hire (€20), trolleys (€3), restaurant, spa and leisure complex with 18-metre indoor swimming pool, tennis courts.
LOCATION: Off the N2, 2 miles south of Carrickmacross.
LOCAL HOTELS: Four-star Nuremore Hotel and Country Club on site.

ROSSMORE GOLF CLUB

Undulating parkland course with ponds and rivers designed by Des Smyth, founded in 1916.

18 holes parkland, 6,025 yards, par 70 (SSS 68).

ADDRESS: Rossmore Park, Cootehill Road, Monaghan, Co. Monaghan.
TELEPHONE & FAX: +353 (0)47 81316.
EMAIL: rossmoregolfclub@eircom.net
PROFESSIONAL: Kieran Smith.
VISITORS: Yes.
GREEN FEES: €30 per round weekdays, €40 at weekends.
CATERING: Bar and snacks.
FACILITIES: Locker rooms, putting green, driving range, pro-shop, buggies, trolleys, club hire.
LOCATION: Off the R188, 11 miles out of Monaghan.
LOCAL HOTELS: Four Seasons Hotel, Riverside House.

COUNTY OFFALY

BEECHLAWN GOLF CLUB

This fairly flat parkland course is easy walking and perfect for beginners. Founded in 2004.

9 holes parkland, 4,748 yards for 18 holes, par 66 (SSS 63). Ladies 4,518 yards, par 66.

ADDRESS: Rahan, Tullamore, Co. Offaly.
TELEPHONE: +353 (0)506 55481.
EMAIL: beechlawngolf@eircom.net
HONORARY SECRETARY: Sean Kinsella.
VISITORS: Yes.

GREEN FEES: €10 for nine holes and €15 for eighteen on weekdays; €15 and €20 at weekends.
FACILITIES: Putting green, practice bunker, driving range, trolleys, club hire.
LOCATION: 4 miles west of Tullamore.

BIRR GOLF CLUB

This undulating parkland course, established in 1893, was part of the estate of the Earl of Rosse. The combination of natural sweeps, hollows, hillocks and fairways winding through avenues of trees provides an exciting challenge.

18 holes parkland, 5,824 metres (6,406 yards), par 70 (SSS 70). Ladies 4,860 metres (5,346 yards), par 72.

SIGNATURE HOLE:
TENTH (325 metres [357 yards], par 4) – running alongside the clubhouse, it is bordered by a wood on the right and has a picturesque approach to an elevated green.

ADDRESS: The Glenns, Birr, Co. Offaly.
TELEPHONE: +353 (0)509 20082.
FAX: +353 (0)509 22155.
EMAIL: info@birrgolfclub.com
WEBSITE: www.birrgolfclub.com
VISITORS: Mondays to Saturdays. Soft spikes.
GREEN FEES: €25 per day weekdays, €32 weekends and public holidays.
CATERING: Restaurant and bar.
FACILITIES: Locker rooms, putting green, driving range, pro-shop, buggies, trolleys, club hire, caddies, tuition.
LOCATION: 2 miles west of Birr on the Birr–Banagher road (R439).
LOCAL HOTELS: County Arms Hotel.

Ireland's Golf Courses

CASTLE BARNA GOLF CLUB

An invigorating course on the banks of the Grand Canal laid out on rolling parkland with plenty of mature trees, subtle water hazards and easy-going terrain.

18 holes parkland, 5,798 metres (6,377 yards), par 72 (SSS 69). Ladies 4,716 metres (5,187 yards), par 72 (SSS 70).

ADDRESS: Daingean, Co. Offaly.
TELEPHONE: +353 (0)506 53384.
FAX: +353 (0)506 53077.
EMAIL: info@castlebarna.ie
WEBSITE: www.castlebarna.ie
SECRETARY/MANAGER: Kieran Mangan.
VISITORS: Always welcome.
GREEN FEES: €20 Mondays to Fridays, €29 Saturdays, Sundays and bank holidays.
CREDIT CARDS ACCEPTED: MasterCard/Visa.
CATERING: Restaurant.
FACILITIES: Locker rooms, practice ground, putting green, pro-shop, buggies (€25), trolleys (€5), club hire (€10).
LOCATION: Not far from the N4, N6 and N7. From Dublin drive to Tyrellspass, turn left at the Tyrellspass Castle and the course is 7 miles through the village of Croghan and into Daingean, situated on the banks of the Grand Canal.
LOCAL HOTELS: Days Hotel, Main Street, Tullamore +353 (0)506 66034, Tyrellspass Village Hotel +353 (0)44 23171.

EDENDERRY GOLF CLUB

This parkland course, founded in 1910, was extended to 18 holes in 1992 and designed by Eddie Hackett. It has long par 4s with some tight fairways and well-protected greens.

18 holes parkland, 6,029 metres (6,631 yards), par 73 (SSS 72). Ladies 4,931 metres (5,424 yards), par 74 (SSS 72).

ADDRESS: Kishawanny, Edenderry, Co. Offaly.
TELEPHONE: +353 (0)46 973 1072.
FAX: +353 (0)46 973 3911.
EMAIL: enquiries@edenderrygolfclub.com
WEBSITE: www.edenderrygolfclub.com
VISITORS: Mondays, Tuesdays, Wednesdays and Fridays are best.
GREEN FEES: €30 per round weekdays, €35 at weekends.
CATERING: Restaurant and bar.
FACILITIES: Locker rooms, putting green, trolleys (€3).
LOCATION: Off the R402.
LOCAL HOTELS: Tullamore Court Hotel, Tullamore +353 (0)506 46666, Wells Hotel.

ESKER HILLS GOLF CLUB

This undulating parkland course with lakes and woodlands was founded in 1996 and designed by Christy O'Connor Jr. No two holes are alike, and it has a links feel with sand-based greens. More than 10,000 years ago the retreating glaciers of the ice age created the sweeping valleys and natural lakes of the spectacular landscape on which Esker Hills was built.

18 holes parkland, 6,618 yards, par 71.

ADDRESS: Tullamore, Co. Offaly.
TELEPHONE: +353 (0)506 55999.
FAX: +353 (0)506 55021.
EMAIL: info@eskerhillsgolf.com
WEBSITE: www.eskerhillsgolf.com
VISITORS: Every day. Soft spikes.
GREEN FEES: €35 per round weekdays, €45 at weekends.
CREDIT CARDS ACCEPTED: MasterCard/Visa.
CATERING: Bar and snacks.
FACILITIES: Locker rooms, putting green, club shop, buggies (€25), trolleys (€3), club hire (€10).
LOCATION: Off the N80, 2½ miles west of Tullamore.

Esker Hills Golf Club

LOCAL HOTELS: Bridge House Hotel,
Tullamore +353 (0)506 22000, Tullamore
Court Hotel, Tullamore +353 (0)506
46666, Days Hotel +353 (0)506 49300.

TULLAMORE GOLF CLUB

Championship parkland course set amongst
mature oak, beech and chestnut trees
on the edge of Tullamore with splendid
fairways, well-manicured rough and new
sand-based, undulating greens. Golf was
first played here in 1860, and the present
course was laid down in 1926. Recently,
Paddy Merrigan has embellished James

Braid's original design and added many new
features, blending the new with the old.
Playable all year round. Views of the Slieve
Bloom Mountains.

18 holes parkland, 6,428 yards, par 70
(SSS 71).

SIGNATURE HOLE:
SIXTEENTH (419 yards, par 4) – dogleg
left. Second shot to an elevated, sloping
green guarded by a stream in front.

ADDRESS: Brookfield, Tullamore, Co.
Offaly.
TELEPHONE: +353 (0)506 21439.

FAX: +353 (0)506 41806.
EMAIL: tullamoregolfclub@eircom.net
WEBSITE: www.tullamoregolfclub.ie
HONORARY SECRETARY: Jo Barber-
Loughnane.
OFFICE SECRETARY: Ann Marie Cunniffe.
PROFESSIONAL: Donagh McArdle.
VISITORS: Yes. Soft spikes.
GREEN FEES: €37 per round weekdays, €48
on Saturdays.
CREDIT CARDS ACCEPTED: Yes.
CATERING: Restaurant and bar.
FACILITIES: Locker rooms, practice ground,
putting green, pro-shop, buggies (€30),
trolleys (€3), club hire (€15).
LOCATION: From Dublin, take the N4 to
Kinnegad, then the N6 to Kilbeggan, then
a left onto the N52 to Tullamore. Take the
left for Kinnitty on the R421 1 mile south
of Tullamore on the N52. Tullamore golf
course is 1 mile south on the right.
LOCAL HOTELS: Bridge House Hotel,
Tullamore +353 (0)506 22000, Tullamore
Court Hotel, Tullamore +353 (0)506
46666.

COUNTY WESTMEATH

BALLINLOUGH CASTLE GOLF CLUB

Undulating parkland with wide fairways on
180 acres. Established in 1998.

18 holes parkland, 6,025 yards, par 69
(SSS 69). Ladies 4,747 yards, par 69 (SSS 68).

ADDRESS: Clonmellon, Co. Westmeath.
TELEPHONE: +353 (0)44 966 4544.
EMAIL: golf@ballinloughcastle.com
WEBSITE: www.ballinloughcastle.com
SECRETARY/MANAGER: Tony Brady.
VISITORS: Yes.

GREEN FEES: €20 per round midweek, €30
at weekends.
CREDIT CARDS ACCEPTED: No.
CATERING: Tea rooms.
FACILITIES: Locker rooms, trolleys,
memberships available.
LOCATION: Off the N52 Kells–Clonmellon
road.

DELVIN CASTLE GOLF CLUB

Opened in 1991, this is a beautiful rolling
parkland course, maturing each year with
many specimen trees, in the estate of
Clonyn Castle. Mix of long and short holes
with water hazards.

18 holes parkland, 6,191 metres (6,810
yards), par 71 (SSS 68). Ladies 4,942 yards,
par 71 (SSS 68).

ADDRESS: Clonyn, Delvin, Co. Westmeath.
TELEPHONE: +353 (0)44 64671.
FAX: +353 (0)44 64315.
EMAIL: delvincastle@golfnet.ie
PROFESSIONAL: David Keenaghan.
VISITORS: Every day except Sundays. Soft
spikes.
GREEN FEES: From €28 per round weekdays,
€38 at weekends.
CATERING: Restaurant and bar.
FACILITIES: Locker rooms, putting green,
pro-shop, buggies, trolleys (€2), club hire
(€8), caddies on request, tuition.
LOCATION: 15 miles north-east of Mullingar,
off the N52.
LOCAL HOTELS: Tullamore Court Hotel,
Tullamore +353 (0)506 46666.

GLASSON GOLF HOTEL AND COUNTRY CLUB

An interesting and challenging parkland
course in an unrivalled setting. It was
designed by Christy O'Connor Jr., who calls

Glasson Golf Hotel and Country Club

Glasson 'one of the most scenic pieces of land I've ever seen in my life, with the first nine overlooking Lough Ree and the second nine in Killinure Bay, there is nothing I've seen that comes close to that'. Glasson has been named in the top ten new Irish golf courses of the past twenty-five years.

18 holes parkland, 7,120 yards, par 72 (SSS 74). Ladies 5,606 yards, par 73.

SIGNATURE HOLE:
FIFTEENTH (185 yards, par 3) – challenging hole with both tee and green situated in the beautiful Lough Ree. The lake is the fairway, and you might be lucky enough to see a brown trout leap in the water.

ADDRESS: Glasson, Athlone, Co. Westmeath.

TELEPHONE: +353 (0)90 648 5120.
FAX: +353 (0)90 648 5444.
EMAIL: info@glassongolf.ie
WEBSITE: www.glassongolf.ie
SECRETARY/MANAGER: Fidelma Reid.
PROFESSIONAL: Colm Moriarty.
VISITORS: Welcome every day. Soft spikes.
GREEN FEES: €60 Mondays to Thursdays, €65 Fridays and Sundays, €75 Saturdays. Group Rates for 20+ golfers: €55 Mondays to Thursdays, €60 Fridays and Sundays, €65 Saturdays.
CREDIT CARDS ACCEPTED: Amex/Diners/ MasterCard/Visa.
CATERING: Restaurant and bar, with full catering facilities available and function room for up to 120 people.
FACILITIES: Locker rooms, 3-hole golf

academy, pitching and putting greens, pro-shop, buggies (€35), trolleys (€3), club hire (€30), leisure centre with sauna, hot tub, gymnasium.

LOCATION: From Dublin, take the M50 westbound and continue on the N6. On the approach to Athlone town, follow Galway signs onto bypass at the first roundabout. On the bypass, take the first exit and follow the signs for Cavan/Longford. Stay on the Cavan–Longford road until Glasson village. At the end of the village beside Glasson Village Restaurant take a left turn. The course is approximately 1 mile down this road.

LOCAL HOTELS: Luxury 65-bedroom hotel on site +353 (0)90 648 5120.

MOATE GOLF CLUB

Tree-lined parkland course on gently rolling countryside. Founded in 1900 and extended to 18 holes in 1993 with a lake on the new section.

18 holes parkland, 5,936 metres (6,529 yards), par 72 (SSS 71). Ladies 4,973 metres (5,470 yards), par 73 (SSS 72).

ADDRESS: Aghanargit, Moate, Co. Westmeath.
TELEPHONE: +353 (0)90 648 1271.
FAX: +353 (0)90 648 2645.
EMAIL: info@moategolfclub.ie
WEBSITE: www.moategolfclub.ie
VISITORS: Mondays, Tuesdays, Thursdays and Fridays are best days. Soft spikes.
GREEN FEES: €25 per round weekdays, €30 weekends and public holidays.
CATERING: Restaurant and bar.
FACILITIES: Locker rooms, putting green, club shop, buggies (€20), trolleys (€3), club hire (€15).

LOCATION: Off the N6, half a mile north of the town.
LOCAL HOTELS: Grand Hotel.

MOUNT TEMPLE GOLF AND COUNTRY CLUB

A championship parkland course built in a traditional style on a unique site offering great all-year round golf with links-type greens and undulating fairways. The course features some preserved ancient sites, including, on the seventh hole, a ring fort, dating back to 500 BC. At the 17th, there is a Franciscan abbey site dating from 1350. The course, established in 1991, is famous for its views of over 50 miles of midlands.

18 holes parkland, 5,927 metres (6,519 yards), par 72 (SSS 72). Ladies 4,804 metres (5,284 yards), par 73 (SSS 71).

SIGNATURE HOLE:
SIXTEENTH ('Heartbreak Hill', 453 metres [498 yards], par 5) – from the tee there is trouble right and left and a strategically placed fairway bunker. Faced with out of bounds right and left on the second shot and a river, a lake and four bunkers to overcome before finding the plateau green.

ADDRESS: Mount Temple Village, Moate, Co. Westmeath.
TELEPHONE: +353 (0)90 648 1841.
FAX: +353 (0)90 648 1957.
EMAIL: mttemple@iol.ie
WEBSITE: www.mounttemplegolfclub.com
SECRETARY/MANAGER: Michelle Allen/ Michael Dolan.
PROFESSIONAL: David Keenan
VISITORS: Welcome any day. Soft spikes.
GREEN FEES: €30 per round weekdays, €35 weekends and public holidays.
CREDIT CARDS ACCEPTED: All major cards.

Mullingar Golf Club

CATERING: Restaurant and bar.

FACILITIES: Locker rooms, putting green, practice ground, driving range (opening in Spring 2006), pro-shop, buggies (€25), trolleys (€3), club hire (€12), caddies, tuition.

LOCATION: Just off the N6, west of Dublin. The course is approximately an hour's drive from both Dublin and Shannon Airports and less than an hour from The K Club. Athlone is 10 minutes away.

LOCAL HOTELS: Hodson Bay Hotel, Athlone +353 (0)90 648 0500, Prince of Wales Hotel, Athlone +353 (0)90 647 7246, Tullamore Court Hotel, Tullamore +353 (0)506 46666, Bridge House Hotel, Tullamore +353 (0)506 22000.

MULLINGAR GOLF CLUB

Designed in 1935 by James Braid, this undulating, championship parkland course has been recently extended and rebunkered. Home of the Mullingar Scratch Cup. Founded in 1894.

18 holes parkland, 6,466 yards, par 72 (SSS 71). Ladies 5,460 yards, par 74 (SSS 73).

SIGNATURE HOLE:
SECOND (189 yards, par 3) – it can take a wood to reach the green depending on the wind.

ADDRESS: Belvedere, Mullingar, Co. Westmeath.
TELEPHONE: +353 (0)44 48366.
FAX: +353 (0)44 41499.
EMAIL: mullingargolfclub@hotmail.com

WEBSITE: www.mullingargolfclub.com
PROFESSIONAL: John Burns.
VISITORS: Mondays, Tuesdays, Thursdays, Fridays and Saturdays are best. Soft spikes.
GREEN FEES: €40 per round weekdays, €45 weekends and public holidays.
CATERING: Restaurant and bar.
FACILITIES: Locker rooms, putting green, driving range, club shop, buggies, trolleys, club hire, caddies on request, tuition.
LOCATION: 3 miles outside Mullingar on the main Kilbeggan road.

COUNTY WICKLOW

ARKLOW GOLF CLUB

A traditional links adjacent to the sea on which the Southern region of the Irish PGA held their 2001 and 2002 championships. Sand warrens, bunkers and large links greens ensure that visitors get the real links experience. The course was established in 1927 by J.H. Taylor, five times winner of the Open Championship. He said, 'It would be difficult to conceive a site for a golf course more beautifully situated.'

18 holes links, 6,387 yards, par 69. Ladies 5,321 yards, par 72.

SIGNATURE HOLE:
FIFTEENTH (453 yards, par 4) – a long tee shot is required, preferably up the left side. Anything short or a lay-up to the lake that protects the green are the safe options but you take your chances on getting your third shot close enough to make par.

ADDRESS: Abbeylands, Arklow, Co. Wicklow.

TELEPHONE: +353 (0)402 32492.
FAX: +353 (0)402 91604.
EMAIL: arklowgolflinks@eircom.net
WEBSITE: www.arklowgolflinks.com
HONORARY SECRETARY: Philip Kavanagh.
VISITORS: Yes.
GREEN FEES: €40 Mondays to Thursdays, €50 Fridays and Saturdays. Husband and wife €65 Mondays to Thursdays, €80 Fridays and Saturdays.
CREDIT CARDS ACCEPTED: Yes.
CATERING: Restaurant and bar.
FACILITIES: Locker rooms, practice ground, putting green, pro-shop, trolleys (€3), club hire (€10).
LOCATION: Off the N11, signposted from town centre.
LOCAL HOTELS: Arklow Bay Hotel +353 (0)402 32309, Woodenbridge Hotel, Woodenbridge +353 (0)402 35146, The Valley Hotel +353 (0)402 35200, The Royal Hotel +353 (0)402 32524, Lawless' Hotel, Aughrim +353 (0)402 36146.

BALTINGLASS GOLF CLUB

This very testing parkland course with tree-lined fairways on the banks of the River Slaney offers spectacular views of the Wicklow Mountains. It has four par 4s of more than 400 yards in length. Founded in 1928.

18 holes parkland, 6,076 yards, par 71 (SSS 69).

ADDRESS: Strangford Lodge, Baltinglass, Co. Wicklow.
TELEPHONE: +353 (0)59 648 1350.
FAX: +353 (0)59 648 2842.
EMAIL: baltinglassgc@eircom.net
VISITORS: Mondays to Fridays. Weekends on request.
GREEN FEES: €25 per round weekdays, €35

The seventh at Blainroe Golf Club

weekends and public holidays.
CREDIT CARDS ACCEPTED: All major cards.
CATERING: Restaurant and bar.
FACILITIES: Locker rooms, putting green, practice ground, buggies (€20), trolleys (€2.50).
LOCATION: 1½ miles north of Baltinglass town on the Dublin road.

BLAINROE GOLF CLUB

Parkland and seaside course with some holes situated right on the coast. Extensive views of the Irish Sea from all 18 holes. The 14th is played over the sea from a cliff promontory. Founded in 1978.

18 holes parkland, 6,175 metres (6,792 yards), par 72 (SSS 72). Ladies 5,450 metres (5,995 yards), par 74 (SSS 73).

ADDRESS: Blainroe, Co. Wicklow.
TELEPHONE: +353 (0)404 68168.
FAX: +353 (0)404 69369.
EMAIL: blainroegolfclub@eircom.net
WEBSITE: www.blainroe.com
PROFESSIONAL: John McDonald +353 (0)404 66470.
VISITORS: Tuesdays to Saturdays.
GREEN FEES: €50 per round weekdays, €70 at weekends.
CATERING: Restaurant and bar.
FACILITIES: Locker rooms, putting green, proshop, buggies, trolleys, club hire, tuition.
LOCATION: 3 miles south of Wicklow on coast road.

Ireland's Golf Courses

BOYSTOWN GOLF CLUB

Parkland course with water features and no severe inclines. Spectacular views of Poulaphuca Reservoir and the Wicklow Mountains. Established in 1998.

9 holes parkland, 6,950 yards for 18 holes, par 72 (SSS 73). Ladies 5,432 yards, par 74 (SSS 73).

ADDRESS: Baltyboys, Blessington, Co. Wicklow.
TELEPHONE: +353 (0)45 867146.
EMAIL: boystowngc@eircom.net
VISITORS: Mondays to Saturdays. Soft spikes.
GREEN FEES: €25 for 18 holes.
CATERING: Snacks.
FACILITIES: Locker rooms, putting green, trolleys.
LOCATION: 3 miles from Blessington on the R758.

BRAY GOLF CLUB

This parkland course with greens to USGA specifications provides spectacular views of the Wicklow Mountains and Killiney Bay.

18 holes parkland, 5,990 metres (6,589 yards), par 71 (SSS 72). Ladies 5,077 metres (5,584 yards), par 72 (SSS 72).

SIGNATURE HOLE:
ELEVENTH (322 metres, [354 yards], par 4) – drive from an elevated tee to an uphill fairway well protected by bunkers. Two-tiered green with bunkers and mounds on both sides.

ADDRESS: Greystones Road, Bray, Co. Wicklow.
TELEPHONE: +353 (0)1 276 3200.
FAX: +353 (0)1 276 3262.
EMAIL: braygolfclub@eircom.net

WEBSITE: www.braygolfclub.com
SECRETARY/MANAGER: Alan Threadgold.
PROFESSIONAL: Ciaran Carroll.
VISITORS: Individuals, groups, societies and corporate outings welcome.
GREEN FEES: €50 for individuals. Group rates available.
CREDIT CARDS ACCEPTED: Yes.
CATERING: Full restaurant.
FACILITIES: Locker rooms, practice ground, putting and chipping green, pro-shop, buggies (€30), trolleys (€4).
LOCATION: Take the Greystones exit from the N11 and continue towards Greystones. The golf course is on the left from Bray to Greystones, less than a mile after turning right at the roundabout at the Ramada Hotel.
LOCAL HOTELS: Ramada Woodlands Court +353 (0)1 276 0258, Esplanade Hotel +353 (0)1 286 2056.

CHARLESLAND GOLF AND COUNTRY CLUB

Championship parkland course skirts the Irish Sea for the best part of the front nine with the back nine being true parkland. The 618-yard 18th with a double-dogleg and water on either side is a fantastic finishing hole. Established in 1992 and designed by Eddie Hackett.

18 holes parkland, 6,159 metres (6,774 yards), par 72 (SSS 72). Ladies 5,046 metres (5,550 yards), par 72.

SIGNATURE HOLE:
THIRTEENTH (229 metres [251 yards], par 3) – spectacular! The highest point of the course. A daunting tee shot to a green 120 feet below.

ADDRESS: Greystones, Co. Wicklow.
TELEPHONE: +353 (0)1 287 4350.

FAX: +353 (0)1 287 4360.
EMAIL: teetimes@charlesland.com
WEBSITE: www.charlesland.com
PROFESSIONAL: Peter Duignan.
VISITORS: Seven days a week.
GREEN FEES: €50 per round weekdays, €60 at weekends.
CREDIT CARDS ACCEPTED: Amex/ MasterCard/Visa.
CATERING: Restaurant and bar.
FACILITIES: Locker rooms, putting green, driving range, pro-shop, buggies, trolleys, club hire, tuition.
LOCATION: Off the N11, 5 miles south of Bray.
LOCAL HOTELS: Charlesland Hotel.

COOLLATTIN GOLF CLUB

Parkland course with large oak trees as a feature. Originally founded in 1962 as a nine-hole course, the new nine holes were designed by Peter McEvoy and built to USGA standards in 1998.

18 holes parkland, 6,148 yards, par 70 (SSS 69). Ladies 5,212 yards, par 71 (SSS 70).

SIGNATURE HOLE:
TWELFTH (124 yards, par 3) – set in a walled garden, the elevated green is surrounded by bunkers with the garden wall coming into play at the back of the green.

ADDRESS: Coollattin, Shillelagh, Co. Wicklow.
TELEPHONE: +353 (0)55 29125.
FAX: +353 (0)55 29930.
EMAIL: coollattingolfclub@eircom.net
WEBSITE: www.coollattingolfclub.com
HONORARY SECRETARY: Billy Stamp.
PROFESSIONAL: Peter Jones.
VISITORS: Yes.

GREEN FEES: €35 weekdays, €40 weekends and public holidays. €30 for groups of 20 plus.
CREDIT CARDS ACCEPTED: Yes.
CATERING: Restaurant and bar.
FACILITIES: Locker rooms, practice ground, putting green, pro-shop, buggies (€20), trolleys (€2).
LOCATION: From the N11, take a right in Gorey for Carnew. In Carnew take a right for Coollattin 3 miles on. From Baltinglass, continue on for Tullow, take a left for Shillelagh, 1 mile from there to golf course.
LOCAL HOTELS: Woodenbridge Hotel, Woodenbridge +353 (0)402 35146, Lawless' Hotel, Aughrim +353 (0)402 36146, Millrace Hotel, Bunclody +353 (0)5393 75150.

DELGANY GOLF CLUB

Established in 1908, this is a slightly undulating parkland course with tree-lined fairways and beautiful scenery. Harry Vardon was involved in the original design and Paddy Merrigan remodelled it with sand-based greens and tees to USGA specifications. Delgany claims to be the only club in the world to have produced four Ryder Cup players in Harry Bradshaw, Jimmy Martin, John O'Leary and Eamonn Darcy.

18 holes parkland, 5,473 metres (6,020 yards), par 69 (SSS 68). Ladies 4,914 metres (5,405 yards), par 70 (SSS 70).

SIGNATURE HOLE:
TWELFTH (386 metres [424 yards], par 4) – a tough two shots to an elevated green with no bunkers.

ADDRESS: Delgany, Co. Wicklow.
TELEPHONE: +353 (0)1 287 4536.

Delgany Golf Club

FAX: +353 (0)1 287 3977.
EMAIL: delganygolf@eircom.net
WEBSITE: www.delganygolfclub.com
PROFESSIONAL: Gavin Kavanagh +353 (0)1 287 4697.
VISITORS: Mondays, Thursdays and Fridays are best. Soft spikes.
GREEN FEES: €45 per round weekdays, €55 weekends and public holidays.
CREDIT CARDS ACCEPTED: Yes.
CATERING: Restaurant and bar.
FACILITIES: Locker rooms, putting green, pro-shop, buggies, trolleys, club hire, tuition.
LOCATION: 30 minutes from Dublin, just off the N11 to Wexford.

LOCAL HOTELS: Delgany Inn, Glenview Hotel.

DJOUCE GOLF CLUB

Parkland course with a unique setting in the Wicklow Mountains, close to Djouce Mountain, Vartry Reservoir and Sugarloaf Mountain. Although in a mountainous environment, it is relatively flat. Founded in 1995.

9 holes parkland, 6,358 yards for 18 holes, par 72 (SSS 70). Ladies 5,480 yards, par 74 (SSS 72).

ADDRESS: Roundwood, Co. Wicklow.

The 18th at Druids Glen Golf Resort

TELEPHONE & FAX: +353 (0)1 281 8585.
EMAIL: djoucegc@eircom.net
PROPRIETOR: Donal McGillycuddy.
VISITORS: Mondays, Wednesdays,
    Thursdays, Fridays and Saturdays, and
    Tuesday and Sunday afternoons. Soft
    spikes.
GREEN FEES: €20 for 18 holes weekdays, €25
    at weekends.
CATERING: Bar.
FACILITIES: Locker rooms, putting green,
    club shop, buggies, trolleys, club hire.
LOCATION: 3 miles from Roundwood village
    on the Bray road.

DRUIDS GLEN GOLF RESORT

Druids Glen is one of the finest of the
new breed of majestic parkland courses
that have enhanced Ireland's reputation
as a venue for great golf. And it is a great
success story. In 2004, it added the Druids
Heath course to an estate which nestles
between the Irish Sea and the Wicklow
Mountains in the 'Garden of Ireland' and

became a Marriott resort in the same year.
In 2005, it was voted the IAGTO European
Golf Resort of the Year. Golf here is an
experience.

Referred to by many as the 'Augusta
of Europe', Druids Glen is a magnificent
undulating and well-wooded parkland
course. Designers Tom Craddock and Pat
Ruddy have made full use of the sylvan
setting and water features to fashion
a course that matches its illustrious
American counterpart in colour and
substance. While Augusta is known for its
azaleas, Druids Glen has an abundance
of plant life, and its clubhouse, a 1770
manor house, must be one of the finest
anywhere. Even the name of the course
hints at romance. It is named after the
Druids Altar – a stone altar dating back
before Christianity – which overlooks the
much-photographed and amphitheatre-
like 12th hole.

Seve Ballesteros is full of praise for the
course, and it was here that his compatriot,
Sergio García, won his first professional
tour victory in the Irish Open in 1999. That

www.druidsglen.ie

Ceann na Draoice

DRUIDS GLEN
GOLF RESORT
COUNTY WICKLOW

Voted European
Golf Resort of the Year
2005

IAGTO
INTERNATIONAL ASSOCIATION OF GOLF TOUR OPERATORS

For Reservations or Further Information Please Contact:
Druids Glen Golf Resort Newtownmountkennedy, Co. Wicklow, Ireland.
Tel: +353 1 2873600 • Fax: +353 1 287 3699
Email: info@druidsglen.ie • Web: www.druidsglen.ie

was the fourth Irish Open staged here, the first being only a year after it had opened to much acclaim in 1995. Then, in 2000, it won the European Golf Course of the Year award.

Drives that demand technique as much as power, approach shots that employ the old grey matter and fast greens on creeping bent grass – it's got the lot. And it finishes as it starts, testing the golfer to the limits. The 445-yard first gives you no time for acclimatisation and, as architect Ruddy puts it, the green 'lurks like a dangerous woman in the sunlit trees'. The 190-yard second is another tester. The seventeenth, 200 yards across water to an island green, is not for the faint-hearted, while the 450-yard finishing hole will stay in your memory for ever with water cascading down through three ponds towards you as you approach the green. But don't think that this course is just a beginning and an ending. The middle is pretty substantial, too, with its own version of Amen Corner from 12 through the tough 471-yard 13th to the 14th.

The new Druids Heath course, also designed by Pat Ruddy, is a massive 7,434 yards off the back tees. He has combined elements of links and heathland with the natural rock quarries, lakes, trees, streams, gorse and traditional pot-bunkers to create quite a test. The feature holes are the 484-yard par-4 12th, the 420-yard 13th and the 171-yard 14th, carved from a natural quarry and surrounded by rock, gorse and wooden sleepers, with the green across a valley and three small pot-bunkers to the front.

DRUIDS GLEN – 18 holes parkland, 7,046 yards, par 71 (SSS 73). Ladies 5,541 yards, par 73 (SSS 73).

DRUIDS HEATH – 18 holes, parkland, 7,434 yards, par 71 (SSS 74). Ladies 5,528 yards, par 72 (SSS 72).

DRUIDS GLEN SIGNATURE HOLE:
TWELFTH (174 yards, par 3) – from an elevated tee you drive across water to a generous green that slopes from back to front.

DRUIDS HEATH SIGNATURE HOLE:
TWELFTH (484 yards, par 4) – arguably the most natural hole in golf, this is a roller-coaster, which snakes through a valley. Your drive must avoid bunkers and gorse on either side of a fairway shelf. The drama of your approach shot is revealed when you reach the fairway, which sweeps through an idyllic valley down 60 feet to a green protected by a lake on the right.

ADDRESS: Newtownmountkennedy, Co. Wicklow.
TELEPHONE: Druids Glen +353 (0)1 287 3600, Druids Heath +353 (0)1 281 2278.
FAX: Druids Glen +353 (0)1 287 3699, Druids Heath +353 (0)1 281 2279.
EMAIL: Druids Glen – info@druidsglen.ie; Druids Heath – druidsheath@druidsglen.ie
WEBSITE: Druids Glen – www.druidsglen.ie; Druids Heath – www.druidsheath.com
DRUIDS HEATH DIRECTOR OF GOLF: Barry Dowling.
DRUIDS GLEN PROFESSIONAL: George Henry.
VISITORS: Yes, all year round. Soft spikes.
GREEN FEES: Druids Glen – €175 per round; Druids Heath – from €70 to €125.
CREDIT CARDS ACCEPTED: Amex/Diners Club/MasterCard/Visa.
CATERING: Restaurants and bar.
FACILITIES: Locker rooms, putting green, practice ground, pro-shop, buggies (€45), trolleys (€5), club hire (€35), caddies, coaching clinics, 3-hole golf academy (including putting, chipping and driving range).
LOCATION: 25 minutes south of Dublin. Take the N11 exit at Newtownmountkennedy,

The new Druids Heath course

Kilcoole – Druids Glen is signposted.
LOCAL HOTELS: Marriott Druids Glen Hotel
and Country Club +353 (0)1 287 0800.

THE EUROPEAN CLUB

A golfing trip to Ireland would not be
complete without a round at Pat Ruddy's
unique 20-hole links course set in tumbling
dunes along the Irish Sea, which is visible
from 16 of the holes. Since it opened for
play in 1993, it has consistently rated high
in the top 100 courses in the world. The
heart of the round is from holes seven
to thirteen – six very substantial par 4s

followed by an awesome 596-yard par 5
along the very edge of the beach. Five of
those par 4s are more than 400-yards long.
Cover this stretch in par and you can call
yourself an accomplished golfer. In 1999,
Ruddy decided to add two holes, seven A
and twelve A, to his already delightfully
challenging eighteen 'simply because we
like the game enough to play a little extra',
as he puts it. He also made the green on the
original 12th a mighty 127-yards long 'to see
the great three-putt restored to the game'.
Ruddy, who also designed such highly
rated courses as Druids Glen, Ballyliffin,
Rosapenna and Portsalon, owns and

operates the European Club with the help of his family and is rightfully proud of his links creation.

20 holes links, 7,726 yards, par 77, or 18 holes, 7,355 yards, par 71 (SSS 74). Ladies 5,788 yards for 20 holes, par 77, 5,569 yards for 18, par 71.

SIGNATURE HOLE:
SEVENTH (470 yards, par 4) – this is regarded as one of the most daunting par 4s on the planet and was voted one of the 100 Greatest Golf Holes in the World in 2000 by a consortium of golf magazines worldwide. The fairway, which looks tiny from a tee set back in gorse-covered dunes, runs on a narrow spit of sand through a marsh to a green set precariously along the bank of a stream just off the right fringe. Two great strokes and the courage of a lion are required, which is why the hole is named in honour of the bravest of them all, Arnold Palmer.

ADDRESS: Brittas Bay, Co. Wicklow.
TELEPHONE: +353 (0)404 47415.
FAX: +353 (0)404 47449.
EMAIL: info@theeuropeanclub.com
WEBSITE: www.theeuropeanclub.com
SECRETARY/MANAGER: Sidon Ruddy.
VISITORS: Welcome any day but wise to pre-book.
GREEN FEES: €150 April to September, €80 November to March, €200 during the Ryder Cup.
CREDIT CARDS ACCEPTED: Laser/MasterCard/Visa.
CATERING: Full catering service in licensed restaurant.

The eighth at The European Club

FACILITIES: Locker rooms, three putting greens, practice ground, golf shop, buggies (€40), trolleys (€3), club hire (€40).

LOCATION: Take the N11 south from Dublin for 30 miles to Brittas Bay. The course is 1½ miles south of the main beach.

LOCAL HOTELS: Grand Hotel, Wicklow; Arklow Bay Hotel, Arklow; Woodenbridge Hotel, Woodenbridge; Tinakilly House, Rathnew; Hunter's, Rathnew; Chester Beatty's, Ashford; Marriott at Druids Glen, Newtownmountkennedy.

GLEN OF THE DOWNS GOLF CLUB

Established in 1998, this parkland course plays almost like a links. Built to USGA specifications with sand-based greens and tees, designer Peter McEvoy believes that it has 'probably the best set of par 3s ever built'. It also has undulating greens and 90 bunkers.

18 holes parkland, 6,443 yards, par 71 (SSS 71). Ladies 5,280 yards, par 71 (SSS 70).

ADDRESS: Coolnaskeagh, Delgany, Co. Wicklow.
TELEPHONE: +353 (0)1 287 6240.
FAX: +353 (0)1 287 0063.
EMAIL: info@glenofthedowns.com
WEBSITE: www.glenofthedowns.com
VISITORS: Mondays to Sundays. Soft spikes.
GREEN FEES: €65 per round weekdays, €80 at weekends.
CATERING: Bar and restaurant.
FACILITIES: Locker rooms, putting green, buggies, trolleys, club hire, club shop.
LOCATION: Off the N11 Dublin–Wexford road.
LOCAL HOTELS: The Glenview Hotel.

GLENMALURE GOLF COURSE

The course has elevated tees and is carved from the natural landscape of Ireland's Garden County with rolling fairways, natural rock quarries, a lake, trees, streams, gorse and a welcoming fresh breeze at the seventh, ninth and twelfth tees. Founded in 1993.

18 holes parkland, 5,497 yards, par 71. Ladies 4,928 yards, par 71.

SIGNATURE HOLE:
NINTH (488 yards, par 5) – spectacular views of Glenmalure Valley. An accurate tee shot is required with the course boundary on the right and a bank of gorse on the left. Two trees in the centre of the fairway provide more food for thought. The second shot must clear the lake to leave the player with a shot to the green.

ADDRESS: Glenmalure, Greenane, Co. Wicklow.
TELEPHONE: +353 (0)404 46679.
FAX: +353 (0)404 46783.
EMAIL: info@glenmaluregolf.com
WEBSITE: www.glenmaluregolf.com
SECRETARY/MANAGER: Sean Breen.
VISITORS: Welcome (except Sundays before 11 a.m.). Soft spikes.
GREEN FEES: €25 per round weekdays, €30 at weekends.
CREDIT CARDS ACCEPTED: Yes.
CATERING: Bar food.
FACILITIES: Locker rooms, putting green, buggies (€20), trolleys (€3).
LOCATION: From Dublin, follow the N11 past Ashford and turn off at Rathnew towards Glenealy and Rathdrum. Course is 2 miles west of Rathdrum.
LOCAL HOTELS: Woodside B & B +353 (0)404 43605, Brook Lodge Hotel +353 (0)402 36444.

Glen of the Downs Golf Club

GREYSTONES GOLF CLUB

Founded in 1895, this parkland course has a hilly front nine and a more flat homeward nine in what is known as the Garden of Ireland. Surrounded by the Wicklow Mountains with panoramic views of Dublin Bay. The course was upgraded in 1998 to USGA standard greens and tees, and Ron Kirby redesigned the back nine.

18 holes parkland, 5,322 metres (5,854 yards), par 69 (SSS 69). Ladies 4,892 metres (5,381 yards), par 72 (SSS 71).

ADDRESS: Whitshed Road, Greystones, Co. Wicklow.
TELEPHONE: +353 (0) 1 287 4136.
FAX: +353 (0) 1 287 3749.

EMAIL: secretary@greystonesgc.com
WEBSITE: www.greystonesgc.com
PROFESSIONAL: Karl Holmes +353 (0) 1 287 5308.
VISITORS: Mondays, Tuesdays, Fridays and Sundays are best days. Soft spikes.
GREEN FEES: €45 per round Mondays to Thursdays, €50 Fridays to Sundays.
CREDIT CARDS ACCEPTED: MasterCard/ Visa.
CATERING: Restaurant and bar.
FACILITIES: Locker rooms, putting green, pro-shop, buggies, trolleys, club hire, tuition.
LOCATION: Take the N11 out of Dublin towards Wexford.
LOCAL HOTELS: Tinnakilly House Hotel.

Greystones Golf Club

KILCOOLE GOLF CLUB

A flat parkland course with water on six holes, including the signature hole, a par 3 with an island green. This members-owned club was founded in 1992.

9 holes parkland, 5,514 metres (6,065 yards) for 18 holes, par 70 (SSS 69). Ladies 5,082 metres (5,590 yards), par 72.

ADDRESS: Newcastle Road, Kilcoole, Co. Wicklow.
TELEPHONE: +353 (0)1 287 2066.
FAX: +353 (0)1 287 0497.

EMAIL: adminkg@eircom.net
WEBSITE: www.kilcoolegolfclub.com
SECRETARY/MANAGER: Eddie Lonergan.
VISITORS: Mondays, Tuesdays, Thursdays and Fridays.
GREEN FEES: €25 for 18 holes weekdays, €30 at weekends.
CATERING: Restaurant and bar.
FACILITIES: Locker rooms, putting green, driving range, pro-shop, buggies, trolleys, tuition.
LOCATION: 20 miles from Dublin heading south on the N11 in the direction of Wicklow.

MILLBROOK GOLF COURSE

This par-3 course is laid out on 20 acres and has all-weather tees and large greens. It also includes mature trees, bunkers and water features.

18 holes parkland, par 54.

ADDRESS: River Valley, Redcross, Co. Wicklow.
TELEPHONE: +353 (0)404 41647.
FAX: +353 (0)404 41677.
EMAIL: info@rivervalleypark.com
WEBSITE: www.rivervalleypark.com
VISITORS: Mondays to Fridays.
GREEN FEES: On application.
CATERING: Restaurant and bar.
FACILITIES: Locker rooms, club hire.
LOCATION: From Dublin, follow the N11 35 miles south, bypassing Newtownmountkennedy, Ashford and Wicklow.

OLD CONNA GOLF CLUB

This beautiful parkland course, designed by Eddie Hackett, has panoramic seascapes and mountain views with exceptional wooded terrain. Founded in 1986.

18 holes parkland, 6,551 yards, par 72 (SSS 72).

SIGNATURE HOLE:
FIFTEENTH (475 yards, par 4) – toughest hole on the course. You need a long drive down the right side to stand a chance of hitting the green, which has bunkers at front left and front right to catch the underhit approach shot, in two.

ADDRESS: Ferndale Road, Bray, Co. Wicklow.
TELEPHONE: +353 (0)1 282 6055.
FAX: +353 (0)1 282 5611.

EMAIL: info@oldconna.com
WEBSITE: www.oldconna.com
PROFESSIONAL: Michael Langford +353 (0)1 272 0022.
VISITORS: Yes, Mondays, Wednesdays, Thursdays and Fridays. Weekends subject to availability. Soft spikes.
GREEN FEES: €50 per round weekdays, €65 at weekends.
CREDIT CARDS ACCEPTED: MasterCard/Visa.
CATERING: Restaurant and bar.
FACILITIES: Locker rooms, putting green, practice ground, pro-shop, buggies, trolleys, club hire, tuition.
LOCATION: 12 miles south of Dublin on the N11 and 2 miles from Bray.
LOCAL HOTELS: Summerhill House Hotel, The Kingston Hotel, Woodland Court Hotel.

POWERSCOURT GOLF CLUB

Two eighteen-hole championship courses set on the 1,000-acre Powerscourt Estate with an abundance of mature trees, water hazards and fast, tiered greens, developed to USGA specifications. Stunning views dominated by the Sugarloaf Mountain. Established in 1996, the East Course was designed by Peter McEvoy and is a parkland course with moorland and links characteristics, while the West Course, designed by David McLay Kidd, is purely parkland.

EAST COURSE – 18 holes parkland, 6,412 metres (7,053 yards), par 72.
WEST COURSE – 18 holes parkland, 6,345 metres (6,979 yards), par 72.

ADDRESS: Powerscourt Estate, Enniskerry, Co. Wicklow.
TELEPHONE: +353 (0)1 204 6033.
FAX: +353 (0)1 207 61303.
EMAIL: golfclub@powerscourt.ie

Powerscourt Golf Club

WEBSITE: www.powerscourt.ie
PROFESSIONAL: Paul Thompson +353 (0)1
 204 6031.
VISITORS: Seven days. Soft spikes.
GREEN FEES: €130 per round weekdays and
 weekends.
CREDIT CARDS ACCEPTED: All major cards.
CATERING: Restaurant and bar.
FACILITIES: Locker rooms, putting green,
 practice ground, driving range, pro-shop,
 buggies (€40), trolleys (€4), club hire
 (€25), caddies on request, tuition.
LOCATION: 12 miles south of Dublin just off
 the N11 in Enniskerry.
LOCAL HOTELS: Powerscourt Hotel (on the
 course).

RATHSALLAGH GOLF CLUB

The course is set in 252 acres of rolling
parkland with thousands of mature trees.
It also features lakes, streams and excellent
USGA-specified greens. Designed by Peter
McEvoy and Christy O'Connor Jr., the
course has been called 'Augusta without the
azaleas'. Opened in 1996, it is demanding
yet fair and according to O'Connor it
is 'a true championship course'. High
maintenance standards ensure play
throughout the year.

 18 holes parkland, 6,885 yards, par 72
(SSS 74). Ladies 5,483 yards, par 73 (SSS
73).

SIGNATURE HOLE:

TENTH (465 yards, par 4) – demands a very good drive to get close to the water to set up your second shot, which has water on your right and a tree-lined ditch on your left all the way to the green. The green is multi-levelled and contoured and is one of the course's most difficult.

ADDRESS: Dunlavin, Co. Wicklow.
TELEPHONE: +353 (0)45 403316.
FAX: +353 (0)45 403295.
EMAIL: golf@rathsallagh.com
WEBSITE: www.rathsallagh.com
SECRETARY/MANAGER: Joe O'Flynn.
PROFESSIONAL: Brendan McDaid.
VISITORS: All week. Soft spikes.
GREEN FEES: €60 (residents €50) Mondays to Thursdays, €75 (residents €65) Fridays to Sundays and public holidays.
CREDIT CARDS ACCEPTED: Amex/Laser/MasterCard/Visa.
CATERING: Function room, restaurant with full bar menu available daily.
FACILITIES: Locker rooms, putting and pitching greens, driving range, pro-shop, buggies (€35), trolleys (€3), club hire – Ping (€30–35), standard (€20) – Brendan McDaid Golf Academy.
LOCATION: From Dublin, take the M7 south. Exit to the M9 (Carlow and Kilkenny). Take a left for Dunlavin 65 miles from the end of the motorway (passing the Priory Inn on the left after approximately 8 miles). Rathsallagh signposted.
LOCAL HOTELS: Rathsallagh House Hotel.

ROUNDWOOD GOLF CLUB

Founded in 1995, a challenging course built to USGA standards with all-weather greens. Although parkland, yawning fairways and an abundance of gorse and heather gives the course a heathland feel. Sweeping views of the Irish Sea and Roundwood Lakes.
18 holes parkland, 6,685 yards, par 72.

SIGNATURE HOLE:

FIFTEENTH (502 yards, par 5) – a strong drive is required to be able to attack the green in two. The green is set behind a lake and the approach is all carry. There is also water on the left so one cannot be too strong if laying up. A bunker at the back of the green catches over-hit approaches.

ADDRESS: Newtownmountkennedy, Co. Wicklow.
TELEPHONE: +353 (0)1 281 8488/281 8500.
FAX: +353 (0)1 284 3642.
EMAIL: rwood@indigo.ie
WEBSITE: www.roundwoodgolf.com
SECRETARY/MANAGER: Michael McGuirk.
VISITORS: Welcome every day. Soft spikes.
GREEN FEES: €40 weekdays, €55 weekend and holidays.
CREDIT CARDS ACCEPTED: Yes.
CATERING: Restaurant and bar in new clubhouse.
FACILITIES: Locker rooms, practice area, putting green, pro-shop, buggies (€32), trolleys (€4), club hire (€15).
LOCATION: 3 miles from the N11 at Newtownmountkennedy, halfway between Roundwood and Newtownmountkennedy.
LOCAL HOTELS: Marriot Druids Glen, Newtownmountkennedy; Glen View, Glen of Downs.

TULFARRIS HOTEL AND GOLF RESORT

This championship parkland course was designed by Paddy Merrigan. Poulaphuca Lake plays an integral part in the layout of the course, which is set on three peninsulas. As well as the water hazards, there are strategically positioned bunkers and trees.

Roundwood Golf Club

Merrigan says of his creation, 'I think the finished article stands alongside the best golf courses to be found anywhere. The natural beauty of the setting is awesome.' It hosted the Irish Seniors Open Championship in 2000. Situated between the mountains and the lakes, the views here are outstanding.

18 holes parkland, 7,165 yards, par 72 (SSS 74). Ladies 5,696 yards, par 72 (SSS 73).

SIGNATURE HOLE:
EIGHTEENTH (481 yards, par 4) – water runs along the right side of the fairway.

ADDRESS: Blessington Lakes, Blessington, Co. Wicklow.
TELEPHONE: +353 (0)45 867644.

FAX: +353 (0)45 867561.
EMAIL: golf@tulfarris.com
WEBSITE: www.tulfarris.com
DIRECTOR OF GOLF: David Murray.
VISITORS: Yes. Soft spikes.
GREEN FEES: €80 weekdays, €100 at weekends.
CREDIT CARDS ACCEPTED: Yes.
CATERING: Restaurant and bar.
FACILITIES: Locker rooms, driving range, putting green, golf shop, buggies (€40), trolleys, Cobra club hire (€30).
LOCATION: Off the N81 south of Blessington. Dublin Airport and city centre are less than an hour's drive.
LOCAL HOTELS: Tulfarris Country House Hotel.

Wicklow Golf Club

VARTRY LAKES GOLF CLUB

Founded in 1997, the course overlooks the beautiful Vartry Lakes with Sugarloaf Mountain as a backdrop.

9 holes parkland, 5,385 metres (5,923 yards) for 18 holes, par 71 (SSS 70). Ladies 4,539 metres (4,992 yards), par 71 (SSS 70).

ADDRESS: Roundwood, Co. Wicklow.
TELEPHONE: +353 (0)1 281 7006.
FAX: +353 (0)1 281 8054.
EMAIL: vartrylakes@hotmail.com

MANAGER: Joe McDonald.
VISITORS: Yes.
GREEN FEES: €22 for 18 holes weekdays and weekends.
CREDIT CARDS ACCEPTED: No.
CATERING: Weekends only.
FACILITIES: Locker rooms, buggies, trolleys.
LOCATION: From the N11, take the road to Glendalough. The club is in the village of Roundwood.

Ireland's Golf Courses

WICKLOW GOLF CLUB

This seaside course without trees, situated on the cliffs overlooking Wicklow Bay, is parkland but has a links feel. Recently extended to 18 holes, it was founded in 1904.

18 holes parkland, 5,946 yards, par 71 (SSS 70). Ladies 4,926 yards, par 71 (SSS 69).

ADDRESS: Dunbur Road, Wicklow, Co. Wicklow.
TELEPHONE: +353 (0)404 67379.
FAX: +353 (0)404 64756.
EMAIL: info@wicklowgolfclub.ie
WEBSITE: www.wicklowgolfclub.ie
SECRETARY: Joe Kelly.
VISITORS: Yes.
GREEN FEES: €40 weekdays and weekends.
CREDIT CARDS ACCEPTED: Yes.
CATERING: Restaurant and bar.
FACILITIES: Locker rooms, putting green, practice ground, pro-shop, buggies, trolleys, club hire, tuition.
LOCATION: In Wicklow town, just off the main Dublin–Rosslare route (N11).
LOCAL HOTELS: The Grand Hotel, Wicklow Town +353 (0)404 67337.

WOODBROOK GOLF CLUB

Founded in 1927, this parkland course perched on top of 100-foot sea cliffs has cunning placement of fairway and greenside bunkers, and sand-based, bent-grass greens built to USGA specifications. Redesigned by Peter McEvoy, it matches any of Ireland's new generation of courses.

18 holes parkland, 6,956 yards, par 72 (SSS 73). Ladies 6,021 yards, par 74 (SSS 75).

ADDRESS: Dublin Road, Bray, Co. Wicklow.
TELEPHONE: +353 (0)1282 4799.
FAX: +353 (0)1282 1950.
EMAIL: golf@woodbrook.ie
WEBSITE: www.woodbrook.ie
SECRETARY: Patrick F. Byrne.
PROFESSIONAL: Billy Kinsella.
VISITORS: Yes.
GREEN FEES: €95.
CREDIT CARDS ACCEPTED: Laser/Visa.
CATERING: Restaurant and bar.
FACILITIES: Locker rooms, putting green, pro-shop, buggies (€35), trolleys (€5).
LOCATION: Take the North Bray exit off the N11 and follow signs.

Woodbrook Golf Club

WOODENBRIDGE GOLF CLUB

Founded in 1884, this parkland course is set in a valley with wooded slopes on all sides. The Avonmore and Aughrim rivers run through the course and many holes are played over water.

18 holes parkland, 6,400 yards, par 71 (SSS 70). Ladies 5,514 yards, par 72 (SSS 71).

ADDRESS: Vale of Avoca, Woodenbridge, Arklow, Co. Wicklow.
TELEPHONE: +353 (0)402 35202.
FAX: +353 (0)402 35754.

EMAIL: wgc@eircom.net
WEBSITE: www.woodenbridgegolfclub.com
SECRETARY: Pat Smyth.
VISITORS: Mondays, Tuesdays, Wednesdays and Fridays are best. Soft spikes. Maximum handicaps of 28 for men and 36 for ladies.
GREEN FEES: €55 per round weekdays, €65 at weekends.
CATERING: Restaurant and bar.
FACILITIES: Locker rooms, putting green, driving range, club shop, buggies (€30), trolleys (€3).
LOCATION: 5 miles north of Arklow on the Arklow–Rathdrum road.

The South-East

COUNTY CARLOW

BORRIS GOLF CLUB

Testing tree-lined parkland course with sand-based greens founded in 1907. Reputed to be one of the best nine-hole courses in the country, it has just one hill but many sloping lies.

9 holes parkland, 5,680 metres (6,248 yards) for 18 holes, par 70 (SSS 69). Ladies 5,106 metres (5,616 yards), par 72 (SSS 71).

ADDRESS: Deer Park, Borris, Co. Carlow.
TELEPHONE: +353 (0)59 977 3310.
FAX: +353 (0)59 977 3750.
EMAIL: borrisgolfclub@eircom.net
VISITORS: Welcome.
GREEN FEES: €25 per round weekdays and
  weekends. Phone in advance.
CATERING: Bar and catering facilities
  available.
FACILITIES: Locker rooms, putting green,
  practice ground, buggies, trolleys.
LOCATION: 16 miles from Carlow off the
  Dublin Road.
LOCAL HOTELS: Lord Bagenal Hotel,
  Newpark Hotel, Seven Oaks Hotel.

CARLOW GOLF CLUB

Founded in 1899, Carlow is a parkland course but has been described as a natural inland links. It is laid out in a former wild deer park over undulating terrain with numerous elevated tees, several excellent doglegs and small slick putting surfaces. With sandy subsoil, Carlow is playable 12 months of the year. There are many long par 4s and the par-3 17th has been

likened to threading a needle, while the par-5 closing hole offers the chance of a birdie as it tumbles downhill all the way back to the clubhouse. The present course was laid out by Cecil Barcroft in 1922 and redesigned by Tom Simpson in 1937. In 2003, Carlow added the nine-hole Oakpark Course.

DEERPARK COURSE – 18 holes parkland, 5,974 metres (6,571 yards), par 70 (SSS 71). Ladies 5,304 metres (5,833 yards), par 73 (SSS 74).

OAKPARK COURSE – 9 holes parkland, par 35.

SIGNATURE HOLE:
EIGHTH (397 metres [436 yards], par 4) – the most picturesque hole, where the tee shot is played to the west into the setting sun from the highest point on the course down to a sloping fairway. To the left and right are two stone-faced raths, overgrown with adult beech. A straight shot is required to stay out of trouble and an accurate second to avoid the three bunkers protecting the green.

ADDRESS: Deer Park, Carlow, Co. Carlow.
TELEPHONE: +353 (0)59 913 1695.
FAX: +353 (0)59 914 0065.
EMAIL: carlowgolfclub@eircom.net
WEBSITE: www.carlowgolfclub.com
SECRETARY/MANAGER: Donard
  MacSweeney.
PROFESSIONAL: Andy Gilbert.
VISITORS: Every day except Sunday.
GREEN FEES: Deerpark – €50 per round
  weekdays, €60 per round weekends and
  public holidays; Oakpark – €20.
CREDIT CARDS ACCEPTED: Laser/
  MasterCard/Visa.
CATERING: Restaurant and bar.
FACILITIES: Locker rooms, putting green,
  practice ground, pro-shop, buggies (€28),

Carlow Golf Club

trolleys (€3), club hire (€15), tuition.
LOCATION: On the N9, 2 ½ miles north of
    Carlow and 50 miles south of Dublin.
LOCAL HOTELS: Seven Oaks Hotel +353
    (0)59 913 1308, Dolmen Hotel +353
    (0)59 914 2002, Courthouse Hotel +353
    (0)59 913 3243.

KILLERIG CASTLE GOLF AND COUNTRY CLUB

Since opening in 2001, the Killerig course,
designed by Des Smyth assisted by Declan
Brannigan, has earned a reputation for
fine greens. Surrounded by scenic
hinterland landscape and framed on the
west by the Killeshin Hills. Work on a
new clubhouse, hotel and leisure centre
is expected to be completed by July
2006.

18 holes parkland, 6,729 yards, par 72
(SSS 72).

ADDRESS: Killerig, Co. Carlow.
TELEPHONE: +353 (0)59 916 3000.
EMAIL: info@killerig.com
WEBSITE: www.killerig.com
SECRETARY/MANAGER: Jean Fleming.
VISITORS: Yes. Soft spikes.
GREEN FEES: €35 per round weekdays, €45
    at weekends.
CATERING: Restaurant and bar.
FACILITIES: Locker rooms, putting green,
    practice area, club shop, buggies(€30),
    trolleys (€2.50), club hire (€10).

MOUNT WOLSELEY HILTON HOTEL, SPA AND COUNTRY CLUB

This challenging parkland course was designed by Christy O'Connor Jr. and opened in 1997. There are no easy holes, with wide landing areas the only concession to demanding approach shots to almost every generous-sized green. Situated a few hundred yards from the River Slaney, water is in play on 11 holes. This was once the home of the Wolseley family, founders of the eponymous automobile company. O'Connor says, 'Rarely after a first look around a potential site for a golf course had I been so impressed as at Mount Wolseley, not just with the ideal and natural roll of the ground itself but also with the magnificence of this delightful rural countryside. It is an idyllic location. Natural free draining ground, enhanced by the very latest international design standards, ensures that players will face few disappointments with the course conditions irrespective of weather conditions.' The 18th is a particularly good finishing hole, where the fairway is lined with mature trees. It requires an accurate approach uphill across a water hazard to a green overlooked by the hotel.

18 holes parkland, 7,198 yards (Championship tees), par 72 (SSS 73). Ladies 5,599 yards, par 74 (SSS 72).

SIGNATURE HOLE:
ELEVENTH (207 yards, par 3) – with a lake on the right, a long or mid-iron tee shot is hit to a two-tiered green, running towards the water.

ADDRESS: Ardattin Road, Tullow, Co. Carlow.
TELEPHONE: +353 (0)59 915 1674.
FAX: +353 (0)59 915 2123.
EMAIL: billy.murray@hilton.com

WEBSITE: www.hilton.co.uk/mountwolseley
GOLF MANAGER: Billy Murray.
VISITORS: Welcome.
GREEN FEES: €50 Sundays to Fridays, €70 on Saturdays.
CREDIT CARDS ACCEPTED: Yes.
CATERING: Restaurant and bar.
FACILITIES: Locker rooms, practice ground, putting green, pro-shop, buggies (€35), trolleys (€2.50), club hire (€25).
LOCATION: 2 miles south-east of Tullow, 40 miles from Dublin.
LOCAL HOTELS: Mount Wolseley Hilton.

COUNTY KILKENNY

CALLAN GOLF CLUB

Founded in 1929, this parkland course was recently extended by Des Smyth. It is well bunkered with water features on eight holes. Accuracy is required off the tee.

18 holes parkland, 6,362 yards, par 71. Ladies 5,436 yards, par 72.

SIGNATURE HOLE:
SEVENTH (457 yards, par 4) – a dogleg left with a carry of 250 yards over water and a bunker to cut the corner. Approach to an elevated green needs to be accurate as out of bounds is on the right and the green falls off back and left.

ADDRESS: Geraldine, Callan, Co. Kilkenny.
TELEPHONE: +353 (0)56 772 5136.
FAX: +353 (0)56 775 5155.
EMAIL: info@callangolfclub.com
WEBSITE: www.callangolfclub.com
SECRETARY/MANAGER: Liam Duggan.
PROFESSIONAL: John O'Dwyer.

Castlecomer Golf Club

VISITORS: Any day by prior arrangement. Soft spikes.

GREEN FEES: €25 per round weekdays, €30 weekends and public holidays.

CREDIT CARDS ACCEPTED: MasterCard/Visa.

CATERING: Restaurant and bar.

FACILITIES: Locker rooms, putting green, practice ground, driving range, club shop, buggies (€25), trolleys (€3), club hire (€10), caddies, tuition.

LOCATION: 1 mile from Callan on the Knocktopher road.

LOCAL HOTELS: Club House Hotel +353 (0)56 772 1994, Ormonde Hotel +353 (0)56 772 3900, Langton's Hotel +353 (0)56 776 5133, Kilford Arms +353 (0)56 776 1018, Springhill Court +353 (0)56 772 1122, Newpark Hotel +353 (0)56 772 2122, Kilkenny River Court Hotel +353 (0)56 772 3388, Kilkenny Hibernian Hotel +353 (0)56 777 1888.

CASTLECOMER GOLF CLUB

Set in a 200-year-old forest, this new course, designed by Pat Ruddy and completed in 2003, is a true test of golf. In total, 13 new holes were incorporated into the 18-hole layout with tees and greens built to USGA standards. The new holes have sand-based fairways with in-built irrigation, which ensures top-class, year-round playing conditions no matter what the weather is like.

18 holes parkland, 6,175 metres (6,792 yards), par 72 (SSS 72). Ladies 4,951 metres (5,446 yards), par 72.

ADDRESS: Drumgoole, Castlecomer, Co. Kilkenny.
TELEPHONE: +353 (0)56 444 1139/1575.
FAX: +353 (0)56 444 1139.
EMAIL: info@castlecomergolf.com
WEBSITE: www.castlecomergolf.com
SECRETARY/MANAGER: Matt Dooley.
VISITORS: Welcome.
GREEN FEES: €35 weekdays, €40 at weekends.
CREDIT CARDS ACCEPTED: Yes.
CATERING: Restaurant and bar.
FACILITIES: Locker rooms, practice ground, putting green, buggies (€20), trolleys (€3), club hire.
LOCATION: 10 miles north of Kilkenny on the N7 and an hour from Dublin.
LOCAL HOTELS: The Avalon Inn, Castlecomer +353 (0)56 444 1302.

GOWRAN PARK GOLF CLUB

Designed by Jeff Howes and opened in 2001, this parkland course set amongst the old Annaly Estate incorporates a mixture of established woodland and two lakes with tree-lined fairways and good greens. Five holes are located within the Gowran Park racetrack.

18 holes parkland, 6,110 metres (6,721 yards), par 71 (SSS 72). Ladies 4,873 metres (5,360 yards), par 71 (SSS 73).

SIGNATURE HOLE:
FOURTH (440 yards, par 4) – dogleg requiring an accurate drive. Approach requires a good mid-iron over a water hazard with bunkers to the left and back.

ADDRESS: Gowran Park, Gowran, Co. Kilkenny.
TELEPHONE: +353 (0)56 772 6699.
FAX: +353 (0)56 772 6173.
EMAIL: gowranparkltd@eircom.net
WEBSITE: www.gowranpark.ie
SECRETARY/MANAGER: Michael O'Sullivan.
VISITORS: Very welcome.
GREEN FEES: €40 weekdays, €50 at weekends.
CREDIT CARDS ACCEPTED: Yes.
CATERING: Restaurant and bar.
FACILITIES: Locker rooms, practice ground, putting green, pro-shop, buggies (€30), trolleys (€3), club hire (€20).
LOCATION: On the main Waterford–Dublin road (N9). On the Waterford side of Gowran village.
LOCAL HOTELS: Blanchville House +353 (0)56 772 7197, Springhill Court, Kilkenny +353 (0)56 772 1122, Rivercourt +353 (0)56 772 3388, Ormonde +353 (0)56 772 3900, Kilkenny Inn +353 (0)56 777 2828, Hibernian +353 (0)56 777 1888.

KILKENNY GOLF CLUB

Founded in 1896, this is one of the oldest golf clubs in Ireland. A flat parkland course, it has hosted top professional and amateur events. It is sand-based and provides good playing conditions even after very wet weather. It has many interesting holes, including the seventh, which is just short of 400 yards and has out of bounds along the right and a horseshoe-shaped bunker to the left. The thirteenth is another long par 4 of much the same length with the green set in a dip calling for a particularly accurate second shot with a long iron. The 16th is a much shorter par 4, about 380 yards, but it's tight all the way to the green with a wood on the left.

The course is to the north of Kilkenny with views of the Johnswell Hills and the Blackstairs Mountains.

18 holes parkland, 5,908 metres (6,498 yards), par 71 (SSS 70). Ladies 5,101 metres (5,611 yards), par 73 (SSS 73).

SIGNATURE HOLE:
ELEVENTH (399 metres [439 yards], par 4) – tree-lined fairway with a slight dogleg to the left.

ADDRESS: Glendine, Kilkenny, Co. Kilkenny.
TELEPHONE: +353 (0)56 776 5400.
FAX: +353 (0)56 772 3593.
EMAIL: enquiries@kilkennygolfclub.com
WEBSITE: www.kilkennygolfclub.com
SECRETARY/MANAGER: Anne O'Neill.
PROFESSIONAL: Jimmy Bolger.
VISITORS: Mondays to Fridays. Soft spikes.
GREEN FEES: €35 per round weekdays, €45 at weekends.
CREDIT CARDS ACCEPTED: Yes.
CATERING: Restaurant and bar.
FACILITIES: Locker rooms, putting green, practice ground, pro-shop, buggies (€25), trolleys (€3), club hire (€30), tuition.
LOCATION: Just over 1 mile from the centre of Kilkenny, off the Castlecomer road (N77).
LOCAL HOTELS: Berkeley House, The Rafter Dempsey's, Viewmount House.

MOUNTAIN VIEW GOLF CLUB

Picturesque parkland course on a plateau with a lake which comes into play on some holes. Founded in 1995 and recently extended to 18 holes.

18 holes parkland, 5,886 yards, par 70 (SSS 68). Ladies 5,235 yards, par 72 (SSS 72).

ADDRESS: Kiltorcan, Ballyhale, Co. Kilkenny.
TELEPHONE: +353 (0)56 776 8122.
FAX: +353 (0)56 772 4655.
EMAIL: info@mviewgolf.com
WEBSITE: www.mviewgolf.com
SECRETARY/MANAGER: Eddie Harris.
VISITORS: Yes. Soft spikes.
GREEN FEES: €20 per round weekdays, €25 at weekends.
CATERING: Snacks available at all times. Meals by arrangement.
FACILITIES: Buggies, club hire.
LOCATION: 1 mile outside Ballyhale, off the main Waterford–Kilkenny road.

MOUNT JULIET GOLF AND COUNTRY CLUB

Jack Nicklaus, possibly the greatest player the game has known, once said, 'Building a golf course is my total expression. My golf game can only go on so long. But what I have learned can be put into a piece of ground to last beyond me.' With Mount Juliet, he has achieved that and more by creating one of Europe's most renowned courses. It has also been voted the best inland course in Ireland.

This outstanding parkland facility in a stunning setting takes full advantage of the natural beauty of the 1,500-acre estate, dominated by magnificent trees and traversed by the River Nore. There is just a hint of Augusta about the place. Water comes into play on six holes and there are eighty strategically placed bunkers and marvellous sand-based greens. As you would expect from Nicklaus, there is a variety of magnificent holes, each calling for the full panoply of golf skills: from thought-provoking par 3s to outstanding par 5s – one of which, the fifth, has a double dogleg – and a classic closing hole.

Nicklaus opened the course himself in 1991 with an exhibition match against Christy O'Connor Jr. and recognition was immediate. It staged the Irish Open in 1993, 1994 and 1995 and was the venue for the 2002 and 2004 WGC–American Express Championship.

The facility also boasts the first 18-hole, par-53 putting course – with bunkers and water hazards – of its kind in Europe.

18 holes parkland, 7,264 yards, par 72 (SSS 75). Ladies 5,554 yards, par 73 (SSS 73).

SIGNATURE HOLE:
THIRD (182 yards, par 3) – accuracy is essential for the tee shot to a green guarded by a natural stream and lake.

ADDRESS: Mount Juliet, Thomastown, Co. Kilkenny.
TELEPHONE: +353 (0)56 777 3064/3071.
FAX: +353 (0)56 777 3078.
EMAIL: golfinfo@mountjuliet.ie
WEBSITE: www.mountjuliet.com
PROFESSIONAL: Sean Cotter.
VISITORS: Yes. Soft spikes only.
GREEN FEES: €75 to €160 in peak season.
CREDIT CARDS ACCEPTED: Yes.
CATERING: Restaurant and bar.
FACILITIES: Locker rooms, practice ground, putting green, driving range, buggies, trolleys (€5), club hire (€20), caddies on request, tuition.
LOCATION: Just over a mile off the N9 near Thomastown.
LOCAL HOTELS: Mount Juliet Conrad +353 (0)56 777 3000.

The third at Mount Juliet Golf and Country Club

COUNTY TIPPERARY

BALLYKISTEEN GOLF AND COUNTRY CLUB

Attractive rolling parkland course with a stream running across the middle of it. Stunning views of the Galtee Mountains. Founded in 1995 and designed by Des Smyth.

18 holes parkland, 6,765 yards, par 72 (SSS 74). Ladies 5,559 yards, par 73 (SSS 73).

SIGNATURE HOLE:
EIGHTEENTH (546 yards, par 5) – a burn 80 yards short of the green lies in wait for those whose ambition gets the better of them.

ADDRESS: Limerick Junction, Ballykisteen, Co. Tipperary.
TELEPHONE: +353 (0)62 33333.
FAX: +353 (0)62 82587.
EMAIL: golf.ballykisteen@ramadaireland.com
WEBSITE: www.ballykisteen.com
SECRETARY/MANAGER: Josephine Ryan.
PROFESSIONAL: David Reddan.
VISITORS: Welcome, but pre-book.
GREEN FEES: €26 per round weekdays, €32 at weekends.
CATERING: Restaurant and bar.
FACILITIES: Locker rooms, putting green, practice ground, driving range, club shop, buggies, trolleys, club hire, caddies on request.
LOCATION: 3 miles from Tipperary on the Limerick road.
LOCAL HOTELS: The Ramada Hotel and Suites at Ballykisteen

CAHIR PARK GOLF CLUB

Parkland course which crosses the River Suir on the eighth and sixteenth, with water in play on seven holes in total. The third and fifth are challenging par 3s. Founded in 1965.

18 holes parkland, 6,348 yards, par 71 (SSS 71). Ladies 5,400 yards, par 73 (SSS 73).

SIGNATURE HOLE:
SEVENTH (440 yards, par 4) – index 1 and an outstanding long hole with a tight landing area for the drive.

ADDRESS: Kilcommon, Cahir, Co. Tipperary.
TELEPHONE: +353 (0)52 41474.
FAX: +353 (0)52 42717.
EMAIL: management@cahirparkgolfclub.com
WEBSITE: www.cahirparkgolfclub.com
SECRETARY/MANAGER: Michael Duggan.
PROFESSIONAL: Marcus Joseph.
VISITORS: Yes, except on major competition days. Soft spikes.
GREEN FEES: €30 per round.
CATERING: Restaurant and bar.
FACILITIES: Locker rooms, putting green, practice ground, practice facilities, pro-shop, buggies, trolleys.
LOCATION: 1 mile from Cahir on Clogheen Road.
LOCAL HOTELS: Castle Court Hotel, Cahir +353 (0)52 43955, Carrigeen Castle, Cahir +353 (0)52 41370, Kilcoran Lodge Hotel, Cahir +353 (0)52 41288, Cahir House Hotel, Cahir +353 (0)52 43000.

Ballykisteen Golf and Country Club

Dundrum House at County Tipperary Golf and Country Club

CLONMEL GOLF CLUB

Testing parkland course set on the wooded slopes of the Comeragh Mountains. Founded in 1911 and designed by Eddie Hackett.

18 holes parkland, 6,347 yards, par 72 (SSS 71). Ladies 5,516 yards, par 73.

ADDRESS: Lyreanearla, Clonmel, Co. Tipperary.
TELEPHONE & FAX: +353 (0)52 24050.
FAX: +353 (0)52 83349.
EMAIL: cgc@indigo.ie
WEBSITE: www.clonmelgolfclub.com
SECRETARY/MANAGER: Aine Myles-Keating.
PROFESSIONAL: Bob Hayes.
VISITORS: Yes.
GREEN FEES: €25 per round weekdays, €35 at weekends.
CATERING: Bar and restaurant.
FACILITIES: Locker rooms, putting green, practice ground, buggies, trolleys, club hire.

LOCATION: 3 miles from Clonmel.
LOCAL HOTELS: Hotel Minella +353 (0)52 22388, Clonmel Arms Hotel +353 (0)52 21233, Hearns Hotel +353 (0)52 21611, Raheen House +353 (0)52 22140, Mulcahy's Hotel +353 (0)52 22825, Knocklofty House Hotel +353 (0)52 38222, Fennessy's Hotel +353 (0)52 23680.

COUNTY TIPPERARY GOLF AND COUNTRY CLUB

Designed by the 1995 Ryder Cup hero Philip Walton and opened in 1993, this parkland course is set in the mature woodland of the Dundrum House estate with the River Multeen coming into play.

18 holes parkland, 7,006 yards, par 72 (SSS 72). Ladies 5,218 yards, par 72 (SSS 72).

ADDRESS: Dundrum, Cashel, Co. Tipperary.
TELEPHONE: +353 (0)62 71717.
FAX: +353 (0)62 71718.

EMAIL: dundrumgolf@eircom.net
WEBSITE: www.dundrumhousehotel.com
SECRETARY/MANAGER: William Crowe.
VISITORS: Any day but booking advisable. Soft spikes.
GREEN FEES: €50 (€38 residents) per round weekdays, €60 (€42) weekends and public holidays.
CREDIT CARDS ACCEPTED: All major cards.
CATERING: Restaurant and bar.
FACILITIES: Locker rooms, putting green, practice ground, driving range, pro-shop, buggies (€35), trolleys (€4), club hire (€20), caddies on request, tuition.
LOCATION: Off the R505, 5 miles west of Cashel.
LOCAL HOTELS: Dundrum House Hotel (on the course).

NENAGH GOLF CLUB

A mature course with scenic water hazards and 13 new undulating sand-based greens, which are guarded by large bunkers. Sandy subsoil means it is unaffected by poor weather and is open all year round, unless there is a severe frost. Nenagh started out as a nine-hole course designed by Alister Mackenzie, architect of Augusta, in 1929.

18 holes parkland, 6,009 metres (6,609 yards), par 72 (SSS 73). Ladies 5,110 metres (5,621 yards), par 73 (SSS 72).

ADDRESS: Beechwood, Nenagh, Co. Tipperary.
TELEPHONE: +353 (0)67 31476.
FAX: +353 (0)67 34808.
EMAIL: nenaghgolfclub@eircom.net
WEBSITE: www.nenaghgolfclub.com
PROFESSIONAL: Robert Kelly.
VISITORS: Yes. Soft spikes.
GREEN FEES: €30 per round.
CATERING: Restaurant and bar.
FACILITIES: Locker rooms, putting green, practice net, pro-shop, buggies, trolleys, club hire, caddies, tuition.
LOCATION: 4 miles from Nenagh on the old Birr road.
LOCAL HOTELS: Abbey Court Hotel.

ROCKWELL GOLF CLUB

Parkland course founded in 1964.
9 holes parkland, 4,296 yards for 18 holes, par 66 (SSS 60).

ADDRESS: Rockwell College, Cashel, Co. Tipperary.
TELEPHONE: +353 (0)62 61444.
FAX: +353 (0)62 61661.
VISITORS: Welcome.
GREEN FEES: On application.
CATERING: Limited facilities.

ROSCREA GOLF CLUB

Golf at Roscrea dates from 1892. The present course was established in 1911 and upgraded from nine holes in 1991. This is a championship parkland course in the shadows of the Slieve Bloom Mountains. A special feature of the course is the variety of par 3s, the best of which is the 180-yard fourth played almost entirely over a lake. The course has a tough final six holes.

18 holes parkland, 6,353 yards, par 71 (SSS 71).

SIGNATURE HOLE:
FIFTH ('Burma Road', 520 yards, par 4) – the fairway is lined by magnificent trees on both sides and out of bounds all the way up the left.

ADDRESS: Derryvale, Roscrea, Co. Tipperary.
TELEPHONE: +353 (0)505 21130.
FAX: +353 (0)505 23410.

EMAIL: roscreagolfclub@hotmail.com
VISITORS: Yes.
GREEN FEES: €20 per round weekdays, €25 at weekends.
CATERING: Restaurant and bar.
FACILITIES: Locker rooms, putting green, trolleys, club hire, caddies.
LOCATION: On the N7 Dublin–Limerick road, 2 miles from Roscrea.

SLIEVENAMON GOLF CLUB

Flat, firm, tight tree-lined parkland course established in 1999.
18 holes parkland, 4,846 yards, par 67. Ladies 4,590 yards, par 68.

ADDRESS: Clonacody, Lisronagh, Clonmel, Co. Tipperary.
TELEPHONE: +353 (0)52 32213.
FAX: +353 (0)52 32040.
EMAIL: info@slievenamongolfclub.com
WEBSITE: www.slievenamongolfclub.com
PROFESSIONAL: Derry Kiely.
VISITORS: Yes. Soft spikes.
GREEN FEES: €10 per round weekdays, €15 at weekends.
CATERING: Restaurant and bar.
FACILITIES: Locker rooms, putting green, practice area, trolleys, club hire, caddies.

TEMPLEMORE GOLF CLUB

Fairly level parkland course with a testing opening par 5. Founded in 1970.
9 holes parkland, 5,928 yards for 18 holes, par 70 (SSS 69).

ADDRESS: Manna South, Templemore, Co. Tipperary.
TELEPHONE: +353 (0)504 31400.
FAX: +353 (0)504 35450.
EMAIL: tmoregc1@eircom.net
VISITORS: Yes.

GREEN FEES: €15 per round weekdays, €20 at weekends.
CATERING: By arrangement.
FACILITIES: Locker rooms, trolleys, caddies.
LOCATION: Off the N62, half a mile from Templemore centre.
LOCAL HOTELS: Anner Hotel, Grants Hotel, Templemore Arms.

THURLES GOLF CLUB

Established in 1909, this challenging parkland course with a tough finish has played host to national and provincial championships. Demanding par 3s.
18 holes parkland, 6,465 yards, par 72 (SSS 69). Ladies 5,264 yards, par 73 (SSS 71).

ADDRESS: Turtulla, Thurles, Co. Tipperary.
TELEPHONE: +353 (0)504 24599/21983.
FAX: +353 (0)504 24647.
EMAIL: thurlesgolf@eircom.net
WEBSITE: www.thurlesgolfclub.com
SECRETARY: Ciara Murphy.
PROFESSIONAL: Sean Hunt.
VISITORS: Yes.
GREEN FEES: €35 weekdays, €40 at weekends.
CREDIT CARDS ACCEPTED: Yes.
CATERING: Restaurant and bar.
FACILITIES: Locker rooms, practice ground, putting green, pro-shop, buggies (€30), trolleys, club hire.
LOCATION: 1 mile south of Thurles town, on Horse and Jockey Road. If on the main Dublin–Cork road, take the turn for Thurles in the Horse and Jockey village. The club is on the right 4 miles on, 1 mile before Thurles town.
LOCAL HOTELS: Anner Hotel +353 (0)504 21799, Hayes Hotel +353 (0)504 22122, Munster Hotel +353 (0)504 22305, Horse and Jockey +353 (0)504 44192.

Ireland's Golf Courses

TIPPERARY GOLF CLUB

A testing tree-lined parkland course recently extended to 18 holes with water hazards and strategically placed bunkers. Situated in the shadow of Cordangan Woods and the Galtee Mountains. Founded in 1896.

18 holes parkland, 5,846 metres (6,430 yards), par 72 (SSS 71). Ladies 5,024 metres (5,526 yards), par 73 (SSS 73).

ADDRESS: Rathanny, Tipperary, Co. Tipperary.
TELEPHONE: +353 (0)62 51119.
FAX: +353 (0)62 52132.
EMAIL: tipperarygolfclub@eircom.net
SECRETARY/MANAGER: Joe Considine.
PROFESSIONAL: Ger Jones.
VISITORS: Yes, by arrangement. Soft spikes preferable.
GREEN FEES: €30 per round weekdays, €35 at weekends.
CATERING: Restaurant and bar.
FACILITIES: Locker rooms, putting green, practice facilities, driving range, pro-shop, buggies (€25), trolleys (€3), club hire (€13).
LOCATION: Off the R664, 1 mile from the town.

COUNTY WATERFORD

CARRICK-ON-SUIR GOLF CLUB

Parkland course with the Comeragh Mountains on one side and the Suir Valley on the other. Founded in 1939 and recently extended, the course was originally designed by Eddie Hackett.

18 holes parkland, 6,011 metres (6,612 yards), par 72 (SSS 70). Ladies 4,933 metres (5,426 yards), par 73 (SSS 72).

ADDRESS: Garravoone, Carrick-on-Suir, Co. Waterford.
TELEPHONE: +353 (0)51 640047.
FAX: +353 (0)51 640558.
EMAIL: info@carrickgolfclub.com
WEBSITE: www.carrickgolfclub.com
SECRETARY/MANAGER: Aidan Murphy.
VISITORS: Yes. Booking advisable.
GREEN FEES: €25 per round weekdays, €30 at weekends.
CATERING: Restaurant and bar.
FACILITIES: Locker rooms, putting green, practice facilities, buggies, trolleys, club hire, tuition.
LOCATION: 15 miles from Waterford.
LOCAL HOTELS: Carraig Hotel.

DUNGARVAN GOLF CLUB

Set against the backdrop of the Comeragh Mountains and adjacent to Dungarvan Bay, this championship parkland course has seven lakes and strategically placed man-made hazards. Founded in 1924.

18 holes parkland, 6,107 metres (6,717 yards), par 72 (SSS 72). Ladies 4,992 metres (5,491 yards), par 74 (SSS 73).

ADDRESS: Knocknagranagh, Dungarvan, Co. Waterford.
TELEPHONE: +353 (0)58 41605/43310.
FAX: +353 (0)58 44113.
EMAIL: dungarvangc@eircom.net
WEBSITE: www.dungarvangolfclub.com
PROFESSIONAL: David Hayes +353 (0)58 44707.
VISITORS: Every day. Soft spikes.
GREEN FEES: €33 per round weekdays, €45 at weekends.
CATERING: Restaurant and bar.
FACILITIES: Locker rooms, putting green, practice area, pro-shop, buggies, trolleys, club hire.
LOCATION: On the N25, east of Dungarvan.

LOCAL HOTELS: Clonea Strand Hotel, Gold Coast Hotel.

DUNMORE EAST GOLF CLUB

This seaside parkland course has some exhilarating cliff-top tees and greens and many interesting holes, including the 14th (*see below*) and the 15th, which requires a drive across the sea. The course overlooks the village of Dunmore East with panoramic views of the village, the bay, Hook Peninsula and Waterford Harbour estuary. Founded in 1993.

18 holes parkland, 6,070 metres (6,677 yards), par 72 (SSS 70). Ladies 5,011 metres (5,512 yards), par 74 (SSS 73).

SIGNATURE HOLE:
FOURTEENTH (180 metres [198 yards], par 3) – drive downhill into a valley between gorse-covered banks with a backdrop of the sea and the Hook lighthouse.

ADDRESS: Dunmore East, Co. Waterford.
TELEPHONE & FAX: +353 (0)51 383151.
EMAIL: info@dunmoreeastgolfclub.ie
WEBSITE: www.dunmoreeastgolfclub.ie
SECRETARY/MANAGER: Sandra Skehan.
PROFESSIONAL: Derry Kiely.
VISITORS: Yes. Soft spikes.
GREEN FEES: €25 per round weekdays, €30 at weekends.
CREDIT CARDS ACCEPTED: MasterCard/Visa.
CATERING: Bar and snacks.
FACILITIES: Locker rooms, pro-shop, buggies (€30), trolleys (€2), club hire (€10), tuition available on request.
LOCATION: 10 miles from Waterford, overlooking the village of Dunmore. At the entrance to Dunmore, take the first left to Strand, then take the first right and follow signposts to the club.
LOCAL HOTELS: Ocean Hotel +353 (0)51

383136, Strand Inn +353 (0)51 383174, Haven Hotel +353 (0)51 383150.

FAITHLEGG HOUSE HOTEL AND GOLF CLUB

Some wicked slopes and borrows on the immaculate greens, a 432-yard seventeenth which has a host of problems and a dogleg approach to the two-tiered eighteenth green (which has Faithlegg House as a dramatic backdrop) are just some of the features incorporated in this Paddy Merrigan-designed course. Beautifully set on the banks of the River Suir, the philosophy of the architect was that 'the design solution was in the landscape', and he sensitively integrated the course into a setting textured with mature trees, flowing parkland and five lakes. Opened in 1993, it was immediately rated in the top ten of new courses in Great Britain and Ireland. Twice the venue for the ladies Irish Open.

18 holes parkland, 6,629 yards, par 72 (SSS 72). Ladies 5,501 yards, par 73 (SSS 72).

SIGNATURE HOLE:
SIXTEENTH (166 yards, par 3) – large trees either side form a corridor, and the green is guarded by a large bunker at the front.

ADDRESS: Faithlegg, Co. Waterford.
TELEPHONE: +353 (0)51 382000.
FAX: +353 (0)51 382010.
EMAIL: golf@fhh.ie
WEBSITE: www.faithlegg.com
DIRECTOR OF GOLF: Darragh Tighe.
PROFESSIONALS: Darragh Tighe and Ryan Hunt.
VISITORS: Welcome every day subject to availability.
GREEN FEES: €49 per round Mondays to Thursdays, and €61 Fridays, Saturdays, Sundays and public holidays.

CREDIT CARDS ACCEPTED: Yes.
CATERING: Restaurant and bar.
FACILITIES: Locker rooms, putting green, practice ground, pro-shop, golf academy, buggies (€35), trolleys (€3.50), club hire (€28), caddies, tuition.
LOCATION: 6 miles from Waterford city. From Waterford take Dunmore East Road towards Cheekpoint village.
LOCAL HOTELS: Faithlegg House Hotel (on the course).

GOLD COAST GOLF CLUB

Scenic and challenging parkland course bordered by the Atlantic Ocean with unrivalled panoramic views of Dungarvan Bay and the Comeragh Mountains. Established in 1939 and originally a nine-hole course, it was recently extended to eighteen holes. The mature tree-lined fairways of the old course are cleverly mingled with the long and challenging newer holes. This is a real test for the discerning golfer.

18 holes parkland, 6,171 metres (6,788 yards), par 72 (SSS 72). Ladies 5,028 metres (5,530 yards), par 72 (SSS 71).

SIGNATURE HOLE:
FIFTEENTH (361 metres [397 yards], par 4) – a 230-yard carry over the Atlantic into the prevailing wind and an approach to a well-bunkered green.

ADDRESS: Ballinacourty, Dungarvan, Co. Waterford.
TELEPHONE: +353 (0)58 45050.
FAX: +353 (0)58 42880.
EMAIL: goldcoastgolfclub2@eircom.net
WEBSITE: www.goldcoastgolfclub.com
SECRETARY: Tom Considine.
VISITORS: Welcome. Soft spikes.
GREEN FEES: €35 per round weekdays, €45 weekends and bank holidays.

CREDIT CARDS ACCEPTED: Yes.
CATERING: Restaurants and bars.
FACILITIES: Locker rooms, putting green, practice ground, shop, buggies (€35), trolleys (€3), club hire (€15), tuition.
LOCATION: 40 miles east of Cork city, 25 miles west of Waterford city on the N25 and 2 miles out of Dungarvan on the coast road.
LOCAL HOTELS: Gold Coast Golf Hotel (adjacent to the first tee) +353 (0)58 45050, Clonea Strand Hotel +353 (0)58 45555.

LISMORE GOLF CLUB

Tree-lined parkland course with two par 3s and one par 5 established in 1965.

9 holes parkland, 5,367 metres (5,903 yards) for 18 holes, par 69 (SSS 67). Ladies 4,601 metres (5,061 yards), par 70.

SIGNATURE HOLE:
SIXTH (394 metres [433 yards], par 4) – dogleg left playing to a green protected by trees on three sides.

ADDRESS: Ballyin, Lismore, Co. Waterford.
TELEPHONE: +353 (0)58 54026.
FAX: +353 (0)58 53338.
EMAIL: lismoregolfclub@eircom.net
WEBSITE: www.lismoregolf.org
HONORARY SECRETARY: Katherine Moynihan.
VISITORS: At all times. Soft spikes.
GREEN FEES: €20 per round weekdays and weekends.
CREDIT CARDS ACCEPTED: MasterCard/Visa.
CATERING: Bar.
FACILITIES: Locker rooms, putting green, trolleys.
LOCATION: Half a mile from Lismore. Take a left over bridge on way out of town.
LOCAL HOTELS: Lismore Hotel, Pinetree House.

TRAMORE GOLF CLUB

This is a gently undulating championship parkland course by the sea with holes of varying character that will challenge the most enthusiastic golfer. The signature hole (*see below*), the 190-yard par-3 tenth, the 'Garden Hole' (par-4 twelfth) and the seventeenth, which has destroyed many a card, are just some of those holes. The club was founded in 1894 and moved to its present location in 1939. There are magnificent views from the clubhouse which embrace almost the whole course with the Comeragh Mountains in the background. The course has hosted the Irish Dunlop professional tournament and the Carrolls Irish Matchplay Championship twice.

18 holes parkland, 6,055 metres (6,660 yards), par 72 (SSS 72). Ladies 5,164 metres (5,680 yards), par 73 (SSS 73).

SIGNATURE HOLE:
FOURTH (344 metres [378 yards], par 4) – dogleg right playing over a valley from the tee to the fairway and then from the fairway to the green over the same valley.

ADDRESS: Newtown Hill, Tramore, Co. Waterford.
TELEPHONE: +353 (0)51 386170.
FAX: +353 (0)51 390961.
EMAIL: tragolf@iol.ie
WEBSITE: www.tramoregolfclub.com
MANAGER: Ted Power.
PROFESSIONAL: John Byrne.
VISITORS: Mondays to Saturdays.
GREEN FEES: €45 per round weekdays, €60 at weekends.
CREDIT CARDS ACCEPTED: Yes.
CATERING: Restaurant and bar.
FACILITIES: Locker rooms, putting green, practice ground, driving range, pro-shop, buggies (€30), trolleys, club hire, caddies on request, tuition.
LOCATION: 7 miles south of Waterford on the Dungarvan coast road.
LOCAL HOTELS: Majestic Hotel, O'Sheas Hotel, Grand Hotel, Hibernian Hotel.

WATERFORD GOLF CLUB

Attractive undulating parkland course with fine greens. Founded in 1912 with the original nine designed by Willie Park and extended by James Braid in 1934. The front nine demands accuracy from the tee. The back nine is more forgiving and features a great closing stretch with a classic finishing hole.

18 holes parkland, 6,260 yards, par 71 (SSS 70).

SIGNATURE HOLE:
EIGHTEENTH (400 yards, par 4) – drive from an elevated tee to a narrow fairway which winds downhill between gorse.

ADDRESS: Newrath, Waterford, Co. Waterford.
TELEPHONE: +353 (0)51 876748.
FAX: +353 (0)51 853405.
EMAIL: info@waterfordgolfclub.com
WEBSITE: www.waterfordgolfclub.com
PROFESSIONAL: Harry Ewing.
VISITORS: Midweek by arrangement.
GREEN FEES: €40 per round weekdays, €50 at weekends.
CATERING: Restaurant and bar.
FACILITIES: Locker rooms, putting green, practice ground, driving range, club shop, buggies, trolleys, club hire, caddies on request, tuition.
LOCATION: On the N9 from Dublin, a mile from Waterford.
LOCAL HOTELS: Bridge Hotel, Jurys Hotel, The Belfry Hotel, Tower Hotel.

Ireland's Golf Courses

WATERFORD CASTLE GOLF CLUB

Opened in 1992, this gently undulating championship parkland course is laid out in a unique island setting, surrounded by the River Suir and accessed by private ferry. Designer Des Smyth, the former European Tour player, commented after he first viewed the site in 1988 that, 'The Island has a natural undulating landscape with mature forestation and beautiful views of the river. To develop a golf course on The Island would have been a natural decision for anyone with a keen love of the game.' Laid out on 310 acres, it has four water features on the second, third, fourth and sixteenth holes. There is even a 'Swilken Bridge' on the third hole. Two of the more challenging holes are the par 4s at three and twelve. Index one comes at the third, a 407-yard dogleg left, with a tee-shot over 160 yards of water; two very good shots are required here to get up in two. The 456-yard 12th is also a fine test of accuracy and distance.

18 holes parkland, 6,820 yards, par 72 (SSS 71). Ladies 5,583 yards, par 72 (SSS 72).

SIGNATURE HOLE:
SIXTEENTH ('Des's Favourite', 205 yards, par 3) – long par 3 with water down the entire right side to a green protected by three bunkers.

ADDRESS: The Island, Ballinakill, Co. Waterford.
TELEPHONE: +353 (0)51 871633.
FAX: +353 (0)51 871634.
EMAIL: golf@waterfordcastle.com
WEBSITE: www.waterfordcastle.com/golf
DIRECTOR OF GOLF: Michael Garland.
VISITORS: Welcome all year round but avoid Sundays. Booking is advisable.

GREEN FEES: €50 per round weekdays, €60 weekends and public holidays.
CREDIT CARDS ACCEPTED: All major cards.
CATERING: Restaurant and bar.
FACILITIES: Locker rooms, putting green, practice ground, driving range, pro-shop, buggies (€35), trolleys (€3), club hire (€25), tuition.
LOCATION: From Cork, take the N25. From Dublin, take the N9. Only 2 miles from Waterford city centre.
LOCAL HOTELS: Waterford Castle Hotel (on the course) +353 (0)51 878203.

WEST WATERFORD GOLF AND COUNTRY CLUB

The course is built on 150 acres of rolling parkland on the banks of the River Brickey, with the backdrop of the Comeragh Mountains to the east, the Knockmealdowns to the north and Drum Hills to the south. The first nine holes are laid out on a plateau featuring a stream which comes into play at the third and fourth holes. The River Brickey traverses the southern boundary and features at the second, twelfth, fourteenth, fifteenth and sixteenth holes, making them very challenging. Designer Eddie Hackett said of West Waterford, 'I was given the opportunity to design a great course in a unique situation.'

18 holes parkland, 6,712 yards, par 72 (SSS 72). Ladies 5,274 yards, par 73 (SSS 72).

SIGNATURE HOLE:
FOURTEENTH (407 yards, par 4) – dogleg right. Challenging tee shot with trouble right and left, as well as in front of the tee. The approach to a small green has to negotiate the river on the left, a lake front left and a dyke.

ADDRESS: Dungarvan, Co. Waterford.
TELEPHONE: +353 (0)58 43216/41475.
FAX: +353 (0)58 44343.
EMAIL: info@westwaterfordgolf.com
WEBSITE: www.westwaterfordgolf.com
SECRETARY/MANAGER: Tom Whelan.
VISITORS: Yes.
GREEN FEES: €32 weekdays, €44 weekends
    and public holidays.
CREDIT CARDS ACCEPTED: Laser/
    MasterCard/Visa.
CATERING: Restaurant and bar.
FACILITIES: Locker rooms, practice ground,
    putting green, pro-shop, buggies (€35),
    trolleys (€3), club hire (€15).
LOCATION: 4 kilometres west of Dungarvan
    off the N25 bypass (Rosslare–Cork road)
    on the Aglish road (Spring roundabout).
LOCAL HOTELS: Clonea Hotel +353 (0)58
    42416, Gold Coast Golf Hotel +353 (0)58
    42249, Lawlors Hotel +353 (0)58 41122,
    Park Hotel +353 (0)58 42899, Walter
    Raleigh Hotel +353 (0)24 92011.

WILLIAMSTOWN GOLF CLUB

The Waterford municipal golf course.
Gently rolling parkland course with water
hazards. Designed by Eddie Hackett and
opened in 1997.

18 holes parkland, 6,700 yards, par 72
(SSS 71). Ladies 5,470 yards, par 72 (SSS
72).

ADDRESS: Williamstown, Waterford, Co.
    Waterford.
TELEPHONE: +353 (0)51 853131.
FAX: +353 (0)51 843690.
EMAIL: williamstowngolfclub@eircom.net
VISITORS: Yes.
GREEN FEES: €16 per round weekdays, €20
    at weekends.
CATERING: Teas, coffees and light snacks.
FACILITIES: Locker rooms, putting green,

practice area, trolleys, club hire.
LOCATION: Off the R708, 1 mile south of
    Waterford.
LOCAL HOTELS: Granville Hotel, Bridge
    Hotel, Jurys Hotel, The Belfry Hotel,
    Tower Hotel.

COUNTY WEXFORD

COURTOWN GOLF CLUB

This heavily wooded parkland course with
spectacular sea views has four great par 3s,
particularly the eighteenth, and three par
5s, the monstrous ninth being a real tester.
Founded in 1936 and upgraded to 18 holes
in 1974.

18 holes parkland, 5,878 metres (6,465
yards), par 71 (SSS 71). Ladies 4,993 metres
(5,492 yards), par 73 (SSS 72).

ADDRESS: Kiltennel, Gorey, Co. Wexford.
TELEPHONE: +353 (0)55 25166.
FAX: +353 (0)55 25553.
EMAIL: courtown@iol.ie
WEBSITE: www.courtowngolfclub.com
PROFESSIONAL: John Coone +353 (0)55
    25860.
VISITORS: Mondays to Fridays. Soft spikes.
GREEN FEES: €38 per round weekdays, €43
    at weekends.
CREDIT CARDS ACCEPTED: All major cards.
CATERING: Restaurant and bar.
FACILITIES: Locker rooms, putting green,
    practice ground, pro-shop, buggies
    (€20), trolleys (€2), club hire, tuition.
LOCATION: 3 miles from Gorey on the
    Courtown side.
LOCAL HOTELS: Bayview Hotel, Courtown
    Hotel, Marlfield Hotel.

ENNISCORTHY GOLF CLUB

Parkland course designed by Eddie Hackett and founded in 1906. Views of the Black Stairs Mountains.

18 holes parkland, 5,953 metres (6,548 yards), par 72 (SSS 71). Ladies 5,189 metres (5,707 yards), par 74 (SSS 72).

SIGNATURE HOLE:
SEVENTH (380 metres [418 yards], par 4) – from an elevated tee box, the fairway is lined with trees on the left side and small spinneys on the right. The green nestles in a copse of trees, with the Blackstairs Mountains as a backdrop. There is a difficult approach from the left side of the fairway because of a lone oak tree.

ADDRESS: Knockmarshall, Enniscorthy, Co. Wexford.
TELEPHONE: +353 (0)5392 33191.
FAX: +353 (0)5392 37637.
EMAIL: info@enniscorthygc.ie
WEBSITE: www.enniscorthygc.ie
SECRETARY: Austin P. Colley.
PROFESSIONAL: Martin Sludds +353 (0)54 37600.
VISITORS: All welcome. Check for availability Tuesdays, Saturdays, Sundays and public holidays. Soft spikes.
GREEN FEES: €30 Mondays to Thursdays, €40 Fridays to Sundays and public holidays. €20 early bird to 10.15 a.m. Mondays to Thursdays; €17.50 twilight (9–12 holes) after 7.15 p.m. Husband and wife €10 off applicable combined green fee.
CREDIT CARDS ACCEPTED: All, except American Express.
CATERING: Restaurant and bar.
FACILITIES: Locker rooms, putting green, driving range, pro-shop, buggies (€30), electric trolleys (€10), trolleys (€3), club hire (€25), tuition by appointment.
LOCATION: 1½ miles west of Enniscorthy on the N30 (New Ross–Waterford road).
LOCAL HOTELS: Riverside Park Hotel +353 (0)5392 37800, Treacey's Hotel +353 (0)5392 37798, Millrace Hotel, Bunclody +353 (0)5393 75150, Riverbank House Hotel +353 (0)5391 23611, Talbot Hotel +353 (0)5391 22566.

NEW ROSS GOLF CLUB

Many challenging holes on this tight parkland course, founded in 1905 and extended to 18 holes in 1995. Stunning views of New Ross.

18 holes parkland, 5,751 metres (6,326 yards), par 70 (SSS 70). Ladies 5,167 metres (5,683 yards), par 71.

ADDRESS: Tinneranny, New Ross, Co. Wexford.
TELEPHONE: +353 (0)51 421433.
FAX: +353 (0)51 420098.
EMAIL: newrossgolf@eircom.net
WEBSITE: www.newrossgolfclub.net
SECRETARY/MANAGER: Kathleen Daly.
VISITORS: Midweek only. Soft spikes.
GREEN FEES: €30 per round weekdays, €40 weekends and public holidays.
CATERING: Restaurant and bar.
FACILITIES: Locker rooms, putting green, practice facilities, club shop, buggies, trolleys, club hire.
LOCATION: 1 mile from the town centre, off Waterford Road.

ROSSLARE GOLF CLUB

Traditional championship links course beside the Irish Sea with sunken greens and many blind shots. The club has recently done considerable work in upgrading the course. Founded in 1905.

OLD COURSE – 18 holes links, 6,786 yards, par 72 (SSS 72). Ladies 5,660 yards, par 73.

BURROW COURSE – 12 holes links, 3,956 yards, par 46 (designed by Christy O'Connor Jr. in 1992).

ADDRESS: Rosslare Strand, Co. Wexford.
TELEPHONE: +353 (0)53 32203.
FAX: +353 (0)53 32263.
EMAIL: office@rosslaregolf.com
WEBSITE: www.rosslaregolf.com
MANAGER: John Hanrick.
PROFESSIONAL: Johnny Young +353 (0)53 32032.
VISITORS: Welcome by appointment. Soft spikes.
GREEN FEES: €40 per round weekdays, €60 at weekends. Burrow Course €20.
CREDIT CARDS ACCEPTED: All major cards.
CATERING: Restaurant and bar.
FACILITIES: Locker rooms, putting green, practice ground, driving range, club shop, golf academy, buggies (€25), trolleys (€3), club hire (€15), tuition.
LOCATION: 6 miles from Rosslare ferry terminal.

ST HELENS BAY GOLF RESORT

The course, designed by Ryder Cup star Philip Walton and established in 1993, is a mixture of links and parkland and has nine water features on 150 acres of sweeping terrain. It is a fair test of golf with four excellent finishing holes. Overlooking the beautiful St Helen's Bay, the Tuskar Lighthouse is nearby and the local beach, known as Pirates' Cove, was once a haunt of smugglers.

OLD COURSE – 18 holes links/parkland, 6,641 yards, par 72 (SSS 72). Ladies 5,442 yards, par 73.

NINE HOLE COURSE – 3,034 yards, par 36. Ladies 2,534 yards, par 36.

SIGNATURE HOLE:
SEVENTEENTH (210 yards, par 3) – with the beach on the left, you need to be accurate here.

ADDRESS: Kilrane, Rosslare Harbour, Co. Wexford.
TELEPHONE: +353 (0)53 33234.
FAX: +353 (0)53 33803.
EMAIL: golfing@sthelensbay.com
WEBSITE: www.sthelensbay.com
PROFESSIONAL: Liam Bowler.
VISITORS: Any day. Soft spikes.
GREEN FEES: €35 per round weekdays, €42 at weekends.
CREDIT CARDS ACCEPTED: Yes.
CATERING: Restaurant and bar.
FACILITIES: Locker rooms, putting green, floodlit driving range, pro-shop, golf academy, buggies (€40), trolleys (€3), club hire (€15), caddies on request, tuition.
LOCATION: 5 minutes from Rosslare ferry port.
LOCAL HOTELS: On-site cottage-style accommodation.

SEAFIELD GOLF AND COUNTRY CLUB

A rolling woodland and parkland course by the sea. Established in 2002, it was designed by Peter McEvoy to USGA specifications. The mature woodland and water hazards of the front nine are in stark contrast to the long fairways, crosswinds and bunkers of the back nine, which runs down towards the sea and the stunning cliff-top tees on the 11th and 17th holes.

18 holes parkland, 6,533 yards, par 71 (SSS 72). Ladies 5,074 yards, par 72 (SSS 71).

Seafield Golf and Country Club

SIGNATURE HOLE:
ELEVENTH (176 yards, par 3) – stunning
cliff-top hole with the Irish Sea on the right.
A tricky double green.

ADDRESS: Ballymoney, Gorey, Co. Wexford.
TELEPHONE: +353 (0)55 24777.
FAX: +353 (0)55 24837.
EMAIL: info@seafieldgolf.com
WEBSITE: www.seafieldgolf.com
SECRETARY: Simon O'Halloran.
PROFESSIONAL: Patrick Geraghty (non-
    resident).
VISITORS: Yes, every day.
GREEN FEES: €45–105.

CREDIT CARDS ACCEPTED: Yes.
CATERING: Five-star restaurant and bar.
FACILITIES: Locker rooms, practice ground,
    putting green, pro-shop, buggies (€36),
    trolleys (€4), club hire (€25).
LOCATION: On the Wexford/Wicklow
    border in the coastal village of
    Ballymoney, which is between Gorey
    and Arklow. Located off the main N11
    Dublin–Rosslare road. The nearest town
    is Gorey, approximately 3 miles away.
LOCAL HOTELS: New hotel and spa is
    opening at Seafield in 2006. Ashdown
    Park Hotel, Gorey +353 (0)55 80500.

TARA GLEN GOLF AND COUNTRY CLUB

Hilly parkland course set in woodland. Founded in 1984.

9 holes parkland, 6,332 yards for 18 holes, par 72 (SSS 70). Ladies 5,514 yards, par 72 (SSS 70).

ADDRESS: Ballymoney, Gorey, Co. Wexford.
TELEPHONE: +353 (0)55 25413.
FAX: +353 (0)55 25612.
SECRETARY/MANAGER: Marion Siggins.
VISITORS: Yes, by prior arrangement.
GREEN FEES: €22 per round.
CATERING: Bar.
FACILITIES: Locker rooms, putting green, practice ground, trolleys, club hire.
LOCATION: On Ballymoney Road.

WEXFORD GOLF CLUB

Founded in 1960, this parkland course has stunning views of the Wexford Mountains and the coastline. Upgraded by Des Smyth.

18 holes parkland, 5,734 metres (6,307 yards), par 72 (SSS 71). Ladies 4,922 metres (5,414 yards), par 73.

ADDRESS: Mulgannon, Co. Wexford.
TELEPHONE: +353 (0)53 42238.
FAX: +353 (0)53 42243.
EMAIL: info@wexfordgolfclub.ie
WEBSITE: www.wexfordgolfclub.ie
VISITORS: Yes.
GREEN FEES: €32 per round weekdays, €38 at weekends.
CATERING: Restaurant and bar.
FACILITIES: Locker rooms, putting green, practice ground, buggies, trolleys, club hire, caddies on request.
LOCATION: In Wexford town.

The South-West

COUNTY CLARE

CLONLARA GOLF AND LEISURE

Tree-lined parkland course with small greens on the banks of the River Shannon. Designed by Christy O'Connor Jr. and founded in 1993.

12 holes parkland, 5,236 metres (5,759 yards) for 18 holes, par 71 (SSS 71). Ladies 4,854 metres (5,339 yards), par 71 (SSS 71).

ADDRESS: Clonlara, Co. Clare.
TELEPHONE: +353 (0)61 354141.
FAX: +353 (0)61 354143.
EMAIL: clonlaragolf@eircom.net
VISITORS: Welcome.
GREEN FEES: €15 per round Mondays to Thursdays, €20 Fridays to Sundays.
CATERING: Advance notice required.
FACILITIES: Locker rooms, trolleys, club hire, caddies.
LOCATION: 7 miles north-east of Limerick on the Corbally–Killaloe road through the village of Clonlara.
LOCAL HOTELS: Self-catering accommodation available on site.

DOONBEG GOLF CLUB

Greg Norman was a giant amongst golfers. On the beautifully rugged Atlantic coast of County Clare, he has built a giant of a course.

There are some courses that bear the signature of golfing superstars whose only involvement has been on paper or, at best, a single visit to the location of their creation. Not so with Doonbeg, which opened in 2002. Greg Norman, out on the course from 8 a.m. to 4 p.m., marching up and down the dunes, became a familiar sight to the locals. Even lunch had to be taken out to him so that it didn't interrupt his hands-on work. In his determination to get the course just right, he flew over from the States to nearby Shannon in his own jet 23 times to visit the site, set along the golden sands of Doughmore Bay. This magnificent location deserved that at least. And get it right he most certainly did. By modern standards, Doonbeg is not long – 6,870 yards off the blue tees – yet it is a consummate test of even the best player's golfing skills.

As you approach the course, the first forbidding view is of towering dunes, which are the trademark of this coast, and it appears that nowhere could there be room for a course to have been laid down. Once on the elevated first tee there is a sensuous feel to Doonbeg. It flows over mounds and valleys as if painted on the landscape, the sharp sunlight and deep shadows accentuating the curves and swales. Yet like most things of beauty, there is also a high degree of complexity. To the left, the breakers of the Atlantic pile in, and the dunes look like insurmountable obstacles, but it is the ribbons of crisp fairways that most grab your attention. Snaking between those dunes, they are dotted with deep red sand bunkers, which often lie hidden like predators, awaiting the careless shot.

The best thing anyone can say about a new course is that it looks older than it is. This magnificent links is so at one with its environment that it appears to have existed for hundreds of years. Doonbeg's head professional Brian Shaw says, 'A lot of credit must go to Greg Norman, who used every bit of land with the least disturbance. It's like it's been here forever. The green sites are awesome. You come off fascinated. It's like meeting an interesting person – you want to see them again.'

The 14th at Doonbeg Golf Club

Great local courses like Ballybunion and Lahinch have built immense reputations, but already Doonbeg is catching them up, and like any great links, it can be a fickle beast. It offers every kind of test you can imagine – deep pot bunkers, tall marram grasses, blind shots, brooks, burns, great sweeping greens and always a capricious wind. In winter you could face a 40 mph gale, in summer, with a light breeze off the sea, there can be no finer place to spend a few hours, especially if the sun is setting over the magnificent clubhouse as you finish your round on the roller-coaster of a home hole.

The test of a course is how many holes you can remember in detail after the first visit. With Doonbeg most are memorable and a great many spectacular. None more so than the signature hole, the par-3 14th, which clings precariously to the side of the cliffs and gives the impression of being in imminent danger of sliding into the ocean. No hole is a copy of another – each has its own strong character – and Doonbeg's other par 3s are devilish tests of shot making.

The course is a typical out and back links, and the front nine ends with another beauty of a par 3 – 175 yards to a long narrow green with no room for manoeuvre. A pace off the green on the left and you're on the beach, miss it on the right and you tangle with a collection of very deep pot bunkers, leaving a nightmarish shot back. Once on the green, take the opportunity to look back along the crescent of the bay to the impressive lodge and clubhouse, which was completed in 2006.

Bunkers are a major characteristic of Doonbeg, and nowhere is that more in evidence than on the 11th – another par 3 – which is 148 yards from an elevated tee to a raised two-tiered green. It's usually into the wind, which adds to the difficulty, but it's the giant bunker in the face of the green that is most intimidating. Around 16-feet deep, it is claimed that one young man putted out of the hazard, which would be a bit like putting up a cliff face. Bunkers are everywhere, and at the next hole, there's even one in the middle of the large undulating green. A four-putt here is not uncommon.

Doonbeg doesn't afford you the nicety of a gentle start. The 566-yard first is the third hardest hole on the course and ends in an amphitheatre green surrounded by dunes. The second demands a blind and accurate tee shot, and the dunes to the left are fenced off to protect endangered microscopic snails. The fourth is the longest hole on the course at 592 yards and is the second of three par 5s on the outward nine.

But it's not all a slog: the sixth is a good risk/reward hole at only 285 yards off the whites. However, if you go for the green, you have to contend with the breeze off the ocean pushing the tee shot into the grassy dunes on the right and bunkers 40-yards short of the elevated target area.

Every hole deserves a mention and none more so than the 373-yard fifth. Too strong a drive, blind and uphill to a narrow gap between the dunes, will end up in a ravine of knee-high grasses. The approach through a narrow alley to a welcoming green with the ocean behind has to be exact or else the beach beckons.

Then there's the 15th – the designer's favourite – which is 405 yards to a funnel-shaped green surrounded by the highest dunes on the course. Norman says, 'Landing a ball on the front edge of the 150-foot-long green and wondering if it will stop before running off the far end, is far more of a challenge to me than target golf . . . and spinning it back six inches.'

Doonbeg has attracted a lot of attention from abroad: the majority of its overseas members are from North America, and many have bought properties on the course. Perhaps they would agree with Norman, who says of his creation, 'This is a course I want to be identified with, one I will be able to say with pride, "I did that one."'

When he first saw the plot of land, Charles 'Buddy' Darby – Doonbeg's owner who also owns the Kiawah Club in South Carolina – said, 'I can't resist it. It's just too beautiful.' He would find it hard to discover any visitor who would disagree with him.

18 holes links, 6,870 yards, par 72 (SSS 74). Ladies 4,661 yards, par 72 (SSS 67).

SIGNATURE HOLE:
FOURTEENTH (111 yards, par 3) – short but often into the prevailing southerly wind, which makes club selection difficult. The first time Greg Norman played it he had to take a six-iron. It is all carry from dune to dune, and the green is narrow and 32-yards long. Miss it on the left and you are in the dunes, go right and you're in the ocean.

ADDRESS: Doonbeg, Co. Clare.
TELEPHONE: +353 (0)65 905 5600.
FAX: +353 (0)65 905 5247.
EMAIL: links@doonbeggolfclub.com
WEBSITE: www.doonbeggolfclub.com
HEAD PROFESSIONAL: Brian Shaw.
VISITORS: Yes. Soft spikes.
GREEN FEES: €185 per round weekdays, €195 at weekends.
CREDIT CARDS ACCEPTED: All major cards.
CATERING: Restaurant and bar.
FACILITIES: Locker rooms, putting green, practice area, driving range, pro-shop, trolleys (€4), club hire (€30), caddies, tuition.
LOCATION: 43 miles from Shannon Airport. West of Ennis, on the N67 coastal road.

LOCAL HOTELS: Suites to rent in the clubhouse. An Tintean Guesthouse, Doonbeg +353 (0)65 905 5036.

DROMOLAND GOLF AND COUNTRY CLUB

If John F. Kennedy had his Camelot then George W. Bush has his Dromoland Castle. When the US president stayed at the sixteenth-century castle on a visit to Ireland in 2004, he declared it a fine place run by fine people and said that everyone should come and visit. Now you may not be prepared to take George Bush's word for it, but this was definitely one of his better decisions. And you don't have to be a Republican to appreciate the course: President Clinton has also visited Dromoland. George Bush did not have a chance to play, but Clinton did and could perhaps appreciate why Dromoland's claim to be the 'Augusta of Ireland' would brook few arguments.

It is almost like something out of a fairytale as you enter this 375-acre estate and proceed down the drive flanked by the fairways of the second and third holes on its recently rebuilt golf course. Then, as you turn the corner, there across the calm waters of Lough Dromoland in a natural amphitheatre, scooped out in prehistoric times by the movement of a glacier, lies the castle, a tricolour fluttering from its battlements.

The feeling of tranquillity is tangible, as one hardened New York cop, used to the constant 24/7 noise of the Big Apple, discovered. Playing the course on his own, he came in with a few holes left and said, 'The quietness was frightening. I could hear the wind in the trees.' The Irish have a word for it: *ciunas*. It's what a lot of the guests come to this 100-room hotel and resort for;

The seventh at Dromoland Golf and Country Club

or to fish, ride, shoot, play tennis or simply pamper themselves in the well-appointed spa.

The course, rebuilt in 2003, winds through great stands of oak, beech and pines and flirts with the lough and the River Rine. There has been a course at Dromoland since 1962, but this new 6,845-yard par-72 version, masterminded by renowned designers Ron Kirby and J.B. Carr at a cost of £4 million, is now capable of matching the delights of more venerable south-west Ireland tracks like Ballybunion, Waterville and Lahinch.

The great thing about this course is that there are a number of risk/reward holes, giving the player the chance to go for it. There are three very good par 3s, at least two driveable holes for the big hitters and a couple of par 5s where you have to carefully plot your progress to get anywhere near par.

The first climbs steadily for 345 yards, but it's the second that first gives you an indication that this is not going to be just a walk in the park. Downhill with a bunker guarding the dogleg right, the bigger hitters are in danger of running through and into a large bunker on the left at 289 yards from the tee. The approach is to a slightly raised green, which, like most on the course, is hard, fast and difficult to hold; anything hit too strong will go through the back and be in danger of plummeting 30 ft or so from the putting surface.

The 429-yard par-4 fifth is another dogleg right, guarded by a cluster of three deep bunkers. A bunker also snakes around the left side of the green, and there's another on the right for those taking the safe route.

It's when you walk off the sixth green and through an avenue of trees to the seventh tee that you really appreciate the grandeur of the setting. The ninth in front of the clubhouse is the first of the gambler's holes. Although only 298 yards long, the green is tucked in behind a pond with some large trees causing obstructions. It's a 281-yard carry to the front and is somewhat reminiscent of the tenth at The Belfry.

Water – whether it's ponds, the lough or the River Rine – plays a major part in a round of golf here, and it's in evidence again on the tenth with the fairway in front of the crenellated towers of the castle curving to the right and hugging the banks of the lough.

The 11th is quite simply an outstanding hole. A 543-yard par 5, you have two choices – be brave or take the easy route. It doglegs right, and a 250-yard drive will just clear the marsh. Feeling more adventurous? Then take out the marsh and a corner of the water – that's 285 yards. Go for the latter and you'll still have 180 yards or so to a small green tucked over on the right and behind another pond. Definitely a hole to take your par and get out of there.

The 159-yard 13th is another tricky par 3 over a ravine and water to a green surrounded by bunkers, while the 15th encourages any golfer, no matter what their ability, to go for it. At 267 yards

and downhill, it's so inviting, but three cavernous bunkers await anything other than the perfectly executed shot.

Dromoland's finishing three holes would rank with any course. The 455-yard par-4 16th is regarded as the toughest on the course. A blind tee shot, bunkers, trees and the river meandering diagonally across the fairway adds to the degree of difficulty. The 227-yard par-3 17th is all carry over marsh and pond to a green only 21-yards deep, and the last is a murderously difficult but beautiful finishing hole. A par 5 at 572 yards, it is another severe dogleg right with a carry of 200 yards to clear the marsh. Once accomplished, the second shot is down a narrow tunnel of trees with water on the right. A large tree stands sentinel 90 yards from the pin, obscuring the view to the green, which is tucked in on the right on the water's edge with a bunker front left.

Whatever you have achieved in your round, the sheer beauty of the setting takes over as you walk up to the final green almost tucked under the grey walls of the castle.

18 holes parkland, 6,845 yards, par 72 (SSS 72). Ladies 5,301 yards, par 72 (SSS 72).

SIGNATURE HOLE:
SEVENTH (179 yards, par 3) – the tee towers high over the green, with a shamrock bunker to the right and a pond on the left, just waiting to be hit. Beyond is a quite magical view to the lough and the lawns leading up to the castle.

ADDRESS: Newmarket-on-Fergus, Co. Clare.
TELEPHONE: +353 (0)61 368444.
FAX: +353 (0)61 368498.
EMAIL: golf@dromoland.ie
WEBSITE: www.dromoland.ie
PROFESSIONAL: David Foley.
VISITORS: Contact in advance. Soft spikes.

GREEN FEES: €110 per round weekdays, €125 weekends and public holidays.
CREDIT CARDS ACCEPTED: All major cards.
CATERING: Restaurant and bar.
FACILITIES: Locker rooms, practice area, putting green, golf academy, pro-shop, buggies (€50), trolleys (€5), club hire (€40), tuition.
LOCATION: 8 miles from Shannon Airport on the Limerick–Galway road.
LOCAL HOTELS: Dromoland Castle Hotel +353 (0)61 368144 (Email – reservations@dromoland.ie).

EAST CLARE GOLF CLUB

A beautiful parkland course, crafted by the designer Arthur Spring in 1991 and set on 150 acres of unspoilt, rolling countryside with majestic views of East Clare. A championship course, it hosted a European Seniors Tour event in 1998. All 11 lakes play a part on most holes and in particular in front of the short 17th and the final hole.

18 holes parkland, 5,922 metres (6,524 yards), par 71 (SSS 71). Ladies, 4,860 metres (5,346 yards), par 71 (SSS 71).

SIGNATURE HOLE:
EIGHTH (131 metres [144 yards], par 3) – beautiful short hole with a lake in front of the green, flanked by three strategically placed bunkers and mature trees to the left.

ADDRESS: Bodyke, Co. Clare.
TELEPHONE: +353 (0)61 921322.
FAX: +353 (0)61 921717.
EMAIL: eastclaregolfclub@eircom.net
WEBSITE: www.eastclare.com
SECRETARY/MANAGER: Michael O'Hanlon.
VISITORS: Welcome.
GREEN FEES: €30 midweek, €35 weekends and bank holidays.
CREDIT CARDS ACCEPTED: Yes.

CATERING: Full catering.
FACILITIES: Locker rooms, practice ground, putting green, pro-shop, buggies (€30), trolleys (€2.50), club hire (€20), caddies, tuition.
LOCATION: 5 minutes drive from beautiful Lough Derg, about 30 minutes from Shannon Airport and 2 miles from Scariff on the main Scariff–Ennis road (R461).
LOCAL HOTELS: Lakeside Hotel, Killaloe; Kincora Hall Hotel, Killaloe.

ENNIS GOLF CLUB

This parkland course, founded in 1907 and designed by Eddie Hackett, is set in rolling hills with tree-lined fairways and tight greens demanding accurate hitting. Out of bounds is a hazard on a number of holes.

18 holes parkland, 5,592 metres (6,151 yards), par 71 (SSS 69). Ladies 5,008 metres (5,508 yards), par 73 (SSS 73).

ADDRESS: Drumbiggle, Ennis, Co. Clare.
TELEPHONE: +353 (0)65 682 4074.
FAX: +353 (0)65 684 1848.
EMAIL: egc@eircom.net
WEBSITE: www.ennisgolfclub.com
PROFESSIONAL: Martin Ward +353 (0)65 682 0690.
VISITORS: Most times, but check in advance.
GREEN FEES: €35 per round weekdays, €40 weekends and public holidays.
CREDIT CARDS ACCEPTED: MasterCard/Visa.
CATERING: Restaurant and bar.
FACILITIES: Locker rooms, putting green, pro-shop, buggies (€30), trolley hire (€3), club hire (€15), caddies, tuition.
LOCATION: 1 mile from Ennis town centre. Well signposted.
LOCAL HOTELS: Magowna House Hotel, Woodstock Hotel.

Kilkee Golf Club

KILKEE GOLF CLUB

Designed by Eddie Hackett, this pleasant coastal parkland course, situated on the east side of Kilkee Bay, is in excellent condition. It has spectacular cliff-top tees and greens with views over the Atlantic Ocean. Founded in 1888.

18 holes parkland, 5,555 metres (6,110 yards), par 70 (SSS 69). Ladies 4,526 metres (4,978 yards), par 71 (SSS 69).

SIGNATURE HOLE:
THIRD ('Chimney Bay', 319 yards, par 4) – a cliff-top hole where you drive over an inlet; the scenery is spectacular.

ADDRESS: East End, Kilkee, Co. Clare.
TELEPHONE: +353 (0)65 905 6048.
FAX: +353 (0)65 905 6977.
EMAIL: kilkeegolfclub@eircom.net
WEBSITE: www.kilkeegolfclub.ie
SECRETARY/MANAGER: Michael Culligan.
VISITORS: Welcome.
GREEN FEES: €30 per round weekdays, €35 at weekends in July and August. €25 and €30 during the rest of the year.
CREDIT CARDS ACCEPTED: MasterCard/Visa.
CATERING: Restaurant and bar.

FACILITIES: Locker rooms, putting green, driving range, pro-shop, buggies (€25), trolleys (€3), club hire (€15).

LOCATION: On the N72, 2 miles west of Killarney, half a mile from the centre of Kilkee on the east side of Kilkee Bay.

LOCAL HOTELS: Ocean Cove Hotel +353 (0)65 908 3100, Marine Hotel +353 (0)65 905 6722, Kilkee Bay Hotel +353 (0)65 906 0060, Stella Maris Hotel +353 (0)65 905 6455, Halpins Hotel +353 (0)65 905 6032.

KILRUSH GOLF CLUB

This parkland course was founded in 1934 and redesigned in 1994 by Dr Arthur Spring using the natural terrain combined with water, trees and sand bunkers to make a scenic course that is a pleasure to play. The eleventh hole measures 421 yards, but only the brave will take on the water in order to reach the green in two. The closing five holes can be a severe test, depending on the direction of the wind. The club has been described as 'possibly the friendliest club in the whole of Ireland'. The course is in a beautiful setting, looking out on the River Shannon, the Kerry Mountains and the Atlantic Ocean.

18 holes parkland, 5,986 yards, par 70 (SSS 70). Ladies 4,714 yards, par 69 (SSS 68).

SIGNATURE HOLE:
NINTH (168 yards, par 3) – breathtaking! Played from a plateau to a green set in a valley and guarded on three sides by water, with sand on the fourth side.

ADDRESS: Ennis Road, Kilrush, Co. Clare.
TELEPHONE: +353 (0)65 905 1138.
FAX: +353 (0)65 905 2633.
EMAIL: info@kilrushgolfclub.com
WEBSITE: www.kilrushgolfclub.com
SECRETARY/MANAGER: Denis Nagle.

VISITORS: Welcome. Societies by prior arrangement.

GREEN FEES: €30 per round weekdays, €35 at weekends.

CATERING: Restaurant and bar.

FACILITIES: Locker rooms, putting green, practice ground, driving range, buggies, trolleys, club hire, caddies, tuition.

LOCATION: 41 miles from Shannon Airport. Take the N68 from Ennis and it is just before Kilrush.

LOCAL HOTELS: Bellbridge Hotel, Stella Maris Hotel +353 (0)65 905 6455, Halpins Hotel +353 (0)65 905 6032.

LAHINCH GOLF CLUB

Rugged and uncompromising terrain offers a stern test on this traditional out and back links course on the Atlantic coast, which is often referred to as the St Andrews of Ireland. Originally planned by officers of a Scottish regiment, it was designed by Old Tom Morris in 1892 and redesigned by Dr Alister Mackenzie, who also worked on Augusta, Pebble Beach and Cypress Point. He said, 'It will make the finest and most popular course that I, or I believe anyone else, ever constructed.' In 1999, architect Martin Hawtree also undertook a four-year renovation of the Old Course.

Blind shots, huge bunkers and quirky holes – this course has the lot. Back in 1991, Phil Mickelson said it was his favourite links. There are many great holes including the fourth and the fifth, also known as 'Dell', a 154-yard par 3, which calls for a blind tee shot to a green with large sandhills front and back. The dogleg seventh plays to the beach with beautiful Liscannor Bay as the backcloth. The Castle Course is situated opposite the Old Course and has cleverly positioned bunkers and water hazards.

OLD COURSE – 18 holes links, 6,882

Lahinch Golf Club

yards, par 72 (SSS 73). Ladies 5,364 yards, par 74 (SSS 74).

CASTLE COURSE – 18 holes links, 6,117 yards, par 70 (SSS 70).

SIGNATURE HOLE:
FOURTH ('Klondyke', 472 yards, par 5) – second shot is blind over a huge sand dune to a green around 200 yards away, and if you get a birdie here, you feel as if you've struck gold.

ADDRESS: Lahinch, Co. Clare.
TELEPHONE: +353 (0)65 708 1003.
FAX: +353 (0)65 708 1592.
EMAIL: info@lahinchgolf.com
WEBSITE: www.lahinchgolf.com

SECRETARY/MANAGER: Alan Reardon.
PROFESSIONAL: Robert McCavery.
VISITORS: All week. Soft spikes.
GREEN FEES: Old Course – €145 per round weekdays and weekends; Castle Course – €50 per round weekdays.
CATERING: Restaurant and bar.
FACILITIES: Locker rooms, putting green, practice ground, club shop, buggies, trolleys, club hire, caddies on request, tuition.
LOCATION: 34 miles from Shannon Airport. From Ennis, take the N85 and then the N67.
LOCAL HOTELS: Castle View Lodge, Mulcarr House, The Shamrock Inn Hotel, Tudor Lodge.

Ireland's Golf Courses

SHANNON GOLF CLUB

A reasonably flat championship parkland course which has the River Shannon as an impressive backdrop. Water features on five of the holes and combines with strategically placed trees and bunkers to make this a testing and enjoyable course. Established in 1966, it has attracted many top golfers, among them Seve Ballesteros, Nick Faldo, Bernhard Langer and Greg Norman.

18 holes parkland, 6,874 yards, par 72 (SSS 73). Ladies 5,646 yards, par 74 (SSS 74).

SIGNATURE HOLE:
SEVENTEENTH (par 3) – a carry of 216 yards across the Shannon estuary.

ADDRESS: Shannon Airport, Co. Clare.
TELEPHONE: +353 (0)61 471849.
FAX: +353 (0)61 471507.
EMAIL: shannongolfclub@eircom.net
WEBSITE: www.shannongolf.com
SECRETARY: Michael Corry.
PROFESSIONAL: Artie Pyke +353 (0)61 471551.
VISITORS: Any day, but pre-book. Soft spikes.
GREEN FEES: €50 per round weekdays, €60 at weekends.
CREDIT CARDS ACCEPTED: All major cards.
CATERING: Restaurant and bar.
FACILITIES: Locker rooms, practice ground, driving range, club shop, golf academy, buggies (€30), trolleys (€3), club hire (€20), caddies on request, tuition.
LOCATION: Half a mile from Shannon Airport.

SPANISH POINT GOLF CLUB

Seaside course, overlooking Spanish Point beach, with elevated tees and greens. Founded in 1896.

9 holes seaside, 5,059 yards for 18 holes, par 64 (SSS 63).

ADDRESS: Spanish Point, Miltown Malbay, Co. Clare.
TELEPHONE: +353 (0)65 708 4198.
FAX: +353 (0)65 708 4263.
EMAIL: info@spanish-point.com
WEBSITE: www.spanishpointgolf.com
MANAGER: David Fitzgerald.
VISITORS: Weekdays. Soft spikes.
GREEN FEES: €25 per round weekdays, €30 at weekends.
CREDIT CARDS ACCEPTED: All major cards.
CATERING: Snacks.
FACILITIES: Trolleys, club hire, caddies.
LOCATION: 2 miles from Miltown Malbay. Take the R482.

WOODSTOCK GOLF AND COUNTRY CLUB

A challenging championship parkland course opened in 1993, Woodstock has some breathtaking holes around the lake, namely the sixth, seventh and eighth. Many fine trees have been planted, and it's a course that is improving with age. Free-draining soil makes it playable all year.

18 holes parkland, 5,864 metres (6,450 yards), par 71 (SSS 71). Ladies 5,045 metres (5,549 yards), par 73 (SSS 73).

SIGNATURE HOLE:
SEVENTH (430 yards, par 4) – with a drive over a lake and an approach shot also over water, this is a fine example of designer Arthur Spring's craft.

ADDRESS: Shanaway Road, Ennis, Co. Clare.
TELEPHONE: +353 (0)65 682 9463.
FAX: +353 (0)65 682 0304.
EMAIL: woodstock.ennis@eircom.net

WEBSITE: www.woodstockgolfclub.com
SECRETARY/MANAGER: Avril Guerin.
PROFESSIONAL: Nick Obolewicz.
VISITORS: Yes.
GREEN FEES: €45 daily.
CREDIT CARDS ACCEPTED: Yes.
CATERING: Restaurant and bar.
FACILITIES: Locker rooms, putting green, pro-shop, buggies (€30), trolleys (€4), club hire (€20).
LOCATION: 2 miles from Ennis, off the N85 (Lahinch Road) and 20 minutes from Shannon Airport
LOCAL HOTELS: Woodstock Hotel (on the course) +353 (0)65 684 6600, Auburn Lodge +353 (0)65 682 1247, Dromoland Castle Hotel +353 (0)61 368144, Old Ground Hotel +353 (0)65 682 8127, Queen's Hotel +353 (0)65 682 8963, Temple Gate Hotel +353 (0)65 682 3300, West County Hotel +353 (0)65 682 8241.

COUNTY CORK

BANDON GOLF CLUB

This attractive parkland course, set on the undulating slopes of the Bandon Valley, meanders around the ruins of the old Castlebernard, and many of the holes are protected by water and bunkers. Established in 1909.

18 holes parkland, 6,634 yards, par 71 (SSS 72). Ladies 5,561 yards, par 73 (SSS 73).

ADDRESS: Castlebernard, Bandon, Co. Cork.
TELEPHONE: +353 (0)23 41111.
FAX: +353 (0)23 44690.
EMAIL: enquiries@bandongolfclub.com

WEBSITE: www.bandongolfclub.com
PROFESSIONAL: Paddy O'Boyle.
VISITORS: Mondays, Tuesdays and Fridays are best. Soft spikes.
GREEN FEES: €40 per round weekdays and weekends. €45 public holidays.
CREDIT CARDS ACCEPTED: All major cards.
CATERING: Restaurant and bar.
FACILITIES: Locker rooms, putting green, practice ground, pro-shop, buggies, trolleys, club hire, caddies on request, tuition.
LOCATION: 1 mile south-west of Bandon, off the N71.
LOCAL HOTELS: Innishannon House Hotel +353 (0)21 477 5121, The Munster Arms Hotel +353 (0)23 41562.

BANTRY BAY GOLF CLUB

A parkland course in a breathtaking location with 14 holes overlooking the shores of Bantry Bay, where the warm Gulf Stream first touches land on this side of the Atlantic. The mountains of Beara can be seen to the north and Sheep's Head and Mizen to the south. This parkland course on 170 acres, which includes six lakes, was originally designed by Eddie Hackett in 1975 and was recently extended from nine to eighteen holes by Christy O'Connor Jr., who admitted, 'It was a challenge I couldn't refuse.' Bantry offers an interesting variety of holes from a 138-yard par 3 to a 535-yard par 5 with a two-tiered green. Even if you have a bad day's golf, the setting will keep your spirits up.

18 holes parkland, 5,910 metres (6,466 yards), par 71 (SSS 72).

SIGNATURE HOLE:

TWELFTH (408 metres [448 yards], par 4) – the most difficult hole on the course. Out of bounds down the left and a large bunker on the right make for a difficult tee shot. If you're brave enough to go for the two-tiered green in two, you'll need a long iron or wood to carry the lake and bunker guarding the approach to the pin.

ADDRESS: Bantry, Co. Cork.
TELEPHONE: +353 (0)27 50579.
FAX: +353 (0)27 53790.
EMAIL: info@bantrygolf.com
WEBSITE: www.bantrygolf.com
MANAGER: John O'Sullivan.
VISITORS: Welcome all year round. Soft spikes.
GREEN FEES: June to September – €40 weekdays, €45 at weekends. October to May – €35 weekdays, €40 at weekends.
CATERING: Restaurant and bar.
CREDIT CARDS ACCEPTED: MasterCard/Visa.
FACILITIES: Locker rooms, putting green, pro-shop, buggies (€30), trolleys (€3), club hire (€15).
LOCATION: About 1 mile north-west of Bantry off the N71.
LOCAL HOTELS: Westlodge +353 (0)27 50360.

BEREHAVEN GOLF CLUB

Scenic nine-hole links course, founded in 1906 and overlooking Bantry Bay.
9 holes links, 5,121 metres (5,633 yards) for 18 holes, par 68 (SSS 67). Ladies 4,410 metres (4,851 yards), par 70 (SSS 68).

ADDRESS: Millcove, Castletownbere, West Cork, Co. Cork.
TELEPHONE: +353 (0)27 70700.
FAX: +353 (0)27 71957.
EMAIL: admin@berehavengolf.com

WEBSITE: www.berehavengolf.com
VISITORS: Yes, at all times except during major competitions.
GREEN FEES: €20 per round weekdays, €25 at weekends.
CREDIT CARDS ACCEPTED: Yes.
CATERING: Restaurant and bar.
FACILITIES: Locker rooms, trolleys, club hire.
LOCATION: On the main Castletownbere–Glengarriff road, 3 miles from Castletownbere.
LOCAL HOTELS: Cametringane Hotel.

BLARNEY GOLF RESORT

John Daly's first design in Europe, this parkland course is set in the Shournagh Valley. Opening in June 2006.
18 holes parkland, 6,800 yards, par 71.

ADDRESS: Tower, Blarney, Co. Cork.
TELEPHONE: +353 (0)21 438 4472.
FAX: +353 (0)21 438 4599.
EMAIL: blarneygolfresort@ramadaireland.com
WEBSITE: www.blarneygolfresort.com
DIRECTOR OF GOLF: David O'Sullivan.
VISITORS: Any day, but check for availability. Soft spikes.
GREEN FEES: €50–90 per round.
CREDIT CARDS ACCEPTED: All major cards.
CATERING: Restaurant and bar.
FACILITIES: Locker rooms, putting green, club shop, buggies, trolleys, club hire, tuition.
LOCATION: 3 miles from Blarney village.
LOCAL HOTELS: Ramada Hotel and Suites at Blarney Golf Resort (on the course).

CHARLEVILLE GOLF CLUB

Founded in 1941, the West Course, set in heavily wooded parkland at the foot of the

Ballyhours Hills, is challenging and has a good reputation for its greens. The club, which is close to the Limerick border, started out with nine holes. This increased to 12 holes and then 18 in 1981. Now the 191-acre site boasts 27 holes.

WEST COURSE – 18 holes parkland, 6,467 yards, par 71.

EAST COURSE – 9 holes parkland, 3,451 yards, par 36.

SIGNATURE HOLE:
SIXTEENTH (175 yards, par 3) – a challenge with water guarding a heavily contoured green.

ADDRESS: Smiths Road, Ardmore, Charleville, Co. Cork.
TELEPHONE: +353 (0)63 81257.
FAX: +353 (0)63 81274.
EMAIL: charlevillegolf@eircom.net
WEBSITE: www.charlevillegolf.com
SECRETARY/MANAGER: Pat Nagle.
PROFESSIONAL: David Keating.
VISITORS: Welcome.
GREEN FEES: €25 Mondays, €35 Tuesdays to Fridays, and €40 weekends and bank holidays.
CREDIT CARDS ACCEPTED: Yes.
CATERING: Full bar and catering facilities – open all year.
FACILITIES: Locker rooms, driving range, putting green, pro-shop, buggies (€30), trolleys (€3), club hire (€20).
LOCATION: 1 mile from Charleville town on the R515.
LOCAL HOTELS: Springfort Hall +353 (0)22 21278, Woodlands House Hotel +353 (0)61 396118.

COBH GOLF CLUB

This nine-hole parkland course was designed by Eddie Hackett in 1987. The club recently purchased a new site and planned to begin the construction of a completely new 18-hole championship course in the spring of 2006.

9 holes parkland, 5,477 yards for 18 holes, par 67 (SSS 64).

ADDRESS: Ballywilliam, Cobh, Co. Cork.
TELEPHONE: +353 (0)21 481 2399.
WEBSITE: www.cobhgolfclub.ie
SECRETARY/MANAGER: Frank Morrissey.
VISITORS: Yes.
GREEN FEES: €18.
CREDIT CARDS ACCEPTED: Yes.
CATERING: Full bar and catering facilities.
FACILITIES: Locker rooms, practice ground, putting green, pro-shop, buggies, trolleys, club hire.
LOCATION: 1 mile east of Cobh.
LOCAL HOTELS: Commodore Hotel, Cobh; Waters-Edge Hotel, Cobh.

COOSHEEN GOLF CLUB

Founded in 1987, this is a scenic 9-hole seaside parkland course with narrow fairways and tight greens, overlooking beautiful Schull Harbour in West Cork.

9 holes parkland, 4,057 yards for 18 holes, par 63. Ladies 3,673 yards, par 65.

ADDRESS: Schull, West Cork, Co. Cork.
TELEPHONE: +353 (0)28 27758.
EMAIL: coosheengolfclub@eircom.net
WEBSITE: www.coosheengolfclub.com
SECRETARY/MANAGER: Linda Morgan.
VISITORS: Yes, every day from April to October. Soft spikes.
GREEN FEES: €25 per round weekdays and weekends.
CREDIT CARDS ACCEPTED: Yes.
CATERING: Restaurant and bar.
FACILITIES: Locker rooms, trolleys, club hire.

Cork Golf Club

LOCATION: 1 mile east of Schull town and signposted.
LOCAL HOTELS: Colla House Hotel, Grove House.

CORK GOLF CLUB

This parkland championship course in a unique quarry setting has hosted many amateur and professional tournaments. Founded in 1888 and redesigned in 1927 by Alister Mackenzie of Augusta fame.

18 holes parkland, 6,192 metres (6,811 yards), par 72 (SSS 72). Ladies 5,182 metres (5,700 yards), par 74 (SSS 73).

SIGNATURE HOLE:
SIXTH (302 metres [330 yards], par 4) – requires a carry over a rocky outcrop and an approach to a green surrounded by quarry walls.

ADDRESS: Little Island, Co. Cork.
TELEPHONE: +353 (0)21 435 3451.
FAX: +353 (0)21 435 3410.
EMAIL: corkgolfclub@eircom.net
WEBSITE: www.corkgolfclub.ie
SECRETARY: Matt Sands.
PROFESSIONAL: Peter Hickey.
VISITORS: Yes.
GREEN FEES: €80 weekdays, €90 at weekends.
CREDIT CARDS ACCEPTED: Yes.
CATERING: Restaurant and bar.
FACILITIES: Locker rooms, practice ground, putting green, pro-shop, buggies (€40), trolleys (€4), club hire (€30).
LOCATION: 5 miles east of Cork city, off the N25.
LOCAL HOTELS: Rochestown Park +353 (0)21 489 3322.

DONERAILE GOLF CLUB

Tight, reasonably flat parkland course with a river coming into play on two holes. Founded in 1927.

9 holes parkland, 5,324 metres (5,856 yards) for 18 holes, par 68 (SSS 67). Ladies 4,610 metres (5,071 yards), par 71 (SSS 68).

ADDRESS: Doneraile, Co. Cork.
TELEPHONE: +353 (0)22 24137.
VISITORS: Yes. Societies by prior arrangement.
GREEN FEES: €20 per round weekdays and weekends.
CATERING: Restaurant and bar.
FACILITIES: Locker rooms, practice ground, trolleys.
LOCATION: 28 miles from Cork, off the T11.

DOUGLAS GOLF CLUB

A traditional and mature members' club course founded in 1909. Set in lush parkland with magnificent views over Cork city, the course is maintained to the highest standards. The greens and tees are to USGA specifications, making it a good challenge for the keen golfer and a pleasant experience for the less competitive.

18 holes parkland, 5,972 metres (6,569 yards), par 72 (SSS 71). Ladies 4,952 metres (5,447 yards), par 72 (SSS 72).

SIGNATURE HOLE:
FIFTEENTH ('Rosies', 134 metres [147 yards], par 3) – usually plays into the prevailing wind from an elevated tee to a generous green almost surrounded by trees.

ADDRESS: Maryborough, Douglas, Co. Cork.
TELEPHONE: +353 (0)21 489 5297.
FAX: +353 (0)21 436 7200.

EMAIL: admin@douglasgolfclub.ie
WEBSITE: www.douglasgolfclub.ie
SECRETARY/MANAGER: Ronan Burke.
PROFESSIONAL: Gary Nicholson.
VISITORS: Welcome, except Tuesdays and Wednesdays.
GREEN FEES: €45 per round weekdays, €50 at weekends.
CREDIT CARDS ACCEPTED: All major cards.
CATERING: Full bar and restaurant.
FACILITIES: Locker rooms, practice ground, putting green, pro-shop, trolleys, club hire.
LOCATION: Through Douglas village and adjacent to Maryborough House Hotel. The course is 3 miles from Cork.
LOCAL HOTELS: Maryborough House Hotel +353 21 436 5555, Rochestown Park Hotel +353 21 489 0800.

DUNMORE GOLF CLUB

Designed by Eddie Hackett in 1967, this hilly parkland course overlooks the Atlantic.
9 holes parkland, 4,923 yards for 18 holes, par 64 (SSS 61). Ladies 4,364 yards, par 66 (SSS 64).

ADDRESS: Dunmore House, Muckross, Clonakilty, Co. Cork.
TELEPHONE: +353 (0)23 34644.
EMAIL: dunmoremens@eircom.net
VISITORS: Yes, but not on Sundays unless with a member or you are a guest of the hotel. Soft spikes.
GREEN FEES: €25 per round weekdays and weekends.
CATERING: Restaurant and bar in Dunmore House.
FACILITIES: Locker rooms, trolleys, club hire.
LOCATION: 3 miles from Clonakilty.
LOCAL HOTELS: Dunmore House Hotel.

EAST CORK GOLF CLUB

Designed by Eddie Hackett, this tree-lined parkland course is on a former dairy farm. Opened in 1969.
18 holes parkland, 5,581 yards, par 69 (SSS 66). Ladies 5,052 yards, par 70 (SSS 68).

ADDRESS: Gortacrue, Midleton, Co. Cork.
TELEPHONE: +353 (0)21 4631687.
FAX: +353 (0)21 4613695.
EMAIL: eastcorkgolfclub@eircom.net
WEBSITE: www.eastcorkgolfclub.com
PROFESSIONAL: Don MacFarlane.
VISITORS: Yes.
GREEN FEES: €25 per day weekdays, €30 at weekends.
CREDIT CARDS ACCEPTED: MasterCard/Visa.
CATERING: Restaurant and bar.
FACILITIES: Locker rooms, putting green, practice ground, driving range, pro-shop, trolleys, club hire, tuition.
LOCATION: Off the main Cork–Waterford road (N25). Take the Midleton exit, 13 miles east of Cork city. The course is 2 miles north of Midleton on the Fermoy road.
LOCAL HOTELS: Glenview House, Lynwen Lodge, The Brambles.

FERMOY GOLF CLUB

Challenging, undulating parkland course, established in 1892.
18 holes parkland, 6,397 yards, par 70 (SSS 70). Ladies 5,194 yards, par 72 (SSS 70).

SIGNATURE HOLE:
FOURTEENTH (510 yards, par 5) – accuracy off the tee makes this reachable in two for the longer hitters. Watch out for the big valley.

ADDRESS: Corrin, Fermoy, Co. Cork.
TELEPHONE: +353 (0)25 31472.
FAX: +353 (0)25 33072.
EMAIL: fermoygolfclub@eircom.net
SECRETARY/MANAGER: Kathleen Murphy.
PROFESSIONAL: Brian Moriarty.
VISITORS: Welcome.
GREEN FEES: €25 per round weekdays, €35 at weekends.
CREDIT CARDS ACCEPTED: Yes.
CATERING: Seasonal.
FACILITIES: Locker rooms, practice ground, putting green, pro-shop, trolleys (€3), club hire (€10).
LOCATION: Take the main road out of Fermoy towards Cork (N8), then take a right turn about 2 miles outside the town.
LOCAL HOTELS: Grand Hotel +353 (0)25 40966.

FERNHILL GOLF AND COUNTRY CLUB

Parkland course with tree-lined fairways and undulating greens in the scenic Owenabue Valley. Established in 1994.

18 holes parkland, 6,053 yards, par 69. Ladies 5,455 yards, par 71.

ADDRESS: Carrigaline, Co. Cork.
TELEPHONE: +353 (0)21 437 2226.
FAX: +353 (0)21 437 1011.
EMAIL: fernhill@iol.ie
WEBSITE: www.fernhillcountryclub.com
PROFESSIONAL: Wayne O'Callaghan.
VISITORS: All week. Soft spikes.
GREEN FEES: €25 per round weekdays, €32 at weekends.
CREDIT CARDS ACCEPTED: All major cards.
CATERING: Restaurant and bar.
FACILITIES: Locker rooms, putting green, practice ground, club shop, buggies (€30), trolleys (€3), club hire (€15), caddies on request.
LOCATION: Off the N28 to Cork, 2 miles from Carrigaline.
LOCAL HOTELS: Fernhill Hotel (on the course).

FOTA ISLAND GOLF CLUB

This traditional championship parkland course, designed by Christy O'Connor Jr. and the former British amateur champion Peter McEvoy, is a sister property of the renowned Mount Juliet Resort in Kilkenny. Golf has been played at Fota Island since the early 1880s. Fota hosted the 2001 and 2002 Irish Open and is the venue for the 2006 AIB Irish Seniors Open. The course, which features pot bunkers and undulating greens, is maintained to the highest standards. Following the purchase of Fota Island in 1998 by the Killeen Group, an 18-month €2.2 million programme was put in place to upgrade the course. It included rebuilding all 18 greens, the reseeding of all tees and the redesign of eight of the holes.

18 holes parkland, 6,927 yards, par 71 (SSS 73). Ladies 5,520 yards, par 72 (SSS 72).

SIGNATURE HOLE:
EIGHTEENTH ('The Lough', 507 yards, par 5) – tee shot needs to be threaded between a copse of mature beech trees on the left and woodland on the right. The approach shot is downhill to a green protected by bunkers and bordered on three sides by a lake.

ADDRESS: Carrigtwohill, Co. Cork.
TELEPHONE: +353 (0)21 488 3700.
FAX: +353 (0)21 488 3713.
EMAIL: reservations@fotaisland.ie
WEBSITE: www.fotaisland.com
MANAGER: Jonathan Woods.
PROFESSIONAL: Kevin Morris.
VISITORS: Welcome every day.

The 18th at Fota Island Golf Club

GREEN FEES: From €62 to €98.
CREDIT CARDS ACCEPTED: Yes.
CATERING: Spike Bar and Niblicks
  Restaurant.
FACILITIES: Locker rooms, practice ground,
  putting green, pro-shop, buggies (€40),
  trolleys (€4), club hire (€28).
LOCATION: Follow the N25 east of Cork
  (Waterford road) for 12 miles, and take
  the Cobh exit. Fota is 1,000 yards on.
LOCAL HOTELS: Carrigaline Court Hotel,
  Carrigaline; Radisson Hotel, Little Island.

FRANKFIELD GOLF CLUB

Hilly parkland course founded in 1984.
  9 holes parkland, 5,205 yards for 18 holes,
par 68 (SSS 65). Ladies 4,881 yards, par 65
(SSS 65).

ADDRESS: Frankfield, Grange, Co. Cork.
TELEPHONE: +353 (0)21 436 3124/1199.
EMAIL: frankfield@golfnet.ie
VISITORS: Yes. Societies on application.
GREEN FEES: €15 per round weekdays, €18
  at weekends.

Harbour Point Golf Club

CATERING: Bar.
FACILITIES: Locker rooms, putting green, driving range, buggies, trolleys, club hire.
LOCATION: 10 miles south of Cork.

GLENGARRIFF GOLF CLUB

Quite tight and very scenic parkland course overlooking the sea. Founded in 1934.

9 holes parkland, 4,514 yards for 18 holes, par 66 (SSS 62). Ladies 4,202 yards, par 68 (SSS 65).

ADDRESS: Glengarriff, Co. Cork.
TELEPHONE: +353 (0)87 246 8071.
EMAIL: info@glengarriffgolfclub.com
WEBSITE: www.glengarriffgolfclub.com
VISITORS: Yes. Societies by prior arrangement.
GREEN FEES: €20 per round weekdays, €25 at weekends.
CATERING: Restaurant and bar.
FACILITIES: Locker rooms, putting green, trolleys, practice ground, club hire.

LOCATION: On the T65, 55 miles west of Cork.

HARBOUR POINT GOLF CLUB

Rolling parkland course on the banks of the River Lee, with large undulating, sand-based greens and difficult par 3s. This new course design, laid down in 1991, demands a full range of shots.

18 holes parkland, 6,675 yards, par 72 (SSS 72). Ladies 5,714 yards, par 73 (SSS 72).

SIGNATURE HOLE:
EIGHTEENTH (473 yards, par 5) – not until you approach your second shot on this hole are you aware of the trouble that lies ahead. The double water hazard in front of the heart-shaped green has ruined many a card. For the big hitter, the green is certainly on in two, but the psychological effect of the hazard often proves too much.

ADDRESS: Clash Road, Little Island, Co. Cork.
TELEPHONE: +353 (0)21 435 3094.
FAX: +353 (0)21 435 4408.
EMAIL: info@harbourpointgolfclub.com
WEBSITE: www.harbourpointgolfclub.com
SECRETARY/MANAGER: Aylmer Barrett.
PROFESSIONAL: Morgan O'Donovan.
VISITORS: Welcome all year, seven days a week.
GREEN FEES: €40 for individuals at weekends, €35 for groups. Earlybird is €25 midweek.
CREDIT CARDS ACCEPTED: MasterCard/ Visa.
CATERING: Restaurant and bar.
FACILITIES: Locker rooms, practice ground, putting green, driving range, pro-shop, buggies (€35), trolleys (€3), club hire (€15), tuition (€25 per half hour).
LOCATION: Just off the N25, 6 miles east of Cork city on Little Island.
LOCAL HOTELS: Radisson Hotel, Little Island; Hayfield Manor +353 (0)21 431 5600; Jurys Inn, Midleton Park.

KANTURK GOLF CLUB

Parkland course with lots of trees and spectacular views of the local mountains. Founded in 1972.

18 holes parkland, 5,721 metres (6,293 yards), par 72 (SSS 70). Ladies 4,423 metres (4,865 yards), par 71 (SSS 69).

ADDRESS: Fairyhill, Kanturk, Co. Cork.
TELEPHONE: +353 (0)29 50534.
FAX: +353 (0)29 20951.
EMAIL: info@kanturkgolf.com
WEBSITE: www.kanturkgolf.com
VISITORS: Yes, but pre-book.
GREEN FEES: €25 per round weekdays, €30 at weekends.
CATERING: Bar. Restaurant by arrangement.
FACILITIES: Locker rooms, putting green, buggies, trolleys, club hire.

LOCATION: 1 mile from Kanturk via Fairyhill Road.
LOCAL HOTELS: Duhallow Park Hotel, Assolas Hotel.

KINSALE GOLF CLUB

Established in 1912, Kinsale boasts two parkland courses in two diverse locations, ranging from the challenging slopes of Ringenane to the gentle rolling meadows of Farrangalway in the River Bandon valley. The club built its eighteen-hole Farrangalway course, which consists of two loops, in 1993. The first hole maximises the roll of the land, initially eastwards to the boundary of the old Cork–Kinsale railway line. It continues over the incline and flows to the natural waterways on the back nine. The demanding Ringenane (the name means 'headland of the birds') slopes down to the riverbanks and occupies a small circular peninsula.

FARRANGALWAY – 18 holes parkland, 6,609 yards, par 71 (SSS 72). Ladies 5,585 yards, par 72 (SSS 71).

RINGENANE – 9 holes parkland, 5,332 yards for 18 holes, par 70 (SSS 68). Ladies 4,000 yards, par 70.

ADDRESS: Farrangalway, Kinsale, Co. Cork.
TELEPHONE: Farrangalway +353 (0)21 477 4722; Ringenane +353 (0)21 477 2197.
FAX: +353 (0)21 477 3114.
EMAIL: office@kinsalegolf.com
WEBSITE: www.kinsalegolf.com
MANAGER: Michael Power.
PROFESSIONAL: Ger Broderick +353 (0)21 477 3258.
VISITORS: Yes.
GREEN FEES: Farrangalway – €32 per round Mondays to Thursdays, €40 per round Fridays to Sundays; Ringenane – €22 per round weekdays and weekends.

CREDIT CARDS ACCEPTED: All major cards.
CATERING: Restaurant and bar.
FACILITIES: Locker rooms, putting green, practice ground, practice facilities, pro-shop, buggies (€20), trolleys (€2), club hire (€10), caddies on request, tuition.
LOCATION: 18 miles from Cork and 3 miles from Kinsale. For Farrangalway turn right at the Blue Haven Hotel. Follow signs for Cork and take second left after Millwheel pub. For Ringenane, follow the R600 to Cork and turn right after the second bridge.
LOCAL HOTELS: Actons Hotel, Trident Hotel, Blue Haven Hotel.

LEE VALLEY GOLF AND COUNTRY CLUB

Undulating parkland course founded in 1992 and designed by Christy O'Connor Jr. Lee Valley has water features on seven of the holes, many of which are extremely testing.

18 holes parkland, 6,725 yards, par 72 (SSS 72). Ladies 5,451 yards, par 73 (SSS 72).

ADDRESS: Clashanure, Ovens, Co. Cork.
TELEPHONE: +353 (0)21 733 1721.
FAX: +353 (0)21 733 1695.
EMAIL: leevalleygc@eircom.net
WEBSITE: www.leevalleygolfclub.com
PROFESSIONAL: John Savage.
VISITORS: Any day. Soft spikes.
GREEN FEES: €44 per round weekdays, €54 at weekends.
CATERING: Restaurant and bar.
FACILITIES: Locker rooms, putting green, driving range, pro-shop, golf academy, buggies (€35), trolleys (€3), club hire, caddies on request.
LOCATION: On the main Cork–Killarney road, 12 miles from Cork.
LOCAL HOTELS: Blarney Park Hotel, Farran House Hotel.

LISSELAN GOLF CLUB

This challenging parkland course meanders around the majestic Lisselan Gardens, and the trout-filled River Argideen flows through it. Golfers must ride a motorised raft from the eighth fairway to the green, and the course also boasts a railcar to take golfers from the green to the next tee. Opened in 1994 as a six-hole course, it was extended to nine holes in 2004.

9 holes parkland, 6,376 yards for 18 holes, par 72 (SSS 71). Ladies 5,070 yards, par 72 (SSS 70).

SIGNATURE HOLE:
SEVENTEENTH (483 yards, par 5) – playing over the River Argideen twice to reach the green, golfers must thread the ball between the numerous hazards: out of bounds along the left and the meandering river that flows down the right and crosses in front of the island green. To add to the experience, there is a second chance to take a ride on the motorised raft to get from the fairway to the green.

ADDRESS: Lisselan Estate, Clonakilty, Co. Cork.
TELEPHONE: +353 (0)23 33249.
FAX: +353 (0)23 34605.
EMAIL: info@lisselan.com
WEBSITE: www.lisselan.com
SECRETARY/MANAGER: Mark Coombes.
VISITORS: Welcome daily.
GREEN FEES: €30 weekdays, €35 at weekends.
CREDIT CARDS ACCEPTED: Yes.
CATERING: Snacks and light refreshments.
FACILITIES: Locker rooms available, trolleys (€3), club hire (€15).
LOCATION: 3 miles east of Clonakilty town. The entrance is 70 metres off the N71 (main Cork–Clonakilty road). The turn-

off is signposted in both directions, 200 metres before the turn-off from the N71.

LOCAL HOTELS: The Lodge and Spa, Inchadoney Island +353 (0)23 33143, The Emmet Hotel +353 (0)23 33394, Quality Hotel and Leisure Centre +353 (0)23 35400, Randles Hotel +353 (0)23 34749.

MACROOM GOLF CLUB

Founded in 1924, this is a magnificent parkland course with mature trees situated within castle grounds on the winding banks of the River Sullane. With the Kerry Mountains creating a backdrop to the west, Macroom exudes a peaceful beauty.

18 holes parkland, 5,574 metres (6,131 yards), par 72 (SSS 70). Ladies 4,561 metres (5,017 yards), par 72 (SSS 70).

ADDRESS: Lacaduve, Macroom, Co. Cork.
TELEPHONE: +353 (0)26 41072.
FAX: +353 (0)26 41391.
EMAIL: mcroomgc@iol.ie
MANAGER: Cathal O'Sullivan.
VISITORS: Weekdays, except Wednesdays. Soft spikes.
GREEN FEES: €35 per day weekdays, €40 at weekends.
CREDIT CARDS ACCEPTED: MasterCard/Visa.
CATERING: Restaurant and bar.
FACILITIES: Locker rooms, putting green, practice ground, club shop, buggies (€25), trolleys (€3), club hire (€13), caddies.
LOCATION: In the centre of town through the arch of the castle. The course is 25 miles west of Cork city and 30 miles east of Killarney, Co. Kerry.
LOCAL HOTELS: Castle Hotel, Victoria Hotel.

MAHON GOLF CLUB

Public parkland course with water hazards designed by Eddie Hackett in 1980.

18 holes parkland, 5,291 metres (5,820 yards), par 70 (SSS 68). Ladies 4,604 metres (5,064 yards), par 72 (SSS 70).

SIGNATURE HOLE:
FOURTH (127 metres [139 yards], par 3) – played from an elevated tee to a green fronted by two bunkers and water at the rear.

ADDRESS: Cloverhill, Skehard Road, Blackrock, Co. Cork.
TELEPHONE: +353 (0)21 429 2543.
EMAIL: mahongolfclub@eircom.net
WEBSITE: www.mahongolfclub.com
VISITORS: Yes, but by prior arrangement at weekends.
GREEN FEES: €22 per round weekdays, €25 at weekends.
CREDIT CARDS ACCEPTED: Yes.
CATERING: Bar.
FACILITIES: Locker rooms, caddies on request, putting green, club hire.
LOCATION: 2 miles south-east of Cork.

MALLOW GOLF CLUB

This parkland course has exceptional views of both Mushera Mountain and the distant Galtee Mountains. There is a friendly, relaxed atmosphere for both members and visitors. Founded in 1947.

18 holes parkland, 5,960 metres (6,556 yards), par 72 (SSS 72). Ladies 4,897 metres (5,386 yards), par 72 (SSS 72).

SIGNATURE HOLE:
SEVENTH (454 yards, par 4) – a dogleg right and a sloping fairway puts a premium on an accurate drive to the left. This leaves

a long second shot to a green guarded by a bunker and large trees.

ADDRESS: Ballyellis, Mallow, Co. Cork.
TELEPHONE: +353 (0)22 21145.
FAX: +353 (0)22 42501.
EMAIL: golfmall@gofree.indigo.ie
SECRETARY/MANAGER: David Curtin.
PROFESSIONAL: Sean Conway.
VISITORS: Midweek only.
GREEN FEES: €45 per round weekdays, €50 weekends and public holidays.
CREDIT CARDS ACCEPTED: MasterCard/Visa.
CATERING: Restaurant and bar.
FACILITIES: Locker rooms, putting green, practice round, driving range, pro-shop, buggies (€35), trolleys (€4), club hire (€20), tuition.
LOCATION: 1 mile from Mallow town centre and 20 minutes from Cork.

MITCHELSTOWN GOLF CLUB

This picturesque parkland course, founded in 1908, has good quality traditional greens. The level, easy-walking course has stunning views of the surrounding countryside and the Galtee Mountains.

18 holes parkland, 5,773 metres (6,350 yards), par 71. Ladies 4,890 metres (5,379 yards), par 73.

SIGNATURE HOLE:
EIGHTH (490 metre [539 yards], par 5) – accurate drive required with a demanding second shot over a river.

ADDRESS: Gurrane, Mitchelstown, Co. Cork.
TELEPHONE: +353 (0)25 24072.
EMAIL: info@mitchelstown-golf.com
WEBSITE: www.mitchelstown-golf.com
VISITORS: Yes, all days by appointment. Soft spikes.

GREEN FEES: €25 per round/day weekdays, €30 at weekends.
CATERING: Restaurant and bar.
FACILITIES: Locker rooms, putting green, practice area, buggies, trolleys.
LOCATION: 1 mile from Mitchelstown, off the N1 (Dublin–Cork road).
LOCAL HOTELS: Firgrove Hotel.

MONKSTOWN GOLF CLUB

A fine parkland course with great greens founded in 1908. The front nine offer magnificent views of Cork Harbour. The back nine has a number of holes with water features and a very difficult finishing stretch.

18 holes parkland, 5,642 metres (6,206 yards), par 70 (SSS 69). Ladies 4,838 metres (5,321 yards), par 73 (SSS 73).

ADDRESS: Parkgariffe, Monkstown, Co. Cork.
TELEPHONE: +353 (0)21 484 1376.
FAX: +353 (0)21 484 1722.
EMAIL: office@monkstowngolfclub.com
WEBSITE: www.monkstowngolfclub.com
MANAGER: Hilary Madden.
PROFESSIONAL: Batt Murphy +353 (0)21 486 3912.
VISITORS: Mondays, Thursdays and Fridays. Saturdays and Sundays after 12 p.m. only. Soft spikes.
GREEN FEES: €40 per round weekdays, €47 at weekends.
CATERING: Restaurant and bar.
FACILITIES: Locker rooms, putting green, practice ground, driving range, pro-shop, buggies (€40), trolleys (€2.50), club hire (€15), caddies, tuition.
LOCATION: 6 miles east of Cork city.

Ireland's Golf Courses

MUSKERRY GOLF CLUB

The River Shournagh comes into play several times on this parkland course founded in 1897. The par-3 sixth and fifteenth are the signature holes.

18 holes parkland, 5,808 metres (6,388 yards), par 71 (SSS 71). Ladies 4,972 metres (5,409 yards), par 75 (SSS 74).

ADDRESS: Carrigrohane, Co. Cork.
TELEPHONE: +353 (0)21 438 5297.
FAX: +353 (0)21 451 6860.
EMAIL: muskgc@eircom.net
SECRETARY/MANAGER: Hugo Gallagher.
PROFESSIONAL: Martin Lehane +353 (0)21 438 1445.
VISITORS: Mondays, Tuesdays, Wednesdays (mornings), Thursdays (afternoons) and Fridays (before 4.30 p.m.).
GREEN FEES: €40 per round weekdays, €50 at weekends.
CREDIT CARDS ACCEPTED: All major cards.
CATERING: Restaurant and bar +353 (0)21 438 5104.
FACILITIES: Locker rooms, putting green, practice ground, pro-shop, buggies (€30), trolleys (€2), club hire, tuition.
LOCATION: 7 miles west of Cork and 4 miles from Blarney.

OLD HEAD GOLF LINKS

Dramatic! This challenging cliff-top links, configured as two returning loops of nine holes, is set on a 220-acre promontory, complete with a famous lighthouse, that juts out 2 miles into the Atlantic. Eight of the holes run along the cliff tops, 200 feet above the Atlantic Ocean, matching the rugged beauty of Cypress Point or Pebble Beach. Joe Carr, Ron Kirby, Paddy Merrigan, Eddie Hackett and Liam Higgins were all involved in the design of the course, which opened for play in 1997. On the back nine there is a 258-yard par 3 and a 632-yard par 5. There are six to eight tees for every hole, and these are set up every day to allow for prevailing wind conditions. Birdies abound – cormorants, peregrine falcons and guillemots.

18 holes links, 7,215 yards, par 72 (SSS 74). Ladies 5,132 yards, par 72 (SSS 72).

ADDRESS: Kinsale, Co. Cork.
TELEPHONE: +353 (0)21 477 8444.
FAX: +353 (0)21 477 8022.
EMAIL: info@oldheadgolf.ie
WEBSITE: www.oldheadgolflinks.com
SECRETARY/MANAGER: John Dwyer.
PROFESSIONAL: Danny Brassil.
VISITORS: Yes.
GREEN FEES: €275 per round, €450 for 36 holes.
CREDIT CARDS ACCEPTED: Yes.
CATERING: Restaurant and bar.
FACILITIES: Locker rooms, practice ground, putting green, pro-shop, buggies (€60), club hire (€40), caddies (€50), soft spikes (€10).
LOCATION: 20 miles south of Cork. From Kinsale, take the R600 and R604.
LOCAL HOTELS: Trident Hotel, Kinsale +353 (0)21 477 2301, Blue Haven Hotel, Kinsale +353 (0)21 477 2209, Perryville House, Kinsale +353 (0)21 477 2731, Blindgate House, Kinsale +353 (0)21 477 7858, Fridaysars Lodge, Kinsale +353 (0)21 477 7384.

RAFFEEN CREEK GOLF CLUB

This seaside/parkland course, with two waterholes and recently upgraded greens, offers magnificent views of Cork Harbour. Designed by Eddie Hackett in 1988.

9 holes seaside/parkland, 5,146 metres (5,630 yards) for 18 holes, par 70 (SSS 67).

Ladies 4,412 metres (4,853 yards), par 72 (SSS 70).

ADDRESS: Ringaskiddy, Co. Cork.
TELEPHONE: +353 (0)21 437 8430.
EMAIL: raffeengca@eircom.net
WEBSITE: www.raffeencreekgolfclub.com
VISITORS: Yes, weekdays. Afternoons only at weekends.
GREEN FEES: €30 per round weekdays, €35 at weekends.
CATERING: Bar and food.
FACILITIES: Locker rooms, putting green, trolleys.
LOCATION: 1 mile from the Ringaskiddy ferry.

SKIBBEREEN AND WEST CARBERY GOLF CLUB

Founded in 1905, the club moved to its present location in 1935. This parkland course was extended to 18 holes in 1992 and offers a variety of interesting holes. The new nine is now much shorter but also much tighter.

18 holes parkland, 5,967 yards, par 71 (SSS 69). Ladies 5,062 yards, par 72 (SSS 70).

ADDRESS: Licknavar, Skibbereen, Co. Cork.
TELEPHONE: +353 (0)28 21227.
FAX: +353 (0)28 22994.
EMAIL: info@skibbgolf.com
WEBSITE: www.skibbgolf.com
MANAGER: Seamus Brett.
VISITORS: Welcome every day.
GREEN FEES: €40 per round.
CREDIT CARDS ACCEPTED: All major cards.
CATERING: Restaurant and bar.
FACILITIES: Locker rooms, putting green, practice ground, buggies (€25), trolleys (€4), club hire (€20), caddies on request, tuition.
LOCATION: 2 miles west of Skibbereen on the Baltimore road.

WATER ROCK GOLF COURSE

A parkland course designed by Paddy Merrigan on the banks of the River Owencurra and opened in 1994. It has no members and operates on a green fee only basis. The course comprises five par 3s and three par 5s in two loops.

18 holes parkland, 6,220 yards, par 70 (SSS 70). Ladies 5,978 yards, par 70 (SSS 69).

SIGNATURE HOLE:
TWELFTH (240 yards, par 3) – known locally as 'Swan Lake'. Intimidating 200-yard carry over water from the back tee.

ADDRESS: Midleton, Co. Cork.
TELEPHONE: +353 (0)21 461 3499.
FAX: +353 (0)21 463 3150.
EMAIL: waterrock@eircom.net
WEBSITE: www.waterrockgolfcourse.com
MANAGER: Con Healy.
VISITORS: Welcome all year round, but advanced booking recommended.
GREEN FEES: €28 weekdays, €34 weekends and public holidays. Senior rate (over 60) is €20 on weekdays only.
CREDIT CARDS ACCEPTED: All major credit cards.
CATERING: Full bar and restaurant facilities.
FACILITIES: Locker rooms, putting green, pro-shop, buggies (€35), trolleys (€3), club hire (€15).
LOCATION: On the outskirts of Midleton, adjacent to the N25. The course is 15 minutes from Cork city, 20 minutes from Cork Airport and 5 minutes from Fota Island Golf Club.
LOCAL HOTELS: Midleton Park Hotel +353 (0)21 463 5100.

Water Rock Golf Course

YOUGHAL GOLF CLUB

Testing parkland course with stunning views of Youghal Bay and the Blackwater estuary. Founded in 1898.

18 holes parkland, 6,102 metres (6,712 yards), par 72 (SSS 72). Ladies 5,205 metres (5,725 yards), par 74 (SSS 73).

ADDRESS: Knockaverry, Youghal, Co. Cork.
TELEPHONE: +353 (0)24 92787.
FAX: +353 (0)24 92641.
EMAIL: youghalgolfclub@eircom.net
WEBSITE: www.youghalgolf.com
PROFESSIONAL: Liam Burns +353 (0)24 92590.
VISITORS: Weekdays, except Wednesdays, are best. Soft spikes.
GREEN FEES: €32 per round weekdays, €42 weekends and public holidays.
CREDIT CARDS ACCEPTED: All major cards.
CATERING: Restaurant and bar.
FACILITIES: Locker rooms, putting green, pro-shop, buggies, trolleys (€3), club hire (€10).
LOCATION: On the N25, between Rosslare and Cork.

COUNTY KERRY

ARDFERT GOLF CLUB

Flat but tricky parkland course with a stream and lake providing natural hazards. Founded in 1994.

9 holes parkland, 5,214 metres (5,735 yards) for 18 holes, par 70 (SSS 68). Ladies 4,680 metres (5,148 yards), par 70 (SSS 68).

ADDRESS: Sackville, Ardfert, Tralee, Co. Kerry.
TELEPHONE: +353 (0)66 713 4744.
EMAIL: ardfertgolfclub@eircom.net
VISITORS: Yes.
GREEN FEES: €25 per round.
CATERING: Snacks.
FACILITIES: Locker rooms, trolleys, club hire.
LOCATION: 15 miles north of Tralee on the R551.

BALLYBUNION GOLF CLUB

Ask an American golfer to name an Irish golf course and it's odds-on he will come up with the magnificent Old Course links of Ballybunion, set amidst towering sandhills alongside the Atlantic Ocean in beautiful County Kerry. For many years, Ballybunion has enjoyed the patronage of Americans. Whether this is because they can fly directly into Shannon (only an hour's drive away), or because a succession of great Americans claim it as their favourite, or simply because it is one of the world's best links courses, is uncertain, but many believe it to be unique.

Former US President Bill Clinton has played here, and Herbert Warren Wind, the great American golf writer, said it was the finest seaside course he had ever seen. But it is perhaps Tom Watson who has done more than anyone to promote the course. He made a habit of warming up for the British Open – and he won five of them – at Ballybunion and was the club captain in the millennium year.

He says, with a considerable amount of affection, 'There is a wild look to the place; the long grass covering the dunes that pitch and roll makes it very intimidating. But the contours on the fairways and the greens are what makes it a great course. You must play accurate shots into the greens, usually to a small target with not a lot of room to miss right or left. It is the best in the world.

Ballybunion is a course on which many golf architects should live and play before they build courses.'

The sandhills running across rather than along the course add to the drama, as it appears, in certain parts, that the ocean is actually attacking the course and, eating into the fairways. These ocean holes compare favourably with any in the world.

Established in 1893, the Old Course was extended to 18 holes in 1926, and, through the years, it has actually been under serious threat from coastal erosion. In 1971, the order of the holes was changed when the new state-of-the-art clubhouse was built, and the course now begins at the original 14th. It's not the most auspicious start, with a graveyard by the first tee perhaps an omen for the golfer not confident about the challenges that lie ahead. What he faces, in fact, is a supreme test of every aspect of his game.

The course begins to show its true strength around the 364-yard sixth. The Shannon estuary comes into play on this dogleg left, and the approach is through a narrow entrance to a plateau green. The power of the ocean dominates the seventh. The tee appears to hang out over the beach and ocean below, which runs down your right side for the full 432 yards of the hole. The 11th, Ballybunion's signature hole, is even more dramatic.

There are five par 3s, but there is no respite at the short holes, especially the 212-yard fifteenth which is not the longest but is perhaps the most daunting. You tee off with the green below appearing to shrink and the huge sandhill on the left and the bunkers on the right appearing to grow larger by the minute. The 17th, doglegging along the shore, is probably the best of the remaining holes because accuracy here is a must.

In the early 1980s, Robert Trent Jones was asked to design a second links, the Cashen Course, and when he saw what he was being given to work with, he exclaimed, 'It's the finest piece of links land I have ever seen.' There are those who believe that the Cashen Course is even more dramatic and challenging than the old one, with its higher dunes, demanding carries and two par 5s to finish.

Whether you play the Old Course or the Cashen Course, there is only one word to describe the experience: unforgettable.

OLD COURSE – 18 holes links, 6,598 yards, par 71 (SSS 72). Ladies 5,300 yards, par 74 (SSS 72).

CASHEN COURSE – 18 holes links, 6,306 yards, par 72 (SSS 73). Ladies 5,031 yards, par 72 (SSS 72).

OLD COURSE SIGNATURE HOLE:
ELEVENTH (453 yards, par 4) – one of the finest and most dramatic par 4s in the world, running along the top of a cliff with the Atlantic to your right. Often exposed to fierce winds, it can be frightening. A huge dune dominates the left of the fairway, which drops to a plateau green guarded by two massive sandhills.

ADDRESS: Sandhill Road, Ballybunion, Co. Kerry.
TELEPHONE: +353 (0)68 27146.
FAX: +353 (0)68 27387.
EMAIL: bbgolfc@iol.ie
WEBSITE: www.ballybuniongolfclub.ie
SECRETARY/MANAGER: Jim McKenna.
PROFESSIONAL: Brian O'Callaghan.
VISITORS: Mondays to Fridays. Handicap limit for men is 24 and 36 for ladies.
GREEN FEES: Old Course – €150 per round; Cashen Course – €110 per round; to play both courses on the same day costs €200.
CREDIT CARDS ACCEPTED: All major cards.

CATERING: Restaurant and bar.
FACILITIES: Locker rooms, putting green, practice ground, driving range, pro-shop, trolleys (€4), club hire (€45), caddies (€40), tuition.
LOCATION: 70 miles from Shannon, 20 miles from Tralee, 40 miles from Killarney and 80 miles from Cork. Off the R551, half a mile south of Ballybunion.
LOCAL HOTELS: Cashen Course Hotel, Iragh Ti Connor, Manor Inn, Ballybunion Golf Hotel, Marine Links Hotel, Cliff House Hotel, Teach De Broc, The Tides.

BALLYHEIGUE CASTLE GOLF CLUB

Founded in 1995, the course, situated on 100 acres of rolling parkland with mature trees in abundance, surrounds the eighteenth-century castle in Ballyheigue. It also overlooks the magnificent Ballyheigue beach with its white sand, and Mount Brandon is a distant backdrop.

9 holes parkland, 6,882 yards for 18 holes, par 72 (SSS 74). Ladies 5,708 yards, par 72.

ADDRESS: Ballyheigue, Co. Kerry.
TELEPHONE: +353 (0)66 713 3555.
FAX: +353 (0)66 713 3147.
EMAIL: ballyheiguecgc@eircom.net
WEBSITE: www.ballyheiguecastlegolfclub. com
SECRETARY/MANAGER: Mary O'Regan.
VISITORS: Yes. Soft spikes.
GREEN FEES: €28 per round weekdays and weekends.
FACILITIES: Locker rooms, buggies, club hire.

BEAUFORT GOLF COURSE

Established in 1994, this parkland course with generous fairways and large greens is set amongst mature trees. The back nine is dominated by the ruins of the twelfth-century Castle Core.

18 holes parkland, 6,598 yards, par 71 (SSS 72). Ladies 5,310 yards, par 71 (SSS 69).

SIGNATURE HOLE:
TWELFTH (482 yards, par 5) – beautiful hole in a sweeping valley with stunning views of MacGillycuddy Reeks.

ADDRESS: Churchtown, Beaufort, Killarney, Co. Kerry.
TELEPHONE: +353 (0)64 44440.
FAX: +353 (0)64 44752.
EMAIL: beaufortgc@eircom.net
WEBSITE: www.beaufortgolfclub.com
SECRETARY: Colm Kelly.
PROFESSIONAL: Keith Coveney.
VISITORS: Welcome every day.
GREEN FEES: €50 per round weekdays, €60 weekends and public holidays.
CREDIT CARDS ACCEPTED: Yes.
CATERING: Restaurant and bar. Food available all day.
FACILITIES: Locker rooms, putting green, practice ground, pro-shop, buggies (€40), trolleys (€3), club hire (€15), caddies on request, tuition.
LOCATION: Off the N72, 7 miles west of Killarney.
LOCAL HOTELS: Castlerosse Hotel +353 (0)64 31144, Gleneagle Hotel +353 (0)64 31870, Aghadoe Heights Hotel +353 (0)64 31766, Killarney Park +353 (0)64 35555.

Beaufort Golf Course

CASTLEGREGORY GOLF CLUB

Founded in 1989, this parkland course is set between the sea and a freshwater lake.

9 holes parkland, 5,264 metres (5,790 yards) for 18 holes, par 68 (SSS 68). Ladies 4,076 metres (4,483 yards), par 68 (SSS 67).

ADDRESS: Stradbally, Castlegregory, Co. Kerry.
TELEPHONE: +353 (0)66 713 9444.
EMAIL: castlegregorygolf@oceanfree.net
SECRETARY/MANAGER: Martin Lynch.
VISITORS: Yes.
GREEN FEES: €28 per round.
CATERING: Snacks.
FACILITIES: Locker rooms, putting green, practice ground, trolleys, club hire.
LOCATION: 2 miles west of Castlegregory.

CASTLEISLAND GOLF CLUB

Established in 2000 and built on 200 acres, the course commands a panoramic view of the MacGillicuddy's Reeks and surrounding lands. All the undulating fairways, tees and greens were built to USGA specifications, which makes the course playable all year round.

18 holes parkland, 6,041 metres (6,645 yards), par 71 (SSS 73). Ladies 4,922 metres (5,414 yards), par 71 (SSS 71).

SIGNATURE HOLE:
SEVENTH (404 metres [444 yards], par 4) – drive must carry 165 yards over a river. Approach is to a green with a stream in front.

ADDRESS: Doneen, Castleisland, Co. Kerry.
TELEPHONE: +353 (0)66 714 1709.
FAX: +353 (0)66 714 2090.
EMAIL: managercastleislandgolfclub@eircom. net
WEBSITE: www.castleislandgolfclub.com
SECRETARY/MANAGER: Michael Coote.

VISITORS: Welcome.
GREEN FEES: €35 weekdays, €40 at weekends.
CREDIT CARDS ACCEPTED: Yes.
CATERING: Yes.
FACILITIES: Locker room, putting green, pro-shop, buggies (€30), trolleys (€3), club hire (€25).
LOCATION: On the N21, 2 kilometres from Castleisland town and 7 kilometres from Kerry Airport. Travelling from Shannon Airport or Adare, the course is 15 miles from Killarney on the N21.
LOCAL HOTELS: River Island Hotel +353 (0)66 714 2555.

CASTLEROSSE HOTEL, GOLF AND LEISURE CLUB

Founded in 2000 on the shores of the Lakes of Killarney, this parkland course adjoins Killarney Golf and Fishing Club on one side and the Killarney National Park on the other. Greens are to USGA standard.

9 holes parkland, 6,000 yards for 18 holes, par 72 (SSS 69). Ladies 5,134 yards, par 72 (SSS 71).

ADDRESS: Castlerosse Hotel, Fossa, Killarney, Co. Kerry.
TELEPHONE: +353 (0)64 31144.
FAX: +353 (0)64 31031.
EMAIL: res@castlerosse.ie
WEBSITE: www.castlerosse.com
VISITORS: Yes. Soft spikes.
GREEN FEES: €28 for 18 holes.
CATERING: Restaurant and bar.
FACILITIES: Locker rooms, putting green, practice ground, golf shop, buggies (€25), trolleys (€3), club hire (€15).
LOCATION: Just over a mile from Killarney town.
LOCAL HOTELS: Castlerosse Hotel (on the course).

DINGLE GOLF LINKS (*CEANN SIBÉAL*)

Running alongside the Atlantic, this is a traditional championship links course and the most westerly course in Europe. It is carved out of the natural landscape with tricky undulations and swales and many hazards, including a burn which winds through the entire course. Founded in 1924, it was redesigned by Eddie Hackett in 1972 and by Christy O'Connor Jr. in 1988. O'Connor says, 'It has everything that St Andrews has to offer and more.' It boasts scenic views of the Dingle Peninsula and the Blasket Islands.

18 holes links, 6,737 yards, par 72 (SSS 71). Ladies 5,227 yards, par 73 (SSS 71).

ADDRESS: Ballyferriter, Dingle Peninsula, Co. Kerry.
TELEPHONE: +353 (0)66 915 6255.
FAX: +353 (0)66 915 6409.
EMAIL: dinglegc@iol.ie
WEBSITE: www.dinglelinks.com
SECRETARY/MANAGER: Steve Fahy.
VISITORS: Welcome.
GREEN FEES: €65 per round weekdays, €85 at weekends in high season.
CREDIT CARDS ACCEPTED: Yes.
CATERING: Restaurant and bar.
FACILITIES: Locker rooms, putting green, pro-shop, buggies (€35), trolleys (€3), club hire (€25).
LOCATION: Take the main road from Dingle town to Ventry, and then take the first right turn after Ventry to Ballyferriter. Continue through the village and take the first right turn.
LOCAL HOTELS: Dingle Skellig Hotel +353 (0)66 915 0200, Dingle Benners Hotel +353 (0)66 915 1638, Óstán Ceann Sibéal +353 (0)66 915 6433.

DOOKS GOLF CLUB

Kerry's oldest club – golf has been played here since 1889 when the game was introduced to the local aristocracy by officers from the Royal Horse Artillery who were attending compulsory training at the nearby Glenbeigh artillery range. Dooks is a charming links course set out on one of three stretches of sand dunes at the head of Dingle Bay. In the immediate foreground are the sand-dune peninsulas of Rossbeigh and Inch – and just a few miles away are the whitewashed houses of Cromane fishing village. South-eastwards are the famed MacGillycuddy's Reeks, to the south-west are the Cooms and hills of Glenbeigh, and across the bay to the north are the Slieve Mish and Dingle Mountains.

18 holes links, 6,401 yards, par 71 (SSS 69). Ladies 5,339 yards, par 72 (SSS 69).

SIGNATURE HOLE:
THIRTEENTH ('Saucer', 150 yards, par 3) – this saucer-shaped green makes putting a pleasure, an adventure or a hair-raising experience.

ADDRESS: Glenbeigh, Co. Kerry.
TELEPHONE: +353 (0)66 976 8205.
FAX: +353 (0)66 976 8476.
EMAIL: office@dooks.com
WEBSITE: www.dooks.com
SECRETARY/MANAGER: Declan Mangan.
VISITORS: Yes, except on Sundays.
GREEN FEES: €70 per round weekdays and weekends.
CREDIT CARDS ACCEPTED: Amex/Diners Club/MasterCard/Visa.
CATERING: Restaurant and bar.
FACILITIES: Locker rooms, putting green, pro-shop, trolleys (€3), caddies (€25).
LOCATION: On the Ring of Kerry road (Killarney 20 miles, Glenbeigh 3 miles).

Kenmare Golf Club

LOCAL HOTELS: Towers Hotel, The Glenbeigh Hotel.

DUNLOE GOLF COURSE

Set amid the glaciated valley of the famous Gap of Dunloe, this nine-hole parkland course, established in 1999, offers spectacular views of Killarney's lakes and mountains.

9 holes parkland, 4,706 metres (5,176 yards) for 18 holes, par 68 (SSS 65). Ladies 4,024 metres (4,426 yards), par 68 (SSS 67).

ADDRESS: Dunloe, Beaufort, Killarney, Co. Kerry.
TELEPHONE: +353 (0)64 44578.
FAX: +353 (0)64 44733.
EMAIL: enquiries@dunloegc.com

WEBSITE: www.dunloegc.com
SECRETARY/MANAGER: Denis P. Moriarty.
PROFESSIONAL: Kieran P. Crehan.
VISITORS: Yes.
GREEN FEES: €25.
CREDIT CARDS ACCEPTED: MasterCard/Visa.
CATERING: Snack bar.
FACILITIES: Locker rooms, practice ground, putting green, pro-shop, trolleys (€2.50), club hire (€7).
LOCATION: N72 from Killarney to Killorglin.
LOCAL HOTELS: Hotel Dunloe Castle, Hotel Europe, Killarney Valley Hotel.

KENMARE GOLF CLUB

This parkland course beside the River Roughty estuary is often described as 'Ireland's best-kept secret'. It was

Kenmare Golf Club

O ver 100 years old and steeped in golfing history, Kenmare Golf Club welcomes visitors from all over the world, with a friendliness that has become the club's trademark. The famous old course is a fair test of golf and is unique in that it suits all standards of golfers. Playable all year, the course is always maintained to the highest standards which allows for greater enjoyment and appreciation of the course. The scenery and location of Kenmare Golf Club is second to none. The beautiful views of Kenmare Bay and the surrounding mountains take one's breath away. Kenmare town is home to some of Ireland's finest restaurants, bars and shops and is located only 30 yards from the golf course.

Kenmare Golf Club
Kenmare
Co. Kerry
Ireland
+353 (0)64 41291
info@kenmaregolfclub.com
www.kenmaregolfclub.com

established in 1903 and extended to a championship layout by Eddie Hackett in 1993. Surrounded by the Kerry Mountains, it is in a glorious setting. Kenmare derives its name from the Gaelic *Ceann Mara* meaning 'Head of The Sea'. The modern Irish name is *An Neidín* ('The little Nest' in English) due to its picturesque location. There are several interesting holes, including the tough par-4 third with the tee rising out of Kenmare Bay, the challenging par-3 eighth and the sixteenth, which is the most exciting hole on the course with the green set into the bay with water on three sides. It is well worth a visit to the clubhouse, which was originally an old Indian hunting lodge brought back to Ireland by Lord Lansdowne.

18 holes parkland, 6,066 yards, par 71 (SSS 69). Ladies 4,924 yards, par 70 (SSS 69).

ADDRESS: Killowen Road, Kenmare, Co. Kerry.
TELEPHONE: +353 (0)64 41291.
FAX: +353 (0)64 42061.
EMAIL: info@kenmaregolfclub.com
WEBSITE: www.kenmaregolfclub.com
MANAGER: Simon Duffield.
VISITORS: Mondays to Fridays.
GREEN FEES: €45 per round Mondays to Saturdays, €55 Sundays and public holidays.
CREDIT CARDS ACCEPTED: MasterCard/Visa.
CATERING: Restaurant and bar.
FACILITIES: Locker rooms, putting green, practice ground, pro-shop, buggies, trolleys (€2), club hire (€15), caddies on request.
LOCATION: Off the N71, the course is a 2-minute walk south of Kenmare.
LOCAL HOTELS: Kenmare Bay Hotel, Park Hotel, The Wander Inn, The White House, Willow Lodge.

KILLARNEY GOLF AND FISHING CLUB

Three classic championship courses on 500 acres adjacent to Lough Lein with the MacGillycuddy's Reeks range of mountains in the background. The courses are parkland, and the fairways are lined with many native tree species and colourful shrubs. All three courses are flat, and both Mahony's Point and Killeen have holes along the lakeshore. Killarney has hosted many top professional and amateur events, including the 1996 Curtis Cup. Nick Faldo, after winning back-to-back Irish Opens here, said, 'Killeen is a fantastic course; Killarney is perfect.' And José Maria Olazábal agrees, saying, 'Killarney is one of the most beautiful places I have ever seen.'

KILLEEN – 18 holes parkland, 6,543 metres (7,197 yards), par 72 (SSS 73). Ladies 4,928 metres (5,420 yards), par 74 (SSS 71).

MAHONY'S POINT – 18 holes parkland, 6,164 metres (6,780 yards), par 72 (SSS 72). Ladies 4,932 metres (5,425 yards), par 74 (SSS 71).

LACKABANE – 18 holes parkland, 6,410 metres (7,051 yards), par 72 (SSS 73). Ladies 5,117 metres (5,628 yards), par 72 (SSS 73).

KILLEEN SIGNATURE HOLE:
TENTH (156 metres [171 yards], par 3) – lakeside with water from front to left back.

MAHONY'S POINT SIGNATURE HOLE:
EIGHTEENTH (179 metres [198 yards], par 3) – played over the lake to a small green, Gene Sarazen described it as 'one of golf's most memorable holes'.

ADDRESS: Mahony's Point, Killarney, Co. Kerry.
TELEPHONE: +353 (0)64 31034.

FAX: +353 (0)64 33065.
EMAIL: reservations@killarney-golf.com
WEBSITE: www.killarney-golf.com
SECRETARY/MANAGER: Tom Prendergast.
PROFESSIONAL: Tony Coveney.
VISITORS: Yes.
GREEN FEES: €80 per round weekdays and
weekends.
CREDIT CARDS ACCEPTED: Yes.
CATERING: Restaurant and bar.
FACILITIES: Locker rooms, putting green,
practice ground, pro-shop, buggies
(€50), trolleys (€3.50), club hire (from
€16 to €40), caddies, tuition.
LOCATION: Take the N72 west of Killarney
town for 2 miles.
LOCAL HOTELS: Aghadoe Heights Hotel
+353 (0)64 31766, Cahernane Hotel
+353 (0)64 31895, Castlerosse Hotel +353
(0)64 31144, Hotel Dunloe Castle +353
(0)64 44111, Gleneagle Hotel +353 (0)64
31870, Great Southern Hotel +353 (0)64
31262, International Hotel +353 (0)64
31816, Lake Hotel +353 (0)64 31035,
Killarney Park Hotel +353 (0)64 35555.

KILLORGLIN GOLF CLUB

Challenging parkland course founded in
1993 and designed by Eddie Hackett.
18 holes parkland, 5,913 metres (6,504
yards), par 72 (SSS 71). Ladies 4,752 metres
(5,227 yards), par 74 (SSS 72).

ADDRESS: Steelroe, Killorglin, Co. Kerry.
TELEPHONE: +353 (0)66 976 1979.
FAX: +353 (0)66 976 1437.
EMAIL: kilgolf@iol.ie
MANAGER: Billy Dodd.
VISITORS: Every day.
GREEN FEES: €30 per round weekdays, €35
weekends and public holidays.
CREDIT CARDS ACCEPTED: All major cards.

CATERING: Restaurant and bar.
FACILITIES: Locker rooms, putting green,
practice ground, club shop, buggies
(€20), trolleys (€3), club hire (€10),
tuition.
LOCATION: 2 miles from the bridge at
Killorglin on the N70.
LOCAL HOTELS: Bianconi Inn, Grove Lodge,
Riverside House.

LISTOWEL GOLF CLUB

Established in 1994, this parkland course
with tree-lined fairways is developing well.
Three holes run alongside the picturesque
River Feale.
9 holes parkland, 5,698 yards for 18
holes, par 69 (SSS 68). 4,958 yards, par 72
(SSS 70).

SIGNATURE HOLE:
FOURTH (182 yards, par 3) – challenging
and very tight hole on the river bank.

ADDRESS: Feale View, Listowel, Co. Kerry.
TELEPHONE: +353 (0)68 21592.
FAX: +353 (0)68 23387.
EMAIL: listowelgc@eircom.net
VISITORS: At all times.
GREEN FEES: €20 per round weekdays and
weekends.
CREDIT CARDS ACCEPTED: Amex/
MasterCard/Visa.
CATERING: Light meals.
FACILITIES: Locker rooms, putting green,
trolleys, club hire.
LOCATION: In Listowel town, follow
signposts.
LOCAL HOTELS: Arms Hotel, Racecourse
Hotel, Three Mermaids.

The Ring of Kerry Golf and Country Club

PARKNASILLA GOLF CLUB

Established in 1898, this seaside course is quite hilly in places and has sand-based greens. Owned by the Great Southern Hotel.

12 holes parkland, 6,039 yards for 18 holes, par 70 (SSS 70).

ADDRESS: Parknasilla, Sneem, Co. Kerry.
TELEPHONE: +353 (0)64 45195.
FAX: +353 (0)64 45323.
EMAIL: parknasilla@golfnet.ie
SECRETARY/MANAGER: Maurice Walsh.
VISITORS: Yes.
GREEN FEES: €35 for 18 holes weekdays and weekends.
CATERING: In the Great Southern Hotel.
FACILITIES: Locker rooms, putting green, trolleys (€2), club hire (€6.50).
LOCATION: 2 miles east of Sneem on the Ring of Kerry road.
LOCAL HOTELS: Great Southern Hotel.

THE RING OF KERRY GOLF AND COUNTRY CLUB

Designed by Eddie Hackett and opened in 1998, this 18-hole course is on heathland, but the sand-based fairways give it a links feel. Overlooks the spectacular Kenmare Bay.

18 holes heathland, 6,814 yards, par 72 (SSS 73). Ladies 5,400 yards, par 72 (SSS 72).

SIGNATURE HOLE:
THIRTEENTH (233 yards, par 3) – play from an elevated tee with a panoramic view of the River Kenmare and the Beara Mountains. A stream runs across the front of the green.

ADDRESS: Templenoe, Kenmare, Co. Kerry.
TELEPHONE: +353 (0)64 42000.
FAX: +353 (0)64 42533.
EMAIL: reservations@ringofkerrygolf.com

WEBSITE: www.ringofkerrygolf.com
SECRETARY/MANAGER: Ed Edwards.
PROFESSIONAL: Adrian Whitehead.
VISITORS: Yes.
GREEN FEES: €70 per round weekdays, €80
    at weekends.
CREDIT CARDS ACCEPTED: Amex/
    MasterCard/Visa.
CATERING: Restaurant and bar. Limited
    catering available in winter, full in season.
FACILITIES: Locker rooms, driving range,
    putting green, pro-shop, buggies (€30 in
    winter, €40 in season), trolleys (€4), club
    hire (€25 or €40 for premium clubs).
LOCATION: 4 miles west of Kenmare on the
    N70, Ring of Kerry road.
LOCAL HOTELS: The Park Hotel, Kenmare
    +353 (0)64 41200, Sheen Falls Lodge,
    Kenmare +353 (0)64 41600, Brook Lane
    Hotel, Kenmare +353 (0)64 42077,
    Kenmare Bay, Kenmare +353 (0)64
    41300, Lansdown Arms, Kenmare +353
    (0)64 41368.

ROSS GOLF CLUB

A tough and challenging parkland course
with tree-lined fairways and very little room
for error. A picturesque setting beside Ross
Castle, with the River Flesk running through
the course. Founded in 1995.

9 holes parkland, 6,450 yards for 18
holes, par 72 (SSS 73). Ladies 5,284 yards,
par 72 (SSS 72).

SIGNATURE HOLE:
EIGHTH (154 yards, par 3) – surrounded
by water with a bale-out area to the right
side of the green.

ADDRESS: Ross Road, Killarney, Co. Kerry.
TELEPHONE: +353 (0)64 31125.
FAX: +353 (0)64 31860.

EMAIL: rossgolfclub@eircom.net
MANAGER: John Looney.
PROFESSIONAL: Alan O'Meara.
VISITORS: Any day. Soft spikes.
GREEN FEES: €16 for nine holes, €25 for 18.
CREDIT CARDS ACCEPTED: Yes.
CATERING: Bar and snacks.
FACILITIES: Locker rooms, putting green,
    practice ground, pro-shop, trolleys (€3),
    club hire (€15), tuition.
LOCATION: Half a mile from Killarney town
    centre.
LOCAL HOTELS: Gleneagle Hotel, Killarney
    Avenue Hotel, International Hotel, Great
    Southern Hotel.

SKELLIG BAY GOLF CLUB

This parkland course designed by Ron
Kirby and opened in 2005 has nine holes
along the River Fionnglassa and nine on an
Atlantic promontory. Many holes are lined
by stone walls.

18 holes parkland, 6,550 metres (7,205
yards), par 72. Ladies 5,075 metres (5,582
yards), par 72.

ADDRESS: Waterville, Co. Kerry.
TELEPHONE: +353 (0)66 947 4133.
FAX: +353 (0)66 947 4680.
EMAIL: info@skelligbay.com
WEBSITE: www.skelligbay.com
MANAGER: Jim O'Brien.
VISITORS: Any day. Soft spikes.
GREEN FEES: €60 per round.
CREDIT CARDS ACCEPTED: All major cards.
CATERING: Bar and snacks.
FACILITIES: Locker rooms, club shop,
    buggies, trolleys, club hire.
LOCATION: Between Kenmare and
    Cahirciveen on the Ring of Kerry road.
LOCAL HOTELS: Waterville Lake Hotel.

Tralee Golf Club

TRALEE GOLF CLUB

They have a saying locally about the course: 'Created by God, designed by Arnold Palmer'. This magnificent links was the first golf course Palmer designed in Europe in the early 1980s. At the time, he said, 'I have never come across a piece of land so ideally suited for the building of a golf course. I am happy we have one of the world's great links here.' The stunning setting was even used in the filming of *Ryan's Daughter*. Bounded by water on three sides, there is a clear view of the Atlantic Ocean from every hole, and the Slieve Mish mountain range is to the south.

The front nine are relatively flat holes, set on a cliff top, while the back nine are built on dunes. Undulating greens and difficult traps make it most challenging with the back nine especially so. The longest hole on the course is the second, which snakes along the coast. The eighth, the difficult twelfth, where it appears there's no room to land the second shot but on the green, the thirteenth and the seventeenth are all classic holes.

18 holes links, 6,975 yards, par 72 (SSS 74). Ladies 5,481 yards, par 72 (SSS 72).

SIGNATURE HOLE:
THIRD ('The Castle', 194 yards, par 3) – named after the adjacent fourteenth-century castle, this hole is a slender finger of green rising from the crashing waves and

a truly demanding par 3 requiring nerve and skill. Wind dictates club selection, and the green is protected by three pot bunkers. Out of bounds is on the right.

ADDRESS: West Barrow, Ardfert, Co. Kerry.
TELEPHONE: +353 (0)66 713 6379.
FAX: +353 (0)66 713 6008.
EMAIL: info@traleegolfclub.com or reservation@traleegolfclub.com
WEBSITE: www.traleegolfclub.com
SECRETARY: Anthony Byrne.
PROFESSIONAL: David Power.
VISITORS: Yes.
GREEN FEES: €160 per round.
CREDIT CARDS ACCEPTED: Amex/ MasterCard/Visa.
CATERING: The upstairs bar and restaurant has one of the most remarkable views of any golf clubhouse. A wide variety of meals are available.
FACILITIES: Locker rooms, practice ground, putting green, pro-shop, trolleys (€3.50), club hire (€45).
LOCATION: From Shannon/Dublin, follow the signs to Limerick, then take route 21 to Tralee. From the town, follow the signs to the golf club.

WATERVILLE GOLF LINKS

There is a saying that 'Whoever can conquer Waterville can play on any golf course in the world'. Over the years, many invaders have tried but few have mastered this magnificent championship links, laid lovingly on a strip of land bordered by the Inny estuary and the Atlantic Ocean on three sides. It is a mystical place, perhaps due in some part to its role in the mythology of ancient Ireland. The *Book of Invasions*, written about a thousand years ago, claimed that Noah's granddaughter Cessair landed in Ballinskelligs Bay after the Flood. In 700 BC, the Milesians then settled here and were responsible for many of the archaeological sites in the area.

In recent times, the invaders have been more peaceful with only golf, and perhaps a bit of fishing, on their minds. These visitors include American presidents Gerald Ford and Richard Nixon, comedians Bob Hope and Jack Lemmon, and, more recently, Tiger Woods, David Duval, Mark O'Meara and the late Payne Stewart (to whom a statue has been dedicated). Ray Floyd, the former US Ryder Cup captain and Masters champion, was so enamoured of the links that he ranked it behind only Augusta National, Cypress Point, Pebble Beach and the Old Course at St Andrews in his list of great courses.

The club was founded in 1885 when golf was introduced to the area with the arrival of the trans-Atlantic telegraph cable from the United States; a nine-hole course was put down at this time. However, today's course is down to the vision of one man and the design skills of Ireland's most prolific architect. Irish-American Jack Mulcahy bought the course in 1968, and five years later, he fashioned a masterpiece with Eddie Hackett, who called the course a 'beautiful monster'.

The fairways undulate gently as they wind through valleys between elevated tees and massive sand dunes, which at times do their best to hide the large and relatively flat greens. The drama of the dunes is matched by the beauty of the surroundings, which include the MacGillycuddy's Reeks mountain range to the north-east. Although the Gulf Stream provides a mild climate, there is a battle with the elements, as is the case with any links course. But such is the depth

Waterville Golf Links

of the valleys between the dunes that on some fairways (like the signature hole 11th, appropriately called 'Tranquillity') it is possible to believe that the rest of the world is a million miles away. Head for the highest point at about 250 feet above the ocean. The tee of the par-3 17th is called Mulcahy's Peak because the owner used it as a vantage point to check building progress, and from here, you can appreciate the rugged beauty and contours of the course. When it's time to play, it's from an elevated tee to a plateau green with nothing but 'jungle' in between.

All the par 3s are marvellous holes and each has a story of its own – like the 200-yard 12th known as the 'Mass Hole', where Irish Catholics held their church services (banned under British rule) in secret. They congregated in a deep depression just short of the green, and any tee shot which doesn't have the legs ends up here. The 179-yard fourth, bordering on Inny Bay, is where the dune holes begin.

But there is not a weak hole on the course. The aforementioned 11th lives long in the memory, while 'Liam's Ace', the 386-yard 16th where resident professional Liam Higgins holed in one, runs alongside

the estuary. The final two holes brave the capricious Atlantic, with the 594-yard 18th on the shores of Ballinskelligs Bay offering memorable views of the fishing village of Waterville.

Only the remoteness of Waterville has prevented this great course from hosting its fair share of major championships. As the locals say, 'It is so far south and so far west that you can see Boston on a clear day.'

18 holes links, 7,309 yards, par 72 (SSS 74). Ladies 5,276 yards, par 73 (SSS 72).

SIGNATURE HOLE:
ELEVENTH ('Tranquillity', 506 yards, par 5) – surrounded by high natural sand dunes. It is possible for big hitters to make it in two in calm conditions but most have to be content to lay up with the fairway narrowing severely about 100 yards from the green.

ADDRESS: Waterville, Co. Kerry.
TELEPHONE: +353 (0)66 947 4102.
FAX: +353 (0)66 947 4482.
EMAIL: wvgolf@iol.ie
WEBSITE: www.watervillegolflinks.ie
SECRETARY/MANAGER: Noel Cronin.
PROFESSIONAL: Liam Higgins.

VISITORS: Welcome every day. Soft spikes.

GREEN FEES: €150. Early and late green fees on Mondays to Thursdays before 8 a.m. and after 4 p.m. are €105.

CREDIT CARDS ACCEPTED: Amex/Laser/MasterCard/Visa.

CATERING: Restaurant and bar.

FACILITIES: Locker rooms, putting green, practice ground, driving range, pro-shop, buggies (€50), trolleys (€4), club hire (€35), caddies on request. For lessons, contact Brian Higgins.

LOCATION: 1 mile west of Waterville, 50 miles from Kerry Airport.

LOCAL HOTELS: Waterville House (on the course) +353 (0)66 947 4244, Butler Arms Hotel +353 (0)66 947 4144.

COUNTY LIMERICK

ABBEYFEALE GOLF CLUB

Rolling parkland course opened in 1992 and designed by Dr Arthur Spring. At weekends, the driving range is closed to extend two holes to par 5s.

9 holes parkland, 4,072 metres (4,479 yards) for 18 holes, par 62 (SSS 62).

ADDRESS: Abbeyfeale, Co. Limerick.

TELEPHONE: +353 (0)68 32033.

FAX: +353 (0)68 51871.

EMAIL: info@abbeyfealegolfclub.com

WEBSITE: www.abbeyfealegolfclub.com

PROFESSIONAL: Mark Heinemann.

VISITORS: All times.

GREEN FEES: €10 for nine holes, €15 for eighteen.

CATERING: Sandwiches/snacks.

FACILITIES: Locker rooms, driving range, trolleys, club hire, caddies, tuition.

LOCATION: Take the N18 to Limerick and then the N21.

ADARE MANOR GOLF CLUB

Established in 1900 when a nine-hole course was built by Ben Sayers. The current rolling parkland course was designed and laid down by Eddie Hackett in 1992. The ruins of Desmond Castle, built in 1200, are a magnificent backdrop to the first and fifteenth greens, while the ruins of an abbey dominate the centre of the course.

18 holes parkland, 5,764 yards, par 69 (SSS 69). Ladies 5,053 yards, par 70 (SSS 70).

ADDRESS: Adare, Co. Limerick.

TELEPHONE: +353 (0)61 396204.

FAX: +353(0)61 396800.

EMAIL: info@adaremanorgolfclub.com

WEBSITE: www.adaremanorgolfclub.com

VISITORS: Yes.

GREEN FEES: €35 per round weekdays and weekends.

CATERING: Bar food.

FACILITIES: Locker rooms, putting green, practice ground, club shop, trolleys, club hire, caddies, tuition.

LOCATION: 10 miles south-west of Limerick on the N21.

LOCAL HOTELS: Fitzgeralds Woodlands Hotel, Knockanes +353 (0)61 396118, Adare Manor Hotel, Adare +353 (0)61 605200, Adare Avona, Adare +353 (0)61 396323, Berkeley Lodge, Adare +353 (0)61 396857, Carrabawn House, Adare +353 (0)61 396007.

ADARE MANOR HOTEL AND GOLF RESORT

A masterpiece of a parkland championship course, opened in 1995 and designed by

The 18th at Adare
Manor Hotel and
Golf Resort

Robert Trent Jones, sen. (architect of 45 of the top 100 golf courses worldwide). It stretches over 230 acres of the 840-acre Adare Manor estate around the ruins of an Augustine abbey, dating from 1313, and a Franciscan friary, dating from 1464. Set amidst mature trees, the course has three lakes – including one of 14 acres which dominates the front nine – and features Jones's signature clover-leaf bunkers. The River Maigue comes into play on three holes, meandering through the back nine and creating a special challenge, particularly on the par-3 eleventh and par-5 eighteenth.

18 holes parkland, 7,125 yards, par 72 (SSS 74). Ladies 5,419 yards, par 72.

SIGNATURE HOLE:
EIGHTEENTH (548 yards, par 5) – a dramatic finish. Jones believes the 18th to be perhaps the best par 5 in the world. It is possible to make the green in two, but it requires a long shot diagonally across the river.

ADDRESS: Adare Manor, Adare, Co. Limerick.
TELEPHONE: +353 (0)61 395044.
FAX: +353 (0)61 396987.
EMAIL: golf@adaremanor.com
WEBSITE: www.adaremanor.com
VISITORS: Every day. Soft spikes.
GREEN FEES: €130 per round, €115 for residents.
CREDIT CARDS ACCEPTED: All major cards.
CATERING: Restaurant and bar.
FACILITIES: Locker rooms, putting green, practice ground, driving range, pro-shop, buggies (€45), trolleys (€5), club hire (€40), caddies subject to availability, tuition.
LOCATION: On the N21, 10 miles from Limerick.

LOCAL HOTELS: Adare Manor Hotel, Adare +353 (0)61 605200 (on site).

CASTLETROY GOLF CLUB

Superbly maintained parkland course, with excellent fairways and greens, which underwent a major development programme in 2005 under the supervision of Eddie Connaughton. The new layout includes 18 new green and tees to USGA specification with water features and fairway bunkering. Some of the outstanding holes include the par-5 sixth, with water to the right and the back of the green, the par-3 fourteenth, played from an elevated tee to a green surrounded by water, and the tough par-4 finishing hole. Founded in 1937.

18 holes parkland, 6,890 yards, par 72 (SSS 71).

ADDRESS: Golf Links Road, Castletroy, Co. Limerick.
TELEPHONE: +353 (0)61 335753.
FAX: +353 (0)61 335373.
EMAIL: cgc@iol.ie
SECRETARY/MANAGER: Patrick Keane.
VISITORS: Yes. Soft spikes.
GREEN FEES: €50 per round weekdays, €60 at weekends.
CREDIT CARDS ACCEPTED: Yes.
CATERING: Restaurant and bar.
FACILITIES: Locker rooms, putting green, practice ground, buggies (€30), trolleys (€3), club hire (€20), caddies by arrangement.
LOCATION: 2 miles from Limerick, off the N7 to Dublin.
LOCAL HOTELS: Castletroy Park Hotel, Kilmurry Lodge Hotel.

LIMERICK GOLF CLUB

Interesting, gently undulating parkland course, designed by Dr Alister Mackenzie, with water hazards, out of bounds and plenty of trees but no steep hills. It has been the venue of several Irish professional championships, and Tiger Woods has played here. Limerick is one of the oldest golf clubs in Ireland having been founded in the same year as the Golfing Union of Ireland in 1891. The club occupied eight other sites before coming to Ballyclough in 1919.

18 holes parkland, 5,965 metres (6,561 yards), par 72 (SSS 71). Ladies 5,111 metres (5,622 yards), par 74 (SSS 74).

SIGNATURE HOLE:
FOURTH (371 metres [408 yards], par 4) – demanding left to right dogleg to a sloping, elevated green.

ADDRESS: Ballyclough, Co. Limerick.
TELEPHONE: +353 (0)61 415146.
FAX: +353 (0)61 319219.
EMAIL: lgc@eircom.net
WEBSITE: www.limerickgc.com
SECRETARY: Pat Murray.
PROFESSIONAL: Lee Harrington.
VISITORS: Yes. Soft spikes.
GREEN FEES: €50 per round Mondays to Thursdays, €70 Fridays to Sundays and public holidays.
CREDIT CARDS ACCEPTED: Yes.
CATERING: Restaurant and bar.
FACILITIES: Locker rooms, putting green, practice ground, pro-shop, buggies (€25), trolleys (€3), club hire (€20), tuition.
LOCATION: 3 miles south-east of Limerick on the R511 road to Fedamore.
LOCAL HOTELS: South Court Hotel +353 (0)61 487428, Clarion Hotel +353 (0)61 444100.

LIMERICK COUNTY GOLF AND COUNTRY CLUB

Undulating championship parkland course with water features on eight holes and well-bunkered contoured greens. Originally designed by Des Smyth in 1994, Declan Brannigan redesigned five holes, which opened in April 2005. The sand-based greens and tees are all to USGA specifications.

18 holes parkland, 5,876 metres (6,463 yards), par 72 (SSS 71). Ladies 4,661 metres (5,127 yards), par 72 (SSS 72).

ADDRESS: Ballyneety, Co. Limerick.
TELEPHONE: +353 (0)61 351881.
FAX: +353 (0)61 351384.
EMAIL: lcgolf@iol.ie
WEBSITE: www.limerickcounty.com
MANAGER: Gerry McKeon.
PROFESSIONAL: Donal McSweeney.
VISITORS: Yes.
GREEN FEES: €40 per round weekdays and weekends.
CREDIT CARDS ACCEPTED: Yes.
CATERING: Restaurant and bar.
FACILITIES: Locker rooms, putting green, practice ground, 20-bay driving range, club shop, buggies (€35), trolleys (€3), club hire (€25), caddies, tuition.
LOCATION: Off the R512, 5 miles south of Limerick.
LOCAL HOTELS: Clarion Hotel +353 (0)61 444100.

NEWCASTLE WEST GOLF CLUB

Founded in 1938 and extended to 18 holes in 1994, this parkland course is built on 150 acres of sandy, free-draining soil and features gentle slopes, lakes, trees and streams.

18 holes parkland, 6,444 yards, par 71 (SSS 72). Ladies 5,203 yards, par 72 (SSS 71).

ADDRESS: Ardagh, Co. Limerick.
TELEPHONE: +353 (0)69 76500.
FAX: +353 (0)69 76511.
EMAIL: ncwgolf@eircom.net
SECRETARY/MANAGER: Eamon Cregan.
PROFESSIONAL: Tom Murphy.
VISITORS: Mondays to Fridays. Soft spikes.
GREEN FEES: €35 per round weekdays, €40 at weekends.
CATERING: Restaurant and bar.
FACILITIES: Locker rooms, putting green, practice ground, driving range, club shop, buggies, trolleys, club hire, caddies on request, tuition.
LOCATION: 6 miles from Newcastle West, off the N21.
LOCAL HOTELS: Courteney Lodge, Devon Inn, Rathkeale House Hotel.

RATHBANE GOLF CLUB

Founded in 1998, this parkland course is built on 125 acres with modern sand-based greens and some memorable par 5s. It is Limerick's first municipal course.

18 holes parkland, 6,201 yards, par 70 (SSS 69). Ladies 5,302 yards, par 71 (SSS 71).

ADDRESS: Rathbane, Co. Limerick.
TELEPHONE & FAX: +353 (0)61 313655.
EMAIL: info@rathbane.com.
WEBSITE: www.rathbanegolf.com
PROFESSIONAL: Barbara Hackett.
VISITORS: Yes. Soft spikes.
GREEN FEES: €20 per round weekdays, €25 at weekends.
CATERING: Coffee shop.
FACILITIES: Locker rooms, putting green, practice ground, driving range, pro-shop, buggies, trolleys, club hire, caddies, tuition.
LOCATION: 1 mile from the centre of Limerick, off the R512.

The West

COUNTY DONEGAL

BALLYBOFEY AND STRANORLAR GOLF CLUB

Undulating parkland course with three holes on the shores of Lough Alann. Panoramic views of the Donegal Mountains. Founded in 1954.

18 holes parkland, 5,377 metres (5,914 yards), par 68 (SSS 68). Ladies 4,781 metres (5,259 yards), par 69 (SSS 69).

ADDRESS: The Glebe, Stranorlar, Co. Donegal.
TELEPHONE: +353 (0)74 913 1093.
FAX: +353 (0)74 913 0158.
VISITORS: Weekdays, and weekends by arrangement.
GREEN FEES: €25 per round weekdays, €30 at weekends.
CREDIT CARDS ACCEPTED: All major cards.
CATERING: Restaurant and bar.
FACILITIES: Locker rooms, putting green, practice ground, club shop, buggies, trolleys, club hire, caddies.
LOCATION: Off the Strabane–Ballybofey road, 15 miles from Strabane.
LOCAL HOTELS: Dirgefield House, Fir Trees Hotel.

BALLYLIFFIN GOLF CLUB

Nick Faldo described the Old Links at Ballyliffin, set amidst towering dunes bordering the North Atlantic, as 'the most natural golf links I have ever played' when he visited in 1993. Two years later, Pat Ruddy and Tom Craddock upstaged it by designing the Glashedy Links (named after the Glashedy Rock offshore) at Ireland's most northerly golf club on Donegal's Inishowen Peninsula. The designers had promised that they would create one of the world's finest golf courses, and the new course, on a 365-acre site, can certainly claim to be one of the best to be built since 1945. It is an exciting challenge, wending between massive sandhills and huge undulating greens protected by deep bunkers. There is a particularly taxing stretch between the 12th and 15th holes, and level par here is an achievement. The Old Links, recently upgraded by Nick Faldo, also offers a marvellous experience, especially the fifth ('The Tank') and eighteenth holes.

OLD LINKS – 18 holes links, 6,600 yards, par 71.
GLASHEDY LINKS – 18 holes links, 7,217 yards, par 72 (SSS 74).

OLD LINKS SIGNATURE HOLE:
FIFTH (176 yards, par 3) – tricky tee shot to an elevated green.

GLASHEDY LINKS SIGNATURE HOLE:
SEVENTH (183 yards, par 3) – elevated tee to a lakeside green with panoramic views of the entire complex.

ADDRESS: Ballyliffin, Inishowen, Co. Donegal.
TELEPHONE: +353 (0)74 937 6119.
FAX: +353 (0)74 937 6672.
EMAIL: info@ballyliffingolfclub.com
WEBSITE: www.ballyliffingolfclub.com
SECRETARY: John Farren.
PROFESSIONAL: John Dolan.
VISITORS: Welcome subject to booking.
GREEN FEES: Glashedy – €70 per round midweek, €80 at weekends; Old Links – €60 per round midweek, €65 at weekends.

Ballyliffin Golf Club

CREDIT CARDS ACCEPTED: Yes, except Amex.
CATERING: Full restaurant.
FACILITIES: Locker rooms, practice ground,
    putting green, pro-shop, buggies (€35),
    trolleys (€3), club hire (€25).
LOCATION: 30 miles north of Derry and 6
    miles from Cardonagh on the R238.
LOCAL HOTELS: Ballyliffin Lodge and Spa
    +353 (0)74 937 8200, Strand +353 (0)74
    937 6107, Ballyliffin Hotel +353 (0)74 937
    6106, Pollan Beach Hotel +353 (0)74 937
    8840, Carlton Redcastle +353 (0)74 938
    5555.

BUNCRANA GOLF CLUB

This is the oldest nine-hole course in
Ireland established in 1890. A links course
on the banks of the 'White Strand', it
overlooks Lough Swilly. It is a challenge to
golfers of all abilities.

9 holes links, 4,250 yards for 18 holes, par 62
(SSS 62). Ladies 4,201 yards, par 66 (SSS 64).

SIGNATURE HOLE:
THIRD (240 yards, par 3) – with out of bounds
on both sides and the green set in a valley, this
is one of the toughest short holes around.

ADDRESS: Railway Road, Ballymacarry,
    Buncrana, Co. Donegal.
TELEPHONE: +353 (0)74 936 2279/932 0749.

EMAIL: buncranagc@eircom.net
SECRETARY/MANAGER: Francis McGrory.
PROFESSIONAL: Jim Doherty.
VISITORS: Yes.
GREEN FEES: €13 for men, €8 for women.
CREDIT CARDS ACCEPTED: No.
CATERING: By arrangement.
FACILITIES: Locker room, putting green,
    pro-shop, trolleys.
LOCATION: First left after the Inishowen
    Gateway Hotel coming into Buncrana.
LOCAL HOTELS: Inishowen Gateway Hotel
    +353 (0)74 936 1144.

BUNDORAN GOLF CLUB

Founded in 1894 and designed by Harry
Vardon, this is a combination of links
and parkland situated on the cliffs above
Bundoran beach. The course has almost
no trees, and holes eight to twelve run
alongside the Atlantic.

18 holes links/parkland, 5,688 metres
(6,256 yards), par 70 (SSS 70). Ladies 5,116
metres (5,627 yards), par 70.

ADDRESS: Bundoran, Co. Donegal.
TELEPHONE: +353 (0)71 984 1302.
FAX: +353 (0)71 984 2014.
EMAIL: bundorangolfclub@eircom.net
WEBSITE: www.bundorangolfclub.com
SECRETARY: John McGagh.
PROFESSIONAL: David Robinson.
VISITORS: Yes.
GREEN FEES: €45 per round weekdays, €55
    at weekends.
CATERING: Bar and snacks.
FACILITIES: Locker rooms, putting green,
    driving range, pro-shop, buggies, trolleys,
    club hire, caddies, tuition.
LOCATION: 22 miles north of Sligo on the
    Sligo–Derry road.
LOCAL HOTELS: Atlantic View House,
    Portnason House.

CLOUGHANEELY GOLF CLUB

Opened in 1997, this undulating nine-hole
parkland course is in the grounds of the
old Ballyconnell Estate. The fairways are
surrounded by mature trees of every variety,
which come into play on most of the holes.
The fairways are generous, but the semi-
rough is tough, and the sand-based greens
are tricky.

9 holes parkland, 6,088 yards for 18
holes, par 70 (SSS 69). Ladies 5,454 yards,
par 72.

SIGNATURE HOLE:
SEVENTH ('Heartbreak', 147 yards, par 3)
– a sheltered hole with out of bounds to the
right and behind the green. Once the ball
gets above the tree line, the wind comes
into play.

ADDRESS: Ballyconnell Estate, Falcarragh,
    Letterkenny, Co. Donegal.
TELEPHONE & FAX: +353 (0)74 916 5416.
EMAIL: falcarraghgolfclub@eircom.net
SECRETARY: Michael Murray.
VISITORS: Welcome, but avoid Sunday
    mornings.
GREEN FEES: €15 weekdays, €20 at
    weekends.
CREDIT CARDS ACCEPTED: No.
CATERING: Bar, tea and coffee.
FACILITIES: Locker rooms, trolleys (€3),
    club hire.
LOCATION: North-west from Letterkenny,
    30 miles from Falcarragh. Turn right in
    the centre of Falcarragh through the
    stone pillars of Ballyconnell Estate. If
    coming from Carigfin Airport (20 miles
    approximately), go through Anagry to
    Falcarragh and turn left in the centre of
    town.
LOCAL HOTELS: Lough Altan, Gortahork
    +353 (0)74 91 35267, An Bear Mor,

Donegal Golf Club (Murvagh)

Gortahork +353 (0) 74 91 35259, An Cuirt, Dunlewy +353 (0) 74 95 32900.

CRUIT ISLAND GOLF CLUB

Situated on cliffs overlooking the Atlantic, the wind is an additional hazard on this links course on the Island of Cruit, which is linked by a bridge to the mainland. Founded in 1986.

9 holes links, 5,141 metres (5,655 yards) for 18 holes, par 68 (SSS 66). Ladies 4,296 metres (4,725 yards), par 68 (SSS 66).

SIGNATURE HOLE:
SIXTH (137 metres [150 yards], par 3) – spectacular with its inlet and sea arches.

ADDRESS: Cruit Island, Kincasslagh, Co. Donegal.

TELEPHONE: +353 (0) 74 954 3296.
EMAIL: cruitgc@eircom.net
WEBSITE: www.cruitislandgolfclub.com
VISITORS: Welcome.
GREEN FEES: €22 per round.
CATERING: Restaurant and bar.
FACILITIES: Locker rooms, practice ground, buggies, trolleys.
LOCATION: 4 miles from the village of Kincasslagh.
LOCAL HOTELS: Viking House Hotel.

DONEGAL GOLF CLUB (MURVAGH)

The challenging Murvagh Links is set on a peninsula in Donegal Bay and, as one of the longest courses in Ireland, suits big hitters who have to contend with the ocean breezes. Peter Dobereiner, one of golf's

Ireland's Golf Courses

finest writers, described it as, 'Hauntingly beautiful and an excellent test of golf.' The course offers marvellous views of the Blue Stack Mountains.

18 holes links, 6,753 metres (7,428 yards), par 73 (SSS 75). Ladies 5,429 metres (5,971 yards), par 75.

SIGNATURE HOLE:
FIFTH ('Valley of Tears', 179 metres [196 yards], par 3) – you can see only the top of the flag from the tee. The shot to the plateau green has to be good.

ADDRESS: Murvagh, Laghey, Co. Donegal.
TELEPHONE: +353 (0)74 973 4054.
FAX: +353 (0)74 973 4377.
EMAIL: info@donegalgolfclub.ie
WEBSITE: www.donegalgolfclub.ie
SECRETARY: Grainne Dorrian.
PROFESSIONAL: Leslie Robinson.
VISITORS: Welcome every day.
GREEN FEES: €55 per round Mondays to Thursdays, €70 per round Fridays, Saturdays and Sundays.
CREDIT CARDS ACCEPTED: Amex/MasterCard/Visa.
CATERING: Restaurant and bar.
FACILITIES: Locker rooms, practice ground, putting green, pro-shop, buggies (€40), trolleys (€3), club hire (€13).
LOCATION: 7 miles outside Donegal town on the N15 towards Sligo.
LOCAL HOTELS: Abbey Hotel +353 (0)74 972 1014, Millpark Hotel +353 (0)74 972 2880, Sandhouse +353 (0)71 985 1777.

DUNFANAGHY GOLF CLUB

This seaside links course, designed by Harry Vardon in 1905, runs along a three-mile stretch of beach next to a beautiful lagoon on Sheephaven Bay. Golf was first played here 25 years or so after the setting-up of

St Andrews in Scotland. Stewart of Horn Head, a local landlord, was one of the founding fathers of St Andrews. The playing of the modern game was first recorded here in 1896. European Tour players Darren Clarke and Paul McGinley often practise here. There is magnificent scenery with the Derryveagh mountain range to the south and Horn Head to the north.

18 holes links, 5,740 yards, par 68 (SSS 66). Ladies 4,988 yards, par 69 (SSS 67).

SIGNATURE HOLE:
NINTH (132 yards, par 3) – play from elevated tee over the beach to a two-tiered green. Bunker on one side, bank at rear.

ADDRESS: Kill, Dunfanaghy, Co. Donegal.
TELEPHONE: +353 (0)74 913 6335.
FAX: +353 (0)74 913 6684.
EMAIL: dunfanaghygolf@eircom.net
WEBSITE: www.dunfanaghygolfclub.com
SECRETARY: Sandra McGinley.
VISITORS: Welcome.
GREEN FEES: €30 weekdays, €40 at weekends.
CREDIT CARDS ACCEPTED: Yes.
CATERING: Snacks only.
FACILITIES: Locker rooms, practice ground, putting green, pro-shop, buggies (€30), trolleys (€3), club hire (€60, €50 deposit).
LOCATION: 30 miles west of Letterkenny on the N56.
LOCAL HOTELS: Arnolds Hotel +353 (0)74 913 6208.

GREENCASTLE GOLF CLUB

Challenging public seaside course founded as a nine-hole layout in 1892. It was extended to 18 holes in 1912, and in 1987, Eddie Hackett added the finishing touches. Bordered on one side by Lough Foyle with panoramic views across to the mountains of Derry, and on the other side there are equally spectacular views up into the hills of County Donegal.

18 holes seaside, 5,211 metres (5,732 yards), par 69 (SSS 67). Ladies 4,590 metres (5,049 yards), par 70 (SSS 69).

ADDRESS: Greencastle, Moville, Co. Donegal.
TELEPHONE: +353 (0)74 938 1013.
FAX: +353 (0)74 938 1015.
EMAIL: greencastlegolfclub@eircom.net
VISITORS: Yes.
GREEN FEES: €25 per round weekdays, €35 at weekends.
CATERING: Restaurant and bar.
FACILITIES: Locker rooms.
LOCATION: On the L85, 23 miles north-east of Londonderry through Moville.
LOCAL HOTELS: Castle Inn, Greencastle Fort, Redcastle Hotel, Tardrum Country House, The Inishowen Gateway Hotel.

GWEEDORE GOLF CLUB

Founded in 1926, this seaside course at the edge of Gweedore Bay was designed by Eddie Hackett. It is challenging with a couple of good par 3s and a tough par 5.

9 holes seaside, 6,302 yards for 18 holes, par 71 (SSS 69). Ladies, 5,387 yards, par 71 (SSS 69).

ADDRESS: Magheragallon, Derrybeg, Co. Donegal.
TELEPHONE: +353 (0)74 953 1140.
VISITORS: Yes.
SECRETARY/MANAGER: Ann Curran.
GREEN FEES: €20 per round.
CATERING: Yes.
FACILITIES: Locker rooms, putting green, practice green, buggies, trolleys, club hire.

LOCATION: The L82 from Letterkenny or T72 from Donegal.

LETTERKENNY GOLF CLUB

This parkland course, situated by Lough Swilly, is reasonably flat with wide fairways. Founded in 1913 and designed by Eddie Hackett.

18 holes parkland, 6,274 yards, par 71 (SSS 70).

ADDRESS: Barnhill, Letterkenny, Co. Donegal.
TELEPHONE: +353 (0)74 912 1150.
FAX: +353 (0)74 912 1175.
EMAIL: letterkennygc@eircom.net
VISITORS: Yes.
GREEN FEES: €25 per round weekdays, €30 at weekends.
CREDIT CARDS ACCEPTED: MasterCard/Visa.
CATERING: Restaurant and bar.
FACILITIES: Locker rooms, practice area, putting green, club shop, buggies, trolleys (€3), club hire, caddies on request, tuition.
LOCATION: On the T72, 2 miles north of Letterkenny.

NARIN AND PORTNOO GOLF CLUB

Established in 1930, this scenic links in a beautiful seaside resort in south-west Donegal meanders over and around dunes with every hole presenting its own special features. The par-4 fifth demands a perfectly placed drive to get a sight of the narrow entrance to an elevated green. Cross winds from the Atlantic Ocean and tight fairways can make some of the par 4s difficult to reach with two woods. There are sweeping views of Gweebarra Bay. The course is being upgraded to a par 72 in 2006.

18 holes links, 5,396 metres (5,935 yards),

par 69 (SSS 69). Ladies 4,490 metres (4,939 yards), par 70 (SSS 68).

SIGNATURE HOLE:
EIGHTH (130 metres [143 yards], par 3) – elevated tee to an elevated, two-tiered green with a chasm to cross.

The eighth at Narin and Portnoo Golf Club

ADDRESS: Narin, Portnoo, Co. Donegal.
TELEPHONE: +353 (0)74 954 5107.
FAX: +353 (0)74 954 5994.
EMAIL: narinportnoo@eircom.net
WEBSITE: www.narinportnoogolfclub.ie
MANAGER: Sean Murphy.
VISITORS: Welcome.
GREEN FEES: €30 weekdays, €35 at
    weekends.
CREDIT CARDS ACCEPTED: Laser/
    MasterCard/Visa.
CATERING: Bar, soup and sandwiches.
FACILITIES: Practice net, locker rooms,
    putting green, shop, buggies (€25),
    trolleys (€3), club hire (€20).
LOCATION: 6 miles northwest of Glenties, 8
    miles north of Ardara, through the village
    of Narin and keep right. The nearest

airport is Donegal International Airport at Carrickfinn.
LOCAL HOTELS: Narin Inn +353 (0)95
    45108, Lake House Hotel +353 (0)95
    45123, Nesbitt Arms +353 (0)95 41103,
    Highlands Hotel +353 (0)95 51111.

NORTH WEST GOLF CLUB

This is a challenging links course with excellent greens. Established in 1891, it has often been dubbed the 'St Andrews of Ireland'. Like the Scottish links, it features concealed runs, humps and hollows in the approach to its greens, which look deceptively easy. The holes are varied with many sandy knolls, concealed bunkers and undulations. Lying between the sea and the Mouldy Mountains, it is generally flat with two loops of nine each ending at the clubhouse. Club member Brian McElhinney won the 2005 British Amateur Championship.

18 holes links, 5,759 metres (6,334 yards), par 70 (SSS 70). Ladies 4,982 metres (5,480 yards), par 71 (SSS 71).

ADDRESS: Lisfannon, Fahan, Co. Donegal.
TELEPHONE: +353 (0)74 936 1715.
FAX: +353 (0)74 936 3284.
EMAIL: secretary@northwestgolfclub.com
WEBSITE: www.northwestgolfclub.com
SECRETARY: Dudley Coyle.
PROFESSIONAL: Seamus McBriarty.
VISITORS: Mondays, Tuesdays and Fridays
    are best.
GREEN FEES: €28 per round weekdays, €33
    weekends and public holidays.
CATERING: Restaurant and bar.
FACILITIES: Locker rooms, putting green,
    pro-shop, buggies, trolleys, club hire,
    caddies, tuition.
LOCATION: Situated on the shores of Lough
    Swilly. On the left-hand side of the

Derry–Buncrana road, about 1 mile north of Fahan village.

LOCAL HOTELS: Inishowen Gateway, Lake of Shadows.

OTWAY GOLF CLUB

This parkland course on the west shores of Lough Swilly was founded in 1893 and is claimed to be one of the five oldest clubs in Ireland.

9 holes parkland, 4,234 yards for 18 holes, par 64 (SSS 64).

ADDRESS: Saltpans, Rathmullan, Co. Donegal.
TELEPHONE: +353 (0)74 915 8593.
EMAIL: otway_golf_club@iolfree.ie
VISITORS: Yes.
GREEN FEES: €15 per round.
CATERING: Bar.
FACILITIES: Locker rooms.
LOCATION: 15 miles north-east of Letterkenny by Lough Swilly.
LOCAL HOTELS: Fort Royal Hotel, Pier Hotel, Rathmullan House Hotel.

PORTSALON GOLF CLUB

This natural seaside links course, established in 1891 and one of the founder members of the Golfing Union of Ireland, has stunning views of Ballymastocker Bay and Lough Swilly.

18 holes links, 7,080 yards, par 72. Ladies 5,703 yards, par 75.

ADDRESS: Portsalon, Fanad, Co. Donegal.
TELEPHONE: +353 (0)74 915 9459.
FAX: +353 (0)74 915 9919.

EMAIL: portsalongolfclub@eircom.net
SECRETARY/MANAGER: Cathal Toland.
VISITORS: Seven days by prearranged booking. Soft spikes.
GREEN FEES: €40 per round weekdays, €50 weekends and public holidays.
CATERING: Restaurant and bar.
FACILITIES: Locker rooms, putting green, club shop, buggies (€30), trolleys (€3), club hire.
LOCATION: 20 miles north of Letterkenny.
LOCAL HOTELS: Fort Royal Hotel, Pier Hotel, Rathmullan House Hotel.

REDCASTLE GOLF CLUB

A parkland course on the shores of Lough Foyle with water hazards. It is flat for the first three holes but then starts to climb. Founded in 1983.

9 holes parkland, 6,152 yards for 18 holes, par 72 (SSS 69).

ADDRESS: Redcastle Hotel, Redcastle, Moville, Co. Donegal.
TELEPHONE: +353 (0)74 938 2073.
FAX: +353 (0)74 938 2214.
EMAIL: redcastle.hotel@oceanfree.net
WEBSITE: www.redcastlehotel.com
VISITORS: Welcome.
GREEN FEES: €20 per round weekdays, €25 at weekends.
CATERING: Restaurant and bar.
FACILITIES: Locker rooms, club shop, trolleys, club hire.
LOCATION: 4 miles from Moville on the Londonderry road.
LOCAL HOTELS: Redcastle Hotel (on the course).

The sixth at Rosapenna Hotel Golf Club

ROSAPENNA HOTEL GOLF CLUB

Two challenging eighteen-hole links courses. The Old Course is not the work of just one great name of golf but three. It was first designed by Old Tom Morris in 1893, but Harry Vardon and James Braid have since done their best to improve on it. In 2002, a second course named Sandy Hills Links was designed by Pat Ruddy with spectacular elevated tees and large greens.

OLD TOM MORRIS LINKS – 18 holes, 6,476 yards, par 70 (SSS 71). Ladies 5,493 yards, par 74 (SSS 72).

SANDY HILLS LINKS – 18 holes, 7,155 yards, par 71. Ladies 4,868 yards, par 71.

ADDRESS: Rosapenna Hotel, Downings, Co. Donegal.
TELEPHONE: +353 (0) 74 915 5301.
FAX: +353 (0) 74 915 5128.
EMAIL: mailbox@rosapennagolflinks.ie

WEBSITE: www.rosapennagolflinks.ie
PROFESSIONAL: Bryan Patterson.
VISITORS: Yes, every day.
GREEN FEES: Old Tom Morris – €50 per
   round; Sandy Hills Links – €75 per
   round.
CATERING: Restaurant and bar.
FACILITIES: Locker rooms, putting green,
   practice ground, driving range, club
   shop, buggies (€35), trolleys (€3), club
   hire (€20), caddies (€45), tuition.
LOCATION: 25 miles north of Letterkenny.
LOCAL HOTELS: Rosapenna Hotel (on the
   course).

ST PATRICK'S LINKS

A 36-hole links on the rugged coastline
of north-east Donegal. The two courses
lie amongst the sandy hills of Sheephaven
Bay. Maheramagorgan is named after the
local townland and is the creation of Eddie
Hackett. Trá Mór was designed by Joanne
O'Haire, the only course in Ireland to be
designed by a woman.
   MAHERAMAGORGAN COURSE – 18
holes links, 7,108 yards, par 72.
   TRÁ MÓR COURSE – 18 holes links,
5,822 yards, par 71.

ADDRESS: Maheramagorgan, Carrigart, Co.
   Donegal.
TELEPHONE: +353 (0)74 915 5114.
FAX: +353 (0)74 915 5250.
EMAIL: info@stpatricksgolflinks.com
WEBSITE: www.stpatricksgolflinks.com
VISITORS: Yes.
GREEN FEES: €25 (hotel residents free).
CREDIT CARDS ACCEPTED: Yes.
CATERING: Yes.
LOCATION: 20 miles north of Letterkenny.
LOCAL HOTELS: Carrigart Hotel (2 miles
   from course) +353 (0)74 55114.

COUNTY GALWAY

ARDACONG GOLF CLUB

Private parkland course with undulating greens. The newer back 9 is possibly trickier with water hazards. Tough but fair.

18 holes parkland, 5,229 metres (5,751 yards), par 70 (SSS 68). Ladies 4,588 metres (5,046 yards), par 68 (SSS 67).

ADDRESS: Milltown Road, Tuam, Co. Galway.
TELEPHONE: +353 (0)93 25525/24343.
EMAIL: ardaconggc@eircom.net
VISITORS: Yes. Soft spikes.
GREEN FEES: €15 per round weekdays, €20 at weekends.
CATERING: Light refreshments available.
FACILITIES: Locker rooms, trolleys, club hire.
LOCATION: 1 mile from Tuam centre. The entrance is on the N17.

ATHENRY GOLF CLUB

Founded in 1902, this flat tree-lined course is a mixture of parkland and heathland. It was extended to 18 holes by Eddie Hackett in 1991.

18 holes parkland/heathland, 5,687 metres (6,255 yards), par 70 (SSS 70). Ladies 4,966 metres (5,462 yards), par 72.

SIGNATURE HOLE:
TWELFTH (175 metres [192 yards], par 3) – from an elevated tee through a corridor of beech and pine trees.

ADDRESS: Palmerstown, Oranmore, Co. Galway.
TELEPHONE: +353 (0)91 794466.
FAX: +353 (0)91 794971.
EMAIL: athenrygc@eircom.net
WEBSITE: www.athenrygolfclub.net
PROFESSIONAL: Raymond Ryan.
VISITORS: Yes, but not on Sundays.
GREEN FEES: €35 per round weekdays, €40 at weekends.
CREDIT CARDS ACCEPTED: Amex/ MasterCard/Visa.
CATERING: Restaurant and bar.
FACILITIES: Locker rooms, putting green, practice facilities, driving range, pro-shop, buggies, trolleys, club hire.
LOCATION: 5 miles from Athenry on the N6 (Dublin–Galway road).

BALLINASLOE GOLF CLUB

Founded in 1894, Eddie Hackett expanded this parkland course from nine to eighteen holes in 1984 with Eddie Connaughton responsible for recent improvements, notably the water features on the eleventh and twelfth.

18 holes parkland, 5,874 metres (6,461 yards), par 72 (SSS 70). Ladies 5,057 metres (5,562 yards), par 73 (SSS 72).

ADDRESS: Portumna Road, Ballinasloe, Co. Galway.
TELEPHONE: +353 (0)90 964 2126.
FAX: +353 (0)90 964 2538.
EMAIL: ballinasloegolfclub@eircom.net
WEBSITE: www.bgc.ie
VISITORS: Pre-book Mondays to Saturdays.
GREEN FEES: €25 per round weekdays, €30 at weekends.
CATERING: Restaurant and bar.
FACILITIES: Locker rooms, putting green, practice ground, driving range, buggies (€20), trolleys (€2), club hire (€20), tuition.
LOCATION: 2 miles off the N6 on the Portumna road.
LOCAL HOTELS: Haydens Hotel.

BEARNA GOLF AND COUNTRY CLUB

This course is set amidst the beauty of the west of Ireland landscape on the fringe of Connemara and enjoys commanding views of Galway Bay, the Burren, the Aran Islands and rugged hinterland. Bearna golf course, inaugurated in 1996, is already being hailed as one of Ireland's finest. The inspired creativity of its designer Robert J. Browne in the siting of tees and sand-based greens throughout more than 100 hectares of unique countryside bounded by Lough Inch has resulted in generously proportioned fairways, many elevated tees and some splendid carries. The designer has left the famine ridges undisturbed, which is clear proof of nearby habitation in the recent past. Water comes into play on 13 of the 18 holes, each one boasting unique features which test the golfer's repertoire of skills. The final four holes provide a spectacular finish.

18 holes parkland, 6,174 metres (6,791 yards), par 72 (SSS 73). Ladies 4,684 metres (5,152 yards), par 70 (SSS 70).

SIGNATURE HOLE:
ELEVENTH ('*Ionnsai na hInse*' [The Attack on Lough Inch], 350 metres [385 yards], par 4) – approach shot requires a carry over Lough Inch to a well-protected green.

ADDRESS: Corboley, Bearna, Co. Galway.
TELEPHONE: +353 (0)91 592677.
FAX: +353 (0)91 592674.
EMAIL: info@bearnagolfclub.com
WEBSITE: www.bearnagolfclub.com
VISITORS: Any day.
GREEN FEES: €35 per round Mondays to Thursdays, €50 Fridays to Sundays.
CREDIT CARDS ACCEPTED: All major cards.
CATERING: Restaurant and bar.
FACILITIES: Locker rooms, putting green, practice ground, pro-shop, buggies (€35), trolleys (€3), club hire (€25), tuition.
LOCATION: 5 miles west of Galway city. Turn right at Twelve Pins Hotel in Bearna village.
LOCAL HOTELS: Twelve Pins Hotel.

CONNEMARA GOLF LINKS

Set amidst ruggedly beautiful terrain along the Atlantic coast on the west tip of Galway, this is a challenging links with great greens. The outward nine is fairly flat, but the homeward nine is a more severe test with 17 and 18 being challenging par 5s. The 27 holes designed by Eddie Hackett have breathtaking views of the Atlantic and the Twelve Bens mountain range. Founded in 1973.

COURSES A AND B – 18 holes links, 7,055 yards, par 72 (SSS 75). Ladies 5,370 yards, par 72 (SSS 71).

COURSE C – 9 holes links, 3,145 yards, par 35. Ladies 2,495 yards, par 35.

SIGNATURE HOLE:
THIRTEENTH (212 yards, par 3) – testing short hole. From an elevated tee to a sloping green with pot bunkers all around.

ADDRESS: Ballyconneely, Co. Galway.
TELEPHONE: +353 (0)95 23502/23602.
FAX: +353 (0)95 23662.
EMAIL: links@iol.ie
WEBSITE: www.connemaragolflinks.com
SECRETARY/MANAGER: Richard Flaherty.
PROFESSIONAL: Hugh O'Neill.
VISITORS: Welcome.
GREEN FEES: €60.
CREDIT CARDS ACCEPTED: Amex/Laser/ MasterCard/Visa.
CATERING: Full bar and restaurant facilities.
FACILITIES: Locker rooms and showers, practice ground, putting green, pro-shop,

Connemara Golf Links

buggies (€35), trolleys (€3), club hire (€20).

LOCATION: Take the N59 from Galway city via Clifden and Ballyconneely. 60 miles from Galway.

LOCAL HOTELS: Abbeyglen Castle Hotel, Rockglen Hotel, Foyle's Hotel.

CONNEMARA ISLES GOLF CLUB

Founded in 1995, this beautiful parkland island course has some of the finest golf holes in the country.

9 holes parkland, 5,260 yards for 18 holes, par 70 (SSS 67). Ladies 4,368 yards, par 68 (SSS 67).

SIGNATURE HOLE:

NINTH (186 yards, par 3) – along the edge of the Atlantic, hitting over an inlet towards the whitewashed thatched cottage of the clubhouse.

ADDRESS: Lettermore, Connemara, Co. Galway.

TELEPHONE & FAX: +353 (0)91 572498.

EMAIL: clynch@eircom.net

WEBSITE: www.connemaraislesgolfclub.com

MANAGER: Tony Lynch.

VISITORS: Every day.

GREEN FEES: €20 per round weekdays, €25 at weekends.

CREDIT CARDS ACCEPTED: All major cards.

CATERING: Restaurant and bar.

FACILITIES: Locker rooms, practice area,

putting green, pro-shop, buggies, trolleys (€2), club hire (€5).

LOCATION: 25 miles from Galway city along the coast road, through Bearna, Spiddal and Forbacha; turn right at Costelloe, and the golf course is signposted (9 kilometres).

LOCAL HOTELS: Carraroe Hotel, Zetland House Hotel, Cashel +353 (0)95 31111.

CURRA WEST GOLF CLUB

Parkland course with a couple of climbs and ponds on the ninth and eighteenth holes. Founded in 1995.

18 holes parkland, 4,868 metres (5,354 yards), par 67. Ladies 4,346 metres (4,780 yards), par 70.

ADDRESS: Curra, Kylebrack, Loughrea, Co. Galway.
TELEPHONE & FAX: +353 (0)90 97 45121.
EMAIL: admin@currawest.com
WEBSITE: www.currawest.com
VISITORS: Yes. Soft spikes.
GREEN FEES: €15 per round weekdays, €20 at weekends.
CATERING: Bar (meals can be arranged).
FACILITIES: Locker rooms, putting green, practice ground, buggies, trolleys, club hire.
LOCATION: 5 miles south of Loughrea.

DUNMORE DEMESNE GOLF CLUB

A scenic parkland course, opened in 1998, and set in an old estate of mature trees. It was designed by Eddie Hackett, who described it as a 'little gem'. The ruins of the Deering Estate, known locally as Dunmore House, lie at the heart of the course.

9 holes parkland, 5,278 metres (5,805 yards) for 18 holes, par 70 (SSS 68). Ladies

4,764 metres (5,240 yards), par 70 (SSS 68).

SIGNATURE HOLE:

FIFTH ('The Cedars', 475 metres [522 yards] par 5) – a challenging hole which doglegs around a copse of trees. Possible to go for the green in two, but it is surrounded by water drains.

ADDRESS: The Green, Dunmore, Co. Galway.
TELEPHONE: +353 (0)93 38709.
EMAIL: ddgc@eircom.net
SECRETARY/MANAGER: Oliver Turner.
VISITORS: Any time. Soft spikes.
GREEN FEES: €15 per round.
CATERING: Food and presentation facilities are available locally.
FACILITIES: Locker rooms, buggies.
LOCATION: In the centre of Dunmore, 9 miles north of Tuam, 12 miles from Ballyhaunis and Claremorris.
LOCAL HOTELS: Gallaghers Hotel.

GALWAY GOLF CLUB

This tight tree-lined parkland course, designed by Dr Alister Mackenzie, has some raised greens and overlooks Galway Bay and the Burren. Established in 1895.

18 holes parkland, 6,560 yards, par 70.

ADDRESS: Blackrock, Salthill, Co. Galway.
TELEPHONE: +353 (0)91 522033/523038.
FAX: +353 (0)91 529783.
EMAIL: galwaygolf@eircom.net
WEBSITE: www.galwaygolf.com
SECRETARY/MANAGER: Padraic Fahy.
PROFESSIONAL: Don Wallace.
VISITORS: Yes.
GREEN FEES: €50 Mondays to Fridays, €60 at weekends when available.
CREDIT CARDS ACCEPTED: Yes.
CATERING: Restaurant and bar.

FACILITIES: Locker rooms, practice ground, putting green, pro-shop, buggies (€30), trolleys (€3), club hire (€20).

LOCATION: 3 miles west of Galway.

LOCAL HOTELS: Galway Bay Hotel +353 (0)91 520520, Salthill Hotel +353 (0)91 522711, Spinnaker Hotel +353 (0)91 525425.

GALWAY BAY GOLF RESORT

This championship parkland course, with the Atlantic on three sides, was designed by Christy O'Connor Jr. Only a year after its opening in 1993, it hosted the Irish Professional Championship. As you would expect, it is exposed to the elements, and there is little shelter from the winds sweeping in off the ocean.

18 holes parkland, 6,537 metres (7,190 yards), par 72 (SSS 73). Ladies 5,154 metres (5,669 yards), par 74 (SSS 73).

SIGNATURE HOLE:
THIRTEENTH (162 metres [178 yards], par 3) – Christy dedicated this hole to his famous uncle, Christy O'Connor, sen.

ADDRESS: Renville, Oranmore, Co. Galway.
TELEPHONE: +353 91 790711/2.
FAX: +353 91 792510.
EMAIL: info@galwaybaygolfresort.com
WEBSITE: www.galwaybaygolfresort.com
PROFESSIONAL: Eugene O'Connor +353 (0)91 790503.
VISITORS: Every day. Soft spikes.
GREEN FEES: €55 weekdays, €70 at weekends.
CATERING: Restaurant and bar.
FACILITIES: Locker rooms, putting green, practice ground, driving range, club shop, buggies (€25), trolleys (€3), club hire (€20), caddies on request, tuition.
LOCATION: 7 miles from Galway city.

LOCAL HOTELS: Galway Bay Hotel (on the course).

GLENLO ABBEY GOLF CLUB

Championship pay-and-play parkland course with nine fairways and large double greens. Overlooking Lough Corrib. Founded in 1996.

9 holes parkland, 6,502 yards for 18 holes, par 71 (SSS 71).

ADDRESS: Glenlo Abbey Hotel, Bushy Park, Co. Galway.
TELEPHONE: +353 (0)91 526666.
FAX: +353 (0)91 527800.
EMAIL: info@glenloabbey.ie
WEBSITE: www.glenlo.com
PROFESSIONAL: Bill Daly.
VISITORS: Yes. Soft spikes.
GREEN FEES: €20 per round weekdays, €25 at weekends.
CATERING: Restaurant and bar.
FACILITIES: Locker rooms, putting green, ten-bay driving range, pro-shop, buggies (€30), trolleys (€3), club hire (€15), tuition.
LOCATION: On the N59 Galway–Clifden road.
LOCAL HOTELS: Glenlo Abbey Hotel (on the course).

GORT GOLF CLUB

Established in 1924, a new eighteen-hole parkland course with four challenging par 3s was opened in 1996 set in 160 acres of picturesque parkland on the edge of the world-famous Burren and within 200 yards of the historic monastic settlement of Kilmacduagh.

18 holes parkland, 5,974 metres (6,571 yards), par 71 (SSS 71). Ladies 4,889 metres (5,377 yards), par 72.

Galway Bay Golf Resort

ADDRESS: Castlequarter, Gort, Co. Galway.
TELEPHONE: +353 (0)91 632244.
FAX: +353 (0)91 632387.
EMAIL: info@gortgolf.com
WEBSITE: www.gortgolf.com
SECRETARY/MANAGER: Sean Devlin.
PROFESSIONAL: Alan Devlin.
VISITORS: Yes, but telephone in advance.
GREEN FEES: €25 per round weekdays, €30
    at weekends.
CATERING: Restaurant and bar.
FACILITIES: Locker rooms, putting green,
    club shop, buggies (€25), trolleys (€2),
    club hire (€10), caddies on request.
LOCATION: Off the N18 to Galway.
LOCAL HOTELS: Lady Gregory Hotel,
    Merriman Hotel, Ardilaun House Hotel.

LOUGHREA GOLF CLUB

This parkland course with good greens was
established in 1954 and extended to 18
holes by Eddie Hackett in 1992.

18 holes parkland, 5,856 metres (6,441
yards), par 71 (SSS 70). Ladies 4,961 metres
(5,457 yards), par 72 (SSS 72).

ADDRESS: Graigue, Loughrea, Co. Galway.
TELEPHONE: +353 (0)91 841049.
FAX: +353 (0)91 847472.
EMAIL: loughreagolfclub@eircom.net
SECRETARY/MANAGER: Maura Hawkins.
VISITORS: Yes.
GREEN FEES: €25 per round.
CATERING: Restaurant and bar.
FACILITIES: Locker rooms, putting green,
    practice ground, buggies, trolleys, club
    hire.
LOCATION: On the R350, 1 mile north of
    Loughrea.
LOCAL HOTELS: Meadow Court Hotel.

MOUNTBELLEW GOLF CLUB

Founded in 1929, this natural parkland
course has water and quarry hazards.

9 holes parkland, 5,214 metres (5,735
yards) for 18 holes, par 69 (SSS 66). Ladies
4,469 metres (4,915 yards), par 70 (SSS 68).

SIGNATURE HOLE:
FIRST (155 metres [170 yards], par 3)
– bunkers on both sides of the green and
trees at the back.

ADDRESS: Shankill, Mountbellew,
    Ballinasloe, Co. Galway.
TELEPHONE: +353 (0)90 967 9259.
EMAIL: mountbellewgc@eircom.net
SECRETARY: Joe Keane.
VISITORS: Any day.
GREEN FEES: €15 per round.
CATERING: Bar and meals.
FACILITIES: Locker rooms, putting green,
    trolleys.
LOCATION: Off the N63 between
    Roscommon and Galway.

OUGHTERARD GOLF CLUB

Mature parkland course on the shores of
Lough Corrib with traditional limestone
walls, which are a main feature throughout
the 18 holes. Oughterard was founded in
1973 as a nine-hole course and upgraded to
eighteen in 1983. It has raised greens and
tree-lined fairways.

18 holes parkland, 5,876 metres (6,463
yards), par 70 (SSS 70). Ladies 4,957 metres
(5,452 yards), par 71 (SSS 70).

ADDRESS: Gortreevagh, Oughterard, Co.
    Galway.
TELEPHONE: +353 (0)91 552131.
FAX: +353 (0)91 552733.
EMAIL: oughterardgc@eircom.net

WEBSITE: www.oughterardgolf.com
PROFESSIONAL: Michael Ryan +353 (0)91 557352.
VISITORS: Always welcome. Soft spikes.
GREEN FEES: €40 weekdays and weekends.
CATERING: Restaurant and bar.
FACILITIES: Locker rooms, putting green, practice ground, pro-shop, buggies (€35), trolleys (€3), club hire, caddies on request, tuition.
LOCATION: 16 miles from Galway city off the N59 and 2 miles east of Oughterard.
LOCAL HOTELS: Lake Hotel, River Walk House, The Boat Inn.

PORTUMNA GOLF CLUB

Wooded parkland course established in 1913.

18 holes parkland, 6,222 metres (6,844 yards), par 72 (SSS 72). Ladies 5,415 metres (5,956 yards), par 74 (SSS 74).

ADDRESS: Portumna, Co. Galway.
TELEPHONE: +353 (0)90 974 1059.
FAX: +353 (0)90 974 1798.
EMAIL: portumnagc@eircom.net
PROFESSIONAL: Richard Clarke.
VISITORS: Mondays to Fridays. Soft spikes.
GREEN FEES: €30 per round weekdays, €35 at weekends.
CATERING: Restaurant and bar.
FACILITIES: Locker rooms, practice ground, golf academy, club shop, buggies (€20), trolleys (€3), club hire, tuition.
LOCATION: Off the R352, 2 miles west of Portumna.

TUAM GOLF CLUB

Founded in 1904, this mature parkland course with good greens is a test for high and low handicappers alike.

18 holes parkland, 6,077 metres (6,684 yards), par 72 (SSS 71). Ladies 4,907 metres (5,397 yards), par 72 (SSS 71).

SIGNATURE HOLE:
FIFTEENTH (151 metres [166 yards], par 3] – raised green with a lake in front and bunkers at the back.

ADDRESS: Barnacurragh, Tuam, Co. Galway.
TELEPHONE: +353 (0)93 28993/24091.
FAX: +353 (0)93 26003.
EMAIL: tuamgolfclub@eircom.net
WEBSITE: www.tuamgolfclub.com
SECRETARY/PROFESSIONAL: Mary Burns.
PROFESSIONAL: Larry Smyth +353 (0)93 24091.
VISITORS: Mondays to Fridays.
GREEN FEES: €30 per round.
CREDIT CARDS ACCEPTED: No.
CATERING: Restaurant and bar.
FACILITIES: Locker rooms, putting green, practice ground, pro-shop, buggies (€30), trolleys, club hire, tuition.
LOCATION: 22 miles from Galway city and 2 miles from Tuam on the Athenry road.
LOCAL HOTELS: Corralea Court Hotel +353 (0)93 24188.

COUNTY LEITRIM

BALLINAMORE GOLF CLUB

Challenging parkland course, designed by Dr Arthur Spring, with sand-based greens. A canal comes into play on the first, second, sixth and seventh holes. Founded in 1941.

9 holes parkland, 5,514 metres (6,033 yards) for 18 holes, par 70 (SSS 68). Ladies 4,708 metres (5,178 yards), par 70 (SSS 69).

ADDRESS: Creevy, Ballinamore, Co. Leitrim.
TELEPHONE: +353 (0)71 964 4346.
EMAIL: ballinamoregolfclub@eircom.net
WEBSITE: www.ballinamoregolfclub.com
SECRETARY/MANAGER: Eileen Blessing.
VISITORS: Yes. Soft spikes.
GREEN FEES: €20 per round.
CATERING: Bar and light refreshments.
FACILITIES: Locker rooms, club hire.
LOCATION: 1½ miles north-west of
    Ballinamore.
LOCAL HOTELS: Commercial Hotel,
    McAllisters Hotel.

COUNTY MAYO

ACHILL GOLF CLUB

Original links on the edge of the Atlantic
with 18 tees. Tough when the wind blows.
Founded in 1951.
    9 holes links, 5,424 metres (5,966 yards)
for 18 holes, par 70 (SSS 67). Ladies 4,640
metres (5,104 yards), par 72 (SSS 68).

ADDRESS: Keel, Achill, Co. Mayo.
TELEPHONE: +353 (0)98 43456.
EMAIL: achillgolfclub@eircom.net
SECRETARY/MANAGER: Seán Connolly.
VISITORS: Yes.
GREEN FEES: €15 per round weekdays, €20
    at weekends.
CATERING: Restaurant and bars nearby.
FACILITIES: Locker rooms, putting green,
    practice ground, buggies, trolleys.
LOCAL HOTELS: Atlantic Hotel, McDowall's
    Hotel, Slievemore Hotel, Strand Hotel.

ASHFORD CASTLE GOLF COURSE

Designed by Eddie Hackett with imaginative
integration of natural features and hazards,
the course has some tough par 3s and a
difficult par 5.
    9 holes parkland, 2,996 yards, par 35.

ADDRESS: Ashford Castle, Cong, Co. Mayo.
TELEPHONE: +353 (0)94 954 6003.
FAX: +353 (0)94 954 6260.
EMAIL: ashford@ashford.ie
WEBSITE: www.ashford.ie
VISITORS: Yes.
GREEN FEES: €50 to include club hire and
    buggy. Residents free.
CREDIT CARDS ACCEPTED: All major cards.
CATERING: Restaurant and bar.
FACILITIES: Locker rooms, putting green,
    buggies, trolleys, tuition.
LOCAL HOTELS: Ashford Castle Hotel (on
    the course).

BALLINA GOLF CLUB

Established in 1910, this is a mostly flat
parkland course. Designed by Eddie
Hackett.
    18 holes parkland, 6,132 yards, par 71
(SSS 69). Ladies 5,263 yards, par 72 (SSS
70).

ADDRESS: Mossgrove, Shanaghy, Ballina,
    Co. Mayo.
TELEPHONE: +353 (0)96 21050.
FAX: +353 (0)96 21718.
EMAIL: ballinagc@eircom.net
WEBSITE: www.ballina-golf.com
VISITORS: Every day, except Sunday
    mornings.
GREEN FEES: €30 per round weekdays, €40
    weekends and public holidays.
CATERING: Restaurant and bar.
FACILITIES: Locker rooms, putting green,

practice area, pro-shop, buggies (€30), trolleys (€3), club hire.
LOCATION: Off the R294, 1 mile east of Ballina.
LOCAL HOTELS: Clarinbridge Court Hotel, Quality Hotel.

BALLINROBE GOLF CLUB

Established in 1895, this championship parkland course, designed by Eddie Hackett, is set in the mature woodlands of the historic 300-acre estate surrounding Clooncastle Tower House, which was built circa 1238. It features seven man-made lakes, contoured sand-based greens, traditional stone walls and the River Robe. Ryder Cup star Padraig Harrington says, 'This must be the finest course in the west of Ireland. The par 3s in particular are a delight. My favourite is the fifth which has a marvellous green inset into the River Robe. The tenth hole (set beside the medieval Tower House) has an island green needing a very precise choice of club.'

18 holes parkland, 6,854 yards, par 73 (SSS 72).

SIGNATURE HOLE:
TENTH (401 yards, par 4) – demanding driving hole with out of bounds running down the entire left-hand side.

ADDRESS: Clooncastle, Ballinrobe, Co. Mayo.
TELEPHONE: +353 (0)94 954 1118.
FAX: +353 (0)94 954 1889.
EMAIL: info@ballinrobegolfclub.com
WEBSITE: www.ballinrobegolfclub.com
MANAGER: John McMahon.
PROFESSIONAL: Kortney Kruegar.
VISITORS: Yes.
GREEN FEES: €28 weekdays, €33 at weekends.

CREDIT CARDS ACCEPTED: Yes.
CATERING: Restaurant and bar.
FACILITIES: Locker rooms, 12-bay floodlit driving range, practice ground, putting green, pro-shop, buggies (€30), trolleys (€3), club hire (€25).
LOCATION: Take Claremorris Road from Ballinrobe. The course is 3 kilometres on the right.
LOCAL HOTELS: Fairhill House Hotel +353 (0)94 954 6176.

BALLYHAUNIS GOLF CLUB

This undulating parkland course is playable all year. The elevated greens are protected by well-positioned bunkers and attractive spinneys. Founded in 1928.

9 holes parkland, 5,443 metres (5,987 yards) for 18 holes, par 70 (SSS 68). Ladies 4,898 metres (5,387 yards), par 72 (SSS 69).

ADDRESS: Coolnaha, Ballyhaunis, Co. Mayo.
TELEPHONE: +353 (0)94 963 0014.
EMAIL: ballyhaunisgc1@eircom.net
SECRETARY/MANAGER: Tom Prenty.
VISITORS: Mondays to Fridays.
GREEN FEES: €20 per round.
CATERING: Bar and snacks.
FACILITIES: Locker rooms, putting green, driving range, trolleys (€2).
LOCATION: On the N83, 2 miles from Ballyhaunis.

CARNE GOLF LINKS

Carne's Belmullet links is a glorious adventure. It is Eddie Hackett's last links course – and many believe his greatest. The present roller-coaster of a course opened in 1995 and is set amongst towering dunes, some as high as 70 feet, on the edge of the Atlantic. Hackett said, 'If ever the Lord intended land for a golf course, Carne was

The 16th at Carne Golf Links

it.' There are many blind tee shots to deep valleys, deceptive doglegs and approaches to elevated greens. Carne demands accuracy on the back nine, where the capricious Atlantic wind makes the 11th, 14th and 17th holes, in particular, exacting.

18 holes links, 6,119 metres (6,730 yards), par 72 (SSS 72). Ladies 4,724 metres (5,196 yards), par 73 (SSS 73).

SIGNATURE HOLE:
SIXTEENTH (154 metres [169 yards], par 3) – the green is well below you nestling in a hollow and can be deceptive for distance. Stray off the tee and you might land in the wild orchids after which the hole is named.

There is a huge exposed sand dune on the tee.

ADDRESS: Carne, Belmullet, Co. Mayo.
TELEPHONE: +353 (0)97 82292.
FAX: +353 (0)97 81477.
EMAIL: carngolf@iol.ie
WEBSITE: www.carnegolflinks.com
RESERVATIONS: Mary Tallott.
VISITORS: Any time.
GREEN FEES: €55 per day weekdays, €60 per round weekends and public holidays.
CREDIT CARDS ACCEPTED: All major cards.
CATERING: Restaurant and bar.
FACILITIES: Locker rooms, putting green, practice ground, club shop, buggies

(€35), trolleys (€3), club hire (€8), caddies on request (€35), tuition.

LOCATION: The course is 1½ miles west of Belmullet.

LOCAL HOTELS: Broadhaven Bay Hotel, Belmullet +353 (0)97 20600, Pontoon Bridge Hotel, Pontoon +353 (0)94 925 6120, Teach Iorrais Hotel, Ballina +353 (0)97 86888, Western Strands Hotel, Belmullet +353 (0)97 81096, The Downhill Hotel, Ballina +353 (0)96 21033, Stella Maris Hotel, Ballycastle +353 (0)96 43322, The Sea Rod Inn, Doohoma +353 (0)97 86767.

CASTLEBAR GOLF CLUB

Mature parkland course in a gentle rural setting. Founded in 1910 and redesigned in 2001 by Peter McEvoy with USGA specification greens.

18 holes parkland, 5,907 metres (6,497 yards), par 71 (SSS 71). Ladies 4,840 metres (5,324 yards), par 72 (SSS 71).

ADDRESS: Hawthorn Avenue, Rocklands, Castlebar, Co. Mayo.

TELEPHONE: +353 (0)94 902 1649.

FAX: +353 (0)94 902 6088.

EMAIL: info@castlebargolfclub.ie

WEBSITE: www.castlebargolfclub.ie

SECRETARY/MANAGER: Joe Staunton.

VISITORS: Thursdays, Fridays and Saturdays are best. Soft spikes.

GREEN FEES: €25 per round weekdays, €32 weekends.

CATERING: Restaurant and bar.

FACILITIES: Locker rooms, putting green, buggies, trolleys, club hire, caddies on request.

LOCATION: Off the N84, 2 miles south-east of Castlebar.

CLAREMORRIS GOLF CLUB

This is a picturesque parkland course with mature trees, water features and rolling hills. Founded 1917 and upgraded to 18 holes in 1998.

18 holes parkland, 6,143 metres (6,757 yards), par 73 (SSS 73). Ladies 4,882 metres (5,370 yards), par 73 (SSS 72).

SIGNATURE HOLE:

SIXTH (440 yards, par 4) – testing hole with the tee on the highest point of the course offering stunning views of Caltra Hill.

ADDRESS: Castlemagarrett, Claremorris, Co. Mayo.

TELEPHONE: +353 (0)94 937 1527.

FAX: +353 (0)94 937 2919.

EMAIL: info@claremorrisgolfclub.com

WEBSITE: www.claremorrisgolfclub.com

SECRETARY/MANAGER: Christina Rush.

VISITORS: Welcome. Soft spikes.

GREEN FEES: €32 per round weekdays, €40 at weekends.

CATERING: Restaurant and bar.

FACILITIES: Locker rooms, putting green, practice ground, buggies (€20), trolleys (€3), club hire (€7).

LOCATION: The course is 1½ miles from Claremorris.

CLEW BAY GOLF COURSE

The course is located in an area of outstanding scenic grandeur with panoramic views of Clew Bay, its islands and Croagh Patrick. A challenge for the proficient golfer and ideal for beginners.

9 holes parkland, 2,774 yards, par 35.

SIGNATURE HOLE:

FIFTH (492 yards, par 5) – plays along an

inlet of Clew Bay, demanding an accurate tee shot and a courageous second.

ADDRESS: Claggan, Kilmeena, Westport, Co. Mayo.
TELEPHONE: +353 (0)98 41730/41739.
EMAIL: clewbaygc@eircom.net
WEBSITE: www.clewbaygolf.com
VISITORS: Yes.
GREEN FEES: €15 per 18 holes.
CATERING: Restaurant and bar.
FACILITIES: Locker rooms, trolleys, club hire.
LOCATION: The course is 5 miles from the centre of Westport.
LOCAL HOTELS: Clew Bay Hotel.

MULRANNY GOLF CLUB

Founded in 1896, this is a natural links course with undulating greens overlooking Clew Bay.
    9 holes links, 5,729 metres (6,301 yards) for 18 holes, par 71 (SSS 69). Ladies 4,368 metres (4,804 yards), par 71 (SSS 69).

ADDRESS: Mulranny, Westport, Co. Mayo.
TELEPHONE: +353 (0)98 36262.
SECRETARY: Declan Nevin.
VISITORS: Yes.
GREEN FEES: €20 per round.
CATERING: Restaurant and bar.
FACILITIES: Locker rooms, buggies (€20), trolleys (€2), club hire (€7).
LOCATION: 15 miles from Westport.

SWINFORD GOLF CLUB

A pleasant parkland course established in early 1910 with difficult par 3s. Holes two and four have recently been upgraded and are now very challenging.
    9 holes parkland, 5,245 metres (5,769 yards) for 18 holes, par 70 (SSS 68).

Ladies 4,245 metres (4,669 yards), par 70 (SSS 68).

SIGNATURE HOLE:
FOURTH (159 metres [174 yards], par 3) – tougher than it may appear at first glance. Trouble left and right with bunkers. Elevated green.

ADDRESS: Brabazon Park, Swinford, Co. Mayo.
TELEPHONE & FAX: +353 (0)92 51378.
EMAIL: regantommy@eircom.net
WEBSITE: www.swinfordgolf.com
SECRETARY/MANAGER: John Sheahan.
VISITORS: Welcome any time of week or weekend but best to avoid early on Sundays.
GREEN FEES: €20 per day.
CREDIT CARDS ACCEPTED: No.
CATERING: By arrangement.
FACILITIES: Locker rooms, practice ground, putting green, trolleys (€2.50).
LOCATION: Only 7 miles from Knock International Airport and 1 mile from the town centre on the Kiltimagh road.
LOCAL HOTELS: The Gateway Hotel +353 (0)92 51328.

WESTPORT GOLF CLUB

A championship course, Westport hosted the 2002 Irish PGA Championship and the Irish Amateur Championship. Although beside the sea, it is not a links course; instead, it is almost pure parkland. Situated in 260 acres with a well-balanced combination of holes, Croagh Patrick and Clew Bay also provide a majestic backdrop. It is a course of two distinct halves: the opening nine is straightforward but the long back nine calls for character. The 15th is an outstanding hole but the 231-yard par-3 12th is almost as challenging, with a tee high on an outcrop with the green 150 feet below. Designed by Fred Hawtree, who also planned the New Course at St Andrews, this course boasts lush fairways and excellent greens. Hawtree says, 'Part inland, part seaside . . . its golfing virtues combine to make Westport uniquely attractive and memorable.'

18 holes parkland, 7,000 yards, par 73 (SSS 74). Ladies 5,625 yards, par 74 (SSS 73).

SIGNATURE HOLE:
FIFTEENTH ('The Reek', 560 yards, par 5) – demands a carry of 200 yards over an inlet of Clew Bay to reach the fairway from a sheltered tee. Sloping fairway with out of bounds all along the left. Well-protected green with bunkers on the left.

ADDRESS: Carrowholly, Westport, Co. Mayo.
TELEPHONE: +353 (0)98 28262.
FAX: +353 (0)98 27217.
EMAIL: wpgolf@eircom.net
WEBSITE: www.golfwestport.com
SECRETARY/MANAGER: Paul O'Neill.
PROFESSIONAL: Alex Mealia.
VISITORS: Welcome every day.
GREEN FEES: €42 per round Mondays to Thursdays, €55 Fridays to Sundays.
CREDIT CARDS ACCEPTED: Yes.
CATERING: Full catering facilities available all year.
FACILITIES: Locker rooms, practice ground, putting green, pro-shop, nine-bay floodlit driving range, buggies (€30), trolleys (€3), club hire (€25).
LOCATION: 2 miles from Westport town.
LOCAL HOTELS: Hotel Westport +353 98 25122, Castlecourt Hotel +353 98 25444.

COUNTY ROSCOMMON

ATHLONE GOLF CLUB

Championship parkland course founded in 1892 and bounded on three sides by the waters of Lough Ree. Its tree-lined fairways and natural undulating terrain make it a true test of golf. The par 3s are particularly difficult. The course exploits the natural beauty of the area, affording panoramic views of the lake from some vantage points and from the modern clubhouse. Athlone has hosted many provincial and national championships, and the Athlone Senior Scratch Cup has been won by many notable golfers, including Padraig Harrington and John O'Leary.

18 holes parkland, 5,973 metres (6,570 yards), par 71 (SSS 72). Ladies 5,045 metres (5,549 yards), par 74 (SSS 73).

SIGNATURE HOLE:
SIXTEENTH (408 metres [448 yards], par 4) – a narrow, tree-lined fairway slopes gently towards a lake on the left with out of bounds on the right. There is a slight dogleg left with the fairway narrowing as you approach the green. The green is protected by a bunker on the right and there is danger both behind and to the left.

ADDRESS: Hodson Bay, Athlone, Co. Roscommon.
TELEPHONE: +353 (0)90 649 2073.
FAX: +353 (0)90 649 4080.
EMAIL: athlonegolfclub@eircom.net
PROFESSIONAL: Kevin Grealy.
VISITORS: Every day but avoid Tuesdays (ladies) and Sundays (competitions).

GREEN FEES: €30 per round weekdays, €35 at weekends.
CATERING: Restaurant and bar.
FACILITIES: Locker rooms, putting green, practice ground, pro-shop, buggies (€25), trolleys (€3), club hire (€15), caddies by arrangement, tuition.
LOCATION: 4 miles from Athlone on the N61 to Roscommon. Take the Hodson Bay junction.
LOCAL HOTELS: Hodson Bay Hotel (adjoining the course).

BALLAGHADERREEN GOLF CLUB

This mature parkland course was founded in 1936. A profusion of trees demands accuracy off the tee, and the greens are small and well protected.

9 holes parkland, 5,339 metres (5,872 yards) for 18 holes, par 70 (SSS 67). Ladies 4,602 metres (5,062 yards), par 70 (SSS 68).

ADDRESS: Aughalustia, Ballaghaderreen, Co. Roscommon.
TELEPHONE: +353 (0)94 986 0295.
EMAIL: corki@iol.ie
WEBSITE: www.ballaghaderreen.com/golf
SECRETARY/MANAGER: John Cawley.
VISITORS: Yes.
GREEN FEES: €15 per round.
CATERING: Bar.
FACILITIES: Locker rooms, putting green, practice facilities, trolleys.
LOCATION: 3 miles west of Ballaghaderreen.

BOYLE GOLF CLUB

Parkland course situated on a low hill with generous fairways and semi-rough. Founded in 1911 and designed by Eddie Hackett.

9 holes parkland, 4,920 metres (5,412 yards) for 18 holes, par 67 (SSS 64). Ladies 4,700 metres (5,170 yards), par 69 (SSS 69).

ADDRESS: Knockadoobrusna, Boyle, Co. Roscommon.
TELEPHONE: +353 (0)71 966 2594.
SECRETARY/MANAGER: Jim Mooney.
VISITORS: Yes.
GREEN FEES: €15 per round.
CATERING: Restaurant and bar.
FACILITIES: Locker rooms, putting green, practice ground, club hire.
LOCATION: On the N61, 2 miles south of Boyle.
LOCAL HOTELS: Forest Park Hotel, Royal Hotel.

CARRICK-ON-SHANNON GOLF CLUB

Founded in 1910, this parkland course overlooks the River Shannon and Drumharlow Lake. Designed by Eddie Hackett to USGA specifications and expanded to 18 holes in 2003.

18 holes parkland, 5,787 metres (6,365 yards), par 70 (SSS 70).

ADDRESS: Woodbrook, Carrick-on-Shannon, Co. Roscommon.
TELEPHONE & FAX: +353 (0)71 966 7015.
EMAIL: ckgc3@eircom.net
WEBSITE: www.carrickgolfclub.ie
SECRETARY/MANAGER: Chris Lowe.
VISITORS: Yes. Soft spikes.
GREEN FEES: €30 per round Mondays to Thursdays, €40 Fridays to Sundays.
CATERING: Restaurant and bar.
FACILITIES: Locker rooms, putting green, driving range, buggies, trolleys, club hire.
LOCATION: On the N4, 5 miles north-west of Carrick.

CASTLEREA GOLF CLUB

Parkland course near the centre of town. Founded in 1904.

9 holes parkland, 5,154 metres (5,669

yards) for 18 holes, par 68 (SSS 66). Ladies 4,240 metres (4,664 yards), par 68 (SSS 68).

ADDRESS: Clonalis, Castlerea, Co. Roscommon.
TELEPHONE: +353 (0)94 962 0068.
FAX: +353 (0)94 962 1214.
EMAIL: castlereagolf@oceanfree.net
SECRETARY/MANAGER: Maura Tully.
VISITORS: Yes.
GREEN FEES: €15 per round.
CATERING: Bar.
FACILITIES: Locker rooms, putting green, driving range, practice ground.
LOCATION: On the main Dublin–Castlebar road.
LOCAL HOTELS: Abbey Hotel.

ROSCOMMON GOLF CLUB

Formidable full-length championship parkland course, set in woodland and featuring a number of man-made lakes with greenside water on three holes. Many long par 4s of which the 444-yard tenth is the toughest hole on the course, being uphill with trees on both sides of the fairway. The course was extended from nine to eighteen holes in 1996.

18 holes parkland, 6,059 metres (6,664 yards) off the championship tees, or 5,901 metres (6,491 yards) off the medal tees, par 72 (SSS 70). Ladies 5,045 metres (5,549 yards), par 74.

SIGNATURE HOLE:
FIFTEENTH (368 metres [404 yards], par 4) – drive to a downhill fairway, trying to avoid water on the right and sand on the left. The approach is to a two-tiered green.

ADDRESS: Mote Park, Roscommon, Co. Roscommon.
TELEPHONE: +353 (0)90 662 6382.
FAX: +353 (0)90 662 6043.
EMAIL: rosgolfclub@eircom.net
VISITORS: Yes.
GREEN FEES: €30 weekdays, €35 at weekends.
CATERING: Restaurant and bar.
FACILITIES: Locker rooms, practice ground, putting green, buggies (€20), trolleys (€5).
LOCATION: Take the N4 to Kinnegad, the N6 to Athlone and the N61 to Roscommon. From the town centre, take Rahara Road. The club is on the left, 1 mile from the roundabout.
LOCAL HOTELS: Abbey Hotel, Hannons Oakwood Hotel, O'Gara's Royal Hotel.

STROKESTOWN GOLF CLUB

Founded in 1995, the club moved to a new location at Bumlin in 1999. It is a flat parkland course set in the side of a hill, which is a famous Irish archaeological site.

9 holes parkland, 5,256 metres (5,781 yards) for 18 holes, par 70 (SSS 66).

ADDRESS: Strokestown, Co. Roscommon.
TELEPHONE: +353 (0)71 963 3528.
PROFESSIONAL: Dave Byrne.
VISITORS: Welcome. Soft spikes.
GREEN FEES: €15 weekdays and weekends.
FACILITIES: Buggies, club hire.
LOCATION: 1 mile out of Strokestown on the Dublin–Westport road.

COUNTY SLIGO

BALLYMOTE GOLF CLUB

Established in 1940, this undulating parkland course was opened in 1993.

9 holes parkland, 5,281 metres (5,809 yards) for 18 holes, par 70 (SSS 68). Ladies 4,647 metres (5,111 yards), par 72 (SSS 70).

ADDRESS: Ballinascarrow, Ballymote, Co. Sligo.
TELEPHONE: +353 (0)71 918 3504/3089.
WEBSITE: www.ballymotegolfclub.ie
SECRETARY/MANAGER: John O'Connor.
VISITORS: Very welcome at all times.
GREEN FEES: €20 per day.
CATERING: Tea and coffee.
FACILITIES: Locker rooms, putting green, buggies, trolleys, club hire.
LOCATION: Off the N4, 14 miles south of Sligo.
LOCAL HOTELS: Sligo Park Hotel, Tower Hotel.

COUNTY SLIGO GOLF CLUB (ROSSES POINT)

When Christy O'Connor, sen., claims a certain hole is one of the finest in Ireland, you'd better believe it. That's his opinion of the 455-yard 17th at County Sligo Golf Club, also known as Rosses Point. Like all good holes, this one demands accuracy. The drive to a small landing area has to be precise to set up a long uphill approach to an amphitheatre green. Not that this is a one-hole course. County Sligo, founded in 1894 and reworked by Harry Colt in 1929, is one of Ireland's great championship links, set above three large beaches on the Atlantic coast in the shadow of Ben Bulben, Ireland's version of Table Mountain.

The term 'undulating' is almost an understatement when describing this course. The first rises gracefully to a protected green, but then the hard work begins with a steep climb to the second. Once there, you feel as if you're on top of the world with a spectacular view of Ben Bulben. Next it's downhill, until the short fourth up to a plateau green. Pause on the fifth tee and take in a simply breathtaking view of the vast plain rolling out before you. Then it's downhill again. The seventh has a hazard of a different kind with any weak approach shot falling into a stream just before the green. At just over 400 yards, the dogleg eighth has the stream popping up again.

The difficult 178-yard 13th across the bay and the testing 433-yard 14th, reputedly Tom Watson's favourite, are a brace of holes that can make a dent in the best of cards, especially when the wind blows. The 15th has a long carry over dunes, and there is little respite at the 16th, the longest par 3 at 216 yards, or the 17th. By the course's standards, the final hole is a reasonably gentle 369-yarder, but after the exertions that preceded it, you will welcome the respite.

18 holes links, 6,041 metres (6,645 yards), par 71 (SSS 72). Ladies 5,259 metres (5,784 yards), par 75. Plus 9-hole Bowmore Course, par 35.

SIGNATURE HOLE:
SEVENTEENTH (414 metres [455 yards], par 4).

ADDRESS: Rosses Point, Co. Sligo.
TELEPHONE: +353 (0)71 917 7134.
FAX: +353 (0)71 917 7460.
EMAIL: jim@countysligogolfclub.ie

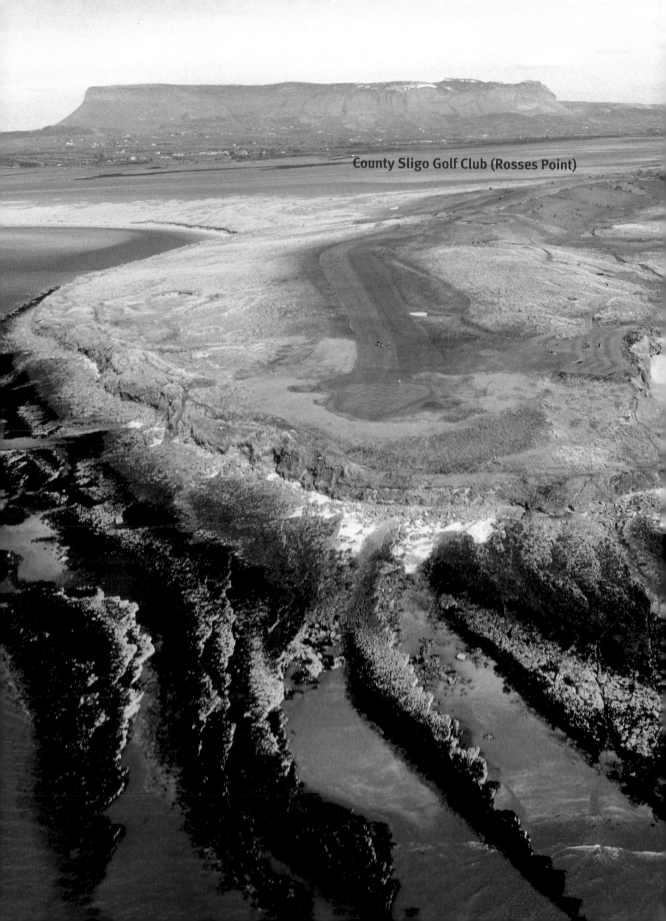

County Sligo Golf Club (Rosses Point)

WEBSITE: www.countysligogolfclub.ie
MANAGER: Jim Ironside.
PROFESSIONAL: Jim Robinson +353 (0)71 917 7171.
VISITORS: Yes, every day. Soft spikes.
GREEN FEES: €70 per round Mondays to Thursdays, €85 Fridays to Sundays; Bowmore Course – €25 for nine holes, €40 for eighteen.
CREDIT CARDS ACCEPTED: MasterCard/Visa.
CATERING: Restaurant and bar.
FACILITIES: Locker rooms, putting green, practice ground, driving range, club shop, buggies (€30), trolleys (€4), club hire (€25), caddies on request, tuition.
LOCATION: Off the R291, 5 miles north of Sligo.
LOCAL HOTELS: Yeats Country Hotel and Leisure Club, Rosses Point +353 (0)71 917 7211, Innisfree Hotel, Sligo +353 (0)71 914 2014, Riverside Hotel, Sligo +353 (0)71 914 8080, Sligo Park Hotel, Sligo +353 (0)71 916 0291, Tower Hotel, Sligo +353 (0)71 914 4000, Clarence Hotel, Sligo +353 (0)71 914 2211, Radisson SAS Hotel, Rosses Point +353 (0)71 914 0008.

ENNISCRONE GOLF CLUB

This championship links course on the shores of Killala Bay has breathtaking views. The traditional links wind through mountainous dunes, and there are many interesting holes which will require you to use all your clubs to negotiate. Founded in 1918, the course was extended to 18 holes by Eddie Hackett in 1974. Recently, a further nine holes were added, designed by Donald Steel.

THE DUNES – 18 holes links, 6,948 yards, par 73 (SSS 73). Ladies 5,634 yards, par 73 (SSS 72).

THE SCURMORE COURSE – 9 holes links, 6,734 yards for 18 holes, par 72.

ADDRESS: Enniscrone, Co. Sligo.
TELEPHONE: +353 (0)96 36297.
FAX: +353 (0)96 36657.
EMAIL: enniscronegolf@eircom.net
WEBSITE: www.enniscronegolf.com
SECRETARY/MANAGER: Michael Staunton.
PROFESSIONAL: Charlie McGoldrick +353 (0)96 36666.
VISITORS: By arrangement – weekdays best.
GREEN FEES: €55 per round weekdays, €70 weekends and public holidays.
CREDIT CARDS ACCEPTED: All major cards.
CATERING: Restaurant and bar.
FACILITIES: Locker rooms, putting green, practice area, driving range, golf shop, buggies (€35), trolleys (€3.50), club hire (€20), caddies available at weekends and during school holidays, tuition.
LOCATION: Off the R297 Enniscrone road, 7 miles from Ballina, 35 miles from Knock Airport and 34 miles from Sligo Regional Airport.
LOCAL HOTELS: Benbulben Hotel, Castle Hotel, Downhill House Hotel.

STRANDHILL GOLF CLUB

This links course is situated between Knocknarea Mountain and the Atlantic. Accuracy is required as the first, sixteenth and eighteenth are par 4s of more than 400 yards. There are also some testing par 3s made more difficult by the wind. Christy O'Connor, sen., on his first visit to the course, described it as 'the hidden jewel of the West'. Established in 1931.

18 holes links, 5,675 metres (6,242 yards), par 69 (SSS 69). Ladies 5,020 metres (5,522 yards), par 72 (SSS 71).

Enniscrone Golf Club

ADDRESS: Strandhill, Co. Sligo.
TELEPHONE: +353 (0)71 916 8188.
FAX: +353 (0)71 916 8811.
EMAIL: strandhillgc@eircom.net
WEBSITE: www.strandhillgc.com
PROFESSIONAL: Anthony Gray +353 (0)71 916 8725.
VISITORS: Weekdays. Soft spikes.
GREEN FEES: €40 per round weekdays, €50 at weekends.
CREDIT CARDS ACCEPTED: All major cards.
CATERING: Restaurant and bar.
FACILITIES: Locker rooms, putting green, driving range, club shop, buggies (€25), trolleys (€4), club hire (€25), tuition.
LOCATION: 5 miles west of Sligo.
LOCAL HOTELS: Ocean View Hotel, Tower Hotel.

TUBBERCURRY GOLF CLUB

Parkland course at the foot of the Ox Mountains with a particularly testing par-3 eighth hole. Established in 1991 and designed by Eddie Hackett.

9 holes parkland, 5,531 metres (6,084 yards) for 18 holes, par 70 (SSS 69). Ladies 4,855 metres (5,340 yards), par 72.

ADDRESS: Tubbercurry, Co. Sligo.
TELEPHONE: +353 (0)71 918 5849.
EMAIL: contact@tubbercurrygolfclub.com
WEBSITE: www.tubbercurrygolfclub.com
VISITORS: Yes.
GREEN FEES: €20 per round.
CATERING: Restaurant and bar.
LOCATION: On the N17 main Galway–Sligo–Derry route. Half a mile outside Tubbercurry.
LOCAL HOTELS: Conleys Hotel.

Northern Ireland

BELFAST

BALMORAL GOLF CLUB

This is a reasonably flat, tree-lined parkland course with a stream coming into play. It is the only course in Ireland that can boast of having bred an Open champion, Fred Daly. Established in 1914.

18 holes parkland, 6,276 yards, par 69 (SSS 70). Ladies 5,562 yards, par 71 (SSS 71).

ADDRESS: 518 Lisburn Rd, Belfast BT9 6GX.
TELEPHONE: +44 (0)28 9038 1514.
FAX: +44 (0)28 9066 6759.
EMAIL: enquiries@balmoralgolf.com
WEBSITE: www.balmoralgolf.com
PROFESSIONAL: Geoff Bleakley.
VISITORS: Welcome.
GREEN FEES: £25 per round weekdays, £35 at weekends.
CATERING: Restaurant and bar.
FACILITIES: Locker rooms, putting green, practice facilities, pro-shop, trolleys, club hire, caddies on request, tuition.
LOCATION: 3 miles south of Belfast city centre, next door to the King's Hall at Balmoral.
LOCAL HOTELS: Beechlawn Hotel.

BELVOIR PARK GOLF CLUB

This classic parkland course, with fairways lined with spruce, was founded in 1927 and designed by Harry Colt, architect of Wentworth's West Course. Belvoir (pronounced 'beaver') has staged many professional championships, including the Irish Open. There are two loops of nine and three tough holes to finish.

18 holes parkland, 6,597 yards, par 71 (SSS 71). Ladies 5,609 yards, par 73.

SIGNATURE HOLE:
EIGHTEENTH (408 yards, par 4) – demands an accurate drive, with a dogleg to the right and trees blocking all but the most perfect placement.

ADDRESS: 73 Church Road, Newtownbreda, Belfast BT8 7AN.
TELEPHONE: +44 (0)28 9049 1693.
FAX: +44 (0)28 9064 6113.
EMAIL: info@belvoirparkgolfclub.com
WEBSITE: www.belvoirparkgolfclub.com
PROFESSIONAL: Michael McGivern +44 (0)28 9064 6714.
VISITORS: Mondays, Tuesday and Thursdays are best.
GREEN FEES: £45 per round weekdays, £55 at weekends.
CREDIT CARDS ACCEPTED: MasterCard/Visa.
CATERING: Restaurant and bar.
FACILITIES: Locker rooms, practice range, pro-shop, buggies, trolleys, club hire, tuition.
LOCATION: 4 miles from Belfast, off the Ormeau road.
LOCAL HOTELS: Stormont Hotel.

CASTLEREAGH HILLS GOLF CLUB

Formerly known as Gilnahirk Golf Club, this parkland course established in 1983 was upgraded to 18 holes in 2005, designed by David Jones.

18 holes parkland, medal tees 5,420 metres (5,962 yards), par 67 (SSS 67).

ADDRESS: Manns Corner, Upper Braniel Road, Gilnahirk, Belfast BT5 7TX.
TELEPHONE: +44 (0)28 9044 8477.

HONORARY SECRETARY: Andy Carson.
PROFESSIONAL: Kenny Gray.
VISITORS: Yes.
GREEN FEES: £15 weekdays, £25 at
   weekends.
CATERING: Restaurant and bar.
FACILITIES: Locker rooms, pro-shop, club
   hire.
LOCATION: 3 miles from Belfast off the
   Ballygowan road.
LOCAL HOTELS: Lamorne House, Stormont
   Hotel.

CLIFTONVILLE GOLF CLUB

Founded in 1911, this is a parkland course
with a river providing water hazards.
   9 holes parkland, 6,232 yards for 18
holes, par 70 (SSS 70). Ladies 5,818 yards,
par 74 (SSS 73).

ADDRESS: 44 Westland Road, Belfast BT14
   6NH.
TELEPHONE: +44 (0)28 9074 6595.
EMAIL: cliftonvillegolfclub@hotmail.co.uk
WEBSITE: www.cliftonvillegolfclub.com
PROFESSIONAL: Peter Hanna.
VISITORS: Welcome except on Saturdays
   and only with a member on Sundays.
GREEN FEES: £14 per round weekdays.
CATERING: Bar facilities.
FACILITIES: Locker rooms, practice range,
   club hire.
LOCATION: from Belfast, take the Antrim
   road for 2 miles, then turn into Cavehill
   Road and left again at the fire station.
LOCAL HOTELS: Lansdowne Court Hotel.

COLIN VALLEY GOLF CENTRE

Formerly known as the Old Dunmurry
Golf Course, the Colin Glen Trust took
over the management of the land in 1994
and restructured the old eighteen holes

as a nine-hole mature parkland course,
featuring the Colin Glen River, densely
wooded plantations and USGA specification
greens.
   9 holes parkland, 5,002 yards for 18
holes, par 68 (SSS 65). Ladies 4,300 yards,
par 68 (SSS 63).

ADDRESS: 115 Black's Road, Belfast BT10
   0NF.
TELEPHONE: +44 (0)28 9060 1133.
FAX: +44 (0)28 9060 1694.
EMAIL: colinvalleygolf@btconnect.com
SECRETARY/MANAGER: Joe McCaffrey.
VISITORS: Welcome.
GREEN FEES: £7.50 weekdays, £9.50 at
   weekends.
FACILITIES: Locker rooms, trolleys, club
   hire, golf shop.
LOCATION: 4 miles west of Belfast city centre,
   with easy access via all major arterial
   routes: M1, Black's Road, Stewartstown
   Road, Lisburn Road.
LOCAL HOTELS: Beechlawn House Hotel.

DUNMURRY GOLF CLUB

This testing parkland course was founded in
1905 and designed by T.J. McAuley.
   18 holes parkland, 6,178 yards, par 70
(SSS 69). Ladies 5,471 yards, par 71 (SSS
72).

ADDRESS: 91 Dunmurry Lane, Dunmurry,
   Belfast BT17 9JS.
TELEPHONE: +44 (0)28 9061 0834.
FAX: +44 (0)28 9060 2540.
EMAIL: dunmurrygc@hotmail.com
WEBSITE: www.dunmurrygolfclub.co.uk
PROFESSIONAL: John Dolan +44 (0)28 9062
   1314.
MANAGER: Tony Cassidy.
VISITORS: Welcome – Mondays and
   Thursdays are best.

GREEN FEES: £27 per round weekdays, £37 at weekends.
CATERING: Restaurant and bar.
FACILITIES: Locker rooms, putting green, practice ground, practice facilities, trolleys, club hire.
LOCATION: From the M1, follow the signs to Dunmurry. Between Upper Malone Road and Lisburn Road, off the B103.
LOCAL HOTELS: Beech Lawn Hotel, Balmoral Hotel.

FORTWILLIAM GOLF CLUB

The club was founded in 1891 (members were allowed to play the nine-hole course only between November and March because the owner required the land for grazing). The club moved to its present site in 1903, and a new parkland course was constructed by the Royal County Down professional Cuthbert Butchart in only a day. In 1923, the course was extended to 18 holes.

18 holes parkland, 6,030 yards, par 70 (SSS 69). Ladies 5,537 yards, par 74 (SSS 72).

ADDRESS: 8a Downview Avenue, Belfast BT15 4EZ.
TELEPHONE: +44 (0)28 9037 0770.
FAX: +44 (0)28 9078 1891.
EMAIL: administrator@fortwilliam.co.uk
WEBSITE: www.fortwilliam.co.uk
PROFESSIONAL: Peter Hanna +44 (0)28 9077 0980.
VISITORS: Welcome – weekday mornings are best.
GREEN FEES: £22 per round weekdays, £29 at weekends.
CATERING: Restaurant and bar.
FACILITIES: Locker rooms, putting green, practice ground, buggies (£12), trolleys, club hire, caddies.
LOCATION: 3 miles north of Belfast, off the Antrim road.

LOCAL HOTELS: Chimney Corner Hotel, Lansdowne Court Hotel.

KNOCK GOLF CLUB

This is a demanding parkland course featuring a variety of interesting trees, a stream and deep bunkers. Designed by Harry Colt, it is a tough par 70 and has hosted many professional events including the Irish Professional Championship. Established in 1895.

18 holes parkland, 6,402 yards, par 70 (SSS 71). Ladies 5,797 yards, par 73 (SSS 73).

SIGNATURE HOLE:
SIXTH (453 yards, par 4) – a challenging hole which is the home of a 72-foot tall monkey-puzzle tree believed to be older than the club.

ADDRESS: Summerfield, Upper Newtownards Road, Dundonald, Belfast BT16 2QX.
TELEPHONE: +44 (0)28 9048 3251.
FAX: +44 (0)28 9048 7277.
EMAIL: knockgolfclub@btconnect.com
SECRETARY: George Managh.
PROFESSIONAL: Gordon Fairweather +44 (0)28 9048 3825.
VISITORS: Best days are Mondays, Wednesdays and Thursday mornings, and Tuesday and Friday afternoons. Soft spikes.
GREEN FEES: £26 per round weekdays, £41 at weekends.
CREDIT CARDS ACCEPTED: Diners Club/ MasterCard/Visa.
CATERING: Restaurant and bar.
FACILITIES: Locker rooms, putting green, practice ground, pro-shop, buggies, trolleys, club hire, tuition.
LOCATION: 4 miles east of Belfast on Upper

The 15th at Malone Golf Club

Newtownards Road and 1 mile east of Stormont off the A20.

LOCAL HOTELS: Stormont Hotel.

MALONE GOLF CLUB

Twenty-seven holes set in 330 acres of rolling wooded parkland. Several holes are bordered by the River Lagan. A 26-acre trout lake comes into play on the back nine, and the tree-lined fairways demand accuracy. The club was founded in 1895 and moved to its current location in 1962. It has staged many professional tournaments and the Irish Amateur Championship.

MAIN COURSE – 18 holes parkland, 6,706 yards, par 71 (SSS 72). Ladies 5,692 yards, par 72 (SSS 73).

EDENDERRY COURSE – 9 holes parkland, 3,160 metres (3,476 yards), par 36. Ladies 2,668 metres (2,934 yards), par 36.

SIGNATURE HOLE:
FIFTEENTH (132 yards, par 3) – a picturesque hole requiring a precise tee shot to a green set into the lake.

ADDRESS: 240 Upper Malone Road, Dunmurry, Belfast BT17 9LB.
TELEPHONE: +44 (0)28 9061 2758.
FAX: +44 (0)28 9043 1394.
EMAIL: manager@malonegolfclub.co.uk
WEBSITE: www.malonegolfclub.co.uk
MANAGER: Nick Agate.
PROFESSIONAL: Michael McGee.
VISITORS: Welcome except Tuesday (ladies' day), Wednesday afternoons, Fridays 12–2 p.m. and Saturdays before 3 p.m.

GREEN FEES: £55 per day weekdays, £60 at weekends.

CREDIT CARDS ACCEPTED: MasterCard/Visa.

CATERING: Restaurant and bar. Full catering available from midday.

FACILITIES: Locker rooms, practice ground, putting green, pro-shop, buggies (£20), trolleys (£2), club hire (£10).

LOCATION: 2 miles south-east of junction 2 off the M1 to Belfast.

LOCAL HOTELS: Wellington Park Hotel +44 (0)28 9038 1111, Malone Lodge Hotel +44 (0)28 9038 8000, Belfast Ramada +44 (0)28 9092 3500.

MOUNT OBER GOLF CLUB

Undulating parkland course which, although short, is a good test of iron play. The seven par 3s are all potential card wreckers, and although the two par 5s are reachable in two, they must also be treated with caution as out of bounds is on the right of both holes. There are excellent views of Belfast city and beyond.

18 holes parkland, 5,281 yards, par 67 (SSS 66). Ladies 5,028 yards, par 70 (SSS 70).

SIGNATURE HOLE:

SIXTH ('Plateau', 386 yards, par 4) – the most challenging hole on the course. A tee shot to the narrowest part of the fairway is required to allow you as short an iron as possible to a long, narrow two-tiered green with danger all around. There is a well-positioned fairway bunker to catch the less-than-perfect tee shot.

ADDRESS: 24 Ballymaconaghy Road, Knockbracken, Belfast BT8 6SB.

TELEPHONE: +44 (0)28 9079 5666/2100.

FAX: +44 (0)28 9070 5862.

WEBSITE: www.mountober.com

SECRETARY: Ena Williams.

PROFESSIONAL: Wesley Ramsay.

VISITORS: Yes.

GREEN FEES: £16 per round weekdays, £18 Sundays and holidays.

CREDIT CARDS ACCEPTED: Yes.

CATERING: Restaurant and bar.

FACILITIES: Locker room, putting green, driving range, trolleys (£1.50), electric trolleys (£5), club hire (half set £5, full set £10).

LOCATION: From Belfast on Saintfield Road, turn left into Cairnshill Road. At the first roundabout, turn right into Ballymaconaghy Road. The course is signposted from there.

LOCAL HOTELS: La Mon House Hotel +44 (0)28 9044 8631, The Ivanhoe Inn and Hotel +44 (0)28 9081 2240, Ramada +44 (0)28 9092 3500.

ORMEAU GOLF CLUB

Flat, tree-lined parkland course founded in 1893. Sir Arthur Conan Doyle played here.

9 holes parkland, 5,376 yards for 18 holes, par 68 (SSS 67). Ladies 5,104 yards, par 70 (SSS 69).

ADDRESS: 50 Park Road, Belfast BT7 2FX.

TELEPHONE: +44 (0)28 9064 0700.

FAX: +44 (0)28 9064 6250.

EMAIL: enquiries@ormeaugolfclub.co.uk

WEBSITE: www.ormeaugolfclub.co.uk

PROFESSIONAL: Bertie Wilson +44 (0)28 9064 0999.

VISITORS: Welcome, except Tuesdays and Saturdays. Soft spikes.

GREEN FEES: £15 per round weekdays, £17.50 weekends and public holidays.

CATERING: Restaurant and bar.

FACILITIES: Locker rooms, putting green, practice ground, trolleys, club hire.

LOCATION: Close to Belfast city centre,

adjacent to Ormeau Road alongside Ravenhill Road and Park Road.

LOCAL HOTELS: Stormont Hotel.

SHANDON PARK GOLF CLUB

Reasonably level parkland course founded in 1926 and designed by Brian Carson.

18 holes parkland, 6,282 yards, par 70 (SSS 70). Ladies 5,676 yards, par 70 (SSS 70).

ADDRESS: 73 Shandon Park, Belfast BT5 6NY.
TELEPHONE: +44 (0)28 9080 5030.
EMAIL: shandonpark@btconnect.com
PROFESSIONAL: Barry Wilson.
VISITORS: Any day except Tuesdays and Saturdays.
GREEN FEES: £40 per round weekdays, £50 at weekends.
CATERING: Restaurant and bar.
FACILITIES: Locker rooms, putting green, practice ground, buggies, trolleys, club hire.
LOCATION: 3 miles from Belfast city centre off the A55.
LOCAL HOTELS: Stormont Hotel.

COUNTY ANTRIM

ABERDELGHY GOLF COURSE

This is a short course, but the emphasis is on accuracy rather than distance. Water comes into play on five holes. Lambeg Golf Club play over the parkland course, which was established in 1986.

18 holes parkland, 4,139 metres (4,552 yards), par 66 (SSS 62). Ladies 3,660 metres (4,026 yards), par 66 (SSS 63).

SIGNATURE HOLE:
THIRD (340 metres [374 yards], par 4)

– a dogleg through tall trees to a green protected by water.

ADDRESS: Bells Lane, Lambeg, Lisburn, Co. Antrim BT27 4QH.
TELEPHONE: +44 (0)28 9266 2738.
FAX: +44 (0)28 9260 3432.
EMAIL: info@mmsportsgolf.com
PROFESSIONAL: Ed Morrison.
VISITORS: Yes. Soft spikes.
GREEN FEES: £13.20 weekdays, £15 weekends and bank holidays.
FACILITIES: Locker rooms, pro-shop, practice area, buggies, trolleys, club hire.
CATERING: Snacks available.
LOCATION: 2 miles from the centre of Lisburn, off the main Lisburn–Belfast A1 road.
LOCAL HOTELS: Forte Post House.

ALLEN PARK GOLF CENTRE

Home of Antrim Golf Club, this is a very flat and open parkland course, with three man-made lakes, set in 143 acres. Established in 1997.

18 holes parkland, 6,683 yards, par 72 (SSS 72).

ADDRESS: 45 Castle Road, Antrim, Co. Antrim BT41 4NA.
TELEPHONE & FAX: +44 (0)28 9442 9001.
EMAIL: allenpark@antrim.gov.uk or info@ antrimgolfclub.com
WEBSITE: www.antrimgolfclub.com
VISITORS: Any day.
GREEN FEES: £16 per round weekdays, £18 weekends and public holidays.
FACILITIES: Locker rooms, putting green, 20-bay floodlit driving range, club shop, trolleys, club hire.
CATERING: Restaurant.
LOCATION: 2 miles from Antrim on the Antrim–Randalstown road.
LOCAL HOTELS: Comfort Hotel Antrim.

Ballycastle Golf Club

BALLYCASTLE GOLF CLUB

Established in 1890 and a founder member of the Golfing Union of Ireland, this combination of parkland and links with undulating greens lies at the foot of Glenshesk, one of the nine glens of Antrim, beside the seaside town of Ballycastle on the Causeway Coast. The opening five holes are parkland, with natural hazards provided by the Margy and Carey rivers. The demanding par-4 second requires an accurate drive over the River Carey, while the par-3 third is adjacent to a thirteenth-century friary. From the fifth, there follows a stretch of links alongside the beach as far as the ninth hole. The tenth is memorable and holes eleven to sixteen are played over an adjacent upland with clear views of Fairhead, Ballycastle Bay and the Mull of Kintyre in Scotland. The testing par-3 17th offers panoramic views of Glenshesk and Ballycastle.

18 holes parkland/links, 5,927 yards, par 71 (SSS 70). Ladies 5,300 yards, par 72.

SIGNATURE HOLE:
TENTH ('The Chasm', 115 yards, par 3) – a pitch across a chasm to an undulating, sloping green with unsurpassed views across the sea to Rathlin Island and the Mull of Kintyre in Scotland.

ADDRESS: 2 Cushendall Road, Ballycastle, Co. Antrim BT54 6QP.

TELEPHONE: +44 (0)28 2076 2536.
FAX: +44 (0)28 2076 9909.
EMAIL: info@ballycastlegolfclub.com
WEBSITE: www.ballycastlegolfclub.com
HONORARY SECRETARY: B.J. Dillon.
PROFESSIONAL: Ian McLaughlin.
VISITORS: Yes.
GREEN FEES: £25 per round weekdays, £35
    at weekends.
CREDIT CARDS ACCEPTED: Yes.
CATERING: Bar and meals in a new
    clubhouse.
FACILITIES: Locker rooms, putting green,
    pro-shop, trolleys (£2).
LOCATION: Between Portrush and
    Cushendall (A2).
LOCAL HOTELS: Marine Hotel +353 (0)28
    2076 2222.

BALLYCLARE GOLF CLUB

Mature parkland course with tree-lined
fairways. Two lakes between the third and
the seventh come into play and a river
meanders across the course. Views of Colin
Mountain to the north and Six-mile Valley
and Cave Hill to the south.

18 holes parkland, 6,314 yards, par 71
(SSS 71).

SIGNATURE HOLE:
ELEVENTH (175 yards, par 3) – deceptive
hole with little room for error. Protected by
water at the front of the green.

ADDRESS: 25 Springvale Road, Ballyclare,
    Co. Antrim BT39 9JW.
TELEPHONE & FAX: +44 (0)28 9332 2696.
EMAIL: info@ballyclaregolfclub.net

WEBSITE: www.ballyclaregolfclub.net
SECRETARY/MANAGER: Michael Stone.
PROFESSIONAL: Colin Lyttle +44 (0)28 9332 4541.
VISITORS: Visitors and societies welcome.
GREEN FEES: £22 per round weekdays, £28 at weekends.
CREDIT CARDS ACCEPTED: No.
CATERING: Restaurant and bar.
FACILITIES: Locker rooms, practice range, putting green, pro-shop, buggies, trolleys.
LOCATION: Take the M2 from Belfast. Take the turn-off for the A57 to Ballyclare. Follow directions from town centre to Ballymena (Rashee Road) approximately 1½ miles. Turn left at the Five Corners Guest Inn.
LOCAL HOTELS: Five Corners Guest Inn +44 (0)28 9332 2657, Rosspark Hotel +44 (0)28 2589 1663, Hilton Templepatrick +44 (0)28 9443 5500, Templeton Hotel +44 (0)28 9443 2984, Fitzwilliam International Hotel +44 (0)28 9445 7000, Adair Arms Hotel +44 (0)28 2565 3674.

BALLYMENA GOLF CLUB

Heathland course with many bunkers. Established in 1902.

18 holes heathland, 5,798 yards, par 68 (SSS 67). Ladies 5,332 yards, par 71 (SSS 70).

ADDRESS: 128 Raceview Road, Ballymena, Co. Antrim BT42 4HY.
TELEPHONE & FAX: +44 (0)28 2586 1487.
EMAIL: ballymena@golfnet.ie
WEBSITE: www.ballymenagolfclub.co.uk
PROFESSIONAL: Ken Revie +44 (0)28 2586 1652.
VISITORS: Any day, except Tuesdays and Saturdays.
GREEN FEES: £17 per round weekdays, £22 Sundays and public holidays.

CATERING: Restaurant and bar.
FACILITIES: Locker rooms, putting green, practice ground, club hire.
LOCATION: 3 miles east of Ballymena, off the A42.
LOCAL HOTELS: Adair Arms, Four Winds, Shanleigh House, The Country House, Tullyglass House.

BENTRA GOLF COURSE

A well-matured course designed by James Braid, with wide fairways and some long holes.

9 holes parkland, 6,084 yards for 18 holes, par 72 (SSS 70).

ADDRESS: Slaughterford Road, Whitehead, Antrim BT38 9TG.
TELEPHONE: +44 (0)28 9337 8996.
EMAIL: mail@bentragolf.co.uk
WEBSITE: www.bentragolf.co.uk
VISITORS: Welcome.
GREEN FEES: £9.50 per round weekdays, £13 weekends and public holidays.
CATERING: Restaurant and bar.
FACILITIES: Locker rooms, club shop, driving range adjacent to course.
LOCATION: 4 miles north of Carrickfergus on the A2.

BURNFIELD HOUSE GOLF COURSE

Tricky parkland course with many bumps and hollows and sloping greens. Established in 1995.

9 holes parkland, 5,800 yards for 18 holes, par 70 (SSS 69).

ADDRESS: Newtownabbey, Co. Antrim BT36 5BN.
TELEPHONE: +44 (0)28 9083 8737.
FAX: +44 (0)28 9083 8448.
EMAIL: michaelhj@ntlworld.com

VISITORS: Any day.
GREEN FEES: Weekdays – £7 for nine holes, £10 for eighteen; Weekends – £8 for nine holes, £14 for eighteen.
CATERING: Bar and meals.
FACILITIES: Locker rooms, trolleys, club hire.
LOCATION: Off the old Carrick Road.
LOCAL HOTELS: Corrs Corner Hotel.

BUSHFOOT GOLF CLUB

Founded in 1890, this nine-hole seaside course with double tees is part links, part parkland and has stunning views. Several of the holes are very tight and challenging.

9 holes links/parkland, 6,075 yards for 18 holes, par 70 (SSS 68). Ladies 5,373 yards, par 70 (SSS 69).

ADDRESS: 50 Bushfoot Road, Portballintrae, Co. Antrim BT57 8RR.
TELEPHONE: +44 (0)28 2073 1317.
FAX: +44 (0)28 2073 1852.
EMAIL: bushfootgolfclub@btconnect.com
SECRETARY/MANAGER: J. Knox Thompson.
VISITORS: Yes, except on competition days.
GREEN FEES: £16 per round weekdays, £20 at weekends.
CATERING: Restaurant and bar. Functions catered for.
FACILITIES: Locker rooms, putting green, pitch-and-putt course, trolleys.
LOCATION: 4 miles east of Portrush on the coast.
LOCAL HOTELS: Beech Hotel, Bushmills Inn, Causeway Hotel.

CAIRNDHU GOLF CLUB

The club was founded in 1928 as Larne Town and moved to Cairndhu in 1958. This parkland course, one of the most scenic in Ireland, has a variety of interesting holes, including the 419-yard third, which has a carry of 180 yards over the headland to a narrow fairway with out of bounds all down the right. The 410-yard tenth is described by the pros as one of the best driving holes in Ireland. Cairndhu is a very fair test of golf with four short par 4s (300–330 yards) which demand accurate tee shots, while there are seven other par 4s which require drives of at least 250 yards to have a chance of reaching the green in two.

18 holes parkland, 5,611 metres (6,138 yards), par 70 (SSS 69). Ladies 4,861 metres (5,347 yards), par 72 (SSS 71).

SIGNATURE HOLE:
SECOND ('The Head', 146 metres [160 yards], par 3) – described by Darren Clarke as 'one of the best eighteen holes in Ireland', it is 500 feet above sea level. He would hit anything from a wedge to a three-iron depending on the wind.

ADDRESS: 192 Coast Road, Ballygally, Larne, Co. Antrim, BT40 2QG.
TELEPHONE & FAX: +44 (0)28 2858 3324.
EMAIL: cairndhugc@btconnect.com
WEBSITE: www.cairndhugolfclub.co.uk
MANAGER: Nat Moore.
PROFESSIONAL: Paul Russell +44 (0)28 2858 3954.
VISITORS: Sundays to Fridays.
GREEN FEES: £20 per round weekdays, £25 at weekends.
CREDIT CARDS ACCEPTED: MasterCard/Visa.
CATERING: Restaurant and bar.
FACILITIES: Locker rooms, putting green, practice ground, pro-shop, buggies, trolleys, club hire, caddies.
LOCATION: 4 miles north of Larne on the coast road leading to the Glens of Antrim.
LOCAL HOTELS: Highways Hotel, Ballygally Castle Hotel, Halfway House Hotel,

Ballygally Holiday Apartments (on the edge of the course).

CARRICKFERGUS GOLF CLUB

Challenging parkland course with water hazards. Founded in 1926.

18 holes parkland, 6,311 yards, par 68 (SSS 68). Ladies 5,265 yards, par 70 (SSS 70).

ADDRESS: 35 North Road, Carrickfergus, Co. Antrim BT38 8LP.
TELEPHONE: +44 (0)28 9336 3713.
FAX: +44 (0)28 9336 3023.
EMAIL: carrickfergusgc@btconnect.com
SECRETARY/MANAGER: John Thomson.
PROFESSIONAL: Gary Mercer +44 (0)28 9335 1803.
VISITORS: Any day except Tuesdays and Saturdays, and Sunday afternoons.
GREEN FEES: £20 per round weekdays, £28 at weekends.
CATERING: Restaurant and bar.
FACILITIES: Locker rooms, putting green, practice ground, trolleys.
LOCATION: 9 miles north-east of Belfast on the North Road.
LOCAL HOTELS: Coast Road Hotel, Dobbins Inn Hotel.

CITY OF BELFAST GOLF COURSE (MALLUSK)

Also known as Mallusk, this flat parkland course has no par 5s. Established in 1992.

9 holes parkland, 4,686 yards for 18 holes, par 64 (SSS 64). Ladies 4,248 yards, par 64 (SSS 62).

ADDRESS: Antrim Road, Glengormley, Newtownabbey, Co. Antrim BT36 4RF.
TELEPHONE: +44 (0)28 9084 3799.
FAX: +44 (0)28 9034 2383.

EMAIL: kevinmcglennon@aol.com
WEBSITE: www.cityofbelfastgolfclub.com
SECRETARY/MANAGER: Kevin McGlennon.
VISITORS: Any day except Saturday mornings.
GREEN FEES: £8.60 per round weekdays, £11.50 at weekends.
CATERING: Snacks.
FACILITIES: Locker rooms, putting green, buggies, trolleys.
LOCATION: From Belfast on the A8 to Antrim. The course is just before Chimney Corner Hotel.
LOCAL HOTELS: Corrs Corner Hotel, Chimney Corner Hotel.

CUSHENDALL GOLF CLUB

Founded in 1937 and designed by Daniel Delargy, this parkland course on the shores of Red Bay has magnificent views across the Sea of Moyle to the Mull of Kintyre on the Scottish coast. With many mature trees and the River Dall creating out of bounds on seven of the holes, the course demands accuracy.

9 holes parkland, 4,797 yards for 18 holes, par 66 (SSS 63). Ladies 4,406 yards, par 66 (SSS 65).

ADDRESS: 21 Shore Road, Cushendall, Co. Antrim BT44 0NG.
TELEPHONE: +44 (0)28 2177 1318.
EMAIL: cushendallgolfclub@hotmail.com
VISITORS: Mondays, Tuesdays and Fridays are best.
GREEN FEES: £13 per round weekdays, £18 at weekends.
CATERING: Bar facilities.
LOCATION: 25 miles north of Larne on the Antrim coast road.
LOCAL HOTELS: Thornlea Hotel.

DOWN ROYAL GOLF CLUB

Situated in the Lagan Valley, this challenging heathland course was founded in 1997. The boundary to the course is the Down Royal racetrack, which was granted the royal charter in 1685. The club's many interesting holes include the second (*see below*) and 'The Pond', the 196-yard par-3 13th. When commenting on the course, former Open champion Fred Daly said, 'To play Muirfield requires every club in the bag. The same could be said of the Down Royal.'

18 holes heathland, 7,021 yards, par 72 (SSS 73). Ladies 5,373 yards, par 72 (SSS 69).

SIGNATURE HOLE:
SECOND ('Canal Turn', 631 yards, par 5) – named by Ireland's professionals as one of the country's best par 5s, this dogleg left requires a long drive as there is a fairway drain at 220 yards and a tight landing area with high rough and gorse bushes on either side.

ADDRESS: Dunygarton Road, The Maze, Lisburn, Co. Antrim BT27 5RT.
TELEPHONE: +44 (0)28 9262 1339.
EMAIL: info@downroyalgolfclub.com
WEBSITE: www.downroyalgolfclub.com
VISITORS: Any day.
GREEN FEES: £17 per round weekdays, £20 at weekends.
CATERING: Bar and restaurant.
FACILITIES: Locker rooms, putting green, driving range, pro-shop, buggies, trolleys, club hire, caddies, tuition.
LOCATION: South-east of Lisburn within the Maze racecourse.
LOCAL HOTELS: The Clubhouse B & B (at the golf course).

GALGORM CASTLE GOLF CLUB

This championship parkland course set in 220 acres surrounds one of Ireland's most historic castles. Designed by Simon Gidman, vice-president of the British Institute of Golf Course Architects, it has been constructed to the highest possible standards with all tees and greens to USGA specifications. It is bordered by the rivers Main and Braid and incorporates an oxbow feature, where there is a horseshoe bend in the River Braid, and five impressive lakes. Large teeing areas make the course suitable for all standards of golfers.

18 holes parkland, 6,736 yards, par 72 (SSS 72). Ladies 5,457 yards, par 72 (SSS 72).

SIGNATURE HOLE:
FOURTEENTH ('Devil's Elbow', 177 yards, par 3) – challenging tee shot to a well-guarded, narrow two-tiered green with water to the right and also at the back. Out of bounds is on the right.

ADDRESS: Galgorm Road, Ballymena, Co. Antrim, BT42 1HL.
TELEPHONE: +44 (0)28 2564 6161.
FAX: +44 (0)28 2565 1151.
EMAIL: golf@galgormcastle.com
WEBSITE: www.galgormcastle.com
PROFESSIONAL: Phil Collins.
VISITORS: Every day. Soft spikes.
GREEN FEES: £32 per round weekdays, £38 weekends and public holidays.
CREDIT CARDS ACCEPTED: All major cards.
CATERING: Restaurant (overlooking the course) and bar.
FACILITIES: Locker rooms, putting green, practice facilities, 24-bay floodlit driving range, pro-shop, golf academy, buggies (£22), trolleys, club hire (£10), caddies (£20), tuition.

LOCATION: 1 mile from Ballymena on the A42, 20 minutes from Belfast and the international airport.

LOCAL HOTELS: Galgorm Manor Hotel, Tullyglass House Hotel, Ross Park Hotel, Adair Arms Hotel.

GRACEHILL GOLF CLUB

This championship course set in beautiful parkland outside the village of Stranocum has American-style water hazards. Founded in 1995.

18 holes parkland, 6,531 yards, par 72 (SSS 73). Ladies 5,641 yards, par 73 (SSS 75).

SIGNATURE HOLE:
FOURTEENTH (211 yards, par 3)
– requires a long carry over water to an undulating green surrounded by whins.

ADDRESS: 141 Ballinlea Road, Stranocum, Ballymoney, Co. Antrim BT53 8PX.
TELEPHONE: +44 (0)28 2075 1209.
FAX: +44 (0)28 2075 1074.
EMAIL: gracehillgc@bigboo.net
WEBSITE: www.gracehillgolfclub.co.uk
SECRETARY/MANAGER: Margaret McClure.
VISITORS: Midweek and weekends if available. Time sheet at weekends.
GREEN FEES: £25 per round weekdays, £30 at weekends.
CREDIT CARDS ACCEPTED: All major credit/debit cards.
CATERING: Restaurant and bar.
FACILITIES: Locker rooms, practice facilities, driving range adjacent to course (not linked), buggies (£20), trolleys (£3), club hire, tuition at driving range.
LOCATION: 7 miles north of Ballymoney on the B147/A2, off the main A26 north from Belfast to the north coast and Giant's Causeway and 40 minutes from Belfast International Airport.

LOCAL HOTELS: Causeway Hotel +44 (0)28 2073 1226.

GREENACRES GOLF CLUB

This challenging parkland course, built into the rolling Antrim countryside, with large greens and lakes on five holes has three par 5s and five par 3s.

18 holes parkland, 5,839 metres (6,422 yards), par 70 (SSS 68). Ladies 5,043 metres (5,547 yards), par 70 (SSS 68).

SIGNATURE HOLE:
SIXTH (158 metres [174 yards], par 3)
– very difficult tee shot over three lakes in front of a large elevated green with bunkers on both sides.

ADDRESS: 153 Ballyrobert Road, Ballyclare, Co. Antrim BT39 9RT.
TELEPHONE: +44 (0)28 9335 4111.
EMAIL: info@greenacresgolfclub.co.uk
WEBSITE: www.greenacresgolfclub.co.uk
VISITORS: Weekdays are best.
GREEN FEES: £16 per round Mondays to Thursdays, £18 on Fridays and £22 at weekends.
CREDIT CARDS ACCEPTED: MasterCard/Visa.
CATERING: Restaurant and bar.
FACILITIES: Locker rooms, putting green, 20-bay floodlit driving range, trolleys, club hire, tuition.
LOCATION: 10 miles north of Belfast via the M2 motorway to Corr's Corner then the B56 signposted to Ballyclare.
LOCAL HOTELS: Chimney Corner Hotel, Dunadry Inn Hotel, Templeton Hotel.

GREENISLAND GOLF CLUB

Hilly parkland course with a river running between the fifth and sixth holes. Founded in 1894.

The 11th at Hilton Templepatrick Hotel and Country Club

9 holes parkland, 6,153 yards for 18 holes, par 71 (SSS 68).

ADDRESS: 156 Upper Road, Greenisland, Carrickfergus, Co. Antrim BT38 8RW.
TELEPHONE: +44 (0)28 9086 2236.
EMAIL: *greenislandgolf@btconnect.com*
VISITORS: Any day except Saturdays.
GREEN FEES: £14 per round for 18 holes weekdays, £18 at weekends.
CATERING: Full clubhouse facilities.
FACILITIES: Locker rooms.
LOCATION: 2 miles from Carrickfergus and 8 miles north of Belfast.
LOCAL HOTELS: Clarion Hotel.

HILTON TEMPLEPATRICK HOTEL AND COUNTRY CLUB

Established in 1999 and set in 220 acres of the beautiful country estate of Castle Upton, this long parkland course, formerly known as Stakis Park, was designed by David Jones and David Feherty to full USGA specifications and boasts strategically placed lakes in tandem with the Six-mile River. The front nine is laid out on the more open part of the estate with water features and mature trees defining the holes, particularly the par-5 third where Neill's Burn runs along the left and at the eighth where the tee shot is right through an ancient tree ring.

241

Ireland's Golf Courses

The back nine enjoys spectacular settings, especially the par-3 eleventh.

18 holes parkland, 7,077 yards, par 71 (SSS 71).

SIGNATURE HOLE:
ELEVENTH (183 yards, par 3) – poplar trees on the left and the Six-mile River on the right make it a narrow entrance to an undulating green.

ADDRESS: Castle Upton Estate, Templepatrick, Co. Antrim BT39 0DD.
TELEPHONE: +44 (0)28 9443 5542.
FAX: +44 (0)28 9443 5511.
EMAIL: lynn.mccool@hilton.com
WEBSITE: www.hilton.co.uk/templepatrick
GOLF DIRECTOR: Lynn McCool.
PROFESSIONALS: Lynn McCool, Eamonn Logue, Marcus Twitchett.
VISITORS: Yes.
GREEN FEES: £45 per person, £28 for residents.
CREDIT CARDS ACCEPTED: Yes.
CATERING: Restaurants and function rooms.
FACILITIES: Locker rooms, practice ground, putting green, pro-shop, buggies (£25), trolleys (£3), club hire (£15).
LOCATION: From Belfast International Airport, a courtesy shuttle bus is provided subject to availability (an approximately 10-minute drive). The course is 12 miles from Belfast city centre. Take the M2 and turn off at the Templepatrick/Airport junction and follow signs for the Hilton Hotel.
LOCAL HOTELS: Hilton Templepatrick on site.

LARNE GOLF CLUB

This part parkland, part links course is situated on the headland of Islandmagee and bounded by water on three sides, which makes the last four holes very tight. It is an extremely scenic course with views of the Antrim coast, and Scotland is visible on a clear day. Founded in 1894.

9 holes parkland/links, 6,288 yards for 18 holes, par 70 (SSS 70). Ladies 6,052 yards, par 74 (SSS 73).

SIGNATURE HOLE:
EIGHTH ('Whins', 417 yards, par 4) – dogleg left, bounded on one side by picturesque whins and on the other by Larne Lough. With the fairway sloping to the water, it takes two perfect shots. Fred Daly claimed it was one of the best holes he had ever played.

ADDRESS: 54 Ferris Bay Road, Islandmagee, Co. Antrim BT40 3RT.
TELEPHONE: +44 (0)28 9338 2228.
FAX: +44 (0)28 9338 2088.
EMAIL: internet@larnegolfclub.freeserve.co.uk
WEBSITE: www.larnegolfclub.co.uk
SECRETARY/MANAGER: Lisa Oldfield.
VISITORS: Yes.
GREEN FEES: £10 per round weekdays, £18 at weekends.
CATERING: Restaurant and bar.
FACILITIES: Locker rooms, putting green, practice ground.
LOCATION: Through Whitehead to the northern end of the Islandmagee peninsula.
LOCAL HOTELS: Magheramorne House.

LISBURN GOLF CLUB

Opened in 1973, this parkland course makes full use of its natural features, such as ground undulations, mature trees and water courses. It comprises two loops of nine, each starting and finishing at the clubhouse and each with two par 5s, two par 3s and five par 4s.

18 holes parkland, 6,647 yards, par 72 (SSS 72). Ladies 5,546 yards, par 72 (SSS 72).

SIGNATURE HOLE:
EIGHTEENTH ('The Garden', 217 yards, par 3) – good finishing hole with bunkers on either side of the green, which slopes from back to front. Club selection is very important.

ADDRESS: 68 Eglantine Road, Lisburn, Co. Antrim BT27 5RQ.
TELEPHONE: +44 (0)28 9267 7216.
FAX: +44 (0)28 92 603608.
EMAIL: info@lisburngolfclub.com
WEBSITE: www.lisburngolfclub.com
HONORARY SECRETARY: Andrew Crawford.
PROFESSIONAL: Stephen Hamill +44 (0)28 9267 7217.
VISITORS: Yes.
GREEN FEES: £30 weekdays, £35 at weekends.
CREDIT CARDS ACCEPTED: Pro-shop only.
CATERING: Restaurant and bar.
FACILITIES: Locker rooms, practice ground, putting green, pro-shop, buggies (£20), trolleys (£2).
LOCATION: On the A1 dual carriageway between Lisburn and Hillsborough – just off junction 7 of the M1.

MASSEREENE GOLF CLUB

Part parkland, part links course founded in 1895 and designed by Fred Hawtree. The front nine is parkland, but the homeward nine, running along Lough Neagh, is more akin to links.

18 holes parkland/links, 6,604 yards, par 72 (SSS 72). Ladies 5,651 yards, par 72 (SSS 72).

ADDRESS: 51 Lough Road, Antrim, Co. Antrim BT41 4DQ.
TELEPHONE: +44 (0)28 9442 8096.
FAX: +44 (0)28 9448 7661.
EMAIL: info@massereene.com
WEBSITE: www.massereene.com
PROFESSIONAL: Jim Smyth +44 (0)28 9446 4074.
VISITORS: Any day, except Fridays and Saturdays.
GREEN FEES: £25 per round weekdays, £30 at weekends.
CREDIT CARDS ACCEPTED: All major cards.
CATERING: Restaurant and bar.
FACILITIES: Locker rooms, putting green, trolleys, club hire, caddies.
LOCATION: 1 mile south of Antrim.
LOCAL HOTELS: Dunadry Inn.

ROYAL PORTRUSH GOLF CLUB

When there are holes with names like 'Calamity Corner', 'Purgatory', 'Himalayas' and 'Giant's Grave', you can be sure of a severe interrogation of your golfing ability. This is very much a case of beauty and the beast. Portrush is a glorious location for a golf course, set in a particularly beautiful part of Ireland with the Giant's Causeway, magnificent white sand beaches and lush countryside nearby. Briar roses colour the rough, the ocean views are magnificent and the course is overlooked by the brooding ruins of Dunluce Castle. But the championship Dunluce Links can be a spectacular monster, winding along narrow fairways between dunes with severe rough and heather and demanding the most accurate of drives. There are six doglegs and tiny well-contoured greens, but although it's a seaside course, you are unlikely to need your bucket and spade as there are only twenty bunkers.

Established in 1888, this is one of the world's great links courses and the only course outside Scotland and England to

Royal Portrush Golf Club

have hosted the British Open (in 1951, when the flamboyant Max Faulkner won). Harry Colt designed the Dunluce Links in 1932 and regarded it as his masterpiece. The first professional golf event in Ireland was staged here in 1895 when Sandy Herd beat Harry Vardon in the final, and in 1960, Joe Carr, that great Dublin golfer, won the Amateur Championship.

Giant's Grave, the 505-yard par-5 second, can be reached in two but needs a long and true drive to give you a chance of carrying the cross bunkers in front of the green. It's not until you reach the tee of the 155-yard third that you can see the full majesty of the links for the first time. The 431-yard seventh is a great challenge with a drive to a narrow landing area and an approach to an elevated green, fronted by cross bunkers. The Himalayas is the 384-yard eighth, requiring a drive over dunes with penal rough and a dogleg right waiting on the other side.

The final three holes are as tough a finish as you will find. A large bunker protects the right side of the green of the 428-yard 16th hole, and if you go left, the slope will carry the ball away from the putting surface. The 17th is a substantial par 5 of 548 yards, while the last is a reasonably flat 469 yards.

When in the area, take the opportunity to visit the Giant's Causeway, the famous basalt outcrop which, according to legend, was the result of giant Finn McCool building a bridge across the sea to his true love on the Hebridean island of Scaffa and, if you need any more persuasion, the world's oldest whiskey distillery.

DUNLUCE LINKS – 18 holes, 6,845 yards, par 72 (SSS 73). Ladies 6,123 yards, par 75 (SSS 75).

VALLEY LINKS – 18 holes, 6,304 yards, par 70 (SSS 70). Ladies 5,494 yards, par 72 (SSS 71).

SIGNATURE HOLE:
FOURTEENTH ('Calamity Corner', 210 yards, par 3) – probably the toughest par 3 in Ireland with rough almost all the way from the tee to green, which has to be hit:

if you're short, the ball will plummet into a chasm 50-feet below.

ADDRESS: Dunluce Road, Portrush, Co. Antrim BT56 8JQ.
TELEPHONE: +44 (0)28 7082 2311.
FAX: +44 (0)28 7082 3139.
EMAIL: info@royalportrushgolfclub.com
WEBSITE: www.royalportrushgolfclub.com
SECRETARY/MANAGER: Wilma Erskine.
PROFESSIONAL: Gary McNeill +44 (0)28 7082 3335.
VISITORS: Every day by prearranged booking. A handicap certificate is required, with a maximum of 18 for men and 24 for ladies.
GREEN FEES: Dunluce – £105 per round weekdays, £120 at weekends; Valley – £35 per round weekdays, £40 at weekends.
CREDIT CARDS ACCEPTED: All major cards.
CATERING: Restaurant and bar.
FACILITIES: Locker rooms, putting green, pitching green, indoor driving range, pro-shop, trolleys (£3.50), club hire (£25–35), caddies (£25, excluding gratuity), tuition.
LOCATION: 1 hour from Belfast Airport. Follow the road to Ballymoney then follow signs to Portrush.
LOCAL HOTELS: Royal Court Hotel, Magherabuoy House Hotel, Causeway Coast Hotel.

WHITEHEAD GOLF CLUB

Undulating parkland course established in 1904.
    18 holes parkland, 6,050 yards, par 70 (SSS 69).

ADDRESS: McCrae's Brae, Whitehead, Carrickfergus, Co. Antrim BT38 9NZ.
TELEPHONE: +44 (0)28 9337 0820.
FAX: +44 (0)28 9337 0825.
EMAIL: info@whiteheadgolfclub.com
WEBSITE: www.whiteheadgolfclub.com
PROFESSIONAL: Colin Farr +44 (0)28 9337 0821.
VISITORS: Any day except Saturdays and Sundays.
GREEN FEES: £17 per round weekdays, £22 weekends and public holidays.
CATERING: Bar and meals.
FACILITIES: Locker rooms, putting green, practice area, trolleys, club hire.
LOCATION: On the Antrim coast between Larne and Carrickfergus.
LOCAL HOTELS: Coast Road Hotel, Magheramorne Hotel.

COUNTY ARMAGH

ASHFIELD GOLF CLUB

Parkland course founded in 1990.
    18 holes parkland, 5,620 yards, par 69 (SSS 67).

ADDRESS: Freeduff, Cullyhanna, Newry, Co. Armagh BT35 0JJ.
TELEPHONE: +44 (0)28 3086 8180.
FAX: +44 (0)28 3086 8111.
EMAIL: ashfield.golfing@virgin.net
SECRETARY: James and Elizabeth Quinn.
PROFESSIONAL: Erill Maney.
VISITORS: Any day.
GREEN FEES: £12 per round weekdays, £15 weekends and public holidays.
CATERING: Bar and snacks.
FACILITIES: Locker rooms, putting green, practice ground, driving range, buggies, trolleys, club hire, caddies on request.
LOCATION: 2 miles north-east of Crossmaglen, off the B30.
LOCAL HOTELS: Canal Court Hotel, Francis Court Hotel.

County Armagh Golf Club

CLOVERHILL GOLF CLUB

This parkland course was extended to 18 holes in July 2002. The combination of narrow dogleg fairways, difficult-to-read greens, water hazards (a river runs through the middle of the course) and sand traps require the golfer to manage his game. Set in the scenic area of the Ring of Gullion, South Armagh.

18 holes parkland, 5,496 yards, par 70.

ADDRESS: Lough Road, Mullaghbawn, Co. Armagh BT35 9XP.
TELEPHONE: +44 (0)28 3088 9374.
FAX: +44 (0)28 3088 9199.
EMAIL: info@cloverhillgc.com

WEBSITE: www.cloverhillgc.com
VISITORS: Everyday. Soft spikes.
GREEN FEES: £12 per round weekdays, £15 weekends and public holidays.
CATERING: Restaurant and bar.
FACILITIES: Locker rooms, club shop, trolleys, club hire.
LOCATION: 8 miles south of Newry. Easily accessible from Belfast and Dublin, being 1 hour from each.
LOCAL HOTELS: Canal Court Hotel.

COUNTY ARMAGH GOLF CLUB

Founded in 1893, this is one of Ireland's oldest clubs. Extended in 1975 to 18 holes, it is a mature and challenging parkland course with breathtaking views of the ancient city of Armagh and surrounding countryside. It has been host to major amateur and professional golf championships. The famous 'Quarry' hole, the picturesque 'Shambles', the intimidating 'Lakes' and the new finishing hole with its backdrop of Armagh's two cathedrals, are four of the most beautiful and testing holes in golf. Situated between the tenth and thirteenth greens is 'The Obelisk'; at 114-feet high, it dominates the course and was erected in 1783 to commemorate the Archbishop of Armagh's patron, the Duke of Northumberland.

18 holes parkland, 6,212 yards, par 70 (SSS 69). Ladies 5,337 yards, par 71 (SSS 70).

SIGNATURE HOLE:
ELEVENTH ('Shambles', 175 yards, par 3) – downhill with a water hazard in front of the green, almost surrounded by trees.

ADDRESS: Newry Road, Armagh, Co. Armagh BT60 1EN.
TELEPHONE & FAX: +44 (0)28 3752 5861.
EMAIL: info@golfarmagh.co.uk
WEBSITE: www.golfarmagh.co.uk
SECRETARY: June McParland.
PROFESSIONAL: Alan Rankin +44 (0)28 3752 5864.
VISITORS: Mondays to Fridays (telephone to check weekend availability). Soft spikes.
GREEN FEES: £17 per round weekdays, £22 weekends and bank holidays.
CREDIT CARDS ACCEPTED: All major cards.
CATERING: Restaurant and bar.
FACILITIES: Locker rooms, putting green, practice ground, pro-shop, buggies (£10), trolleys (£2), club hire (£15), tuition.
LOCATION: On edge of the city of Armagh

on the Newry Road, just past the police station on the road to Dublin via Newry.
LOCAL HOTELS: Armagh City Hotel, Charlemont Arms Hotel.

CRAIGAVON GOLF AND SKI CENTRE

This public parkland course with lakes and streams is played over by Silverwood Golf Club. Founded in 1984.

18 holes parkland, 6,483 yards, par 72 (SSS 71). Ladies 5,596 yards, par 73 (SSS 70). 9-hole par-3 course.

ADDRESS: Turmoyra Lane, Silverwood, Lurgan, Co. Armagh BT66 6NG.
TELEPHONE: +44 (0)28 3832 6606.
FAX: +44 (0)28 3834 7272.
VISITORS: Yes, but not Saturday mornings.
GREEN FEES: £15 weekdays, £18.50 at weekends.
CATERING: Meals and snacks.
FACILITIES: Locker rooms, putting green, floodlit driving range, 12-hole pitch and putt, trolleys, club hire.
LOCATION: Junction 10, off the M1 from Belfast, 2 miles north of Lurgan.
LOCAL HOTELS: Ashburn Hotel, Silverwood Hotel.

EDENMORE GOLF AND COUNTRY CLUB

This gently rolling, mature parkland course, has undergone major alterations in recent years with the addition of a par 3 and par 5 holes. Founded in 1992 and designed by Frank Ainsworth, it is well drained.

18 holes parkland, 6,278 yards, par 71 (SSS 69). Ladies 5,252 yards, par 71 (SSS 70).
SIGNATURE HOLE:

THIRTEENTH ('Edenmore', 481 yards, par 5) – approach shot over water to the green between two large oak trees.

Edenmore Golf and Country Club

ADDRESS: Edenmore House, 70 Drumnabreeze Road, Magheralin, Craigavon, Co. Armagh BT67 0RH.

TELEPHONE: +44 (0)28 9261 9241.

FAX: +44 (0)28 9261 3310.

EMAIL: info@edenmore.com

WEBSITE: www.edenmore.com

SECRETARY/MANAGER: Kenneth Logan.

PROFESSIONAL: Jason Greenaway.

VISITORS: Very welcome.

GREEN FEES: £18 per round weekdays, £24 at weekends.

CREDIT CARDS ACCEPTED: Delta/Switch/Visa.

CATERING: Extensive licensed restaurant.

FACILITIES: Locker rooms, practice ground, putting green, pro-shop, buggies (£15), trolleys (£2), club hire (£10), gym and health suite, seven conference rooms.

LOCATION: 20 miles west of Belfast. Take the Moira exit from the M1 motorway and travel through the village towards Lurgan. In the village of Magheralin, follow the signs for Edenmore.

LOCAL HOTELS: Seagoe Hotel, Craigavon; Newforge House, Magheralin.

LOUGHGALL GOLF CLUB

Set in the mature woodland of Loughgall Country Park, this municipal course, designed by Don Patterson in 2000, provides a challenge for all levels of golfer.

Lurgan Golf Club

Strategically placed bunkers, sloping terrain and water hazards all add to its character.

18 holes parkland, 6,229 yards, par 72 (SSS 70). Ladies 5,686 yards, par 72.

ADDRESS: 11–14 Main Street, Loughgall, Co. Armagh BT61 8HZ.
TELEPHONE: +44 (0)28 3889 2900.
FAX: +44 (0)28 3889 2902.
SECRETARY/MANAGER: Greg Ferson.
VISITORS: Yes.
GREEN FEES: £14.50 weekdays, £16.50 at weekends.
CREDIT CARDS ACCEPTED: All major cards.
FACILITIES: Locker rooms, buggies, trolleys, club hire.

LOCATION: 8 miles west of Portadown on the B77.

LURGAN GOLF CLUB

This challenging parkland course, bordering Lurgan Park lake, is well wooded and the greens are well trapped. With a pond on the seventh fairway, internal out of bounds on some holes and quite a few doglegs, straight driving is essential. Founded in 1893 and designed by Frank Pennink.

18 holes parkland, 6,272 yards, par 70 (SSS 70). Ladies 5,398 yards, par 71 (SSS 71).

ADDRESS: The Demesne, Windsor Avenue, Lurgan, Co. Armagh, BT67 9BN.

TELEPHONE: +44 (0)28 3832 2087.
FAX: +44 (0)28 3831 6166.
EMAIL: lurgangolfclub@btconnect.com
WEBSITE: www.lurgangolfclub.co.uk
SECRETARY/MANAGER: Muriel Sharpe.
PROFESSIONAL: Des Paul.
VISITORS: Yes, except Wednesdays and Saturdays.
GREEN FEES: £17 per round weekdays, £22 weekends and bank holidays.
CATERING: Restaurant and bar +44 (0)28 3832 2087.
FACILITIES: Locker rooms, practice ground, putting green, pro-shop, trolleys.
LOCATION: 1 mile from exit 10 on the M1, signposted from town centre.
LOCAL HOTELS: Ashburn Hotel, Lurgan + 44 (0)28 3832 5711.

PORTADOWN GOLF CLUB

Set on the banks of the River Bann, this is a tree-lined parkland course established in 1900.

18 holes parkland, 6,118 yards, par 70 (SSS 69). Ladies 5,618 yards, par 72 (SSS 72).

ADDRESS: 192 Gilford Road, Portadown, Co. Armagh BT63 5LF.
TELEPHONE: +44 (0)28 3835 5356.
FAX: +44 (0)28 3839 1394.
EMAIL: portadowngc@btconnect.com
WEBSITE: www.portadowngolfclub.co.uk
PROFESSIONAL: Paul Stevenson +44 (0)28 3833 4655.
VISITORS: Any day except Tuesdays and Saturdays. Soft spikes.
GREEN FEES: £17 per round weekdays, £21 at weekends.
CATERING: Bar and meals.

FACILITIES: Locker rooms, putting green, practice ground, buggies, trolleys, club hire.
LOCATION: 2 miles south-east of Portadown, off the A50.
LOCAL HOTELS: Bannview Hotel, Seagoe Hotel.

TANDRAGEE GOLF CLUB

Formidable parkland course with tree-lined fairways beside the River Cusher. It is also picturesque, with views of the ancient Tandragee Castle. Established in 1911, two lakes and four new holes were recently added.

18 holes parkland, 5,531 metres (6,084 yards), par 70 (SSS 70). Ladies 4,930 metres (5,423 yards), par 72 (SSS 72).

ADDRESS: Markethill Road, Tandragee, Co. Armagh BT62 2ER.
TELEPHONE: +44 (0)28 3884 1272.
FAX: +44 (0)28 3884 0664.
EMAIL: info@tandragee.co.uk
WEBSITE: www.tandragee.co.uk
SECRETARY/MANAGER: David Clayton.
PROFESSIONAL: Gary Mercer +44 (0)28 3884 1761.
VISITORS: Any day except Saturdays and Thursday afternoons.
GREEN FEES: £15 per round weekdays, £20 at weekends.
CATERING: Restaurant and bar.
FACILITIES: Locker rooms, putting green, practice ground, buggies, trolleys, club hire.
LOCATION: On the B3 in Tandragee.
LOCAL HOTELS: Bannview Hotel, Carngrove Hotel, Seagoe Hotel.

COUNTY DOWN

ARDGLASS GOLF CLUB

Founded in 1896, this spectacular course with championship-standard greens lies in a fishing village, 30 miles south of Belfast. The first five holes, with the Irish Sea and cliffs tight to the left, should be treated with respect, as anything resembling a hook will meet with disaster. Panoramic views of the Irish Sea and, on a clear day, the Isle of Man.

18 holes links, 6,268 yards, par 70 (SSS 70). Ladies 5,303 yards, par 70 (SSS 70).

ADDRESS: Castle Place, Ardglass, Co. Down BT30 7TP.
TELEPHONE: +44 (0)28 4484 1219.
FAX: +44 (0)28 4484 1841.
EMAIL: info@ardglassgolfclub.com
WEBSITE: www.ardglassgolfclub.com
PROFESSIONAL: Philip Farrell.
VISITORS: Weekdays are best, weekends by arrangement.
GREEN FEES: £35 per round weekdays, £50 at weekends.
CREDIT CARDS ACCEPTED: All major cards accepted.
CATERING: Restaurant and bar in a clubhouse which is a fourteenth century castle.
FACILITIES: Locker rooms, driving range, pro-shop, buggies, trolleys, club hire, tuition.
LOCATION: 7 miles north of Downpatrick, 20 minutes from Newcastle, Co. Down.
LOCAL HOTELS: Slieve Donard Hotel +44 (0)28 4372 1066.

ARDMINNAN GOLF CLUB

This testing parkland course has two gradual hills, and a river and two ponds come into play on six of the holes. Founded in 1995.

9 holes parkland, 6,053 yards for 18 holes, par 70 (SSS 69).

ADDRESS: 15a Ardminnan Road, Portaferry, Co. Down BT22 1QJ.
TELEPHONE & FAX: +44 (0)28 4277 1312.
SECRETARY/MANAGER: Iris Gowan.
PROFESSIONAL: +44 (0)28 4277 1004.
VISITORS: Yes.
GREEN FEES: £10 per day weekdays, £15 at weekends.
CATERING: Restaurant and bar.
FACILITIES: Locker rooms, trolleys, club hire.
LOCATION: Take the main road from Portaferry to Cloughey.

BANBRIDGE GOLF CLUB

This mature parkland course was founded in 1913 and boasts views of the Mourne Mountains. Its signature holes are the sixth, with a menacing pond, and the tenth.

18 holes parkland, 5,590 metres (6,149 yards), par 69 (SSS 77). Ladies 4,987 metres (5,485 yards), par 70 (SSS 69).

ADDRESS: 116 Huntly Road, Banbridge, Co. Down BT32 3UR.
TELEPHONE: +44 (0)28 4066 2211.
FAX: +44 (0)28 4066 9400.
EMAIL: banbridgegolf@btconnect.com
SECRETARY/MANAGER: J. McKeown.
PROFESSIONAL: Derek Brown +44 (0)28 4062 6189.
VISITORS: Yes.
GREEN FEES: £17 per round weekdays, £22 at weekends.

Ardglass Golf Club

CATERING: Restaurant and bar.
FACILITIES: Locker rooms, putting green, practice ground, pro-shop, trolleys, club hire.
LOCATION: 1 mile from Banbridge.
LOCAL HOTELS: Bannview Hotel, Belmont Hotel, Downshire Arms Hotel

BANGOR GOLF CLUB

This undulating parkland course, overlooking Belfast Lough, was established in 1903 and designed by the five-times Open champion, James Braid. Challenging holes are the long and difficult par-4 fifth and the exhilarating fifteenth where accuracy is paramount. Famous names who have been associated with the club are David Feherty, Norman Drew and Garth McGimpsey.

18 holes parkland, 6,410 yards, par 71 (SSS 71). Ladies 5,689 yards, par 72 (SSS 72).

ADDRESS: Broadway, Bangor, Co. Down BT20 4RH.
TELEPHONE: +44 (0)28 9127 0922.
FAX: +44 (0)28 9145 3394.
EMAIL: bangorgolfclubni@btconnect.com
WEBSITE: www.bangorgolfclubni.co.uk
SECRETARY/MANAGER: David Ryan.
PROFESSIONAL: Michael Bannon +44 (0)28 9146 2164.
VISITORS: Any day, except Tuesdays and Saturdays.
GREEN FEES: £29 per round weekdays, £35 at weekends.
CATERING: Restaurant and bar.
FACILITIES: Locker rooms, putting green, practice ground, club shop, trolleys, club hire, tuition.
LOCATION: 1 mile south of Bangor centre, off the B21.
LOCAL HOTELS: Marine Court Hotel, Royal Hotel.

Bangor Golf Club

BLACKWOOD GOLF CENTRE

Located in Clandeboye Estate, the Hamilton Course is a championship parkland course with man-made lakes. The par-3 Temple Course is designed for novices and experienced golfers alike. Established in 1994.

HAMILTON COURSE – 18 holes parkland, 6,392 yards, par 71 (SSS 70). Ladies 5,323 yards, par 72 (SSS 70).

TEMPLE COURSE – 18 holes parkland, 2,492 yards, par 54.

ADDRESS: 150 Crawfordsburn Road,
Clandeboye, Bangor, Co. Down BT19 1GB.
TELEPHONE: +44 (0)28 9185 2706.
FAX: +44 (0)28 9185 3785.
EMAIL: blackwoodgc@btopenworld.com
VISITORS: Any day.
GREEN FEES: Hamilton – £20 per round
weekdays, £25 weekends and public
holidays; Temple – £12 per round
weekdays, £15 weekends and public
holidays.
CATERING: Restaurant and bar.
FACILITIES: Locker rooms, putting green,
practice ground, floodlit 26-bay driving
range, trolleys, club hire, caddies on
request.
LOCATION: On the A2 towards Bangor from
Belfast. Take the turn to Newtownards.
LOCAL HOTELS: Clandeboye Lodge Hotel.

BRIGHT CASTLE GOLF CLUB

This hilly parkland course, featuring four
formidable par 5s, was founded in 1969 and
designed by Arnold Ennis. It has views of
the Mountains of Mourne.

18 holes parkland, 7,110 yards, par 73
(SSS 73).

SIGNATURE HOLE:
SIXTEENTH (615 yards, par 5) – this
hole was originally a 735-yard par 6,
but it was not recognised for handicap
purposes, so the club reluctantly trimmed
the yardage.

ADDRESS: 14 Coniamstown Road, Bright,
Downpatrick, Co. Down BT30 8LU.
TELEPHONE: +44 (0)28 4484 1319.
EMAIL: bright.castle@virgin.net
HONORARY SECRETARY: John McCawl.
VISITORS: Welcome.
GREEN FEES: £12 per round weekdays, £15
weekends and public holidays.

CATERING: Restaurant and bar.
FACILITIES: Locker rooms, putting green,
practice facilities, buggies, trolleys.
LOCATION: 5 miles south of Downpatrick.
LOCAL HOTELS: Abbey Lodge Hotel.

CARNALEA GOLF CLUB

Meadowland course on the shores of Belfast
Lough, founded in 1927.

18 holes meadowland, 5,647 yards, par 69
(SSS 67). Ladies 5,192 yards, par 70 (SSS 70).

ADDRESS: Station Road, Bangor, Co. Down
BT19 1EZ.
TELEPHONE: +44 (0)28 9127 0368.
FAX: +44 (0)28 9127 3989.
EMAIL: carnaleagolfclub@supanet.com
SECRETARY/MANAGER: Gary Steele.
PROFESSIONAL: Tom Loughran +44 (0)28
9127 0122.
VISITORS: Welcome.
GREEN FEES: £16.50 per round weekdays,
£21 weekends and public holidays.
CATERING: Restaurant and bar.
FACILITIES: Locker rooms, putting green,
practice facilities, trolleys, club hire.
LOCATION: 1½ miles from Bangor, next to
Carnalea Station.
LOCAL HOTELS: Clandeboye Lodge Hotel,
Royal Hotel, Marine Court Hotel,
Crawfordsburn Inn.

CLANDEBOYE GOLF CLUB

Two undulating heathland courses with
clusters of gorse bushes and copses.
Established in 1931 on the hills above
the village of Conlig with views of Belfast
Lough and the Irish Sea.

DUFFERIN COURSE – 18 holes
heathland, 6,559 yards, par 71 (SSS 71).

AVA COURSE – 18 holes heathland,
5,770 yards, par 73 (SSS 68).

ADDRESS: 51 Tower Road, Conlig,
Newtownards, Co. Down BT23 3PN.
TELEPHONE: +44 (0)28 9127 1767.
FAX: +44 (0)28 9147 3711.
EMAIL: contact@cgc-ni.com
WEBSITE: www.cgc-ni.com
PROFESSIONAL: Peter Gregory +44 (0)28
9127 1750.
VISITORS: Weekdays, weekends after 2.30 pm.
GREEN FEES: Dufferin Course – £27.50 per
round weekdays, £33 at weekends; Ava
Course – £22 per round weekdays, £27.50
at weekends.
CATERING: Restaurant and bar.
FACILITIES: Locker rooms, practice facilities,
buggies, trolleys, club hire.
LOCATION: In the village of Conlig off the
Belfast–Bangor road at Newtownards.
LOCAL HOTELS: Clandeboye Lodge Hotel,
Marine Court Hotel, Crawfordsburn Inn.

CROSSGAR GOLF CLUB

This is a tight parkland course with a couple
of hills and only one hole over 400 yards.
Founded in 1994.

9 holes parkland, 4,580 yards for 18
holes, par 64 (SSS 63).

ADDRESS: 231 Derryboy Road, Crossgar,
Downpatrick, Co. Down BT30 9DL.
TELEPHONE & FAX: +44 (0)28 4483 1523.
EMAIL: crossgargolfclub@tiscali.co.uk
WEBSITE: www.crossgargolfclub.co.uk
PROFESSIONAL: +44 (0)28 4483 1629.
VISITORS: Yes. Societies by prior
arrangement.
GREEN FEES: £10 per round weekdays, £12
at weekends.
CATERING: None.
FACILITIES: Locker rooms.
LOCATION: 5 miles south of Saintfield, close
to Crossgar.
LOCAL HOTELS: Millbrook Lodge Hotel.

DONAGHADEE GOLF CLUB

Founded in 1899, this is a mixture of
undulating links and parkland with
spectacular views of the Irish Sea to the
Scottish coast.

18 holes parkland/links, 6,094 yards, par
71 (SSS 69). Ladies 5,645 yards, par 72 (SSS
72).

ADDRESS: 84 Warren Road, Donaghadee,
Co. Down BT21 0PQ.
TELEPHONE: +44 (0)28 9188 3624.
FAX: +44 (0)28 9188 8891.
EMAIL: deegolf@freenet.co.uk
PROFESSIONAL: Gordon Drew +44 (0)28
9188 2392.
VISITORS: Mondays, Wednesdays and
Fridays are best.
GREEN FEES: £22 per round weekdays, £25
at weekends.
CATERING: Restaurant and bar.
FACILITIES: Locker rooms, putting green,
practice ground, trolleys, club hire.
LOCATION: 5 miles south-east of Bangor on
the A2 coast road.
LOCAL HOTELS: Clandeboye Lodge Hotel,
Copeland Hotel.

DOWNPATRICK GOLF CLUB

A classic parkland course, including five
par 3s and two par 5s. Undulating fairways,
strategically placed sand traps and quick-
but-true greens make it a testing, yet
pleasurable, challenge to golfers of all
abilities. It has spectacular views of County
Down, Strangford Lough and even the Isle
of Man on a clear day. Established in 1930.

18 holes parkland, 6,120 yards, par 70
(SSS 69). Ladies 5,270 yards, par 71 (SSS
71).

SIGNATURE HOLE:

SEVENTH ('Downhill', 437 yards, par 4) – out of bounds down the right to an undulating green which is protected by two sand traps. There are trees to the left and panoramic views of all County Down from the tee.

ADDRESS: 43 Saul Road, Downpatrick, Co. Down, BT30 6PA.
TELEPHONE: +44 (0)28 4461 5947.
FAX: +44 (0)28 4461 7502.
EMAIL: info@downpatrickgolfclub.co.uk
WEBSITE: www.downpatrickgolfclub.co.uk
PROFESSIONAL: Robert Hutton.
VISITORS: Yes, ordinarily any day midweek.
GREEN FEES: £22 per round weekdays, £27 at weekends.
CATERING: Restaurant and bar.
FACILITIES: Locker rooms, putting green, practice ground, pro-shop, buggies, trolleys, club hire.
LOCATION: 25 miles south of Belfast on the A7 to Downpatrick. The course is 1 mile from town.
LOCAL HOTELS: Denvir's Hotel +44 (0)28 4461 2012, Abbey Lodge Hotel +44 (0)28 4461 4511, Burrendale Hotel +44 (0)28 4372 2599, Slieve Donard Hotel +44 (0)28 4372 1066, The Mill at Ballyduggan +44 (0)28 4461 3654.

HELEN'S BAY GOLF CLUB

This parkland course on the shores of Belfast Lough has panoramic views from the lough to the Antrim coast and across the Irish Sea to the Mull of Galloway in Scotland. Established in 1896.

9 holes parkland, 5,186 metres (5,704 yards) for 18 holes, par 68 (SSS 67). Ladies 4,854 metres (5,339 yards), par 70 (SSS 70).

ADDRESS: Golf Road, Helen's Bay, Bangor, Co. Down BT19 1TL.
TELEPHONE: +44 (0)28 9185 2815.
EMAIL: mail@helensbaygc.com
WEBSITE: www.helensbaygc.com
SECRETARY/MANAGER: Alan Briggs.
VISITORS: Mondays, Wednesday, Fridays and Sundays are best.
GREEN FEES: £18 per round weekdays, £20 at weekends.
CATERING: Bar and meals.
FACILITIES: Locker rooms, putting green, practice facilities, buggies.
LOCATION: 4 miles west of Bangor, off the B20.
LOCAL HOTELS: Crawfordsburn Old Inn, Clandeboye Lodge, Marine Court Hotel, Culloden Hotel, Ballymullan House.

HOLYWOOD GOLF CLUB

Undulating parkland course founded in 1904.

18 holes parkland, 6,078 yards, par 69 (SSS 68). Ladies 5,289 yards, par 71 (SSS 71).

ADDRESS: Nuns Walk, Demesne Road, Holywood, Co. Down BT18 9LE.
TELEPHONE: +44 (0)28 9042 3135.
FAX: +44 (0)28 9042 5040.
EMAIL: mail@holywoodgolfclub.co.uk
WEBSITE: www.holywoodgolfclub.co.uk
PROFESSIONAL: Paul Gray +44 (0)28 9042 5503.
VISITORS: Any day except Thursdays, which is ladies' day.
GREEN FEES: £18 per round weekdays, £26 weekends and public holidays.
CATERING: Bar and meals.
FACILITIES: Locker rooms, putting green, practice ground, trolleys, club hire, caddies on request.
LOCATION: Off the A2, 6 miles east of Belfast.

LOCAL HOTELS: Culloden Hotel, Park Avenue Hotel, Stormont Hotel.

KILKEEL GOLF CLUB

A parkland course set in 120 acres in the Kilmorey Estate at the foot of the Mountains of Mourne, it was extended to 18 holes by Eddie Hackett in 1993. Founded in 1924.

18 holes parkland, 6,579 yards, par 72 (SSS 72). Ladies 5,906 yards, par 74 (SSS 74).

ADDRESS: Mourne Park, Ballyardle, Kilkeel, Co. Down BT34 4LB.
TELEPHONE: +44 (0)28 4176 2296.
FAX: +44 (0)28 4176 5579.
EMAIL: info@kilkeelgolfclub.org
WEBSITE: www.kilkeelgolfclub.org
SECRETARY/MANAGER: George Graham.
VISITORS: Yes, by prior arrangement.
GREEN FEES: £20 per round weekdays, £25 at weekends.
CATERING: Restaurant and bar.
FACILITIES: Locker rooms, putting green, practice range, buggies, trolleys, club hire, caddies on request.
LOCATION: 3 miles west of Kilkeel, off the A2.
LOCAL HOTELS: Kilmorey Arms, Cranfield House Hotel, Slieve Donard Hotel, Burrendale Hotel.

KIRKISTOWN CASTLE GOLF CLUB

This links course, featuring elevated greens on the coast of County Down, was designed by five-times Open champion James Braid and founded in 1902. It offers a variety of fair and testing holes. The course dries quickly after bad weather and is often open when others are closed.

18 holes links, 5,596 metres (6,122 yards), par 69 (SSS 70). Ladies 5,207 metres (5,727

yards), par 73 (SSS 73).

SIGNATURE HOLE:
TENTH (397 metres [437 yards], par 4) – tough hole with a small pulpit green 10-metres above the fairway. When played into the wind, it's more like a par 5.

ADDRESS: 142 Main Road, Cloughey, Co. Down BT22 1JA.
TELEPHONE: +44 (0)28 4277 1233.
FAX: +44 (0)28 4277 1699.
EMAIL: kirkistown@supanet.com
WEBSITE: www.linksgolfkirkistown.com
CLUB ADMINISTRATOR: Rosemary Coulter.
PROFESSIONAL: Richard Whitford +44 (0)28 4277 1004.
VISITORS: Any day, except Saturdays.
GREEN FEES: £25 per round weekdays, £30 at weekends.
CATERING: Restaurant and bar.
FACILITIES: Locker rooms, putting green, practice grounds, pro-shop, trolleys, club hire, tuition.
LOCATION: Approximately 45 minutes from Belfast, 16 miles from Newtownards on the A2.
LOCAL HOTELS: Lough Cowey Lodge, Portaferry Hotel.

MAHEE ISLAND GOLF CLUB

This undulating parkland course with Scrabo Tower in the background is almost surrounded by water and has scenic views of Strangford Lough. There is only one par 3 on the course. Founded in 1929.

9 holes parkland, 5,822 yards for 18 holes, par 70 (SSS 70). Ladies 5,564 yards, par 72 (SSS 71).

ADDRESS: 14 Mahee Island, Comber, Newtownards, Co. Down BT23 6ET.
TELEPHONE: +44 (0)28 9754 1234.

EMAIL: adrian.ross@ntlworld.com
WEBSITE: www.maheeislandgolfclub.com
VISITORS: Any time, except Saturdays
before 5 p.m.
GREEN FEES: £12 per round/day weekdays,
£17 per round at weekends.
CATERING: Meals by arrangement.
FACILITIES: Locker rooms, putting green,
pro-shop, trolleys, club hire.
LOCATION: From Comber, take the A22 to
Killyleagh. After half a mile, turn left for
Mahee Island. Approximately 15 miles
from Belfast.

RINGDUFFERIN GOLF CLUB

Parkland course founded in 1993.
18 holes parkland, 5,093 yards, par 68
(SSS 66). Ladies 4,668 yards, par 68 (SSS 68).

ADDRESS: Ringdufferin Road, Toye,
Killyleagh, Co. Down BT30 9PH.
TELEPHONE & FAX: +44 (0)28 4482 8812.
VISITORS: Any day, except Saturdays. Soft
spikes.
GREEN FEES: £12 per round.
CATERING: Restaurant and bar.
FACILITIES: Locker rooms, putting green,
practice facilities, driving range, trolleys,
club hire.
LOCATION: 2 miles north of Killyleagh on
the Comber road.
LOCAL HOTELS: Dufferin Arms.

ROCKMOUNT GOLF CLUB

Founded in 1995, this undulating parkland
course covers 120 acres with water coming
into play on the 11th and 14th holes.
18 holes parkland, 6,410 yards, par 72
(SSS 71). Ladies 5,524 yards, par 73 (SSS 73).

ADDRESS: 28 Drumalig Road, Carryduff,
Co. Down BT8 8EQ.

TELEPHONE & FAX: +44 (0)28 9081 2279.
EMAIL: admin@rockmountgolfclub.com
WEBSITE: www.rockmountgolfclub.com
SECRETARY/MANAGER: Diane Patterson.
VISITORS: Mondays, Tuesdays, Thursdays,
Fridays and Sundays are best.
GREEN FEES: £23 per round weekdays, £27
weekends and public holidays.
CATERING: Restaurant and bar.
FACILITIES: Locker rooms, putting green,
practice net, pro-shop, buggies, trolleys.
LOCATION: 1 mile south of Carryduff, off the
A24.
LOCAL HOTELS: Ivanhoe Inn and Hotel.

ROYAL BELFAST GOLF CLUB

Although it is the oldest club in Ireland,
founded in 1881, this Harry Colt-designed
parkland course alongside Belfast Lough
was opened in 1927. Mature trees,
strategically placed bunkers and good
greens make it a course worthy of hosting
many top professional events. It was
upgraded by Donald Steel in 1988.
18 holes parkland, 6,306 yards, par 70
(SSS 71). Ladies 5,540 yards, par 72 (SSS
72).

SIGNATURE HOLE:
FIRST (415 yards, par 4) – considered to be
one of the best opening holes in Irish golf.
A slight dogleg left rising to a green which is
probably the most difficult on the course.

ADDRESS: Station Road, Craigavad,
Holywood, Co. Down BT18 0BP.
TELEPHONE: +44 (0)28 9042 8165.
FAX: +44 (0)28 9042 1404.
EMAIL: enquiries@royalbelfast.com
WEBSITE: www.royalbelfast.com
SECRETARY/MANAGER: Susanna Morrison.
PROFESSIONAL: Chris Spence +44 (0)28
9042 8586.

Royal Belfast Golf Club

VISITORS: Any day, except Wednesday and
   Saturdays (by appointment).
GREEN FEES: £46 per round weekdays, £56
   weekends and public holidays.
CREDIT CARDS ACCEPTED: All major cards.
CATERING: Restaurant and bar.
FACILITIES: Locker rooms, putting green,
   practice ground, buggies (£25), trolleys
   (£3), club hire, caddies, tuition.
LOCATION: 2 miles east of Holywood on the
   A2, 7 miles from the centre of Belfast.
LOCAL HOTELS: Culloden Hotel; Olde Inn,
   Crawfordsburn.

ROYAL COUNTY DOWN GOLF CLUB

In 1889, Old Tom Morris was paid the
princely sum of four guineas to create a
golf course in this most beautiful of all
settings along Dundrum Bay in the town of
Newcastle where the romantic Mountains
of Mourne do indeed sweep down to the
sea. That equally legendary champion
Harry Vardon improved on it in 1908, and
although inflation has gone through the
stratosphere since then, time has not been
able to devalue what is simply one of the
world's great links courses.

   This classic links country, which will

Royal County Down Golf Club

host the 2007 Walker Cup, has imposing sand dunes covered in gorse and heather, narrow fairways, small undulating greens and an unwelcome number of blind shots. But there are also magnificent views of Dundrum Bay and the town, and the 3,000-foot-high Slieve Donard, the highest of the Mountains of Mourne, which towers menacingly above you at all times.

The mark of a really good golf course is how many of the holes you can remember after your first visit and in what detail. With Royal County Down, every one stays in your memory. Whether they are fond memories or otherwise depends on your experience of this magnificent links; it is the ultimate test of golf. The American magazine *Golf* once rated it third behind Muirfield and Pebble Beach. With nine of the par 4s exceeding 400 yards and many carries over dunes and gorse, this is a course that calls for long, accurate driving. It isn't the traditional 'out and back' links; instead, two loops of nine each finish at the clubhouse. The outward

nine is undoubtedly the more challenging and, off the championship tees, is a tough start. You can, though, get off to a flyer on the 539-yard par-5 first (which lies closest to the sea) if the wind is with you, but beware the narrow green.

Then comes a couple of those tough par 4s at 444 and 477 yards. You face a drive over sandhills on the second hole with an approach to a tiny green protected by pot bunkers to the left and a slope to the right. The third is even tougher, and the view from the tee, with the sea hard on your right, is intimidating. Again, the green has sentry bunkers, and the sandhills seem to creep in from left and right. The fourth, played towards the Mountains of Mourne, is a par 3, and if you expected a breather, forget it; it is almost all carry over 213 yards of gorse. The fifth is another 440-yard par 4.

At 145 yards, the seventh is a welcome sight, but 'short' doesn't necessarily mean 'easier'. The green is domed and hard to hold, and the tee shot needs little encouragement to run away into bunkers or gorse. Normal service is resumed at the eighth and ninth (430 and 486 yards), with the former requiring an accurate approach through a narrow entrance to the green, while the latter has more than its fair share of difficulties. It is as good an outward nine as you can experience, and Tom Watson agrees: 'It is a tremendous test of golf, and the outward half especially is as fine a nine holes as I have ever played.'

From this point onwards, the course is that bit further away from the sea, and the dunes are not quite as threatening. The par-5 12th is definitely birdie territory if you manage to carry a depression with your drive. The 13th, which doglegs right, is one of the most beautiful holes on the course, and it is necessary to find a path through the heather. The 15th is probably the toughest of the remaining holes, while, finally, the 16th is a short par 4 of a mere 337 yards, almost from hill to hill. The final hole into the prevailing wind needs care as it is pitted with bunkers.

One of Royal County Down's most enduring stories is that of Eric Fiddian. Playing in the final of the 1933 Irish Amateur Championship, he holed in one in the morning and then again in the afternoon round but still lost. Perhaps that's as much as anyone can expect from Royal County Down – victory and defeat in almost the same breath. One thing is certain though – this is one of golf's essential experiences.

CHAMPIONSHIP COURSE – 18 holes links, 7,181 yards, par 71 (SSS 74). Ladies 6,243 yards, par 75 (SSS 76).

ANNESLEY LINKS COURSE – 18 holes links, 4,800 yards, par 66 (SSS 63).

SIGNATURE HOLE:
NINTH (486 yards, par 4) – to pick a favourite hole at Royal County Down is difficult, but this one-time par 5 is the perfect example of the course's degree of difficulty. The drive is uphill and blind. If you find the flat of the fairway in the valley on the other side, you have a fair chance of making the plateau green in two. It is the highest point of the course, and the views of Slieve Donard are awesome.

ADDRESS: 36 Golf Links Road, Newcastle, Co. Down BT33 0AN.
TELEPHONE: +44 (0)28 4372 3314.
FAX: +44 (0)28 4372 6281.
EMAIL: golf@royalcountydown.org
WEBSITE: www.royalcountydown.org
SECRETARY: James Laidler.
PROFESSIONAL: Kevan Whitson +44 (0)28 4372 2419.
VISITORS: Mondays, Tuesdays, Thursdays, Fridays and Sundays.
GREEN FEES: Championship Course – £125 per round weekday mornings, £110 weekday afternoons, £140 on Sundays; Annesley Course – £30 per round weekdays, £35 at weekends.
CREDIT CARDS ACCEPTED: Amex/MasterCard/Visa.
CATERING: Restaurant and bar.
FACILITIES: Locker rooms, putting green, pro-shop, trolleys (£3), club hire (£30), caddies.
LOCATION: 30 miles south of Belfast on the A24, 90 miles north of Dublin via the N1 to Newry, and 25 miles east of Newry via the A25.
LOCAL HOTELS: Slieve Donard Hotel +44 (0)28 4372 1066, Burrendale Hotel +44 (0)28 4372 2599, Donard Hotel +44 (0)28 4372 2203, Glassdrumman Lodge Hotel +44 (0)28 4376 8585, Enniskeen Hotel +44 (0)28 4372 2392.

Ireland's Golf Courses

SCRABO GOLF CLUB

Founded in 1907, this parkland course winds its way around Scrabo Hill and Tower, one of the best-known County Down landmarks. It demands accurate shot making as it has narrow fairways lined by heather and gorse. There are magnificent views of Strangford Lough and the Mountains of Mourne.

18 holes parkland, 6,227 yards, par 70 (SSS 71). Ladies 5,216 yards, par 72 (SSS 71).

SIGNATURE HOLE:
FIRST (459 yards, par 4) – Christy O'Connor, sen., once nominated it as the best opening hole in Ireland.

ADDRESS: 233 Scrabo Road, Newtownards, Co. Down BT23 4SL.
TELEPHONE: +44 (0)28 9181 2355.
FAX: +44 (0)28 9182 2919.
EMAIL: admin.scrabogc@btconnect.com
WEBSITE: www.scrabo-golf-club.org
SECRETARY/MANAGER: Bill Brown.
PROFESSIONAL: Paul McCrystal.
VISITORS: Yes, but avoid Saturdays and Wednesdays 4.30 p.m. to 6.30 p.m.
GREEN FEES: £19 per round weekdays, £24 at weekends.
CREDIT CARDS ACCEPTED: MasterCard/Visa.
CATERING: Restaurant and bar. Full catering except Mondays.
FACILITIES: Locker rooms, practice ground, putting green, pitch and putt, pro-shop, buggies (£10), trolleys (£1.50), club hire (£8).
LOCATION: 10 miles from Belfast off the main Belfast–Newtownards road. Follow the signs to Scrabo Country Park.
LOCAL HOTELS: Strangford Arms +44 (0)28 9181 4141.

SPA GOLF CLUB

Wooded parkland course with views of the Mourne Mountains. Established in 1907.

18 holes parkland, 6,469 yards, par 72 (SSS 72). Ladies 5,390 yards, par 72 (SSS 72).

ADDRESS: 20 Grove Road, Ballynahinch, Co. Down BT24 8PN.
TELEPHONE: +44 (0)28 9756 2365.
FAX: +44 (0)28 9756 4158.
EMAIL: spagolfclub@btconnect.com
SECRETARY/MANAGER: Terry Magee.
VISITORS: Yes.
GREEN FEES: £18 per round weekdays, £23 at weekends.
CATERING: Bar, meals by arrangement.
FACILITIES: Locker rooms, putting green, practice ground, trolleys, club hire.
LOCATION: 1 mile from Ballynahinch, 10 miles south of Belfast.
LOCAL HOTELS: White Horse Hotel, Millbrook Lodge Hotel.

TEMPLE GOLF AND COUNTRY CLUB

This parkland course set in the rolling drumlins of County Down, with views of Slieve Croob and the Mountains of Mourne, has nine holes but eighteen tees. Established in 1994.

9 holes parkland, 5,388 yards for 18 holes, par 68 (SSS 69). Ladies 5,119 yards, par 69 (SSS 70).

ADDRESS: 60 Church Road, Boardmills, Lisburn, Co. Down BT27 6UP.
TELEPHONE: +44 (0)28 9263 9213.
FAX: +44 (0)28 9263 8637.
EMAIL: info@templegolf.com
WEBSITE: www.templegolf.com
SECRETARY/MANAGER: Peter Hunt, sen.
VISITORS: Yes.
GREEN FEES: Weekdays – £9 for nine holes, £13

Scrabo Golf Club

for eighteen; weekends and public holidays
– £11 for nine holes, £17 for eighteen.
CREDIT CARDS ACCEPTED: MasterCard/Visa.
CATERING: Restaurant and bar.
FACILITIES: Locker rooms, pro-shop
(limited), buggies (£10 for nine holes, £16
for eighteen), trolleys (£2), club hire (£5).
LOCATION: From Belfast, follow the A24
towards Carryduff and Ballynahinch. The
course is on the right, approximately 4
miles from Carryduff.
LOCAL HOTELS: Ivanhoe Hotel, Millbrook
Hotel.

WARRENPOINT GOLF CLUB

This is a challenging parkland course with
three par 5s in the first four holes and
beautiful views of the Mourne Mountains
and Cooley Peninsula. Established in 1893.

18 holes parkland, 6,173 yards, par 71
(SSS 70). Ladies 5,377 yards, par 72 (SSS 71).

SIGNATURE HOLE:
FIFTEENTH (500 yards, par 5) – tough,
but also the most picturesque hole on the
course. It sweeps from left to right, and
there are no bunkers at the green.

ADDRESS: Lower Dromore Road,
Warrenpoint, Co. Down BT34 3LN.
TELEPHONE: +44 (0)28 4175 3695.
FAX: +44 (0)28 4175 2918.
EMAIL: office@warrenpointgolf.com
WEBSITE: www.warrenpointgolf.com
SECRETARY: Marian Trainor.

PROFESSIONAL: Nigel Shaw +44 (0)28 4175 2371.
VISITORS: Yes.
GREEN FEES: £28 per round weekdays, £34 weekends and public holidays.
CREDIT CARDS ACCEPTED: Yes.
CATERING: Restaurant and bar.
FACILITIES: Locker rooms, putting green, practice ground, driving range, pro-shop, trolleys, club hire, tuition.
LOCATION: Travelling through Newry from Dublin, go straight through the traffic lights. Turn right at the first roundabout, take the second turn at the second roundabout and the second turn at third roundabout. Then take the first left onto Lower Dromore Road.
LOCAL HOTELS: Canal Court Hotel +44 (0)28 3025 1234.

COUNTY FERMANAGH

CASTLE HUME GOLF CLUB

Extended to 18 holes in 1992, this championship parkland course has large greens. Situated on the shores of Lower Lough Erne, rivers and lakes also come into play.

18 holes parkland, 5,932 metres (6,525 yards), par 72 (SSS 71). Ladies 4,941 metres (5,435 yards), par 72 (SSS 72).

ADDRESS: Ballyhose, Castle Hume, Enniskillen, Co. Fermanagh BT93 7ED.
TELEPHONE: +44 (0)28 6632 7077.
FAX: +44 (0)28 6632 7076.
EMAIL: info@castlehumegolf.com
WEBSITE: www.castlehumegolf.com
PROFESSIONAL: Shaun Donnelly.
VISITORS: Any day, but book in advance. Soft spikes.

GREEN FEES: £25 per round weekdays, £30 at weekends.
CREDIT CARDS ACCEPTED: All major cards.
CATERING: Restaurant and bar.
FACILITIES: Locker rooms, putting green, practice ground, driving range, pro-shop, buggies (£25), trolleys (£3), club hire (£10), tuition.
LOCATION: 5 miles from Enniskillen on the Donegal road.
LOCAL HOTELS: Fort Lodge Hotel, Killyhevlin Hotel.

ENNISKILLEN GOLF CLUB

Established in 1896, this mature tree-lined parkland course is set in the heart of Fermanagh's Lakeland beside Castlecoole Estate. There are panoramic views over Enniskillen town and the surrounding countryside. Upgraded to eighteen holes in 1989, the new front nine is hilly with a stream crossing the first – which can be intimidating – seventh, eighth and ninth fairways.

18 holes parkland, 6,230 yards, par 71 (SSS 69). Ladies 5,438 yards, par 72 (SSS 72).

SIGNATURE HOLE:
SEVENTH (306 yards, par 4) – drive from an elevated tee to a tree-lined fairway with a lake on the right and a drain running across the fairway. A bunker guards the green.

ADDRESS: Castlecoole, Enniskillen, Co. Fermanagh BT74 6HZ.
TELEPHONE: +44 (0)28 6632 5250.
FAX: +44 (0)28 6632 9269.
EMAIL: enniskillengolfclub@mail.com
WEBSITE: www.enniskillengolfclub.com
SECRETARY/MANAGER: David McKechnie.
VISITORS: Welcome but with restricted times at the weekend.
GREEN FEES: £18 weekdays, £22 weekends and bank holidays.

Enniskillen Golf Club

CREDIT CARDS ACCEPTED: Yes.
CATERING: Full bar service. Sandwiches, coffee and tea are always available.
FACILITIES: Locker rooms, practice ground, putting green, buggies (£20), trolleys (£2), club hire (£5).
LOCATION: Within easy walking distance of Enniskillen town centre, on Castlecoole Road beside the Castlecoole Estate just off the main A4.
LOCAL HOTELS: Belmore Court Motel +44 (0)28 6632 6633, Killyhevlin Hotel +44 (0)28 6632 3481, Ashberry Hotel +44 (0)28 6632 0333.

LISNARICK GOLF CLUB

Established in 1998.
9 holes parkland, 4,334 yards for 18 holes par 66 (SSS 62). Ladies 3,995 yards, par 66 (SSS 62).

ADDRESS: Drumarky, Lisnarick, Co. Fermanagh BT94 1PN.
TELEPHONE: +44 (0)28 6862 8091.
FAX: +44 (0)28 6862 8030.
EMAIL: lisnarick@golfnet.ie
VISITORS: Yes.
GREEN FEES: £15 weekdays and weekends.
CATERING: Restaurant and bar.
FACILITIES: Locker rooms, practice bunker, putting green, six-bay floodlit driving range, pro-shop, buggies, club hire.

COUNTY LONDONDERRY

BROWN TROUT GOLF CLUB

On the banks of the River Agivey, this heavily wooded parkland course crosses water seven times. Opened by Norman Drew in 1973.

9 holes parkland, 5,488 yards for 18 holes, par 70 (SSS 68). Ladies 4,734 yards, par 70 (SSS 67).

SIGNATURE HOLE:
FIFTH (510 yards, par 5) – the toughest hole on the course. Tee shot over water and then a sharp dogleg left.

ADDRESS: 209 Agivey Road, Aghadowey, Coleraine, Co. Londonderry BT51 4AD.
TELEPHONE: +44 (0)28 7086 8209.
FAX: +44 (0)28 7086 8878.
EMAIL: bill@browntroutinn.com
WEBSITE: www.browntroutinn.com
PROFESSIONAL: Ken Revie.
VISITORS: Any day. Soft spikes.
GREEN FEES: £10 per day weekdays, £15 at weekends. £3 discount for groups.
CREDIT CARDS ACCEPTED: Amex/Diners Club/MasterCard/Visa.
CATERING: Restaurant and bar. Attached to the Brown Trout Inn and open for food from 8 a.m. to 10 p.m.
FACILITIES: Locker rooms, putting green, practice ground, trolleys, club hire, tuition.
LOCATION: On the A54, 7 miles from Kilrea. On the main road to Coleraine at intersection of the A54 and B66.
LOCAL HOTELS: Brown Trout Golf and Country Inn.

CASTLEROCK GOLF CLUB

Founded in 1901, Castlerock on the Causeway Coast has two courses: the challenging Mussenden, an eighteen-hole links set among rolling sandhills with five par 5s, and the nine-hole Bann course, which offers a more relaxed game but includes a 540-yard par 5.

MUSSENDEN – 18 holes links, 6,747 yards, par 73 (SSS 72). Ladies 5,904 yards, par 75 (SSS 73).

BANN – 9 holes links, 4,892 yards for 18 holes, par 68 (SSS 66). Ladies 4,466 yards for 18 holes, par 68 (SSS 64).

SIGNATURE HOLE:
FOURTH ('Leg O' Mutton', 200 yards, par 3) – out of bounds on both sides with a railway line on the right and a burn on the left.

ADDRESS: 65 Circular Road, Castlerock, Co. Londonderry BT51 4TJ.
TELEPHONE: +44 (0)28 7084 8314.
FAX: +44 (0)28 7084 9440.
EMAIL: admin@castlerockgc.co.uk
WEBSITE: www.castlerockgc.co.uk
SECRETARY/MANAGER: Mark Steen.
PROFESSIONAL: Ian Blair.
VISITORS: Yes.
GREEN FEES: £50 per round weekdays, £70 weekends and bank holidays.
CREDIT CARDS ACCEPTED: Amex/ MasterCard/Visa.
CATERING: Restaurant and bar.
FACILITIES: Locker rooms, practice ground, putting green, pro-shop, buggies (£25), trolleys (£3), club hire (£15), caddies.
LOCATION: 5 miles west of Coleraine on the north coast.
LOCAL HOTELS: Golf Hotel +44 (0)28 7084 8777 (fax +44 (0)28 7084 8295).

The ninth at Castlerock Golf Club

CITY OF DERRY GOLF CLUB

This parkland course was first designed
as a nine-hole layout by Willie Park Jr. in
1911 and features much gorse and mature
woodland. Fred Daly, winner of the 1947
British Open, was the professional here
from 1939 to 1944.

PREHEN COURSE – 18 holes parkland,
6,429 yards, par 71 (SSS 71). Ladies 5,388
yards, par 72.

DUNHUGH COURSE – 9 holes
parkland, 4,708 yards for 18 holes, par 63.

ADDRESS: 49 Victoria Road, Londonderry
BT47 2PU.
TELEPHONE: +44 (0)28 7134 6369.
FAX: +44 (0)28 7131 0008.
EMAIL: info@cityofderrygolfclub.com
WEBSITE: www.cityofderrygolfclub.com
PROFESSIONAL: Michael Doherty +44 (0)28
7131 1469.
VISITORS: Mondays to Fridays.
GREEN FEES: £25 per round weekdays, £30
at weekends.
CREDIT CARDS ACCEPTED: All major cards.
CATERING: Restaurant and bar.
FACILITIES: Locker rooms, putting green,
practice ground, driving range, club

shop, trolleys, club hire, caddies on request, tuition.

LOCATION: Off the A5, 3 miles south of Derry.

LOCAL HOTELS: Tower Hotel, Derry.

FAUGHAN VALLEY GOLF CLUB

The course, situated on the banks of the meandering River Faughan, is not long but hidden water hazards test even the experienced player. Established in 2000.

18 holes parkland, 5,722 yards, par 69 (SSS 68). Ladies 5,129 yards, par 70 (SSS 70).

ADDRESS: 9a Carmoney Road, Campsie, Londonderry BT37 3JH.

TELEPHONE: +44 (0)28 7186 0707.

EMAIL: david@faughanvalleygolf.com

WEBSITE: www.faughanvalleygolf.com

SECRETARY/MANAGER: David Forbes.

VISITORS: Yes.

GREEN FEES: £9 weekdays, £11 at weekends.

FACILITIES: Locker rooms, pro-shop, buggies, club hire.

FOYLE INTERNATIONAL GOLF CENTRE

Championship parkland course with two lakes and stunning views. Greens to USGA specifications. Founded in 1994.

EARHART COURSE – 18 holes parkland, 6,678 yards, par 72 (SSS 71). Ladies 5,507 yards, par 72 (SSS 72).

WOODLANDS COURSE – 9 holes parkland, 2,698 yards for 18 holes, par 54.

ADDRESS: 12 Alder Road, Londonderry, Co. Londonderry BT48 8DB.

TELEPHONE: +44 (0)28 7135 2222.

FAX: +44 (0)28 7135 3967.

EMAIL: mail@foylegolfclub24.co.uk

WEBSITE: www.foylegolfcentre.co.uk

PROFESSIONAL: Kieran McLaughlin.

VISITORS: Any day.

GREEN FEES: Earhart Course – £14 per round weekdays, £17 weekends and public holidays; Woodlands Course – £5 weekdays, £7 at weekends.

CREDIT CARDS ACCEPTED: Yes.

CATERING: Restaurant and bar.

FACILITIES: Locker rooms, putting green, practice ground, 19-bay floodlit driving range, club shop, trolleys (£2), club hire (£5), caddies on request, tuition.

LOCATION: 2 miles north of Londonderry, off Culmore Road.

LOCAL HOTELS: Waterfoot Hotel, White Horse Inn.

KILREA GOLF CLUB

Established in 1919, this is an undulating parkland course with tight fairways and small greens.

9 holes parkland, 5,489 yards for 18 holes, par 70 (SSS 67). Ladies 5,016 yards, par 70 (SSS 69).

ADDRESS: Kilrea, Co. Londonderry.

TELEPHONE: +44 (0)28 2954 0044.

EMAIL: secretary@kilreagolfclub.co.uk

WEBSITE: www.kilreagolfclub.co.uk

VISITORS: Best days are Sundays to Fridays, except Tuesday and Wednesday afternoons.

GREEN FEES: £20 per round weekdays and weekends.

CATERING: By prior arrangement.

LOCATION: Half a mile from village of Kilrea on the road to Maghera.

LOCAL HOTELS: Portneal Lodge +44 (0)28 2954 1444.

MANOR GOLF CLUB

This is a parkland course with a few hills and water coming into play on a couple of holes. Founded in 1990.

9 holes parkland, 4,174 metres (4,591 yards) for 18 holes, par 64 (SSS 62). Ladies 4,040 metres (4,444 yards), par 64 (SSS 62).

ADDRESS: 69 Bridge Street, Kilrea, Coleraine, Co. Londonderry BT51 5RR.
TELEPHONE: +44 (0)28 2954 1636.
VISITORS: Yes.
GREEN FEES: £9 per round weekdays, £10 at weekends.
CATERING: Restaurant and bar.
FACILITIES: Locker rooms, buggies, trolleys, club hire.

MOYOLA PARK GOLF CLUB

This mature parkland course is set on both sides of the River Moyola in the 130 acres of the Shanemullagh Estate. Founded in 1977.

18 holes parkland, 6,519 yards, par 71 (SSS 71). Ladies 5,653 yards, par 72.

SIGNATURE HOLE:
EIGHTH ('The River', 421 yards, par 4) – this testing dogleg left requires an accurate tee shot for the approach through a gap between mature trees. The River Moyola comes into play 30-yards short of a green guarded by two bunkers.

ADDRESS: 15 Curran Road, Shanemullagh, Castledawson, Co. Londonderry BT45 8DG.
TELEPHONE: +44 (0)28 7946 8468.
FAX: +44 (0)28 7946 8626.
EMAIL: moyolapark@btconnect.com
WEBSITE: www.moyolapark.com
SECRETARY/MANAGER: F.G. Kearney.

PROFESSIONAL: Bob Cockcroft +44 (0)28 7946 8830.
VISITORS: Yes, by arrangement. Handicap certificates preferred. Soft spikes.
GREEN FEES: £20 per round Mondays to Thursdays, £25 Fridays and £30 at weekends.
CATERING: Restaurant and bar.
FACILITIES: Locker rooms, putting green, practice ground, club shop, buggies, trolleys, club hire, caddies on request, tuition.
LOCATION: 35 miles north of Belfast along the M2. Go through Toomebridge towards Derry. Turn right at first large roundabout and take a left for Castledawson.
LOCAL HOTELS: Glenavon Hotel, The Inn at Castledawson.

PARK GOLF COURSE

This parkland course has two par 3s and seven par 4s, one of which is to be upgraded to a par 5 in 2006.

9 holes parkland, 4,816 yards, par 68 for 18 holes.

ADDRESS: Tireighter Road, Park, Co. Londonderry BT47 4BA.
TELEPHONE: +44 (0)28 7778 1293.
VISITORS: Any day.
GREEN FEES: £7 per round.
FACILITIES: Trolleys, club hire.
LOCATION: 8 miles from Dungiven on the B44.

PORTSTEWART GOLF CLUB

Established in 1894, Portstewart now has three eighteen-hole links courses. The Strand Course, opened in 1992, has imposing dunes and is a true test of links golf. It offers magnificent views of the blue

Portstewart Golf Club

Donegal hills, the Atlantic and the River Bann estuary. The Old Course, situated at the eastern end of Portstewart, begins and ends at the site of the original course, where golf was first played in 1889. Portstewart was a qualifying course when the 1951 British Open was played at Royal Portrush. Some claim that Portstewart has the best opening hole in golf.

STRAND COURSE – 18 holes links, 6,895 yards, par 72 (SSS 73). Ladies 5,853 yards, par 74 (SSS 73).

OLD COURSE – 18 holes links, 4,730 yards, par 64 (SSS 62).

RIVERSIDE COURSE – 18 holes links, 5,725 yards, par 68.

ADDRESS: 117 Strand Road, Portstewart, Co. Londonderry BT55 7PG.
TELEPHONE: +44 (0)28 7083 2015.
FAX: +44 (0)28 7083 4097.
EMAIL: info@portstewartgc.co.uk
WEBSITE: www.portstewartgc.co.uk
SECRETARY: Michael Moss.

PROFESSIONAL: Alan Hunter +44 (0)28 7083 2601.

VISITORS: Seven days by prearranged booking.

GREEN FEES: Strand Course – £65 per round weekdays, £85 at weekends; Riverside Course – £18 per round weekdays, £23 at weekends; Old Course – £10 per round weekdays, £15 at weekends.

CREDIT CARDS ACCEPTED: MasterCard/Switch/Visa.

CATERING: Restaurant and bar.

FACILITIES: Locker rooms, putting green, pitching green, practice range, pro-shop, buggies, trolleys, caddies on request.

LOCATION: Off the A2, 3 miles north-west of Coleraine.

LOCAL HOTELS: Edgewater Hotel, O'Malley's Wateredge Inn, The Anchorage Inn.

RADISSON ROE PARK HOTEL AND GOLF RESORT

This parkland course has three ponds, the Mullagh Hill at its centre and is set amidst the beautiful countryside of the Roe Valley – with mountains to the south and the sea to the north. Established in 1992 and designed by Frank Ainsworth.

18 holes parkland, 6,283 yards, par 70 (SSS 70). Ladies 5,033 yards, par 70 (SSS 69).

ADDRESS: Radisson SAS Roe Park Resort, Limavady, Co. Londonderry BT49 9LB.

TELEPHONE: +44 (0)28 7776 0105.

FAX: +44 (0)28 7772 2313.

EMAIL: drgolf@radissonroepark.com

WEBSITE: www.radissonroepark.com

PROFESSIONAL: Sean Devenaugh.

VISITORS: Yes.

GREEN FEES: £25 per round weekdays, £30 at weekends.

CATERING: Restaurant and bar.

FACILITIES: Locker rooms, floodlit driving range, putting green, pro-shop, indoor golf academy, buggies (£20), trolleys (£2), club hire (£12), caddies on request.

LOCATION: On the A2 Londonderry–Limavady road, 15 miles from Londonderry.

LOCAL HOTELS: Radisson Roe Park Hotel and Golf Resort (on the course).

TRAAD PONDS GOLF CLUB

Parkland course with many water hazards running into nearby Lough Neagh. Founded in 1998.

9 holes parkland, 4,888 metres (5,376 yards) for 18 holes, par 66 (SSS 64). Ladies 3,642 metres (4,006 yards), par 66 (SSS 64).

ADDRESS: 122a Shore Road, Magherafelt, Co. Londonderry BT45 6LR.

TELEPHONE: +44 (0)28 7941 8865.

VISITORS: Yes.

GREEN FEES: £10 for 18 holes weekdays, £12 weekends and public holidays.

CATERING: Can be arranged.

FACILITIES: Locker rooms, putting green.

LOCATION: 4 miles out of Magherafelt in the village of Ballyronan.

LOCAL HOTELS: O'Neill Arms Hotel, Clearwater House.

COUNTY TYRONE

AUGHNACLOY GOLF CLUB

Parkland course in the Clogher Valley with one steep hill and a river. Established in 1995.

9 holes parkland, 5,489 yards for 18 holes, par 70 (SSS 68).

Radisson Roe Park Hotel and Golf Resort

ADDRESS: 99 Tullyvar Road, Aughnacloy, Co. Tyrone BT69 6BL.
TELEPHONE: +44 (0)28 8555 7050.
FAX: +44 (0)28 8556 8629.
VISITORS: Any day, except Saturdays.
GREEN FEES: £15 per round weekdays, £20 Sundays and public holidays.
CATERING: Restaurant and bar.
FACILITIES: Locker rooms, putting green, practice ground, driving range, buggies, trolleys, club hire.
LOCATION: 2 miles from Aughnacloy and signposted.

BENBURB VALLEY GOLF CLUB

Parkland course established in 1998.
9 holes parkland, 6,408 yards for 18 holes, par 72 (SSS 72).

ADDRESS: Maydown Road, Benburb BT71 7LJ.
TELEPHONE: +44 (0)28 3754 9868.
VISITORS: Any day.
GREEN FEES: £8 for nine holes weekdays, £11 for eighteen; £10 for nine holes weekends, £14 for eighteen.
CATERING: Bar and meals.
FACILITIES: Locker rooms, caddies.
LOCATION: A quarter of a mile east of Benburb.
LOCAL HOTELS: Charlemont House Hotel.

DUNGANNON GOLF CLUB

The club, established in 1890, was a founder member of the Golfing Union of Ireland a year later. It is also where Ryder Cup star Darren Clarke learned the game. Now an Honorary Life Member, he officially opened the new clubhouse in 2000. It is a classic parkland course with tree-lined fairways, great greens and a couple of tough par 5s – the 558-yard third and the 554-yard seventeenth.

18 holes parkland, 6,061 yards, par 72 (SSS 69). Ladies 5,419 yards, par 72 (SSS 72).

SIGNATURE HOLE:
NINTH ('Darren Clarke', 161 yards, par 3) – features a fairly narrow, ribbon-like crescent-shaped green which is protected from the tee by a pond.

ADDRESS: 34 Springfield Lane, Dungannon, Co. Tyrone BT70 1QX.
TELEPHONE: +44 (0)28 8772 2098.
FAX: +44 (0)28 8772 7338.
EMAIL: info@dungannongolfclub.com
WEBSITE: www.dungannongolfclub.com
PROFESSIONAL: Alastair Fleming +44 (0)28 8772 7485.
VISITORS: Mondays, Thursdays and Fridays are best.
GREEN FEES: £20 per round weekdays, £25 weekends and public holidays.
CATERING: Restaurant and bar.
FACILITIES: Locker rooms, putting green, practice ground, buggies, trolleys.
LOCATION: From the M1, follow signs for the town centre and then the B43 to Donaghmore. The course is approximately 2 miles from the town centre.
LOCAL HOTELS: Glengannon Hotel, Oaklin House Hotel.

FINTONA GOLF CLUB

This is an attractive parkland course with a trout stream that comes into play on some of the holes. Founded in 1904.
9 holes parkland, 5,765 metres (6,307 yards) for 18 holes, par 72 (SSS 70). Ladies 5,507 metres (6,057 yards), par 74 (SSS 73).

ADDRESS: Fintona, Co. Tyrone BT78 2BL.
TELEPHONE: +44 (0)28 8284 0777.
FAX: +44 (0)28 8284 1480.

EMAIL: fintonagolfclub@tiscali.co.uk
PROFESSIONAL: Paul Leonard.
VISITORS: Welcome on weekdays.
GREEN FEES: £10 per round weekdays, £15 at weekends.
CATERING: Restaurant and bar.
FACILITIES: Locker rooms, putting green, trolleys.
LOCATION: 9 miles south-west of Omagh.
LOCAL HOTELS: Silver Birches Hotel.

KILLYMOON GOLF CLUB

Founded in 1889 and one of the founder members of the Golfing Union of Ireland. It is a mainly parkland course set on high ground with a picturesque first hole skirting the woods of Killymoon Castle.

18 holes parkland, 5,496 metres (6,045 yards), par 70 (SSS 69). Ladies 4,939 metres (5,432 yards), par 71 (SSS 71).

ADDRESS: 200 Killymoon Road, Cookstown, Co. Tyrone BT80 8TW.
TELEPHONE & FAX: +44 (0)28 8676 3762.
EMAIL: killymoongolf@btconnect.com
PROFESSIONAL: Gary Chambers +44 (0)28 8676 3460.
VISITORS: Yes, but must have handicap certificate.
GREEN FEES: £21 per round weekdays, £26 at weekends.
CATERING: Restaurant and bar.
FACILITIES: Locker rooms, putting green, practice ground, practice facilities, pro-shop, trolleys, tuition.
LOCATION: 1 mile south of Cookstown town centre. Turn left at Killymoon Road off the Cookstown main street. Continue down the road to the golf course.
LOCAL HOTELS: Glenavon House Hotel, Greenvale Hotel, Central Inn Royal Hotel.

NEWTOWNSTEWART GOLF CLUB

This challenging parkland course, founded in 1914, is situated in the Baronscourt Estate amidst an abundance of flora and fauna at the foot of the Sperrin Mountains with panoramic views of the Donegal hills.

18 holes parkland, 5,341 metres (5,875 yards), par 70 (SSS 69). Ladies 4,603 metres (5,063 yards), par 71 (SSS 69).

ADDRESS: 38 Golf Course Road, Newtownstewart, Co. Tyrone BT78 4HU.
TELEPHONE: +44 (0)28 8166 1466.
FAX: +44 (0)28 8166 2506.
EMAIL: newtown.stewart@lineone.net
SECRETARY: Diane Cooke.
VISITORS: Weekdays are best.
GREEN FEES: £17 per round weekdays, £25 at weekends.
CREDIT CARDS ACCEPTED: MasterCard/Visa.
CATERING: Bar and snacks.
FACILITIES: Locker rooms, putting green, practice ground, pro-shop, buggies, trolleys, club hire, caddies.
LOCATION: Signposted from Strabane Road (A57) at Newtownstewart. The course is 2 miles west of Newtownstewart on the B84.
LOCAL HOTELS: Clanabogan House, Fir Trees Hotel, Hawthorn House.

OMAGH GOLF CLUB

This undulating parkland course on the banks of the River Drumnagh was founded in 1910.

18 holes parkland, 5,638 metres (6,201 yards), par 71 (SSS 70). Ladies 4,749 metres (5,223 yards), par 72 (SSS 71).

ADDRESS: 83a Dublin Road, Omagh, Co. Tyrone BT78 1HQ.
TELEPHONE & FAX: +44 (0)28 8224 3160.
EMAIL: omaghgolfclub@tiscali.co.uk

SECRETARY/MANAGER: Florence Caldwell.

VISITORS: Always welcome.

GREEN FEES: £15 per round weekdays, £20 at weekends.

CATERING: Bar.

FACILITIES: Locker rooms, putting green.

LOCATION: On the A5, outside Omagh. Leave Omagh on the A5 for Dublin. The golf course is 2 kilometres along this road on the right-hand side.

LOCAL HOTELS: Silver Birch Hotel.

STRABANE GOLF CLUB

Founded in 1908, this is a testing parkland course, designed by Eddie Hackett, with the River Mourne coming into play on some holes.

18 holes parkland, 5,610 metres (6,171 yards), par 69 (SSS 69). Ladies 4,844 metres (SSS 5,328 yards), par 72 (SSS 70).

ADDRESS: 33 Ballycolman Road, Strabane, Co. Tyrone BT82 9PH.

TELEPHONE: +44 (0)28 7138 2007.

FAX: +44 (0)28 7188 6514.

EMAIL: strabanegc@btconnect.com

SECRETARY/MANAGER: Claire Keys.

VISITORS: Weekdays, except Tuesdays.

GREEN FEES: £15 per round weekdays, £17 at weekends.

CATERING: Bar, meals by arrangement.

FACILITIES: Locker rooms, putting green, practice ground, buggies, trolleys, caddies on request.

LOCATION: On the A5, 1 mile south of Strabane.

LOCAL HOTELS: Fir Trees Hotel, Beech Tree House.

Index

Vartry Lakes, Roundwood 119
Virginia, Virginia 30

Warrenpoint, Warrenpoint 263
Water Rock, Midleton 173
Waterford, Waterford 139
Waterford Castle, Ballinakill 140
Waterville, Waterville 188
West Waterford, Dungarvan 140
Westmanstown, Dublin 57
Westport, Westport 218

Wexford, Mulgannon 145
Whitehead, Carrickfergus 245
Wicklow, Wicklow 120
Williamstown, Waterford 141
Woodbrook, Bray 120
Woodenbridge, Arklow 121
Woodlands, Naas 75
Woodstock, Ennis 158

Youghal, Youghal 175

Picture Credits

Photographs courtesy of:

COVER The K Cub
SPINE Roundwood Golf Club
BACK COVER Steve Uzzell/Doonbeg Golf Club

Ireland's Golf Courses

189	Lynne Connolly
191	Adare Manor Hotel and Golf Resort
197	North & West Coast Links
199	North & West Coast Links
202	Narin and Portnoo Golf Club
204	North & West Coast Links
208	North & West Coast Links
211	Fáilte Ireland
216	North & West Coast Links
223	North & West Coast Links
225	North & West Coast Links
231	Malone Golf Club
234	Northern Ireland Tourist Board
235	Northern Ireland Tourist Board
241	Hilton Templepatrick Hotel and Country Club
244	Northern Ireland Tourist Board
246	Northern Ireland Tourist Board
248	Edenmore Golf and Country Club
249	Northern Ireland Tourist Board
252	Northern Ireland Tourist Board
253	Northern Ireland Tourist Board
259	Royal Belfast Golf Club
260	Northern Ireland Tourist Board
263	Scrabo Golf Club
265	Northern Ireland Tourist Board
267	North & West Coast Links
270	North & West Coast Links
272	Radisson Roe Park Hotel and Golf Resort